Knowledge and Power

Knowledge and Power

Essays on Politics, Culture, and War

Gordon A. Craig

Edited by Bruce Thompson, Carolyn Halladay,
and Donald Abenheim

Society for the Promotion of Science and Scholarship
Palo Alto, California
2013

The Society for the Promotion of Science and Scholarship, Inc.
Palo Alto, California

© 2013 The Society for the Promotion of Science and Scholarship

The Society for the Promotion of Science and Scholarship is a
nonprofit organization established for the purposes of scholarly
publishing, to benefit both academics and the general public.

This book has been published with the assistance of the Stanford
History Department and a number of private donors.

Library of Congress Cataloging-in-Publication Data

Craig, Gordon Alexander, 1913-2005.
  Knowledge and power : essays on politics, culture, and war / Gordon A.
Craig ;
edited by Bruce Thompson, Carolyn Halladay, and Donald Abenheim.
    p. cm.
  Includes bibliographical references and index.
  ISBN 0-930664-30-2 (alk. paper)
  1. Germany--Politics and government--1871-1933. 2. Germany--Politics and
government--1933-1945. 3. Politics and culture--Germany--History--19th
century. 4. Politics and culture--Germany--History--20th century. 5.
Liberalism--Germany--History. 6. Militarism--Germany--History. 7. Political
leadership--Germany--History. 8. Germany--Intellectual life. 9. Germany--
Military policy. 10. War and society--Germany--History. I. Thompson, Bruce
A. (Bruce Allan), 1955- II. Halladay, Carolyn. III. Abenheim, Donald, 1953-
IV. Title.

  DD221.C685 2013
  943.08--dc23
                        2012040207

Contents

Editors' Introduction

When Gordon A. Craig was born in Glasgow in November 1913, George V was King of Great Britain and Emperor of India, and the Habsburg, Hohenzollern, and Romanov emperors were still on their thrones. Many decades later, when he was the J. E. Wallace Sterling Professor of Humanities at Stanford University, Craig liked to tease his students by reminding them that the year of his birth was the last year of "the long nineteenth century," the year before the First World War began. But why should the books and essays of an author born a century ago continue to attract readers in the second decade of the twenty-first century?

The short answer, of course, is that Craig was one of the finest historians of his time, and that everything he wrote is worth reading and re-reading. His first book, *The Politics of the Prussian Army*, published by Oxford University Press in 1955, is still in print more than half a century later. He belonged to the generation of scholars who fought in the Second World War, and more particularly to an elite group who served in the Research and Analysis Branch of the Office of Strategic Services. For these young scholars, the most urgent historical problem at the beginning of their careers was the German question: Why Hitler? Why did liberalism falter and democracy fail so catastrophically in Germany?

Gordon Craig had begun to ponder the problem even before the Second World War began, while he was still an undergraduate at Princeton:

> The first time I saw Germany was in 1935, when I went there at the end of my junior year in college to do research for the senior thesis that I was expected to submit in the spring of the following year. The subject that I had chosen for this piece of work was "The Rise and Fall of the Weimar Republic," for that ill-fated experiment in democracy had ended in failure two years earlier, and it was, in my view, high time that someone wrote the definitive account of its collapse. There was no doubt in my mind that a few months in Germany would enable me to uncover all the materials necessary to supply this felt want.[1]

What struck him forcibly during his first visit was the startling contrast between the German cultural legacy he had already begun to cherish—the beautiful walled towns, the art of Dürer and Cranach, the treasures of Dresden, the plays of Goethe and Kleist, the theater of Max Reinhardt—and the appalling barbarism of the Nazis. As a young man in his early twenties, Craig had begun to think about a problem that would engage him not for months but for decades.[2] He published his first major essay in 1943, when he was not yet thirty, and his last (included in this volume) in 2004, when he was over ninety. To read him is to have the pleasure of following a great historian's reflections on modern German and European history over a period of sixty years.

A longer answer to the question of why certain works of history are worth re-reading comes from Gordon Craig himself, in a memorial tribute he composed in 1970 for one of his teachers, the eminent British historian E. L. Woodward:

> All of [Woodward's] works belong to those rarities of historical scholarship which can be reread with pleasure and profit. To do this with [any of his books] is to be reminded that erudition can be combined with elegance and economy of style and to see demonstrated again, in the work of a master, how historians should organize and present their material, how they should proceed with the delicate business of dealing with causality, and how they can be fair without being noncommittal. Woodward was a firm believer in the historian's obligation to take a stand on the controverted issues of the past and he never made the error of supposing that to pass

moral judgment upon an historical figure's character or actions was to violate the principle of objectivity.[3]

This view of the historian's craft has antecedents not only in Woodward's example but also in the work of the great historians of the eighteenth and nineteenth centuries whom Craig most admired: Gibbon and Macaulay, Ranke and Burckhardt. The historian who hopes to reach beyond the academy should strive to combine the essential work of analysis and explanation with the pleasures of an engaging style and skillful narrative construction. But most noteworthy here is the emphasis on moral judgment: Craig's forthright insistence that evaluating political actors as moral agents is one of the historian's chief responsibilities.[4]

In his essay on "History as a Humanistic Discipline," which concludes this volume, he returned to the theme of moral judgment and quoted Jakob Burckhardt on the importance of writing for an educated public: "At the risk of being considered unscientific by the population of pedants, I am firmly determined from now on to write in a *readable* fashion. . . . Against the sneers of the contemporary scholarly generation, one must armor oneself with a certain indifference, so that one will perhaps be bought and read, and not merely be the subject of bored note-taking in libraries." With Burckhardt's view in mind, Craig concluded that "a humanistic discipline deserves to be presented in a humane way, as a story about human beings in circumstances, told with grace and energy, its analytic rigor heightened by clarity and logic, its argument persuasive rather than strident." This was the credo that served him so well as a writer and teacher over the course of his long career. It enabled him to flourish not only as an academic historian but also as a public intellectual, writing for a broad audience of educated readers in both America and Europe.

As his colleague James J. Sheehan observed in a superb memorial essay,[5] Craig developed his distinctive style by immersing himself in the literature and historical writing of the nineteenth century and by submitting to the discipline of reviewing books for a general audience. He began reviewing regularly for *The New York Herald Tribune* during the 1950s, wrote for *Commentary*, *The Reporter*, *The Atlantic Monthly*, *The New Republic*, *Foreign Affairs*, and *The New York Times Book Review* in subsequent decades, and finally found his favorite forum in *The New York Review of Books*, for which he began to write in 1981.

Many of the *New York Review* pieces collected in this volume, and in its two predecessors, *Politics and Culture in Germany: Essays from the New York Review of Books* (2000), and *Tact and Intelligence: Essays on Diplomatic History and International Relations* (2008), and particularly the essays on Hitler and the Nazis, show how he refined his views on German and European history in light of recent scholarship. Others offer shrewd analyses of political leadership and keen reassessments of writers and reformers who swam against the current: Prussian reformers, dissident writers, German-Jewish philosophers and scientists.

Like his near-contemporary A. J. P. Taylor (1906–1990), Craig devoted much of his career to the study of German diplomacy and the European balance of power.[6] Both men were spellbinding lecturers and masters of narrative history, as well as prolific essayists. Both insisted on the primacy of politics and the crucial role of political leadership, and each combined analysis of conflicts and crises in modern European history with brilliant biographical portraits of statesmen and diplomats. Taylor favored brisk, declarative sentences and a dynamic, propulsive style, like the one he attributed to Macaulay: "mobility, velocity, momentum, and the flash of deadly fire."[7] Craig, in contrast, was one of the few twentieth-century historians—Hugh Trevor-Roper was another—who could bend the bow of Gibbon, writing longer, gracefully cadenced periodic sentences leavened by irony.[8]

Taylor, identifying with the British radical Dissenting tradition that descends from Tom Paine, was an instinctive revisionist. He was eager not only to challenge but to invert conventional views on major issues, and to assert the role of accident and contingency in history. "He thought," according to David Cannadine, that "most men in authority were neither admirable nor exemplary; instead, they were knaves or fools, fudging and blundering their way through events."[9]

For Craig, in contrast, the keywords are balance, perspective, and proportion. Where Taylor often "corruscated on very thin ice,"[10] Craig was among the most judicious of historians. As Fritz Stern observed in a review of Craig's contribution to the Oxford History of Modern Europe, *Germany 1866–1945*, "he is hard on causes he would tend to favor—such as the Social Democrats—and understanding of men and movements he abhors."[11] Like his favorite German novelist, Theodor Fontane, he wrote with a combination of empathy and objectivity about a variety of personalities and social types. And he was equally effective in writing about both constructive and catastrophic examples of political leadership, as several essays in this volume demonstrate.[12]

Unlike Taylor, who believed that statesmen's ideas were usually irrelevant, Craig took ideas and ideology seriously. The complex relationship between theory and practice was a recurrent concern in his work: "The translation of ideas into action and theory into practice and the subtle ways in which they are modified and transformed in the process by the play of circumstance, chance, and individual idiosyncrasy is one of the most difficult problems that confronts the historian."[13] Although he held that "ideas are elusive and chameleon-like,"[14] he was far closer to John Maynard Keynes's view that "the ideas of economists and political philosophers, both when they are right and when they are wrong, are more powerful than is commonly understood," than he was to Taylor's skepticism about the role of ideas in politics. Craig could never have made the mistake of minimizing the importance of Hitler's *Weltanschauung*, as Taylor notoriously did.

More generally, the fraught relationships between culture and power, and between intellectuals and politics, were among the principal concerns of Craig's scholarship. Having begun his career as a historian of military and diplomatic affairs, he devoted increasing attention to intellectual and cultural history during his retirement years after 1980. But there is a sense in which he was always an intellectual historian, not only when writing about high culture, but also in his magisterial narratives of political and military history and his deft portraits of diplomats and statesmen.[15]

The theme of power was the common thread that linked almost all of his studies in political, military, diplomatic, and intellectual history.[16] The tendency of German liberals to allow power to trump principle was a leitmotif of his work on the nineteenth century. The tendency of German conservatives to fetishize power was another major theme. But he was equally critical, particularly in his studies of Weimar intellectuals, of the radical Left in German politics. Unlike Taylor, who found among the "troublemakers" of the British Left a tradition of principled dissent that he could admire, Craig regarded the intellectuals of the Weimar Left as fatally irresponsible, erratic, and shrill.[17] His experience of the Second World War and the reconstruction of Germany and Europe that followed in its wake confirmed Craig's own liberalism,[18] although (as several of the essays in this volume show) he was acutely aware of liberalism's failures and limitations as well.[19]

During the 1990s Craig published *The Politics of the Unpolitical: German Writers and the Problem of Power* (1995), a book that showed how some of the greatest German intellectuals thought incisively and creatively about the problem of power,[20] and *Theodor Fontane: Literature and History in the Bismarck Reich* (1999), a study of the German novelist who focused "most consistently upon the problems that had fascinated Dickens and Trollope and would later challenge the imagination of Proust—the decline of the aristocracy, the insidious effect of parvenuism on the middle class, and the general deterioration of values that flowed from all of this."[21] Like the distinguished scholar of Russian politics Leonard Schapiro, who permitted himself in retirement to write a book about Ivan Turgenev as an antidote to his studies of Bolshevism and totalitarianism, Gordon Craig paid tribute in his retirement to Fontane's tolerant, humane spirit as a counterpoise to Heinrich Treitschke and other writers who had contributed to Germany's disastrous *trahison des clercs*. Fontane was also a subtle guide to the moral corruption that followed in the wake of Prussia's military success. Craig studied the classics of European literature not only as essential sources for the history of mentalities, but also as deep reservoirs of social criticism. His double portrait of Fontane and Heinrich Mann, "Irony and Rage in the German Novel," included in this volume, brilliantly illuminates those novelists' critiques of the disintegration of values and the confusion of power and culture in Imperial Germany.

In 1989, planning a collection of lectures and essays that he had composed during the 1980s—several of which appear here for the first time—Gordon Craig chose the title "Knowledge and Power." Those two words might call to mind the work of Michel Foucault, whose influential books exposed the hidden relationship between the production of "knowledge" and the disciplines of social control. But a diligent search of Gordon Craig's more than 800 publications is unlikely to turn up a single mention of the great French philosopher.

His inspiration here, instead, was Francis Bacon, founder of the British empirical tradition of philosophy and scientific investigation. He chose an epigraph from Bacon's *Novum Organum* (1620): "Knowledge and human power are synonymous, since the ignorance of the cause frustrates the effect."

The epigraph from Bacon signaled Gordon Craig's commitment to the European Enlightenment, of which Bacon was a progenitor. The Enlightenment faith in the idea that rational inquiry produces objective knowledge, so vigorously challenged by Foucault, was central to Craig's view of scholarship. In an unpublished lecture entitled "Knowledge and Power: The Universities," delivered at the Library of Congress in 1988, Craig offered a succinct summary of his view of the relationship between knowledge and power in German history before 1945: "In brief, the balanced relationship of *Wissen* and *Macht* that Hegel and Fichte envisaged was distorted into one in which power manipulated knowledge for its own purposes, and knowledge not only abdicated its critical function but in the end actually abandoned its very ideals in a willing servitude to tyranny and inhumanity."[22]

Burckhardt warned his fellow historians that "the man who walks one road of limited interest too long may fall by the wayside. Buckle's study of the Scottish divines of the seventeenth century caused him his paralysis of the brain."[23] Such a fate could never have befallen Gordon Craig. The essays in this book, all written during the years of his retirement, exhibit the same insatiable curiosity and unflagging energy that characterized his entire career. On the cusp of his tenth decade he was planning a book on the culture and literature of Berlin. Hints of what that final book might have been appear in several of the essays included in this volume. All of them are examples of the author's conception of history as a humanistic discipline, alert to the ever-present possibilities of corruption and catastrophe in human affairs, but also committed to "a warm and instinctive sympathy for such qualities as fortitude, steadfastness, endurance, civic virtue, dedication to the greater good, and service to humanity when they are embodied in historical movements and personalities."[24]

As scholar, teacher, and public intellectual, Gordon Craig embodied this conception of humanism in his own life and work. Born the year before Imperial Germany took its fateful plunge into the First World War, he lived long enough to applaud the reunification of Germany after the Cold War[25] and the rebirth of a vibrant cultural life in his beloved Berlin. He continued to produce his superb essays as recently as 2004, his eyesight dimming, but his prose as clear and trenchant as ever.

Part One

Politics

1

The Nineteenth Century: The Triumph and Crisis of Liberalism

I am going to talk to you today about the nineteenth century, an age that may seem remote to you. Even if we define the nineteenth century as historians often do, as extending from 1815, the end of the Napoleonic period, to 1914, the beginning of the First World War, that's far back: seventy-four years, three full generations. And yet this is a lot closer than you might think. Because, as Eric Hobsbawm has written recently [1987], part of our own memory, although though we don't often think of this, is bound up with that century. Some of you have grandfathers and grandmothers who were born in the nineteenth century: that is, before 1914. If so they may have talked to you about their fathers and mothers, or told you stories that they heard about people and events even further back than that. And by this process, by this tie of relationship, and by this office of transmitted memory, which may extend a surprisingly long way, the nineteenth century, or bits of it, becomes part of your personal recollection.

A lecture for the Stanford Alumni Association's series entitled "Origins of Modern Society: Capstone Lectures in Western Culture," delivered in 1989. Published by permission of the estate of Gordon Craig and the Stanford Alumni Association.

I was born in the last year of the nineteenth century, that is, in 1913. From my parents I heard a good deal about life in Scotland in the eighties and the nineties and the reasons why after their marriage they decided to emigrate. From my mother I listened to stories about the political preferences of her father and thus at an early age I came to know the name and something of the character of the great British liberal William Ewart Gladstone. And much later in Oxford when I was having lunch one day with my tutor in All Souls College, he, who was already a man well stricken in years, told me that in that very place he had once talked with a man who had known another man who, when he was twenty, had been in Paris during the revolution of 1830. And after that time I always felt I had a special connection with the revolution of 1830 and knew a lot more about it than I could possibly get out of books, which was quite erroneous, but pleasant to think. Whether or not we enjoy that kind of backward projection into the nineteenth century, the nineteenth century inevitably projects itself into our lives. That is because the great majority of the movers and shakers of our own century were products of that time. Adolf Hitler, the man who more than any other single individual shaped the world in which we have to live, with all of its dreadful perplexities, was already twenty-five years old in 1914, Lenin was forty-four, Stalin was thirty-five, Benito Mussolini was thirty-one, Franklin Delano Roosevelt was thirty, Winston Churchill was forty, Konrad Adenauer was thirty-eight, Charles de Gaulle was twenty-four, Mahatma Gandhi was forty-five, Mao Zedong was twenty-one.

A listing of those who have shaped our tastes and our thinking about the world would show the same result. Einstein was thirty-five in 1914, Sigmund Freud was fifty-eight, Stravinksy was thirty-two and Schoenberg forty, Picasso was thirty-three, and James Joyce thirty-two. All of these people, whose actions or creations or theories have had such profound effects on our century, were mature individuals before the end of the last one. Their ideas and ambitions were shaped by its political, social, and intellectual currents and projected through them onto our own.

To be more precise, and here I come to the principal subject of my remarks today, all of them one way or another were influenced in their thinking and actions by nineteenth-century liberalism, by its ideals and principles, by its achievements, by its failures and dilemmas. Franklin

Roosevelt was a believer in the humanitarian impulse of liberalism, which he inherited via Woodrow Wilson from William Ewart Gladstone. Winston Churchill's career after 1918 was profoundly influenced by his membership in the last great Liberal cabinet in England before 1914. Lenin inherited from Karl Marx a determination to destroy the capitalistic economic system, which was the result of liberal energy and liberal principles. Mussolini built the fascist movement as a complete repudiation of what he considered to be liberalism's materialism, its lack of nobility and heroism. Adolf Hitler's political ideas and techniques grew naturally out of the idealization of violence and the cult of irrationality, which as we shall see, eroded the foundations of liberalism in the last years before World War I.

Let's talk, then, about European liberalism in the nineteenth century, and let's start with a definition: historically, liberalism was the amalgam of beliefs developed by the middle class as it made its way upward to the position of political and social prominence that it enjoyed in the nineteenth century. It was a philosophy that was determined by the proud individualism of that class and the intensity of its struggle against all forms of institutional and legal restriction. The liberals—the word seems to have originated in Spain at the beginning of the nineteenth century but was widely adopted—were drawn for the most part from university-trained elites and the administrative and judicial bureaucracy, from the professions—doctors, lawyers, professors, and journalists—and, not least important, from the more progressive members of the business class—merchants and pioneers of the new industrial revolution. All of these people shared the conviction that freedom, in all of its forms—freedom from absolutism and feudalism, from economic regimentation and religious obscurantism, from occupational restriction and limitations of speech and assembly—would improve the quality of society and the well-being of all its members. And they all believed that their knowledge of this, in distinction to the reactionary conservatism of the aristocratic classes, validated their claims to political power, indeed gave them a stronger claim to political power than any other section of society.

The liberals believed in freedom because they believed in individuality. And one of their most eloquent spokesmen, the Englishman John Stuart Mill, wrote in his great essay *On Liberty* in 1859, "in proportion to the development of his individuality, each person becomes more valuable to himself and is therefore more capable of becoming more valuable to others." Because of this faith in the free individual they believed in progress. "Once men were free," the Frenchman Condorcet wrote, they would advance "with a firm and sure step on the pathway of truth, of virtue, and of happiness. There was no limit set to the perfecting of the powers of man. Human perfectibility was in reality indefinite. The progress of this perfectibility had no other limit than the duration of the globe upon which nature has placed us."

The liberals were not economic egalitarians, nor were they democrats. They remembered the excesses of the French Revolution, and distrusted democracy because it placed power in the hands of the least responsible members of society. That the education of the masses would in time correct this, they professed to believe. And the ardor with which they advocated educational reform indicated that their professions were genuine. Meanwhile, however, they were inclined to the view that government should be in the hands of people like themselves, that is men of intelligence and *Bildung*, men who because they owned property had a real stake in society. This was not selfishness. In his fight against the English aristocracy in the 1840s, Richard Cobden cried "the sooner the power in this country is transferred from the landed oligarchy which has so misused it and is placed absolutely, mind I say absolutely, in the hands of the intelligent, middle, and industrious classes, the better for the condition and destiny of this country." When Cobden said that he was not intimating that the middle class would govern in its own interest. Like the Frenchman, Sieyès, who said that the Third Estate was the nation, Cobden believed that the demands of the middle class were in the interest of all classes and would bring to all of them guarantees of human rights, and law and justice, and opportunities to improve their material lot.

We can be a bit more specific than this and say that the liberals and the liberal parties, when they were formed, subscribed in general to the following list of principles and beliefs (*mutatis mutandis*, of course, because there were always different national emphases and the British liberals, for instance, didn't always subscribe to the beliefs of their continental brothers). But roughly speaking we can say this: first, in economics, they believed in the principle of laissez faire, that is, the belief that there should be no interference with the natural laws of supply and demand and that trade, commerce and production should be free from external regulation and restriction; and in the principle of modernization, meaning the removal of feudal encumbrances, trade barriers, and other artificial hindrances to economic growth. Second, in politics, the belief in civil liberties guaranteed by an equitable judicial system and by written constitutions (here the British were an exception because they didn't have a constitution); a belief in representative government with suffrage based on education and property and limited to males because women had no political rights until the twentieth century; and in the separation of church and state. Third, in social policy, as was logical in a philosophy that put such a premium upon individuality, a general belief in self-improvement, rather than government-directed reform—a principle that was, however, tempered by a belief in state-supported educational reform and a strong humanitarian impulse that was directed toward the vulnerable classes of society. Fourth, in foreign policy, opposition to adventurism, to militarism, and to overseas expansion, combined with strong feelings of antipathy toward absolutist regimes, a general sympathy for movements of national self-determination and a faith in the compatibility of such national movements with internationalism and peace. And finally, in general, faith in progress, which was strengthened by a firm belief that all problems are capable of solution by the use of human reason. Liberalism was the heir of the European Enlightenment from which it derived its faith in secular rather than divine or mystical authority and in rationality above all else.

The age of liberalism can be said to have begun in 1830 with the revolutions in Belgium, France, and Switzerland, which brought liberal parties to power in those countries, and with the passage of the Great Reform Bill in Great Britain in 1832, which started a political revolution that was completed by the repeal of the Corn Laws in 1846. The apogee of liberalism came in the late sixties and seventies, the time of Gladstone's so-called "Great Ministry," the time when the National Liberal Party in Germany was the largest party in the Reichstag with 155 seats, and when liberal parties, sometimes under different names, to be sure, dominated the political scene in Austria, Belgium, Italy, Spain, and at the end of the seventies, France. The waning of liberalism

began in the 1880s. We can almost date it precisely: in 1882 a character
in Gilbert and Sullivan's *Iolanthe* sang:

> I often think it's comical
> fa la la lal, fa la la lal,
> how nature always does contrive
> fa la la lal, fa la la lal,
> that every boy and every gal
> that's born into the world alive
> is either a little Liberal
> or else a little Conservative.

The truth of this was confounded almost immediately. Of the last
twenty-five years of the nineteenth century, all but nine were years of
conservative domination. And elsewhere too liberal parties were generally in disarray. The once powerful National Liberal Party in Germany
had lost more than two-thirds of its parliamentary seats by 1882 and it
never recovered. The liberal age in Austria came to end at the same
time, and the strong Swiss liberal movement even earlier, although its
eclipse was not so complete. In Belgium the only thing that kept the
once dominant liberal party from being totally wiped out by the conservative and socialist parties, was the fact that the Belgian constitution
provided for proportional representation. In short, by the last years of
the nineteenth century organized liberalism was in full retreat to that
condition of obscurity and ineffectiveness that it was to enjoy in the
twentieth century.

Before we try to explain the causes and consequences of that precip-
itous decline, let's consider for a moment the achievements of liberalism and liberal parties in their years of ascendancy, because these
achievements were notable. We don't have to try to give anything like
the complete record of liberal reforms, but again we can content ourselves with listing what they accomplished under four headings.

The field of economic growth: everyone, I suppose, is entitled to his
opinion about the social and moral effects of the extension of industri-
alization. But whatever can be said about that, there can be no doubt
that it made accessible to the masses commodities that were once beyond their reach and increased the material comforts and conveniences
of life in society in general. The liberal contribution to this was notable,

for the extension and expansion of industrialism benefited not only from the liberal philosophy of free trade which was ascendant until the late seventies and from their abolition of both internal and external tariff and customs barriers, but also wherever formally atomized and federalized countries became united states, as was true of Switzerland in 1848 and Italy and Germany in the sixties, from liberal programs of national public works, improvement of national transportation, and standardization of such things as weights and measures and currency.

Even more important was the way liberal regimes set about establishing credit facilities in the interest of economic growth. It should also be remembered that the great age of liberalism was also the great age of the railway. In 1830 there were virtually no European railways at all. Indeed as late as the middle 1840s there were only 1,750 kilometers of railway in Germany, 882 in France, and none in Switzerland at all. Yet by the 1870s, Europe was covered with integrated rail systems and one could travel from Paris to Constantinople with speed and comfort. Now this would have been quite impossible if railroad entrepreneurs had had to depend upon the kind of private banking houses that existed at the beginning of the century. What was needed was the kind of bank that had large accumulations of funds that came from selling shares to the public, and then using its funds not to pay out big dividends, but to make investments in the national economy by supporting new industries and large-scale enterprises like the railway. In countries like Germany and Switzerland when liberal regimes came into power, such banks were founded, the Schweizerische Kreditanstalt, founded in Zürich in 186 and still existing, was a prime example. The liberal regimes also helped the expansion of industry and commerce, by reforming company laws, reducing the risks of investment by legitimizing the principle of limited liability, to give only one example.

In the second place the impulse toward modernization not only gave benefits to business but measurably increased the area of individual liberty. Liberals were ruthless in their abolition of feudal remnants and encumbrances and rural populations profited from this as they did from liberal attacks upon the system of tithing from which peasants on church lands had long suffered. The latent anticlericalism of liberal parties also often led to the abolition of religious foundations and the conversion of their wealth to civic improvement and the building of hospitals and almshouses. Liberal abolition of guild restrictions provided a freer labor market for business and increased opportunities for skilled workers. Notable also was the zeal with which liberals tore down the ancient and sometimes not so ancient fortifications of walled towns like Rastatt in Baden or Zürich in Switzerland, to give only two examples. And it is typical of the mixed motives of the liberal reformers in general that in 1832, when the liberal party in the canton of Zürich in Switzerland began its campaign for the leveling of old fortifications, they used a combination of economic, humanitarian, and ideological arguments, claiming that the walls were a relic of militarism, that they must be removed on that account, that they were a barrier to the equality of the city and the countryside which the liberals had vowed to promote, and that they were an impediment to traffic and an obstacle to the natural expansion of the city, which if allowed to take its own course would both lower rents and improve public health. All of these arguments were quite sincere, and as a matter of fact, quite sound. Modernization also took the form of a rigorously utilitarian approach to institutions inherited from the past. Courts of chancery and circumlocution offices, however venerable and fixed in tradition would, the liberals insisted, not be tolerated unless they worked effectively. And this attitude led to a healthy overhauling of public administration to long overdue reform of judicial systems and to the codification of laws, all of which improved guarantees of individual liberties.

In the third place the liberal achievement of opening education to the masses was absolutely epoch-making. At the beginning of the liberal era systems of free compulsory elementary education existed only in Prussia, some of the north German states and some of the Scandinavian countries. Elsewhere the rate of illiteracy, even in so-called advanced countries like England and France, was stupendous: in England and France, for instance, over forty percent as late as the 1850s, in Italy and Spain closer to seventy percent in the 1870s. This situation the liberals recognized as the problem of the century, arguing that only by extending education to the masses could they be made decent, intelligent, industrious, and capable in the sharing of political responsibility. And the liberals set out to accomplish this by a series of notable reforms: Guizot's education law of 1833 in France (Guizot was the man who said, "the opening of every schoolhouse closes a jail"); a series of Swiss laws in the same decade, which led the Englishman Matthew Arnold to hail Swiss elementary and secondary education as the best in Europe; the Foster Education Act in England in 1871; laws extending the compulsory principle in Italy, Belgium, and Holland in the late seventies; and at the same time a notable expansion of the primary schools in France under the inspiration of Léon Gambetta and Jules Ferry. These reforms were often opposed by the Church, which the liberals sought to exclude from school direction, and by the conservatives, but even so, they made their way.

Finally, among the achievements of the liberals we must include their contribution to the cause of national integration. It was the liberals who led the fight to break down the atomized condition of countries like Switzerland and Italy and Germany, and the victory of the national principle in the transformation of the Swiss *Eidgenossenschaft* into the new *Bundesstaat* and the creation of the kingdom in Italy and the new German Reich was largely due to the public support that they generated in its behalf. These achievements were impressive, but they were not unalloyed as we shall see when we turn to the complex of causes that led to the decline of liberalism and the erosion of liberal ideals at the end of the century, which had consequences reaching into our own century.

The decline of liberalism had its roots in the world economic crisis of 1873 and the subsequent economic malaise that lasted until the nineties. The halcyon days of liberalism after all had been during the boom of the years 1853 to 1873 when everything was gas and gaiters, when no enterprise seemed capable of failure, when there was general prosperity. The economic atmosphere that reigned after the crash of '73 bred all sorts of new problems that confused liberals and challenged their loyalty to their own economic principles. But this was not the only reason for their troubles at the end of the century. Their troubles were compounded by inherent contradictions in their basic philosophy and to a very great extent by the very success of the programs that they had launched earlier, which now had some very curious effects that disappointed their authors.

With respect to the economic situation, there is no doubt that European businessmen, who had always been the backbone of liberal parties, regarded the years that stretched from 1873 down into the nineties as one long depression. Despite the paradoxical fact that during those years industrialism never stopped expanding, that the American and German industrial economies registered significant gains, that the industrial revolution penetrated Sweden and Russia for the first time, and that investment in Latin America reached dizzying heights. But the businessmen of this period seemed to be much less interested in growth than they were in profitability; their minds were set on the depression in prices and interest and hence profits, of which agriculture was the principal victim, although by no means the only one. They became obsessed with the idea of propping up prices. And they urged the liberal leadership to make alliances with the agricultural parties for that purpose.

Now that was bad enough, because the agricultural parties were traditionally conservative and aristocratic, and the liberals had come to power in the first place by opposing them, as the British liberals under Richard Cobden had done in the fight over the Corn Laws in the 1840s, but in the eighties and nineties, businessmen were no longer interested in the old principles of the party. And to protect their own interests, they demanded that their liberal parties come out in favor of such things as protectionism by tariff legislation, of combination in the form of monopolies and trusts, and in order to gain new markets, of imperialism or the acquisition of colonies overseas. Now these policies were all in variance with liberal principles and when the parties tended to yield to the demands of their businessmen, they lost the support of members who were more interested in principle than they were in profit. There were quite a number of these people, and this hurt the liberal parties. It was the selfishness of the business contingent of British liberalism that turned John Stuart Mill into a socialist. It was the fight over the abandonment of free trade that broke the German National Liberal party in two and it never recovered. The abandonment of the principle of laissez faire that was involved in asking governments to pass tariff bills, and protect businesses by legitimizing the formation of trusts and cartels, was resented by many members who left the party because they had always set their faces against any government role in economic affairs, and who in any case regarded monopoly and other forms of combination as a potent threat to small business. As for the new advocacy of imperialism, this revolted the conscience of old liberals who regarded this as an encouragement of militarism and war, as of course, it was. And many English liberals who regarded William Ewart Gladstone as their greatest and indeed destined leader withdrew their support from him when he seemed to compromise the liberal anti-imperialist philosophy by his occupation of Egypt in 1882. By all of these issues liberal parties were riven, and all of them caused fissiparous tendencies and general decline.

Meanwhile, the whole nature of politics was changing, and liberals could no longer claim as Abbé Sieyès had done, that the Third Estate was the nation. The extension of the suffrage in all major countries from the 1870s onward had the result not only of creating large working class parties but also of producing sizable numbers of unattached voters, predominantly lower middle class, who tended to drift toward the right and provide a basis for the rejuvenation of conservatism on a new and radical basis. The day of mass political parties now dawned. In it, the more questionable effects of the greatest liberal achievements of the century now manifested themselves. The extension of education to the masses had doubtless increased literacy: that is, many more people could now read. But because most children left school at an early age the price of literacy was a large degree—a dangerous degree—of gullibility. And this was played upon by government propaganda, by the sensationalism of the new popular press, and by the blandishments of a new breed of demagogic and charismatic leaders.

And this is one of the reasons why the last quarter of the nineteenth century, a time of such material progress and scientific accomplishment and cultural glory that it was later nostalgically called La Belle Époque, "the beautiful era," was also an age of xenophobic nationalism, political extremism, and racism. Newspaper editors who wanted large press runs found that they could get them by playing on the masses' yearning for excitement, by printing lurid descriptions of colonial wars, or dramatizing the threat posed by other nations to their own interests. Governments interested in getting new arms appropriations or funds to build new battle fleets could use the same tactics and they often appealed to the untutored masses to break the opposition of political parties that sought to stem the dangerous tendencies of the age by reasoned argument. Political leaders of the right played on the hidden resentments of the masses to win a following of their own, often using racist arguments against their own countrymen. It's no accident that it was in the last quarter of the nineteenth century that racist anti-Semitism (once a Jew always a Jew and never a full citizen), as opposed to the older religious anti-Semitism (which held that you ceased to be a Jew if you were baptized as a Christian) came into its own: in France, in the Dreyfus case of the 1890s; in Austria, where Karl Lueger built a political career on the basis of anti-Semitism, greatly impressing a young countryman of his called Adolf Hitler; in Germany, where there was actually an anti-Semitic party of fifteen members in the German Reichstag in the 1890s. In the European subconscious the evil seed was already germinating for the dreadful flowering in the twentieth century.

This was a time in short, when governments, politicians and intellectuals alike were discovering the usefulness of irrationality, and when the respected political scientist in Great Britain, Graham Wallas, warned students of politics not "to exaggerate the intellectuality of mankind." And along with the spread of irrationality went a growing belief that the problems of the age were to be solved not by reason but by power. There was a new respect for violence. I think one could say that there was in this time an idealization of violence. It was to be found in the prevalent Social Darwinism, which attempted to justify international war and colonial competition, and domestic strife, as natural and tolerable manifestations of the struggle for existence. It was to be found in Marxism with its insistence on class struggle and revolution and the overthrow of bourgeois society. It was to be found in syndicalism, with its belief in the resolution of labor disputes by direct action, that is machine-breaking, and its leader Georges Sorel's myth of the general strike. It was to be found in anarchism, which horrified and fascinated Europe in the eighties, which emphasized the use of violence for its own sake and whose founder Mikhail Bakunin had ecstatic visions of the whole of Europe—St. Petersburg, Paris, and London—transformed into a gigantic rubbish heap. All of these intellectual tendencies, and at the end of the century Bergsonian philosophy, with its emphasis upon *élan vital* rather than reflection, and Freudian psychology, with its insistence that man is not moved by reason but by dark instinctual forces that he finds difficult to control, wore away the old belief typically stated in John Stuart Mill's *On Liberty*, that man is a responsible being capable of improving himself by his own efforts and solving his own difficulties by his own mind. That vision of purpose and responsibility, seemed now to be yielding to the despairing view expressed by the German moralist Friedrich Nietzsche, who wrote in 1888, "our whole European culture has for a long time been moving with a tortured tension that increases from decade to decade as if towards a catastrophe. Agitated, violent, headlong, like a river that longs for its mouth, but no longer has time for deliberation, that is afraid of deliberation."

When Graham Wallas said what he said about not exaggerating the intellectuality of mankind, he was, as Eric Hobsbawm has recently noted, consciously writing the epitaph of European liberalism. There is no doubt that by the nineties the liberal bourgeoisie was caught up in a crisis of identity. New directions in economics had made their cardinal principles of free trade and laissez-faire meaningless, the coming of mass politics and the rejuvenation of the right on a charismatic demagogic basis had undermined the strength of their parties, had indeed created a polarization of the political process in which they were drained of members and political inspiration and squeezed relentlessly between the extremes. At the same time the decline of established religion, to which they had themselves in their heyday contributed, the weakening of the Puritan ethic, which had once sustained them, and the loosening of family ties eroded their moral assurance. As if that were not enough, new tendencies in the social sciences and in art and literature—what was one to make after all of Richard Strauss's *Salomé* or the stories of Oscar Wilde?—confirmed their fears that the rule of reason that they had inherited from the enlightenment and had accepted as a guide to public and private conduct had lost its legitimacy.

All of this was reflected now in the political attitudes of the old liberal middle class. Amid the bewildering shift of values they began to feel that the realities of their time were passing them by, and they tried to retrieve their position either by the abandonment of principle or by the rationalization of positions that they had hitherto changed only in part. This is how they accommodated themselves to imperialism, which they had at one time stoutly opposed, but which they now found diverse and contradictory reasons for supporting, resolutely closing their eyes to the fact that the European scramble for profits in Africa and the Far East and Persia and the Ottoman Empire and Morocco could not be squared with the traditional humanitarianism of liberalism, and aside from that could hardly leave the European balance of power, which was the support of peace, unaffected because it was subjected to a continual strain of international confrontations.

And this is how when the final crisis came the liberals accommodated themselves to the demands of nationalism. There had been a time when the liberal bourgeoisie were at the height of their influence, when they had regarded the nation, including their own nation, as merely a temporary way-station on the journey that would eventuate in a truly international society: likely one that was described by Alfred Lord Tennyson in that quintessential liberal poem "Locksley Hall," in which he had a vision of seeing "the heavens fill with commerce, argosies of magic sails,/Pilots of the purple twilight, dropping down with costly bales, . . . Till the war-drum throbb'd no longer, and the battle flags were furl'd/ In the Parliament of man, the Federation of the world."

There had been a time in which, despite their support of national self-determination, liberals had been skeptical of the claims to national independence of what they regarded as unviable or small peoples, like the Serbs, who caused so much dreadful trouble in 1914. And as for war, there had been a time when, while willing to admit that it might sometimes be necessary, the liberals had nevertheless insisted that it was something to be avoided, something that aroused enthusiasm only among the militaristic nobility and the uncivilized.

But that was then. In 1914 to most liberals in all countries such notions were an embarrassment, and because they were, the liberals were wholly ineffectual in deterring Europe's heedless plunge into catastrophe, toward a holocaust that was to bequeath so many intractable problems to future generations.

2

Politics of a Plague

Asiatic cholera, one of humanity's greatest scourges in the modern period, came to Europe for the first time in the years after 1817, traveling by ship and caravan route from the banks of the Ganges, where it was endemic, to the Persian Gulf, Mesopotamia and Iran, the Caspian Sea and southern Russia, and then—thanks to troop movements occasioned by Russia's wars against Persia and Turkey in the late 1820s and its suppression of the revolt in Poland in 1830–1831—to the shores of the Baltic Sea. From there its spread westward was swift and devastating, and before the end of 1833 it had ravaged the German states, France, and the British Isles and passed on to Canada, the western and southern parts of the United States, and Mexico.

Statistics for morbidity and mortality in this first great cholera epidemic are unreliable, for there was generally no means of collecting and tabulating them on a large scale, but on the basis of what we have it appears that Russia suffered over 100,000 deaths in 1830–1831 and that, in Germany, Berlin alone had 2,000 deaths out of a population of

Review of *Death in Hamburg: Society and Politics in the Cholera Years, 1830–1910*, by Richard J. Evans, *The New York Review of Books*, June 30, 1988, pp. 9–10, 12–13. Reprinted with permission from *The New York Review of Books*. Copyright © 1988, NYREV, Inc.

230,000, while in France there were 39,000 cases of cholera in Paris, with 18,000 deaths, a mortality rate of 21.8 per thousand of population. In Great Britain, the Black Country was particularly affected, with heavy death rates in towns like Bilston, Manchester, and Liverpool, while Glasgow and Dublin had mortality rates of 15 and 30 to the thousand respectively. In Canada one in every thirteen inhabitants of Montreal died in 1832, and in the United States there were 5,000 cases in New Orleans. Nor was this the end of the matter, for the disease returned in 1848–1849, when there were 668,000 deaths in Russia and heavy losses in Italy and France; in 1854, when there were 5,000 deaths in Liverpool; in 1866–1867; in 1873, when half a million Hungarians died of the disease; in 1884; and in 1892.

Cholera was by no means the greatest of the killer diseases of the nineteenth century; tuberculosis had a far higher incidence and claimed nearly four million victims in England and Wales alone between 1851 and 1910, and typhoid, smallpox, and measles had higher mortality rates. But there is no doubt that its psychological impact was unequaled. William H. McNeill has written that the cholera bacillus produced

> violent and dramatic symptoms—diarrhea, vomiting, fever and death—often within a few hours of the first signs of illness. The speed with which cholera killed was profoundly alarming, since perfectly healthy people could never feel safe from sudden death when the infection was anywhere near. In addition, the symptoms were peculiarly horrible: radical dehydration meant that a victim shrank into a wizened caricature of his former self within a few hours, while ruptured capillaries discolored the skin, turning it black and blue. The effect was to make mortality uniquely visible: patterns of bodily decay were exacerbated and accelerated, as in a time-lapse motion picture, to remind all who saw it of death's ugly horror and utter inevitability.[1]

Nor did the disease respect class or degree. It struck down the prominent as well as the humble—among its victims in 1831 were the French prime minister Casimir Perier, the German philosopher Hegel, Napoleon's great antagonist August Neithardt von Gneisenau, the military theorist Clausewitz, the Russian grand duke Constantine, and the commander who suppressed the Polish revolt, General Diebitsch. It also had the power to undermine the foundations of apparently stable regimes, as it did in the canton of Zurich in 1867, when an unforeseen outbreak of cholera, which affected the poorer districts of the city most grievously, raised a storm of indignation that helped to overthrow the government and ended the liberal era that had lasted since 1830. It was no accident that preoccupation with the disease affected literature and supplied both the pulpit and the language of politics with new analogies and symbols. When Bismarck said that preventive war was like committing suicide because you are afraid to die, he was thinking of an old lady in Berlin during the epidemic of 1831 who had done precisely that. When Theodor Mommsen sought an effective way of describing his feelings about anti-Semitism, his mind turned in the same direction, and he said, "It is a horrible epidemic like cholera—one can neither explain nor cure it. One must patiently wait until the poison consumes itself and loses its virulence."

In an influential article in *Past and Present* in April 1961, Asa Briggs called upon historians to turn their attention to cholera's deadly nineteenth-century progress, which they had until then largely neglected. He insisted that when they did so they would have to undertake far more than a mere exercise in medical epidemiology, for cholera was a disease of society in the most profound sense:

> It hit the poor particularly ruthlessly, thriving on the kind of conditions in which they lived. Whenever it threatened European countries, it quickened social apprehensions. Wherever it appeared, it tested the efficiency and resilience of local administrative structures. It exposed relentlessly political, social and moral shortcomings. It prompted rumours, suspicions and at times violent social conflicts.

Richard Evans's new book, which concentrates on the cholera epidemic in Hamburg in 1892, is precisely the kind of study that Briggs had in mind. A brilliantly written work of great analytical penetration, which is based on very extensive reading, it is not a mere description of the Hamburg epidemic of 1892 (which, even with its 17,000 cases and 8,600 deaths and its mortality rate of 13.4 per thousand, was far less severe than the epidemics in Montreal in 1832 or in Hungary in 1873), but rather an investigation of why the harbor city on the Elbe, alone of the great European cities, suffered a major outbreak in that year. Evans finds the answer to that question in the peculiar combination of political, economic, social, and medical circumstances that prevailed in Hamburg at the time, which not only explained the failure to take preventive action before the crisis came but also determined the nature of the response to it and the corrective measures taken after it was over.

The epidemic itself is not really the center of Evans's story, but it was, as he says, "one of those events that, as Lenin once put it, may perhaps be ultimately insignificant in themselves, but nevertheless, as in a flash of lightning, illuminate a whole historical landscape, throwing even the obscurest features into sharp and dramatic relief." More graphically than other epidemics, it demonstrated the helplessness of traditional patterns of authority to meet the challenge posed by the social and environmental consequences of rapid industrial and urban growth, while revealing the structures of social inequality, the operations of political power, and the attitudes and habits of mind of different classes and groups in society with a cold and pitiless clarity.

At the end of the nineteenth century, Hamburg was governed by an eighteen-member Senate and a Citizens' Assembly of 160 members. Both bodies were representative of the population only in the most limited sense, for the Senate, whose members served for life and could not be replaced, filled its vacancies by a process of appointment in which the Citizens' Assembly collaborated, and the latter body was elected half by the tax-paying citizens, who also had to pay a substantial annual citizen's fee, and half by the property owners and the "notables" or citizens serving in civic positions. As Evans writes, "Property thus in a very real sense formed the foundation of direct political power." The wealthiest of the city's merchants, bankers, and lawyers, bound together by familial and social ties, reserved to themselves the executive power in the Senate. The middling bourgeoisie of lesser merchants, doctors, apothecaries, lawyers, and teachers, and those members of the lower middle class who owned rentable property, made their influence felt through the Citizens' Assembly, the Chamber of Commerce, the Property-Owners' Association, the Citizens' Clubs, and other organizations.

This was a form of government that worked through leisurely consultation and informal agreement and compromise, but it was at a grave disadvantage when it came to coping with emergency situations or even with the kind of problems that are inevitable in expanding urban conglomerations—public works, communications, housing, and hygiene and sanitation. Unlike the bordering Kingdom of Prussia, it had no professional civil service, the very idea of which was offensive to its tradition of particularism and its liberal philosophy. Almost all of the city's higher administrative work was carried out by the so-called Deputations, of which there were thirty-four, each responsible for a particular aspect of government and each composed of prominent citizens, elected by the Citizens' Assembly and serving without pay under the leadership of one or more senators. Inevitably the work of these bodies was characterized by duplication of effort, conflict over jurisdiction, and, since all senators were not equally competent or energetic, inefficiency and procrastination.

Given the social complexion of the Deputations, and their lack of technical advisers, they were also affected by a baleful myopia when confronted with problems like environmental pollution, to which Hamburg was increasingly prone as it became more industrialized. They were inclined to regard this as a direct physical consequence not of capitalist expansion but of the dirtiness and unhygienic habits of the lower classes, a fixation from which much tragedy was to come. In general, there was no doubt about the civic conscience that animated the political system, but the philosophy underlying this was one of "common sense," which meant doing nothing that violated tradition, or involved needless and costly change—above all nothing that would jeopardize Hamburg's trade, the promotion of which was universally regarded as the end of all policy, even by such outsiders as the Social Democrats (this helps to explain the reformism of that party in Hamburg, despite its revolutionary pronouncements elsewhere in the country).

These institutional weaknesses and habits of mind might have had less tragic results during the crisis of 1892 if there had been a determined and united medical profession capable of making the government face up to realities. But the doctors were slow in winning the confidence of the ruling classes in Hamburg, who were suspicious of their claim to a monopoly in the health market and their attempt to strengthen hygienic and sanitary regulations, and who were in any case, as one doctor wrote in 1863, prone to "a scarcely believable ignorance and indifference...with regard to what one might call public health care."

Typical of the disregard of medical advice is the fact that decades after the introduction of compulsory vaccination against smallpox in the rest of Germany, Hamburg's government continued to rely on voluntary methods of prevention, and when the medical profession pressed for legislation on the subject in the 1860s, and again in 1871, this was rejected by the Citizens' Assembly, with the argument on the latter occasion that compulsory vaccination "encroaches upon personal freedom and liberty, and upon the most basic right of the individual, that of the freedom to dispose of his body as he wishes." Later in the year, soldiers returning from the war against France brought the smallpox virus with them. Four thousand and fifty-three inhabitants of Hamburg died of the disease, more victims than in any local outbreak of typhoid or cholera in the nineteenth century, including the epidemic of 1892.

In the case of cholera, effective pressure for remedial action was made impossible because the medical profession was badly divided on the question of the causes of the disease. The English doctor John Snow had demonstrated that all cases of cholera that occurred in a district of central London during the outbreak of 1854 could be traced to a single contaminated source of drinking water. But his report was regarded as circumstantial and attracted little attention in Germany, where the prevailing theory was that of Dr. Max von Pettenkofer, a flamboyant and stubborn Bavarian advocate of the miasmatic theory, which held that sudden outbreaks of the disease were caused by a miasma that was exuded by corpses and other rotting matter in the earth and was particularly infectious to constitutions weakened by their living conditions or manner of life.

This theory remained unchallenged until 1883, when Robert Koch, the discoverer of the tuberculosis bacillus, claimed to have found a new bacillus responsible for cholera. This discovery was hailed throughout Germany, perhaps more for political than for scientific reasons, for it seemed to be proof of the scientific eminence of the new German Reich, but for the same reasons it had less resonance in particularistic Hamburg, which feared the kind of bureaucratic controls that the contagionist theory would require in time of epidemic. On the other hand, Pettenkofer's views were entirely congenial to Hamburg's liberal philosophy of government, for he declared roundly that prevention by hygienic measures to provide cleanliness, fresh air, and rational diet was the only effective way of coping with cholera, and that, once an epidemic had broken out, nothing could be done by quarantine or special hospitals or the closing of markets and fairs or the compulsory boiling of water to check its progress. His theory of cholera was reassuring because it seemed a guarantee against excessive expenditures and the disruption of trade, and also, as Evans writes, because

> his emphasis on sanitation . . . [was] more than welcome to the German middle classes at a time when the urban environment was rapidly deteriorating, and when bourgeois consciousness of the presence of dirt and excrement, noxious vapours, and polluted or adulterated food was growing stronger. The stress he laid on temperance and regularity accorded strongly with bourgeois values, as did the belief he expressed that hygienic improvement depended above all on the individual.

Moreover, since Pettenkofer was a sound scientist who offered a synthesis of many previous studies and linked his theory to the established scientific principle of fermentation, he persuaded a large part of the medical profession that his views were correct and left others undecided, and hence doubtful of the validity of the contagion theory of Snow and Koch. In the intermittent debate on the construction of a new water and sewage disposal system for Hamburg, which began after the epidemic of 1873 and continued without issue for the next seventeen years, there was no really persistent pressure from the medical profession, even after Koch's discovery increased the advisability of such construction. The doctors do not seem to have protested when new port facilities and a grandiose new town hall were given precedence over a water filtration system, which was not indeed approved until 1890 and was still unfinished when the epidemic came in 1892.

The first part of Evans's discussion of the epidemic itself is aptly called "From Concealment to Catastrophe," and it is a sad story of administrative failure and individual incompetence. Throughout the summer of 1892, local authorities were aware that a new epidemic was threatening their city, and they had been warned by the Imperial Health Office, which by now had completely accepted Koch's views, to institute all of the measures that had been anathema to Pettenkofer: disinfection and quarantine, strict control of the river traffic, the boiling of all water, and the plentiful use of carbolic. But when the first cases appeared, doctors were reluctant to take the responsibility for diagnosing them as *cholera Asiatica*, and were subjected to pressure to prevent them from doing so. The city's chief medical officer, Johann Caspar Kraus, Evans says, followed an "'absolutely definite plan' . . . of not taking cognizance of individual cases."

Kraus and his superior, Senator Gerhard Hachmann, were so dilatory in responding to accumulating evidence of the mounting danger that it was not until August 24, nine days after the appearance of the first case, that the Senate met to consider what measures might be taken, and even then its members seemed more worried about the quarantine measures that foreign ports might impose upon Hamburg shipping if the news got out than about the danger confronting the people of Hamburg. It was by then already too late to prevent the epidemic. It had been a hot summer, and the Elbe was so low that the tide was pushing further upstream than usual, and carrying rapidly multiplying cholera bacilli and excreta from the river's traffic past and into the main intake of the city's unfiltered central water supply, whence it passed into reservoirs and was pumped directly into the city's houses. By August 23 every section of the city was affected and thousands of people were experiencing the first symptoms of the disease. When Robert Koch arrived in the city and inspected its hospitals on August 25, he wrote to his mistress:

> I felt as if I was walking across a battlefield. Everywhere, people who had still been bursting with health a few hours before and had begun the day full of *joie de vivre* were now lying stretched out in long rows, shot down by invisible bullets, some with the characteristic rigid stare of the cholera victim, others with broken eyes, others already dead: no lamentations were to be heard, only here and there a sign or a death-rattle.

Koch was appalled by the delays and confusion and lack of energy that he found in government offices, by the evasiveness and disingenuousness of the city's medical authorities, and by the failure to implement measures long recommended and now proving their worth in Bremen and Altona, which experienced cholera in 1892 but not in epidemic proportions, Bremen suffering only six deaths. Most of all, he was shaken by the conditions of overcrowding, lack of effective sewage disposal, narrow alleys, insanitary courtyards, and stinking waterways that he discovered in a tour of the Alley Quarters in the inner city; and it was here that he made the remark that, Evans says, did more than any other single statement "to discredit the government of Hamburg, its social policy, and the political system on which it rested." "Gentlemen," Koch said, "I forget that I am in Europe."

And yet after the epidemic had run its course, the system was able to survive, with only cosmetic changes, and in Evans's opinion "the power of mercantile, banking, and industrial interests in the city continued undiminished, and even increased." One of the few genuine reforms that can be attributed to the epidemic was the law of November 1896, which broadened the suffrage by abolishing the citizen's fee, but even here income requirements were included to prevent the extension of the voting right beyond the respectable working class. The reform of 1896 also established a higher civil service in Hamburg with a career structure like the Prussian system, which weakened the element of self-government by citizen participation and tended to strengthen the authority of the Senate, as did the granting of new powers to the police "to protect persons and property against emergencies and dangers," a provision intended to guard against any possible threat from the lower and still disenfranchised classes.

The pressure from Berlin for elaborate reform in the sphere of public health was only partially successful. A Hygienic Institute was established to carry on testing of food and drink and eliminate adulteration; the sewage system was greatly improved, but it was many years before a full treatment process was instituted; new medical regulations were written, designed among other things to increase the medical profession's numerical superiority on the medical boards, although these did not come into effect until 1900. These reforms and the institution of an effective water filtration system in 1893 doubtless improved the health of the population in the years before the war. The basic social and political realities in the city, however, remained unchanged.

Given Hamburg's bourgeois-liberal tradition and its opposition to centralization and bureaucratization, which in some part determined the inefficiency of its authorities in 1892, one might think that it would have been strongly opposed to National Socialism. In reality, before 1933 the Nazis received the support not only of its resentful lower middle class, the chief victims of the financial misfortunes of the Weimar Republic, but a significant proportion of the votes of the middle and upper bourgeoisie as well. During the Third Reich, Hamburg was a Nazi stronghold often visited by Hitler and a place where the sterilization and extermination policies of the regime proved easier to carry out than in other parts of Germany. Evans believes that in part this was a reflection of attitudes toward the poor and vulnerable classes of society that had become almost automatic during the epidemics of the nineteenth century, when the well-to-do came, quite illogically, to regard them as the cause of all of society's misfortunes, including epidemic disease. It was, he says,

> the culmination of the fear and contempt with which the state, the bourgeoisie, and increasingly the apparatus of the Social Democratic Party had come to regard people such as the denizens of the Alley Quarters—the last parts of which were pulled down in the Third Reich—until they were ultimately disqualified as human beings altogether.

About the contemporary relevance of this book there can be no question, confronted as we are with an epidemic of yet unknown, but surely staggering, proportions. Current public attitudes toward AIDS are not dissimilar to those that were elicited by the great cholera epidemics of the last century. Today too, as Evans correctly points out, there has been a tendency to blame stigmatized groups, and governments waver between coercion and indifference. Medical opinion sometimes seems as widely divided about the crisis as it was in the nineteenth century; nor has it been immune to political pressure. Governments have been as reluctant to commit the resources that the threat requires as the Hamburg Senate of 1892 showed itself to be. The same lack of energy in grappling with the problem is everywhere evident. The price of such attitudes is clearly written in the historical record. If cholera has disappeared from our society, the mistakes made by governments in dealing with it in the nineteenth century still have something to teach us.

3

Demonic Democracy

I

Max Weber, born in 1864 as the child of a well-to-do Berlin family, began his scholarly career at the end of the 1880s. It was a time of crisis and turbulence in European thought. The great age of liberalism was coming to an end with the rise of mass politics and new kinds of leaders, popular tribunes with charisma (to use a Weberian term) like Georg von Schönerer and Karl Lueger and other precursors of Mussolini and Hitler. Among intellectuals, there was a widespread repudiation of the former faith in historical progress, as well as a tendency to turn away from liberal rationalism to neoromantic forms of philosophical and artistic expression. Characteristic of the crisis, above all, was a deep cultural pessimism, a sense of being trapped in a world of degeneration and decline, of disenchantment with old ideals and a frenetic search for

Review of *Fleeing the Iron Cage: Culture, Politics, and Modernity in the Thought of Max Weber*, by Lawrence A. Scaff; and *Max Weber Briefe 1906–1908*, edited by M. Rainer Lepsius, Wolfgang J. Mommsen, et al.: *The New York Review of Books*, February 13, 1992, pp. 39–43. Reprinted with permission from *The New York Review of Books*. Copyright © 1992, NYREV, Inc.

new forms of self-realization—free-love movements and youth cults, nature worship and vegetarianism. From the very beginning the young scholar was preoccupied with what he called "the fate of our times," and the unifying theme of both his scholarship and his life was the prevailing cultural crisis and the destiny of humankind in the contemporary world.

At least, this is the view of Lawrence A. Scaff in his absorbing new critical study of Weber's life and writings. Mr. Scaff believes that the familiar characterizations of Weber's work, and descriptions of him as the founder of sociology, or the leader of the revolt against positivism, or the theoretician of *Machtpolitik*, and the like, are incomplete and inadequate. He writes:

> As one turns from the comfort of the old and familiar to the life and thought as a whole . . . one cannot fail to sense a dissonance between interpretive generalizations long since taken for granted and the record of actual work and accomplishment. . . . Even to conceive [Weber's] essential questions arrayed along a single axis between "science" and "politics" is already to risk missing what is most important

—namely, what both Karl Jaspers and Karl Löwith sensed, Weber's fundamental philosophical impulse, his search for knowledge of self and the specific historical character of his time. "In my judgment," Mr. Scaff writes, "if we follow Weber's lead in this direction—that is, toward the culture and politics of the modern age—we should be rewarded with the recovery of a much more challenging and unusual body of thought than has generally been encountered before."

The direction taken by Weber's early career clearly supports Mr. Scaff's approach. In her biography of her husband, Marianne Weber tells us that the young jurist's decision in 1894 to leave the University of Berlin, where he seemed likely to receive Levin Goldschmidt's chair in commercial law when Goldschmidt retired, and to accept a chair in political economy at the University of Freiburg was caused not only by his indignation over the disingenuous manner in which the Prussian minister of education, Friedrich Althoff, tried to undercut the Freiburg offer but also by his conviction that his interests would be better served by the change in discipline. He felt, she wrote, that

> as a science political economy [was] still elastic and "young" com-

pared with jurisprudence, and in addition [lay] on the boundary of the most varied scholarly provinces; from it there [were] direct connections with cultural and intellectual history, as well as with philosophical problems; and finally it [was] more rewarding for a political and sociopolitical orientation than the more formal approach of legal thought.[1]

In fact, Scaff writes, Weber had become increasingly interested in political economy since the Eighties. The relatively new discipline seemed to him to offer a means of achieving "a modus vivendi between theoretical work and practical activity." It was a science that investigated "the economic and social conditions of existence" that shape "the quality of human beings," while at the same time imposing restraint upon the currently fashionable emphasis on economic development by means of its strong national component, which sought always to identify, and take as a standard of judgment, "the permanent economic and political *power* interests of the nation." Finally, political economy, in Weber's view, "built its content on characteristics of the modern," not least of all because theory began, he believed, with "the modern occidental type of human being and his economic action."

The general problem that preoccupied Weber in his early writings was the relationship between changes in economic and social structures and those in political authority and rule, and the consequences of such structural changes for the conduct of life in different social strata. This concern marked his early studies of agrarian economies and their role in the rise of capitalism and found eloquent and comprehensive expression in his inaugural lecture at Freiburg in May 1895.

In this closely argued discourse, Weber argued that methods of production currently followed by the East Elbian landowners, in particular their increasing use of Polish day laborers in preference to German agricultural workers, posed a problem that could be judged only by political standards, since it involved the basic interests of the nation, the Germanness of its eastern districts. The economic preferences for Polish labor on the part of the Junkers, the class upon which the monarchy depended for the protection and governance of the state, clearly invalidated their right to continued political authority, since they no longer recognized the national interest.

The difficult question was into whose hands their power would fall in a time when the political will of the old liberal *Bürgertum* seemed broken beyond repair as a result of Bismarck's rule, and when the lower middle class was sunk in philistinism, while the working class was bereft of "the catilinarian energy of the deed." Despite the achievement of the period of unification, the Germans were now burdened by "the heaviest curse that history can give a race . . . the hard fate of being political epigoni." The way out of this cultural crisis, Weber declared, in words clearly influenced by Nietzsche's essay "On the Uses and Disadvantages of History for Life," lay in a new political education that would wean the Germans from their prevalent eudaemonism and make them conscious of their responsibility to history and willing to embark on a *Grosse Politik* like that followed by Britain and France.

> We shall not succeed in banning the curse under which we stand, that of being lateborn in a politically great time, unless we understand how to become something else, the forerunners of a greater one. . . . It is not the epochs of a glorious history whose weight ages a great nation. It remains young when it has the capacity and courage to be true to itself and the great instincts that are given to it and when its leading strata are capable of lifting themselves up to the hard clear air in which the sober work of German politics prospers, which is, however, also inspired by the earnest grandeur of national feeling.

In this address, which had great resonance in the country, not least of all because it accorded with the imperialist fervor of the age, the interrelatedness of the various dimensions of Weber's political economy is clear, as is the primacy of his preoccupation with the cultural crisis.[2]

In 1897 Weber suffered a nervous collapse that forced him to take a long leave of absence from the University of Freiburg and, indeed, put an effective end to his career as a teacher, although he taught briefly at Heidelberg in 1902 and gave intermittent lectures until the end of his life. It was not until 1903 that he was able to return to his methodological studies, and these were frequently interrupted by periods of rest and trips to health resorts. Even so, thanks to his remarkable powers of self-discipline, his greatest work lay before him, and in it the emphasis on culture, always implicit in his earlier writings, became more pronounced. Scaff points out, for example, that in 1904, when Weber, in collaboration with Edgar Jaffé and Werner Sombart, assumed the direction of the *Archiv für Sozialwissenschaft und Sozialpolitik* he wrote a preface (*Geleitwort*) to the new series in which he contrasted the work of the journal from that of other social science publications:

> Above all, today the research domain of the "Archiv" must be fundamentally expanded, something that until now happened only sporadically and from case to case. Our journal will have to consider historical and theoretical knowledge of the *general cultural significance of capitalist development* as the scientific problem whose understanding it serves.

He made his own contribution to this tendency in the essays of 1905–1906 that became the second half of his study *The Protestant Ethic and the Spirit of Capitalism*. Here he traced the history of the ascetic ideal since the Protestant Reformation, showing its relationship to the origins of capitalism and the way in which it was finally defeated by its own projection into the external world of production, labor, and material culture, and by the relentless rationalization of capitalist development. As a result of this process, the modern individual was left a prisoner of vocational activity in a disenchanted world without meaning. In a famous passage, Weber wrote:

> The Puritan wanted to work in a calling; we are forced to do so. For when asceticism was carried out of monastic cells into everyday life, and began to dominate worldly morality, it did its part in building the tremendous cosmos of the modern economic order. This order is now bound to the technical and economic conditions of machine production which today determine the lives of all the individuals who are born into this mechanism, not only those directly concerned with economic acquisition, with irresistible force. Perhaps it will so determine them until the last ton of fossilized coal is burned. In Baxter's view,[3] the care for external goods should only lie on the shoulders of the "saint like a light cloak, which can be thrown aside at any moment." But fate decreed that the cloak should become an iron cage.[4]

The problem that is posed by capitalist development is, therefore, that of finding means of rationalizing or manipulating or adapting to the cultural dilemma in ways that will restore meaning and purpose to modern life. Weber pursued this theme in the section on "Religious Ethics and the 'World'" in *Economy and Society* and, more particularly, in the "Intermediate Reflection" at the end of the first volume of his *Sociology of Religion*.[5] Written sometime after 1909, the latter essay, apart from providing a typology of asceticism and mysticism, elaborated the conclusions of *The Protestant Ethic* in more abstract and generalized form, emphasizing that any system of values that accepted the transformation of the world into "causal mechanism"—the rationalized economic system, for example, which is built upon money, "the most abstract and 'impersonal' thing that exists"[6]—necessarily rejects on principle any way of looking at things that, above all, searches for a "meaning" in what takes place in this world.[7] The "Intermediate Reflection," then, considered the validity of value systems that did profess to make life meaningful—in particular the religious, aesthetic, erotic, and intellectual "spheres of life activity"—and Weber gave a tentative analysis and a rudimentary evaluation of them as possible escapes from the contemporary cultural dilemma.

His views, necessarily sketchy in the "Intermediate Reflection," were fleshed out in a lifetime of scholarly investigation and continuing debate with friends. He analyzed and criticized systems of world-abnegation like Tolstoy's pacifism and the ethically dominated commitment to pure forms of democracy and socialism favored by Robert Michels and Georg Lukács, as well as Marianne Weber's speculations about an autonomous "female culture." The possibility of a life controlled by aesthetic ideals and criteria preoccupied him for a long time. He was powerfully attracted by the poetry and ideas of Stefan George, until the poet's "Maximin experience," his encounter with a fifteen-year-old boy who he believed was an incarnation of the godhead, convinced him that the George circle was little more than an absurd exercise in self-indulgence.[8] Under the influence of Wagner's music, particularly *Tristan und Isolde*, he concluded that music was, in Scaff's words, "the finest and highest expression of amoral and irrational interiority," without, however, being convinced that it, or other forms of art, had any hope of vanquishing, or even escaping, the forces of rationalization. Nor did he find much promise in the *Lebenskult* of eroticism which was so much a part of his time. The Webers encountered this in the circle around the aberrant Freudian Otto Gross in Munich and in the community of artists at Ascona in Switzerland—a haunt, Marianne Weber wrote, which was a refuge for all kinds of extraordinary people who had abandoned bourgeois society, anarchists, nature lovers, vegetarians, and other sectaries who wanted to realize their dreams there and create a new world order[9]—where Weber tried, with characteristic generosity and considerable expenditure of time and energy, to be of help to some of the troubled young residents he came to know there. He asked himself, Scaff writes, whether "the new 'freedom,' based on a critique of sexuality and the erotic life, [could] be anything more than an age-old hedonism," giving none but an evanescent meaning to human existence.

Indeed, whether there was an effective escape from the iron cage at all was always, to one of Weber's skeptical and ironic mind, questionable. In his view, a responsible person had to choose either total rejection of the world or affirmation of it as it was, and either an absolute ethics of brotherliness or a value system that would accept the relativism of actual political conditions. Every choice was accompanied by costs: one had to be prepared to live with fictions or antinomies, incongruities between the ideal and the real or what Scaff calls "the uncertainties of responsibility for consequences of action." In modern culture there were no perfect answers, but by accepting the historical world as it had become and striving to understand it, and by resisting the temptations of inwardness and subjectivism, one might make possible the emergence of "contingently hopeful futures." In the last analysis, Weber's choice among the contending orders or value systems of his time was intellectualism, the reliance on scientific knowledge. He wrote in the "Intermediate Reflection,"

> Although science has created this cosmos of natural causality and has seemed unable to answer with certainty the question of its own ultimate presuppositions, in the name of "intellectual integrity" it has come forward with the claim of representing the only possible form of a reasoned view of the world. Thus, the intellect, like all cultural values, has also created an unbrotherly aristocracy of the rational possession of culture, one that is independent of all personal ethical qualities of humankind.[10]

The decision to join this aristocracy of rational scientific enquiry, Scaff says, was one of Weber's "most fundamental choices . . . [and] represented a specific, permanent and comprehensive answer to the various escape routes of modern discontent."

The second half of Scaff's book is given over to an account of the debates and discussions over this choice and related problems between Weber and members of his circle like Ferdinand Tönnies, Werner Sombart, Robert Michels, and Georg Lukács. Certainly the most fascinating of these chapters is that on Weber's relations with Georg Simmel, the Berlin sociologist of culture and the author of, among other things, the famous treatise on *The Philosophy of Money*. The two men shared a deep respect for Nietzsche, whom Simmel was among the very first to recognize as a moralist rather than an egoist or prophet of a new superman, as a profound critic of the modern age and its incipient nihilism, and as a master psychologist of human existence. Scaff points out that it was probably the brilliant third essay of *The Genealogy of Morals* ("What Do Ascetic Ideals Mean?") that inspired Simmel's conception of responsibility for the self and Weber's attention to the fortunes of asceticism; and one might add that Weber's generally critical opinion of the German professoriate was surely reinforced by Nietzsche's thunderous assaults in that essay upon the moral flabbiness of modern scholarship.[11]

The problems that engaged Weber and Simmel were much alike: urbanization, labor and vocation, the fate of the religious, ethical, and aesthetic systems of value, the prospect for freedom and individuality in a rationalized and disenchanted world, and other essentially cultural problems of modernity. There were profound differences in their approach, Weber being more interested in the specific, while Simmel aspired to know the world in its totality, and in its infinite variety. (Lukács reported that he once complained that there were too few categories just as there were too few sexes.) But they were at one in the questions they asked, and the biggest of these, Scaff writes, was simply,

> What comes next? Should we expect affirmation of modern culture, adaptation to its many modes, an exhaustive search for alternatives, a call for new prophets, a return to old religions, the persistence of familiar wisdom ("meeting the demands of the day"), individual inventiveness ("creating ideals from within our chests"), or simply nothingness?

II

Despite the brilliance of Scaff's analysis of Weber's cultural views, the personality of his subject tends to be rather obscured by the argument. The reader gets only glimpses of Weber's quotidian existence, his likes and dislikes, his working day, his views of contemporary German politics, his controversies, and his passions. Happily these are all on display in Rainer Lepsius and Wolfgang Mommsen's admirable edition of Weber's letters for the years between 1906 and 1908, the first volume of letters to appear in the Weber *Gesamtausgabe*.

The editing of Weber's letters involves a myriad of problems, beginning with their author's handwriting, which has been a source of exasperation and even agony for everyone who has had to decipher it. In addition, over the years the letters have been scattered and many of them lost, while others, like those published by Marianne Weber, have survived in incomplete form. Because of the accidents of time and history, the letters to which Weber was responding have often disappeared. This is true of those of Robert Michels, for example, and of most of Weber's correspondence with Werner Sombart and Georg Simmel. The editors have not been daunted by these difficulties. They have painstakingly restored the text of the surviving letters, provided the reader with admirable notes that explain the circumstances in which each letter was written and its motivation, supplied quotations from letters of the addressee or from other documents that illuminate the text, described contemporary events mentioned in it, and tracked down every historical allusion or literary citation. In addition, in an appendix, they have included a list, and short biographies, of all of the persons mentioned in the letters and a set of genealogical tables that is highly useful for the understanding of Weber's letters about family affairs. Because of these editorial labors, this volume is a constant pleasure to read.

Family letters, particularly those between Weber and his wife, bulk large here, because the couple were often apart, Marianne's interest in the women's movement taking her to frequent conferences, and Weber's ill health necessitating long trips to Sicily and Capri in 1906, the Netherlands in 1907, and the Riviera and Florence in 1908. These letters not only show Weber's deep affection for his wife and his interest in her work but include a considerable amount of interesting social information, about life on the health circuit, for example, and Weber's constant but frustrated search for places that had not yet been invaded by the automobile. One learns a good deal also about the Webers' contacts with the erotic movement and the adventures of friends, like Else von Richthofen Jaffé—*la bella peccatrice*, as they called her—who were more deeply involved in it than they. Weber described the relationship that Else and her sister, Frieda Weekley (who later married D.H. Lawrence), maintained with Otto Gross, the Munich psychiatrist, follower of Freud, drug addict, and cult leader, as *"die nackte Schweinerei"* and when Gross submitted a paper to the *Archiv für Sozialwissenschaft und Sozialpolitik* which was filled with metaphysical speculation, Weber, no great admirer of Freud, wrote to Else Jaffé:

> Every new scientific or technical discovery still has as a consequence the fact that the discoverer, whether it is a matter of beef extract or the highest abstractions of natural science, believes himself called upon to be the discoverer of new values and a reformer of "ethics," just as the inventors of color photography turn themselves into reformers of painting. But that these apparently unavoidable swaddling clothes have to be washed in our Archiv is not in my opinion necessary.

Gross was, he wrote on another occasion, a *Trottel* (addlepate) with whom he wanted as little to do as possible.

The letters to Paul Siebeck, the publisher of the *Archiv*, provide considerable insight into Weber's working habits, which can only be described as hazardous for one of his precarious health. What emerges here about his editorial duties, which involved soliciting articles in the fields of political economy, social history, and psychology and then reading them and generally making painstaking suggestions for improvement and amplification, makes it difficult to understand how he was able to accomplish so much research and writing of his own in these years. The physical effort was, moreover, always accompanied by considerable nervous strain over such matters as Edgar Jaffé's handling of the printing of Weber's articles on the Russian revolution of 1905, which Weber claimed left him 2,000 RM out of pocket because of corrections and additional printing costs. There were frequent contractual disputes and threats to resign, which never came to anything because no one could imagine an *Archiv* without Weber's participation, least of all himself.

Despite his resignation from his professorship at Heidelberg in

1903, Weber remained an influential force there and in the academic profession generally, and his advice was frequently sought on appointments. He was quick to strike out at what he considered to be injustice or prejudice in the behavior of university faculties, and considered the exclusion of Social Democrats from teaching positions in German universities a "shame and a disgrace, for a civilized nation [*Cultur-Nation*]," as he wrote Robert Michels, one of the victims of this rule. He was driven to fury by the tactics that defeated his efforts to secure a professorship in Heidelberg for Georg Simmel, like the letter from Professor Dietrich Schäfer of Berlin to a high official in the Baden Ministry of Culture that stated that Simmel was "an Israelite through and through, not only in external appearance but in his behavior and mentality" and the persistent rumors that his Berlin classes were filled with subversive foreigners.

Weber's defense of his friends when they were unfairly attacked was immediate and unconditional—on hearing that a Marburg professor had made a slur against Michels he wrote: "I am itching in every finger to fetch that *Bengel* one behind the ear!"—but he was no less forthright when no personal factor was involved, as in his defense of the younger faculty of the universities against the often arbitrary behavior of the full professors. He did not hesitate to remonstrate sharply to Lujo Brentano, a man whom he greatly admired, when the Munich economist objected to demands made by junior faculty and said that a *quos ego* or divine threat was needed to bring them to their senses.

Among the most interesting of the letters in this volume are those addressed to Robert Michels, the young social scientist and analyst of political parties who emigrated to Italy after his socialist views made it impossible for him to secure a teaching position in Germany. Weber, the editors of this volume tell us, was interested at first only in winning Michels as a contributor to the *Archiv* in order to widen its political spectrum, but they became friends and continued so after Michels began teaching at the University of Turin. It was a not undisturbed relationship, and on one occasion Michels aroused Weber's indignation by wanting to have views about the German professoriate that Weber had expressed in a private letter printed in a socialist newspaper and telling Weber that the editor had said that Weber might be afraid to allow this. Nothing infuriated Weber more than doubts about his courage, and he once challenged a man who had libeled him to a duel. But his anger on this occasion was compounded by Michels's obtuseness in not understanding the difference between the latitude allowed in private correspondence and the scientific accuracy required of public statements. He refused Michels's request and warned him that its repetition would end the intimacy of their correspondence.

Weber was always disturbed by the romantic and emotional components of Michels's thinking. When Michels wrote an article on urban erotic life in which he claimed that prostitution in France was morally superior to that in Germany, Weber accused him of being "a moralist from head to toe," adding:

> You are unfair to German whores. They have their firm "ethics" just like others, and the Parisian ones seem somewhat idealized. For the rest I am in complete agreement. About the public Knutschen of German lovers I feel much the same as the Italians, although the latter are, in my opinion, all too "prudish."

He was equally critical of the utopian and moralistic cast of Michels's socialism, and in a long letter criticizing an essay of the younger man on "the oligarchic tendencies of society" warned him against the use of meaningless phrases like "the true will of the people" and his failure to realize that talk about revolution and the establishment of a form of democracy that would end the domination of people over people was farcical in modern conditions.

> Any one who wants to live as a "modern person"—and only in the sense that he has his newspaper every day and railroads and electric trams, etc.—renounces all those ideals that hover darkly before your mind, above all as soon as he gives up the position of revolutionary action for its own sake, without any "goal," yes, without the possibility of thinking of a goal. You are a basically honorable fellow and will by yourself…complete the critique that long ago brought me to this way of thinking and by doing so stamped me as a "bürgerlich" politician as long as the little that one as such can will, does not withdraw into the endless distance.

With infinite patience and insistent criticism, Weber sought to make a scientist out of Michels, constantly playing changes on the dictum announced in one of his letters of 1908: "*Scientific* work is not a labor that 'distributes light and shadow,' as you write—and there is no justice there—only *facts* and their *causes*." He constantly urged him to turn his mind to the systematic analysis of institutions, and there can be little doubt that Michels's great work, *Die Soziologie des modernen Parteiwesens*, owed a great debt to Weber's critical oversight.

In German politics, the period covered by this volume saw the personal regime of Emperor William II reach its height. As one who hoped against hope for a turn toward parliamentary government, Weber in 1906 warned his old friend Friedrich Naumann, one of the leaders of the left liberal Freisinnige party, to see to it that his followers did not rally behind the Kaiser in the crisis caused by the Tangier incident of the previous year. He wrote:

> The degree of contempt that our nation increasingly encounters abroad (Italy, America, everywhere!)—and with justice—is the decisive issue. Our submission to this regime of this man is gradually becoming a power issue of "world" importance for us. No man and no party, who in any sense cultivates "democratic" and at the same time "national-political" ideals, dares take upon himself the responsibility for this regime, whose continuation is a greater threat to our world position than all colonial problems of every kind.

The situation did not improve. In one of the last letters in this volume, written to Naumann at the height of the uproar over the Kaiser's irresponsible remarks to a reporter of the English *Daily Telegraph*, Weber expressed the view that the conservatives were responsible for maintaining the personal regime. "Much too much is said about the 'impulsiveness,' etc. of the *person* of the Kaiser," he wrote. "The political *structure* is responsible for that. . . . The decisive thing is that a *dilettante* has the *threads* of power in his hands, and *that's what the conservatives want*." The note of resignation was unmistakable.

III

A month after Weber's death in 1920, Robert Michels wrote in a Basel newspaper:

> Max Weber was a very complex person: a man of strict and exact science, a scholar from head to toe who loved science as passionately as a young bride, a political economist, specialist in public law, sociologist, historian of religion, but also a practical politician, organizer, and not least possessed of a truly daemonic nature.

Michels was wrong about Weber's political gifts, and Wolfgang J. Mommsen has demonstrated that when Weber had a chance to play a part, after the collapse of 1918, in building a new democracy in Germany, he developed doubts and convinced himself that what the country needed was a plebiscitary or Caesarist statesman on the Bismarck model.[12] As for his daemonic nature, this was merely a reflection of the fatalist cast of his thinking. Lawrence A. Scaff has pointed out that Weber was apparently fond of Goethe's poem "Daemon" and that in 1897, in a debate with Karl Oldenburg, he quoted from it in a peroration that ran:

> There are optimists and pessimists in the consideration of the future of German development. Now, I don't belong to the optimists. I also recognize the enormous risk which the inevitable outward economic expansion of Germany places upon us. But I consider this risk inevitable, and therefore I say, "So must you be, you will not escape yourself."

Coming from one who already recognized and feared the irresponsible adventurism of the Wilhelmine regime, this degree of fatalism is off-putting, and reminds us that too many Germans before 1914 and before 1933 and before 1939 talked about their inescapable destiny. There is another passage in Goethe, at the end of his memoirs *Poetry and Truth*, in which he discusses daemonic natures and quotes the lines of his hero Egmont, who was one of them:

> Child, child! No further! As if whipped by invisible spirits, the sunsteeds of time bear onward the frail chariot of our fate, and nothing remains for us but, with courageous composure, to grip the reins firmly and steer the wheels now left, now right, here from the cliffs, there from the abyss. Whither is he hasting? Who knows! Does anyone consider whence he came?[13]

But surely the point of Goethe's drama was that, because of this fatalistic predisposition, Egmont was a foolhardy and irresponsible leader who encompassed his own destruction and that of most of his followers. One cannot accuse Weber of anything of the sort, but it is surely not too much to say that the daemonic nature that Michels attributed to him comported ill with his democratic professions.

It would be unfair to end on this sour note. Like most great men, Weber was a person of paradoxes and contradictions. He was also honest and knew his own weaknesses. Scaff tells us that he recognized his vocational imperative as an *amor fati*, and that he also knew that love of fate was in itself a fatality. He once wrote to Ferdinand Tönnies, "In this respect I feel myself a cripple, a deformed human being, whose inner fate is to have to answer honestly for this."

4

Berlin in the Twenties: The Capital Between
Empire and Third Reich

It is perhaps appropriate, at the beginning of a conference that will deal
in large part with the cultural life of Berlin, to remind ourselves that the
city that we shall be discussing was more than a cultural center. It was,
indeed, preeminently a political one, and life in Berlin in the 1920s was
dominated, not by its cultural and artistic activities, but by its politics.

This was something that the free-floating intellectuals who were
resident in the city, and the painters and novelists and musicians, found
it difficult to acknowledge. Ever since the 1870s, the metropolis had
been enormously attractive to Germans active in the arts. Their exhila-
ration over being part of it was once described by the novelist Conrad
Alberti when he wrote of the "nervous, endlessly quivering Berlin air . . .
which works upon people like alcohol, morphine, cocaine, exciting,
inspiring, relaxing, deadly: the air of the world city."[1]

A lecture for the Conference on Berlin and German Culture, University
of California, Berkeley, April 1984. Published here with the permission
of the estate of Gordon A. Craig and the Department of Special Collections, Stanford University Libraries. The volume editors have prepared the endnotes for this chapter.

But it was the world city that fascinated them, not the politics of the capital, about which they were so completely incurious that in 1910 Heinrich Mann reproached his fellow artists and said that their political irresponsibility merely encouraged the forces that were destroying their country.

Mann's indignation did not make them change their ways. During the First World War, Franz Werfel wrote: "I cannot describe how contradictory to me are the concepts poetry and politics! The politician looks at life coldly; the evil of power has triumphed over him. The writer . . . is endlessly destructive, immeasurably anarchistic. . . . He dare not blow the trumpet for the revolution. He storms other bastilles, O irresistible dynamite of insight! He is there to make life unbearable and holy!"[2] Werfel became one of the so-called Expressionist activists in the first years after the war, but, like most of his fellows, he remained anti-political by conviction, believing that the political process as such stifled man's creative instincts and that institutions, which most of us realize give form and motive force to society, simply victimized and despiritualized human beings. The activism that he and most of his fellow-artists professed was a combination of anarchism and utopianism, and even this did not survive the relative stabilization that took place in German politics at the end of 1923, but was replaced by a profound lack of interest in the political realities of the Weimar Republic. That indifference was doubtless responsible in part for the fact the Republic was so short-lived. Certainly, in any assessment of the role of the intellectuals in the 1920s, their political myopia should not be forgotten.

I have been asked to talk this morning about the "the Capital between the Empire and the Third Reich." It will perhaps underline my earlier statement about Berlin being a preeminently political center if I begin by pointing out that Berlin was not merely one capital but two. It was the capital of Germany, but also the capital of Prussia, and that double function was the source of many problems that contributed powerfully to the weakness, and the eventual collapse, of the Weimar Republic, as we shall see. For the moment, we need merely note that the fact that it was a double capital meant that the executive, legislative, and judicial branches of two separate governments, along with their attendant ministries and ministerial bureaucracies, were located in Berlin. And, as if that were not enough, Berlin had its own communal government as well. The law of 1920, which combined eight cities, 59 *Landgemeinde*, and 27 *Gutsbezirke* into the entity called Great Berlin, provided for an elected city parliament or *Stadtverordnetenversammlung* with 255 seats and a *Magistrat*, elected from this assembly, of 30 members. Hans Herzfeld has written that the existence side by side of three great parliamentary bodies—Reichstag, Prussian Landtag, and the equally turbulent city assembly—was an embarrassment of riches, that was replete with the danger of mutual friction and wounded sensibilities on the part of what Bismarck called "Chamber celebrities" in quiet times and of continual crisis in troubled ones. Moreover, the three bodies were close enough together to exercise a sympathetic attraction upon each other so that incidents that occurred in any one of them were likely to have profound effects in the other two, which happened, for example, at the time of the Sklarek scandal, which I'll mention a little later. For the moment we can confine ourselves to the thought of what it was to have so many elected politicians wandering about in the city at any one time, along with the clouds of lobbyists from trade unions and industrial associations that were also part of the local scene, to say nothing of the staffs and working forces of the various party headquarters. It meant that Berlin was a very political city indeed, and that its life was not concentrated in the Café des Westens or the Romanisches Café, as one might think from reading some of the books on Weimar culture. Indeed, the number of people working at politics in Berlin at any one time probably exceeded the number of practicing painters, sculptors, poets, novelists, dramatists, and film-makers by a good deal.

Three aspects of this political city demand our attention: first, its significance as a political symbol; second, its role as the theater in which the tension and mounting hostility between the Reich on the one hand and Prussia on the other was played out to its dramatic denouement; and, third, the place occupied by Berlin in the thinking of the Nazis and their Führer.

The historian Percy Schramm, who during the Second World War kept the diary of the *Oberkommando der Wehrmacht* [Supreme Command of the Armed Forces] and consequently spent a lot of time at Hitler's *Hauptquartier*, and was forced to listen to his endless harangues on all sorts of subjects, wrote once that, in talking about his grandiose plans for post-war Berlin, Hitler said that he was considering changing its name to Germania. This is not insignificant. With all of his ambivalent feelings toward the city, Bismarck recognized what all politicians in the Weimar recognized, that the identification of Berlin with the Reich was complete and unchangeable. This had been accepted unwillingly by those who had drafted the constitution for the new republic in 1919, some of whom felt that Weimar, the home of Goethe and of the poet who had tried to teach his countrymen that "German Greatness" should be measured not in terms of power but rather of moral conviction and dedication to the cause of freedom, would be the most appropriate capital for their new creation. Such hopes were unavailing. It was generally acknowledged that Berlin was the symbol of the united Germany that Bismarck had created. To choose any other capital would, moreover, as all but the most obtuse could see, amount to an acceptance of the diminished status that the Allies appeared to be seeking to impose upon Germany for all time.

The identification of Berlin with the nation took another political form. It became the basic assumption of the politics of extremism, left and right, that whoever took Berlin ruled Germany. Spartakus Week and the Kapp Putsch of 1920 were the first attempts to prove this, and one might have thought that the results would be discouraging, for both were defeated essentially by counter-action from the provinces, in the form of Free Corps from middle Germany in the former case and a national general strike in the second. But these failures in no way diminished the symbolic importance of Berlin in the eyes of revolutionary movements. To capture Hamburg or Dresden or Munich, they all agreed, would be to register at best an inconclusive triumph. Thus, the anti-republican conspiracy that centered in the paramilitary *Arbeitskommandos* at Küstrin in September 1923 put its hopes in a direct thrust against Berlin, a more successful Kappist *coup de main*. Thus, the conservative forces who made plans in November 1923 to force the fall of the Stresemann government and to replace it with a four-man directorate (in truth, a quasi-military dictatorship) counted on diversions taking place in other cities but regarded Berlin as the center of the action.

Later, when National Socialism resumed its march toward power in the mid-20s, Joseph Goebbels was appointed Gauleiter [regional party leader] of Berlin and given the mission of conquering the city, but

Goebbels's opponents on the extreme left were no less intent on that same objective. In October 1930 Count Harry Kessler wrote in his diary (and it says something that this shrewd political observer did so quite matter-of-factly as if reporting the most natural thing in the world) that he had heard that "the Communists . . . have a plan worked out in detail for a *Putsch* in Berlin in the middle of November. Even the date is firm. They would not be so stupid as to make another *Klamauk* [hullabaloo] in the streets as in 1919, but, based on reliable elements in the *Schupo* [the security police] and the Reichswehr, simply do the thing without a sound in the night. Berlin would wake up and find a new government. They are quite sure of the success of their blow."[3]

Revolutionary politics during the Weimar Republic was, therefore, quite clearly Berlin-oriented; for quite practical reasons but, above all, for symbolic ones, Berlin was the chief goal. In January 1933, when Adolf Hitler was appointed Reichskanzler, the Nazis made a grandiose spectacle of this event, with massed brown-clad columns moving jubilantly with banners and torches and military music down Unter den Linden, along the Wilhelmstrasse and past the Reichskanzlei, for the effect that this apparent capture of Berlin would have upon the country as a whole, preparing it psychologically to accept the real conquest of the country that was to come in the months that lay ahead.

The background of that ultimate Nazi conquest is to be found in another drama that had its setting in Berlin, the conflict between Prussia and the Reich which, until its brutal resolution in July 1932, took the form of a bitter duel between the Reich Chancellery on one side of the Wilhelmstrasse and the Prussian State Ministry on the other.

The roots of this conflict run back to the constitutional debates in the National Assembly in Weimar in 1919 and particularly to a draft proposal prepared at that time by Hugo Preuss, the most distinguished and influential of those jurists who wrote the basic charter of the Weimar Republic. Preuss, a man who often allowed logic to drive him well beyond the limits of common sense, declared in this paper that, in Germany's new political circumstances, the separate existence of Prussia had "lost all meaning," that Prussia had "no inherent right to continued existence, since it was an unnatural construct, the result of successfully ended wars and dynastic legacies."[4] It had outlived its usefulness and should, for economic as well as political reasons, be dissolved.

In practical terms, this would mean that many of the rights and powers formerly reserved to it would pass to the Reich and that, territorially, it would be separated into smaller units, like the separate Rhine province that was desired by Konrad Adenauer, the Lord Mayor of Cologne.

Preuss's views were shared by a fair proportion of liberal and progressive opinion (the historian Friedrich Meinecke was one of his strongest supporters), by the Communists and the left-wing Socialists, and by leading Centrist politicians. In the end, however, they were defeated by the votes of the Majority Socialists, whose leader Friedrich Ebert felt that, at a time when the exact nature of the Peace Terms was still unknown, anything like a dissolution of Prussia might encourage the Entente to be more extreme in their territorial demands than it was feared they would be in any case. It was his view, moreover, that the provisional government was having enough trouble in asserting its authority over the country as a whole without compounding its difficulties by assuming the job of running Prussia's internal affairs as well. The National Assembly agreed that the uncertain situation of Germany's frontiers forbade tampering with the traditional administrative structure of the country.

Unfortunately, once that decision was made, Preuss and the other constitution-makers didn't draw the logical conclusions from it. Prussia had always been the largest of the German states, and even after the losses of territory suffered because of the Versailles Treaty it remained so, with three-fifths of the national population and a realm that extended from Germany's westernmost boundaries to its eastern and northern limits. How were the policies and prerogatives of this giant among federal states to be coordinated with those of the new national government? Even under the Empire, this had been a problem of complexity. Then it had been alleviated by ministerial and other linkages, for the German Emperor had also been the King of Prussia, and the Reich Chancellor had usually been Minister President of Prussia as well as Prussian Foreign Minister. The Weimar Constitution made no provision for such permanent connections and ties, and this was unfortunate, given the quite considerable powers left to the individual states (justice, police, education, and the like). Wolfgang Heine, the Prussian Minister of the Interior, said early on, "It is a misfortune that the question of the new organization of the Reich, and especially the position of

Prussia in the Reich, was left to a theoretician [he meant Hugo Preuss] who didn't have the slightest conception of practical tasks and possibilities and who, instead of making Prussia's strengths useful to the Reich, steered at once into the channel that led to conflict between them."

Since there were no formal links between the two governments, wise men on both sides of the Wilhelmstrasse, who saw the vital necessity of coordinating their policies, suggested that the missing linkages might be supplied by a practice of each government's having observers in the other's cabinet, by having corresponding ministries headed by the same person, and by having joint commissions for important areas of public work. But this would, of course, have been possible only if both Prussia and the Reich were governed by the same political party, or by identical coalitions of parties, and this very quickly ceased to be a practical possibility. After the national elections of June 1920, when the original Weimar Coalition of Socialists, Democrats, and Centrists was defeated so definitively as never to be capable again of piecing together a Reichstag majority, the Reich was governed by coalitions of very mixed loyalties, so much so that people spoke increasingly of Germany being a republic without republicans. On the other hand, Prussia became, and for the whole history of the Weimar Republic remained, Germany's most democratic state, with the Socialists and their Centrist and Democratic allies controlling the Landtag and a Social Democrat, Otto Braun, as Minister President.

This was a sure prescription for conflict, because, as the governments of the Reich became more conservative, disputes were sure to arise over questions of economic policy and internal security and, particularly, over the army's attempts to evade the military clauses of the Versailles Treaty by secret rearmament and other illegal activities, many of which took place on Prussian soil and were bitterly resented by the Social Democrats. For a time, these were prevented from becoming critical by the surprising intimacy that grew up, in the first years after Field Marshal von Hindenburg's election as Reich President in 1925, between him and the Prussian Minister President. Hindenburg was impressed by Otto Braun, an East Prussian with a tall, slightly bowed frame (he was as a matter of fact taller than Hindenburg by a hand), a hooked nose and dark heavy eyebrows, brusque and almost violent in his speech, although not without a grim humor, who resembled the

Junkers of his homeland so closely that it was rumored that his real father was a large landholder (which was not true). The two men found that they had areas of common interest (both were impassioned huntsmen) and enjoyed talking over common problems. Hindenburg once said, "Just think how often you get false information about a person! My friends in Hannover told me that Otto Braun was a fanatical inciter of trouble. And now I see that he is a completely reasonable man with whom one can talk about anything." For a time, with the Reich President consulting the Prussian Minister President on political problems that perplexed him, and more often than not following his advice, the intergovernmental linkage that Hugo Preuss had failed to put into the constitution actually existed. Unfortunately, this didn't last, because Hindenburg was not a strong man, and he fell increasingly under the influence of his class and his profession, and the agrarian conservatives and the soldiers poisoned his mind against Braun.

The agrarians were infuriated by Braun's attempts to derail the *Osthilfe* project, a plan for providing subventions to save the great landowners east of the Elbe from the consequences of their own incompetent husbandry; the army was opposed to him because of his constant interference with their rearmament plans and with their encouragement to paramilitary organizations that Braun regarded as a threat to internal security and to democratic government. Both groups bombarded Hindenburg with arguments intended to prove that Braun intended to expropriate the landowning class in Prussia and to subvert the army's patriotic program for national recovery. The latter argument was particularly effective and, in the end, it was Braun's violent dislike of uniformed demonstrations by veterans' societies and Hitler's Storm Troops, which were becoming a dangerous nuisance in Berlin and other parts of Prussia, that finally brought a break between the two men. In September 1929, a rally of the veterans' organization Stahlhelm in Langenberg in the Rhineland—that is, in the zone that was demilitarized by the terms of the Versailles Treaty—led Braun to declare it an illegal organization and to prohibit it from public activity. Hindenburg was an honorary member of Stahlhelm, and Braun's action ended any hope of effective collaboration between them.

This was unfortunate, because in March 1930 the last Reich government that could be considered a truly democratic one, the Great

Coalition of Hermann Müller, collapsed, and Germany entered a period of great economic distress, of growing political extremism (both the Nazis and the Communists assuming formidable strength), and of serious civil unrest, a time in which close cooperation between Prussia and the Reich was more urgent than ever before. Indeed, in this period, Braun, who believed that Prussia was the last bastion of German democracy, repeatedly suggested to the leaders of Reich cabinets that a renewed attempt be made to establish linkages that would make the fight against the extremist, anti-democratic parties more effective, perhaps by fusing ministries or by having the Prussian Minister President serve as Vice Chancellor and thus building a real bridge across Wilhelmstrasse. The most promising time to have effected this would have been during the Brüning ministry, but Brüning's own position was for long ambivalent and, when he at last put the idea before Hindenburg, the old man brusquely rejected it. Papen and Schleicher, who followed Brüning, were hostile to Braun, feeling that their own elaborate plans to cajole and coopt Hitler were threatened by his more forthright opposition to the Nazis (his insistence, for example, that they be prohibited from appearing in uniform on the streets of Berlin or elsewhere in Prussia). They came to the conclusion that the best way of advancing their plans was to get rid of him and, if possible, to destroy Prussia's autonomy and absorb it in the Reich, along with its large and effective police force.

In 1920 State Secretary Heinrich Albert had predicted that, if policy on both sides of the Wilhelmstrasse could not be brought into harmony, the Reich government might some day feel constrained to use "its always great direct and indirect sources of power—although naturally not including military resources—" to bend Prussia to its will. Albert was a good prophet, although mistaken in believing that military means would be excluded when the crisis came. Twelve years after his prediction, on 20 July 1932, Chancellor Franz von Papen persuaded President von Hindenburg to issue a decree deposing the Prussian government for failing to maintain the public order which Papen himself, by his toleration of Nazi disorders in the streets, had subverted. Papen sent a Reichswehr unit across the Wilhelmstrasse to bar Braun from access to his office and to drive out the other Prussian ministers. Braun had always been considered to be the strong man of Prussia; he did not prove his strength on this occasion. He was later criticized for not resorting to the tactics that had defeated Kapp in 1920, but there was no assurance that the trade unions would have tried a general strike in time of deep depression, and Braun seems to have doubted that his own police would have supported defiance of a presidential decree. He was certainly correct in this last surmise, for reasons that will become clear. But his failure to react strongly meant that the struggle for democracy that had been waged by the two sides of the Wilhelmstrasse was lost by default.[5]

Since the Nazis had provided Papen and Hindenburg with a plausible pretext for the action of 20 July, and since they became its chief beneficiaries (for Papen, who ruled Prussia as Reich Commissioner after July, handed all his powers, including command of the police, over to them as soon as Hitler became Reichskanzler, thus enormously strengthening his hand), we should in conclusion ask what the Nazis and their Leader thought about Berlin and what they did about it.

In an interesting book called *Agrarromantik und Grossstadtfeindschaft* (*Agrarian Romanticism and Hostility to the Big City*),[6] Klaus Bergmann has pointed out that anti-urbanism was a salient characteristic of the Nazi ideology, which is understandable if we remember the movement's roots in small towns and villages and its tendency from the beginning to idealize the Germanness of peasant life. Nazi intellectuals were fond of quoting people like Otto Ammon, W. H. Riehl, Julius Langbehn, Heinrich Söhnrey, Adolf Bartels, Oswald Spengler, and the poet Rainer Maria Rilke, all of whom regarded the city as a threat to German health and community and culture, the center of cosmopolitanism, Jewry, and vice. They were apt to agree with Constantin Frantz who, back in the 70s, had said that Berlin was more suited to be a capital of the Jews than the capital of Germany; and, like Wilhelm Schäfer, the author of an anti-modernist work called "The Thirteen Books of the German Soul,"[7] they found the slogan *"Los von Berlin!"* ["Out of Berlin!"] a congenial one. Many of the Nazi leaders had been members of the *Artamanenbewegung*, a youth movement that was concerned about urbanization and the flight from the land and whose program foreshadowed the *Blut und Boden* ideology of Walther Darré. Darré himself, Hitler's Reich Peasant Leader after 1933, called for an open attack upon big-city culture, capitalism, and the Jews, and a return to the organic rather than the pluralistic state with a vital connection between *Raum* and *Volk*.

Adolf Hitler was not inclined to encourage these prejudices by giving them concrete form. It is clear enough that he did not like Berlin and Berliners, any more than they liked him. The city, he often said, didn't have the atmosphere to be a real *Kunstmetropole* and, for culture's sake, should be rebuilt by southerners. In the last part of the war, looking at the extensive bomb damage with Albert Speer, he commented that the Allies had really done them both a service, for Speer and he would have had to destroy as much after the war in any case. As for Berliners, he did not enjoy their wit and their habit of lampooning him and his comrades in satire (Kurt Tucholsky's pretended schoolboy essay on "Goethe and Hitler," for example) and in music hall song (like the popular "I Wonder What Adolf Has in Store for Us?," with its gibes at the provincialism of National Socialism), and Claire Waldoff's song about Hermann Goering:

Rechts Lametta, links lametta,
Und der Bauch wird imma fetta

[Ornaments on the right, ornaments on the left,
And the belly acquires ever more heft]

But he was a realist. He recognized Berlin as the capital, and resolved that it would be *his* capital. He rejected the slogan "*Los von Berlin!*" and adopted another one coined by the pre-war agricultural romanticist Leonhard, "*Bestürmt wird nun die schwarze Stadt!*" ["Now will the black city be stormed!"] And, as we have seen, he sent Joseph Goebbels to Berlin in 1926 to conquer the city.

In the strictest sense, Goebbels never accomplished that, but he accumulated enough strength in the city, and was clever enough in his uses of propaganda, to contribute powerfully to its political turbulence in the years of the Great Depression and to the progressive breakdown of the morale of its public services. His *dramatic* slogans ("*Adolf Hitler frisst Karl Marx!*") ["Adolf Hitler devours Karl Marx!"]; his carefully planned street battles with the Communists, touched off by provocative invasions of working class districts; his transformation of the pimp Horst Wessel into a martyr and a myth (thanks in part to the appeal of the Horst Wessel Song, the tune of which was adapted from one in a

Communist song book); his campaign against the police by means of persistent calumniation of the Deputy Police President, Dr. Bernhard Weiss (always referred to in the Goebbels newspaper as "Isidor Weiss, the most prominent Jew in the government")—these and other Goebbels inspirations put the Nazis on the map in Berlin.

The first impressive success came with the eruption of the so-called Sklarek scandal in 1929–30. The brothers Sklarek owned a firm that supplied the city with various kinds of uniforms, but they were not content with this lucrative business and decided to increase their profits by charging the city for goods never delivered and by falsifying their records in many ingenious ways. They made a special point of ingratiating themselves with city officials by making handsome gifts to them, a practice to which even the Lord Mayor Gustav Böss proved susceptible, for he permitted the Sklarek brothers to sell him a fur coat for his wife at a ridiculously low price. It was not long before all of this became public, and the sensational revelations encouraged the Nazis to organize a series of mass demonstrations in which mobs of what Count Harry Kessler called "catilinarian existences" ran amok in the city shouting anti-Jewish slogans. Before it was over, the Sklarek affair caused stormy debates in all three of Berlin's parliamentary bodies. More important, it forced a major reorganization of the city government, while at the same time weakening its confidence and its will to resist attacks on the democratic order.

The main support of that order was, of course, the Berlin security police (*Schutzpolizei*), a well-armed and disciplined force of 14,000 to 16,000 men, comprising precinct police and 42 riot brigades, whose officers for the most part had actual military experience. Until 1929, this force had had no difficulty in preventing dangerous political demonstrations in the capital; after that time they found themselves caught between two antagonists equally determined to wrest control of the streets from them. In late 1931 and the first months of 1932, the incidence of Nazi and Communist violence in the city was already so great that the physical and moral resources of the police were overtaxed. Some relief was afforded when the Brüning government, by presidential decree, dissolved the Nazi SA and SS in April 1932, enabling the police to shut down their local headquarters. But this merely encouraged the Communists to retake the offensive and, in any case, in

June 1932 the Papen government lifted the ban on Hitler's storm troops, and there was a resurgence of general violence. In an interview in the *Vossische Zeitung* on 8 July, Police President Albert Grzsesinski talked about the struggle for control of Berlin with a note of resignation, admitting that, while the capital was not yet in a state of civil war, the police were down to their last resources. This speech explains, as much as anything can, why the police, all but demoralized now, did not resist on 20 July 1932 when, at the President's orders, they were taken over by General Gerd von Rundstedt, commander of the third military district, and that action in turn gave the Nazis a victory that facilitated Hitler's coming to power six months later.

It is interesting to note that, while all this was going on, the Nazis never did very well in the communal elections in Berlin. In November 1929, they were represented for the first time in the city assembly but with only 13 seats, compared with 56 for the Communists and 64 for the SPD. In none of the elections from 1930 on, did they come close to matching their percentage of the vote in national elections. Even in March 1933, they managed to win only 86 of the 225 seats in the assembly. It is clear that the city voters were to the end opposed to handing the capital over to the Nazis.

Not that this expression of their will did any good. The expulsion of the Communists and the Socialists soon gave the Nazis control of the assembly; and six months later there was no assembly, for it was replaced by a 45-member communal council with purely advisory powers, whose members were appointed by the Lord Mayor at the suggestion of the Gauleiter. After 1935, Berlin had a National Socialist mayor, and, in addition, Gauleiter Joseph Goebbels had been empowered to make sure that there was "harmony and accord between city administration and party." Like all other organizations of democratic nature and independent will, Berlin had been *gleichgeschaltet* ["bought into line," i.e., "forcibly coordinated"].

In 1943, when the Allied bombing offensive began in earnest, it is said that a song was sung in the industrial regions of western Germany that ran:

Lieber Tommy, fliege weiter.
Wir sind alle Bergarbeiter.
Fliege weiter nach Berlin,

Die haben alle "Ja." geschrien.

[Dear Tommy, fly farther!
We are all workers in the mines.
Fly farther to Berlin
They are the one who all shouted "Ja!"]

Well, they hadn't all shouted "Ja," but that didn't spare them the sorrows that befell their city during Hitler's war. But one thing they were spared. Hitler, I said, didn't like Berlin and was resolved that, after the war had been won, it would be re-created. Along what lines, we can gather from Albert Speer's memoirs and other sources. Berlin was spared that awful metamorphosis, which would probably have destroyed its spirit as completely as it would certainly have destroyed its beauty, and was permitted—at least, part of it was permitted—to make a new start and to forge new ties with the best of its political and cultural tradition.

5

"Working Toward the Führer"

In the introduction to his book about the popular appeal of National Socialism, Peter Fritzsche tells how in 1930, in a café in Munich, the photographer Heinrich Hoffmann showed Adolf Hitler the pictures he had taken of the excited crowd that had assembled before the Feldherrnhalle on the first day of mobilization for war in 1914. Hitler leafed through them and then said abruptly, "I, too, stood in this crowd." An ardent Nazi himself, Hoffmann was excited by the thought of the political advantage that might be made of this if it could be proved and subjected his prints to painstaking examination, finally discovering the face of his Führer, disheveled and intensely excited, near the bottom edge of the last photo.

"This fortuitously discovered shot," Fritzsche writes, "caught the precise moment when the Third Reich became possible." That is perhaps too sweeping a statement, but it is not entirely wrong. Hoffmann's

Review of *Germans Into Nazis*, by Peter Fritzsche; *Hitler, 1889–1936: Hubris*, by Ian Kershaw; *Hitler's Vienna: A Dictator's Apprenticeship*, by Brigitte Hamann, translated by Thomas Thornton; and *Where Ghosts Walked: Munich's Road to the Third Reich*, by David Clay Large: *New York Review of Books*, March 18, 1999, pp. 32–35. Reprinted with permission from *The New York Review of Books*. Copyright © 1999, NYREV, Inc.

photograph documents in a remarkable way the sense of national solidarity that marked the August Days of 1914, a feeling that persisted later through the long years of defeat, revolution, and political frustration as a memory and a felt need. As we look at it, we are reminded also that the unkempt young man in the corner of Hoffmann's photograph would become the leader of the political movement that was to respond most effectively to that longing and, because it did, to win the mass political support that was not the least important factor in bringing him to power in January 1933. Why this was true is the subject of Fritzsche's book.

I

Even if the war had not ended in military defeat and the abdication of the Kaiser, it would have changed the political culture of Germany profoundly. The bitterness of the conflict and the sacrifices it demanded strengthened the feeling of national identity, while defining it in increasingly populist and racist terms. The ideal of the *Volksgemeinschaft* was a product of the war, and the rhetoric that accompanied it encouraged Germans to think of themselves as citizens rather than subjects, inspired by an equal temper of heroic hearts, and as members of a compact that depended for its existence upon the achievements and self-reliance of ordinary Germans. During the war these ideas inspired a degree of voluntarism and civic activism that was unknown before 1914, when such initiatives were left to constituted authorities. They found expression also in the rising expectations of ordinary citizens and the widely held belief that the war would do away with traditional inequalities and forms of subordination.

During the revolution of 1918, these ideas persisted, and they did not disappear after Germany moved by way of anti-republican coups and the trauma of the inflation to the relative stability of the mid-Twenties. They animated in particular the mass of non-Socialist, Protestant voters in the small towns and rural areas of the country who in the end constituted the primary dynamic of German politics in the last days of the Weimar Republic. These were the voters who assured Hindenburg's election as president of the Republic in 1925, an election widely misrepresented, in Fritzsche's view, as determined by the longing for the good old days of the Empire. The fact that the same voters abandoned Hindenburg for Hitler in 1932 indicates, he says, that they were not looking for a return to the past but "fashioning a populist nationalism that Hitler ultimately embodied much more plausibly than Hindenburg."

Why did National Socialism succeed in winning over these voters? Partly because of the proliferation of party branches in every part of the country (3,400 by 1929), and the Nazis' success in ingratiating themselves in small towns (honoring local celebrities, sponsoring band concerts, erecting maypoles and Christmas trees, and otherwise being good neighbors). Partly also because of the sheer political energy with which they pushed their message (2,370 public meetings across Germany in 1925, 1,300 meetings in the last thirty days before Saxony's Landtag election in 1929). More important, however, was their ideological appeal.

The Nazis, Fritzsche writes, "developed an image of themselves as a party that was constructive, that would move forward and bring Germans together in a militant *Volksgemeinschaft* reminiscent of August 1914." This attracted middle-class women, who believed (falsely, as it turned out) that the victory of the party would give them once more the opportunities and responsibilities that they had enjoyed during the war. It also appealed increasingly to workers disenchanted with the doctrinal rigidities of the parties of the left and increasingly susceptible to Nazi slogans (one of every ten Nazi voters in the summer of 1932, Fritzsche claims, was an ex-Social Democrat). And it was a magnet as well to young people, who were impressed by the confidence in imminent victory that characterized the mass rallies of the party and were not put off by the brutality with which Nazis dealt with their opponents.

The party profited from the fact that its conservative rivals seemed incorrigibly tied to the past, while the Social Democrats were timid and unimaginative in the solutions they offered for the country's economic ills. In contrast, the Nazis claimed to speak for the future, for a radical reformation of the nation that would give all Germans an equal place in the new *Volksgemeinschaft*. This new Germany would be as technologically advanced as any other nation on earth and would guarantee social justice to all of its members, provided, of course, they had the proper *völkisch* credentials. The envisaged economic reforms were not clearly stated, but this vagueness was obscured by the nationalistic rhetoric in which they were presented.

Fritzsche is firm in insisting that it was not an accident that so many Germans became Nazis. Nor was it the result of the Versailles Treaty, or the inadequacy of the Republic and its leaders, or the *Inflationszeit*, or the Great Depression. Anti-Semitism, he says several times, had little to do with their support of Nazism, although most Germans learned to live with it in exacerbated forms after 1933. On the contrary, he writes, "It should be stated clearly that Germans became Nazis because they wanted to become Nazis and because the Nazis spoke so well to their interests and inclinations." Or, more precisely, the Nazis responded effectively to broad demands for popular sovereignty and social recognition, while insisting that "these could only be achieved through national union, which would provide Germans with an embrasive [*sic*] sense of collective identity and a strong role in international politics."

II

Fritzsche's book suffers from its flat and repetitive style and the fact that he has very little (and nothing very interesting) to say about Adolf Hitler. These complaints cannot be made about the first volume of Ian Kershaw's biography, in which the Nazi leader is rarely far from the center of the stage, and which is written in a prose that is clear and direct and a pleasure to read. There can be little doubt that this will become the classic Hitler biography of our time, not only because of the author's mastery of the sources and of the staggeringly voluminous secondary literature, but because he has corrected and amplified the historical record and significantly altered the perspective from which Hitler and his actions have been seen by previous biographers.

For the greatest of these, Alan Bullock and Joachim Fest, Hitler was always the prime mover in the events described. Bullock made this clear even in his title, *Hitler: A Study in Tyranny*. Fest's more psychological approach heightened this tendency, and it is significant that, perhaps under the influence of Burckhardt, he devoted a good deal of space to the question of whether Hitler could be considered to possess historical greatness. Kershaw believes that this question is both irrelevant and potentially an apology for Hitler and that, given what we now know about the social history of Germany in the first half of this century, it is not enough to think of Hitler as the author of his own destiny. What is required of the modern biographer, he writes, is an examination of Hitler's power—"how he came to get it, what its character was, how he exercised it, why he was allowed to expand it to break all institutional barriers, why resistance to that power was so feeble." And these, he adds, are questions that cannot be answered by focusing exclusively on Hitler, but only by analyzing German society.

Hitler's own attempts to portray his career as a triumph of the will Kershaw views with the most extreme skepticism. Hitler claims in *Mein Kampf* that his despair over the state of his country in 1918 and 1919 made him decide to become a politician. In a brilliant reconstruction of the events in Munich in 1919, however, Kershaw shows that during the revolutionary troubles Hitler was without political conviction or initiative and intent only upon avoiding anything that would lead to his being mustered out of the army and returned to civilian life. He was saved from this when Captain Karl Mayr, the head of the army's Information Department in Munich, sent him to an anti-Bolshevik instruction course in the university and then used him as an instructor to indoctrinate troops. This led adventitiously to his involvement with Anton Drexler's German Workers Party, where his political career began. But none of this was determined by a sense of mission on Hitler's part or a triumph of his will. Captain Mayr wrote later in life that when he met Hitler "he was like a tired stray dog looking for a master" and was "ready to throw in his lot with anyone who would show him kindness," adding that "he was totally unconcerned about the German people and their destinies." Kershaw comments that Hitler's course had been

> shaped by circumstance, opportunism, good fortune and, not least, the backing of the army. . . . It was indeed the case . . . that Hitler did not come to politics, but that politics came to him—in the Munich barracks.

Nor was this the only time in his career when Hitler's course was determined less by his own wishes than by external forces. In the crisis year 1923, which began with the French invasion of the Ruhr and saw headlong inflation in Germany, a Communist attempt to infiltrate the government of Saxony, and attempted coups in Küstrin and Hamburg, Hitler, now a rising politician in Munich, felt driven to attempt a revolt against the national government because of the pressure of his growing but highly volatile supporters, who had been inflamed by his anti-republican rhetoric and were now demanding action. But he had no control over the forces he needed to guarantee success—the Bavarian government, the police, and the local army garrison—and when their leaders, after posing as allies, betrayed him, he marched into disaster.

This might have been the end of him had it not been for his opportunism and his ability to turn the fiasco into a legend and a promise, as he did in his sensational performance during his jury trial for treason in the People's Court in Munich in February and March 1924. (Kershaw tells us that after Hitler's first speech, one of his judges said, "What a tremendous chap, this Hitler!") What he learned from the experience was that he could not hope to seize power in Germany by means of force and that only propaganda and mass mobilization would open the way to the national revolution. This was the line he followed after he had served his short sentence in Landsberg prison and emerged to reorganize his divided party and to establish his mastery over it. Kershaw has some very acute things to say about this process, particularly about the Bamberg party conference of February 1926, which decided that the party would be subordinated not to its program but to its leader, a move that effectively reduced squabbling over doctrinal points within the ranks. This creation of a *Führerpartei* was the first step toward the creation of the Hitler myth—the readiness of his followers to see heroic qualities in him and to place all their faith and expectations in him, which is the essence of charismatic power.

The reorganized party grew slowly and did not make a significant breakthrough until the fall of 1930. In analyzing the motivating factors behind support for the NSDAP, Kershaw agrees in general with Fritzsche. On the basis of an examination of the life stories of 581 members of the party made in 1934, he writes that in a third of the cases the idea of national consolidation promised by the Nazis was the strongest theme. It was clear also that many were moved by the idealistic vision of a new Germany that the Nazis alone of the parties of the right were offering. In contrast, only one eighth seem to have been motivated primarily by anti-Semitism. He also notes, however, that two thirds of the biographies he examined revealed some form of dislike of Jews. Perhaps the most significant of these findings was that one fifth of the members seem to have been motivated solely by the Hitler cult.

On January 30, 1933, Hitler became Reich chancellor, after a political confrontation in which, despite his party's electoral strength, he had no more control over events than he had had in 1923. As Henry Turner has pointed out, there was nothing inevitable about this elevation.[1] At the end of 1932, despite his electoral strength, he had maneuvered himself into an apparently hopeless position. He had alienated Reich President von Hindenburg by refusing to undertake any political responsibility unless he were given the chancellorship. As the stalemate continued, there were signs of disaffection among Hitler's followers and the beginning of a significant downturn in his electoral fortunes. Political observers had begun to say that he had overplayed his hand and lost his chance. He was saved by the ambitions of a small group of rightist politicians led by the President's friend Franz von Papen, who gambled on their ability to control Hitler after giving him the prize he had sought for so long. "We have hired him!" Papen said cynically when the new cabinet was formed. This was a fateful mistake on their part, and Hitler soon outmaneuvered them and concentrated all power in his own hands.

This was an astonishing example of how fortune shaped Hitler's career. As Kershaw says:

> What he had been unable to achieve himself, his "friends" in high places had achieved for him. The "nobody of Vienna," "unknown soldier," beerhall demagogue, head of what was for years no more than a party on the lunatic fringe of politics, a man with no credentials for running a complicated state-machine, practically his sole qualification the ability to muster the support of the nationalist masses whose base instincts he showed an unusual talent for rousing, had now been placed in charge of government of one of the leading states in Europe.

The question now was how he would use the power that had fallen into his hands.

Here it must be noted that Hitler's daily regimen had not changed significantly since his days as a rising politician in Munich. He rose late, lunched in the early afternoon, and unless he was engaged in writing a speech, which always commanded his complete attention, spent much of the afternoon sitting in cafés talking with close associates, and then, after dinner, watched movies. In the details of the so-called Nazi Revolution, for instance, he was not interested, and, as far as possible, he avoided them. "The extraordinary economic recovery that rapidly formed an essential component of the Führer myth was not," Kershaw tells us, "of Hitler's making." Until the end of May 1933 he gave no backing to the work-creation programs developed in the Labor Ministry; and then, when under the strong urging of ministers and economic experts, he embodied them in a "Law for the Reduction of Unemployment," he was interested only in their propaganda effects. His program for making automobile manufacturing Germany's chief industry, hailed as "the turning-point in the history of German motorization," proved not to be a program at all but merely some ideas he aired in a speech to the International Automobile and Motor-Cycle Exhibition in Berlin.

Similarly, the reordering of German cultural life along Nazi lines (*Gleichschaltung*) was largely self-generating—left to the initiatives of local party members—and its effects upon German universities and museums and culture in general were all the more horrendous because of this. Nothing was done to issue national guidelines and restrictions. This would have been alien to Hitler's whole style of governing, which, Kershaw says, produced "a most extraordinary phenomenon, a highly modern, advanced state without any central coordinating body and with a head of government largely disengaged from the machinery of government." Yet, although Hitler was rarely involved in the transformation of Germany in the spring and summer of 1933, he was, Kershaw argues, the chief beneficiary. Popular adulation of the new chancellor reached new levels. "The Führer cult was established, not now just within the party, but throughout state and society, as the very basis of the new Germany."

Meanwhile, a new kind of voluntarism became manifest. In February 1934, Werner Willikens, state secretary in the Prussian Agriculture Ministry, made a speech in which he argued that it was difficult for the Führer to order from above everything that he intended sooner or later to carry out. The resultant tendency to await such orders, therefore, should come to an end.

> Rather, however, it is the duty of every single person to attempt, in the spirit of the Führer, to work towards him. Anyone making mistakes will come to notice it soon enough. But the one who works correctly towards the Führer along his lines and towards his aim

will in the future as previously have the finest reward of one day suddenly attaining the legal confirmation of his work.

This suggestion, coming from a ministerial source and never disavowed by anyone in the party hierarchy, set off a Darwinian struggle between agencies and persons within agencies hoping to increase their influence in the state hierarchy. At a time when the racial and expansionist goals of the Nazi ideology were coming more sharply into focus, it also led to a progressive increase in the violence and unconditionality of politics. Kershaw says that working toward the Führer "invited radical initiatives from below and offered such initiatives backing, so long as they were in line with [the Führer's] broadly defined goals." This led to disingenuousness of a high order, as in 1935, when an eruption of anti-Jewish incidents and demands that Jews be excluded from citizenship and punished by death for "racial defilement" and other offenses was tolerated, and indeed encouraged, by the government until the police complained about the increase in public disturbances and the president of the Reichsbank, worried that they would jeopardize the country's economic recovery, called for legislation to regulate anti-Semitic activity. Hitler then forbade further public outrages but at the same time partially appeased them by instituting the process that led to the Nuremberg Laws, a significant and ominous curtailment of Jewish rights.

In general, "working toward the Führer" enabled Hitler to accomplish things that he wanted to accomplish without relying on institutional means, and this enhanced his personal mastery over party and state. Important in this respect were his first successes in foreign policy. This was a field of activity in which Hitler's knowledge was exiguous. Even so, he had no lack of confidence, and he possessed gifts that are of major importance in diplomacy, particularly a sense of its limits, a skill in the uses of ingratiation and bluff, shrewdness in assessing the weak spots of his opponents, and, when it was needed, great daring.

When he came to power, he was aware that the revisionism and expansion on which his heart was set could be pursued only after the home front had been stabilized and Germany's armed forces built up. While the *Gleichschaltung* process was being carried out, therefore, Hitler encouraged foreign states to believe that his government would effect no radical break with the foreign policy of the past. His public pronouncements were pacific and disarming and even when he shocked Europe by withdrawing from the League of Nations and the Disarmament Conference in October 1933, he was able to avoid antagonizing the other powers by professing willingness to enter any schemes of arms limitation that they might propose.

But in the next two years he had a series of successes that belied those assurances. His pact with Poland in January 1934 drove a wedge in France's eastern alliance system; his announcement in March 1935 that he would no longer abide by the arms clauses of the Versailles Treaty and was proceeding to build an air force and an army of thirty-six divisions ended any hopes of European disarmament; and his success in persuading the British to conclude a naval agreement in June 1935 effectively split the Stresa Front and destroyed the last possibility of reprisals against him for his proclamation in March.

These successes were greeted with the wildest enthusiasm in his own country, and this became shriller when in March 1936, disregarding the cautionary preachments of his own officers, he sent troops into the demilitarized Rhineland, effectively destroying the Locarno Treaty of 1925, in which Germany promised to respect established European borders. The Hitler myth now assumed its most extreme form, and the Führer's infallibility became an article of faith.

Unfortunately, Hitler had begun to believe it himself. It was after the Rhineland coup that he said, before an immense gathering in Munich, "I go with the certainty of a sleepwalker along the path laid out for me by Providence." Nothing now seemed impossible to him. Kershaw ends this volume with the words, "Hubris—that overweening arrogance which courts disaster—was inevitable. The point where nemesis takes over had been reached by 1936." That story will come in the sequel.

III

Readers of Kershaw's impressive biography may find some fascinating elaboration of its earlier chapters in two books: Brigitte Hamann's account of Hitler's life in Vienna after he left Linz in February 1908, and David Clay Large's lively book on the Munich that Hitler officially designated as the Capital of the Movement.

A well-known historian of the Habsburg Empire, particularly in its final days, Hamann has undertaken here to write a cultural and social history of Vienna in the last years before the First World War as it was seen by a young man from the provinces, combining this with a biography of her subject up to the time when he left for Munich at the age of twenty-four. The Vienna she describes, is not, she says at the outset, the artistic-cultural *fin-de-siècle* Vienna, which has become a cliché, but the Vienna of the "little people" who confronted the *Wiener Moderne* with incomprehension, and rejected it as degenerate, without any real tie to the *Volk*, and too international, too "Jewish," and too liberal. It was also a city of mass politics, of prophets and hot-gospelers and popular demagogues, of bitter ethnic rivalries (particularly between the Pan-Germans and the Czech minority), and of rampant anti-Semitism.

In this city, Hamann is convinced, Hitler acquired important elements of his *Weltanschauung*. This he did by observation—he spent a lot of time in the Austrian parliament watching the endless and fruitless wrangling of the parties and was a faithful attendant of the speeches of Karl Lueger, a masterful popular tribune beloved of Vienna's Christian Socialist population—and by endless reading of newspapers and pamphlets, acquiring miscellaneous information that he impressed upon his memory by repeating what he read to exasperated acquaintances. His philosophy was made up of a number of strongly held general ideas based on fragments of arguments that were sometimes taken out of context. Thus, in one of those debates in which he became involved in the men's hostels in which he lived in Vienna, he once quoted Schopenhauer and was told by his *vis à vis* that he should not talk about things that he did not understand.

Hamann believes that Hitler's fondness for bipolar theories of master and slave peoples, of strong and weak, of blond and dark, and of good and evil originated in Vienna and found corroboration in his memory of his favorite author Karl May's *Ardistan and Dschinnistan* and in sentences that stuck in his mind from books like Otto Weininger's *Sex and Character*, a work that he understood as imperfectly as he did Schopenhauer, which did not prevent him in later life from citing it for his own purposes. His tendency to see politics in friend-foe terms and his belief that evil is always bent on destroying good, fighting not openly in a fair *Heldenkampf* [heroic struggle] but "after the manner of the *Untermenschen*, with bacillae, parasites, *Schmarotzer* [spongers] or defilement of morals or blood," were clearly influenced by the political struggles he witnessed in Vienna and by the rhetoric of the Pan-German leaders like Georg Ritter von Schönerer and mystics like Guido von List. And his lifelong belief that the downfall of the weak was as inevitable as the victory of the strong was rooted in the Darwinian atmosphere of Vienna at the turn of the century and in the rhetoric of people like his hero Lueger.

Despite Hitler's professions in *Mein Kampf*, however, Hamann refuses to believe that his anti-Semitism originated in Vienna. There is no doubt that he thought deeply about the Jewish question and spent a lot of time discussing it with others. But as often as not, in debates about the Jews and their place in Austria he was on the side of the Jews rather than that of their opponents. Hamann tells of a stormy discussion in 1910 about Empress Elizabeth's veneration for Heinrich Heine, in which Hitler defended the poet and regretted that there were no statues to him in Germany. In other discussions in the men's hostel, he was reported to have praised Maria Theresa's great reforming minister Joseph von Sonnenfels and Jewish musicians like Mendelssohn and Offenbach. He had Jewish friends with whom he discussed religious questions and the future of the Zionist movement and upon whom he could rely for loans and other help in his worst times. He always preferred to sell his watercolors to Jewish dealers, because he thought that they were more honest and gave him better prices. No reliable source has reported Hitler making any anti-Semitic remarks in his Vienna period; on the contrary, he was known to have expressed admiration for the courage with which the Jews had withstood a long history of persecution.

Nevertheless, Vienna was a profoundly anti-Semitic city and the Jews were the favorite targets of the politicians whom Hitler admired and studied most. Hamann concludes that it was only during the revolutionary disturbances in Munich in 1918–1919 that the young politician Hitler found it profitable to adopt anti-Semitism himself. And she adds, "It was then that he could use everything that he had learned in Vienna under the rubric, '*Die Juden sind an allem schuld.*' [The Jews are to blame for everything.]"

In the history of National Socialism, Munich took a larger part than any other German city. It was there that Hitler entered politics and founded the NSDAP, and it was there that the party had its first martyrs, during the 1923 Putsch. In 1935 Munich was officially designated as the Capital of the Movement, and in September 1938 it was the place where the Munich Conference, Hitler's last great diplomatic success, was held.

Why did this particular city come to play the central role that it did in the development of the Nazi movement? In the nineteenth century it had been widely hailed as a beautiful city of broad avenues, baroque architecture, and more painters and sculptors than Berlin and Vienna combined. It was a city in which social divisions seemed to be less pronounced than in other parts of the country, a fact that the American consul in 1874 attributed to its most famous product, beer, which he said was "a great constitutional, political, and social leveler." In the brisk survey of the city's nineteenth-century history with which David Large begins his book *Where Ghosts Walk*, he expresses doubts about this, pointing out that the city's beer halls were frequently the scenes of violent battles between opponents hurling great stone mugs, and that this was symptomatic of the tensions and rage that lay beneath the surface of the city even in its Golden Age.

Before the First World War, in the district called Schwabing, Munich possessed a bohemia for artists and writers that was as free and unrestrained as Montmartre. (Large has a splendid chapter on this in which he describes the antics of eccentrics like Oscar Panizza and Fanny zu Reventlow, the founding of the satirical journal *Simplicissimus*, and the daring bill of fare provided by the cabaret "The Eleven Executioners.") But the reaction to Schwabing's cultural norms by the general public was not much different than that of Vienna's to the so-called *Wiener Moderne*. Similarly, Munich had acute social problems, evidenced in the numbers of beggars and prostitutes on the public streets and the virulent anti-Semitism that followed the sudden growth of the Jewish population after the turn of the century, when there was an influx of new migrants from Galicia, Poland, and Russia. The propensity to social and racial resentments and the willingness to consider violent solutions to alleviate them were present long before they were exacerbated by the war and the revolutions that followed it. It is not difficult to understand why the Nazi Party (NSDAP) found the city's atmosphere congenial.

Not all of the party's members were as enamored of the city as Hitler, however, and after the failure of the 1923 Putsch there was a protracted fight led by north German leaders like Gregor Strasser and Joseph Goebbels against the domination of the party by what they called "the dumbest city in the world." Hitler, however, won the day, for reasons that Large makes clear, and Munich became the center of the movement and, for Nazi *Bonzen* in their relaxed moments, a third-class Babylon on the Isar, where one might, if one were lucky, catch a glimpse of the Führer gobbling ravioli at the Osteria Bavaria while Unity Mitford lurked in the doorway trying to catch his eye.

That the citizens of Munich delighted in their city's position and the honors and festivities that it brought them, like the "2,000 Years of German Culture Parade" in 1937, which Large says "broke new ground in the field of Nazi kitsch," is all too clear, although they had reason to regret this when their special tie with Hitler became one of the reasons for the particular attention that Allied bombers paid them in the last two years of the war. Large is very good on the war years, and particularly on Munich's only serious attempt at active resistance to Nazism, the White Rose Movement of Hans and Sophie Scholl, which was repudiated by the very university students to whom it was directed. As for most of the population, while doing a lot of complaining, they were loyal to Hitler to the end. When the Allied bombardment was at its height they attributed this not to anything he had done or any fault of their own but took it to be a confirmation of everything that Hitler had told them about the inveterate Jewish desire to destroy the Aryan race.

In a sardonic epilogue Large describes Munich's astonishing rise from the ashes after 1945, so that by the 1960s it was the richest, fastest growing, most culturally ambitious city in the Federal Republic, drawing 1.7 million foreign tourists a year. This growth was accompanied by a remarkable amnesia about the past and a speedy disappearance of physical signs of the recent Nazi presence. During the days of the "economic miracle," *Vergangenheitsbewältigung*—mastering the Nazi heritage—was not a matter of concern to most Müncheners. It was not until the 1990s that a new generation began to demand a reckoning with the ghosts of the past.

6

Founding Father

I

In the fall of 1944, in the wake of the bomb plot against Hitler, Konrad Adenauer was arrested by the Gestapo on the mistaken assumption that he had been an accomplice and was taken to a prison at Brauweiler. After he had been deprived of his braces, shoe laces, necktie, and pocket knife, and put in a narrow unheated cell, the warden said to him, "Now please do not commit suicide. You would cause me no end of trouble. You're seventy years old and your life is over anyway."

In the circumstances this was a not unreasonable remark, and the warden would have been astonished had he been able to guess the truth. For his prisoner had almost twenty years of active political life before him, during which time he was to serve as chancellor of Germany for two years longer than Adolf Hitler, to contribute largely to the overcoming of the traumatic effects of the Führer's reign, and to transform West Germany from a beaten foe to a respected ally.

Review of *Adenauer: The Father of the New Germany*, by Charles Williams, *The New York Review of Books*, November 1, 2001, pp. 19–21. Reprinted with permission from *The New York Review of Books*. Copyright © 2001, NYREV, Inc.

The accomplishments of Adenauer's old age were indeed so extraordinary that they have tended with the passage of time to obscure everything that went before, leaving the impression that it was unimportant and irrelevant to his late triumphs. It is not the least of the merits of Charles Williams's biography that he does not make this assumption, but sets himself the task of demonstrating that Adenauer's tenure as mayor of Cologne between 1917 and 1933 was the school in which he developed the talents that were so conspicuously successful in his postwar career.

Konrad Adenauer was born in Cologne in January 1876, the third son of a father who had served for fifteen years in the Prussian army and been decorated for bravery at Königgrätz, and who had then risen to become a senior clerk in the Prussian judicial service. His sons grew up in an atmosphere of discipline and deep Roman Catholic religious faith, which in Konrad's case was a principal source of the inveterate self-assurance that marked him from his earliest years. He was educated in the law at Freiburg, Munich, and Bonn, and in 1902 won a position as junior prosecutor in the state prosecutor's office in Cologne.

In the same year he met Emma Weyer, the daughter of a prosperous, well-established family, whom he married two years later. It was a happy marriage, but it made him increasingly discontented with his modest and badly paid position as a lawyer, and in 1906, when an opening occurred in the city government, he applied for it, despite his complete lack of political experience. What Williams calls his "effrontery" worked; aided by his growing reputation as an eloquent and combative trial lawyer and the influence of his wife's family connections, Adenauer was elected by the city council. This marked a decided improvement in his financial and social position, and he made the most of it by the energy with which he threw himself into his work. In 1909, when the position of first deputy to the mayor fell vacant, the Center Party successfully pushed Adenauer for the job.

By this time Germany was rushing toward war. Later in life Adenauer was to say that "the 1914–1918 war was . . . brought about by the stupidity of everyone," but Williams finds no evidence that he feared the coming of the conflict or was particularly percipient about the special problems that it would pose for Cologne. It was only after the fighting had begun, and after the mayor, who believed in keeping a low profile and delegating difficult jobs to others, had placed the organization of the city in the hands of his first deputy, that Adenauer was inspired to set about creating a cross-party alliance of Social Democrats, Centrists, and Liberals to run the city during the conflict.

This arrangement—the first of many that Adenauer would negotiate in his long career—and the diplomatic skill and stubbornness that enabled him to preserve it during the hardest days of the war enhanced his reputation, and in September 1917, after the mayor had gone to Berlin to become Under-Secretary of State in the Ministry of the Interior, the Cologne city council elected Adenauer as his successor by fifty-two out of a possible fifty-four votes. It was a position that he was to hold until 1933.

For Adenauer and for Cologne the first months of his tenure were a difficult time. After bearing him three children, his wife died of cancer at the end of 1916, and he had to face the myriad problems caused by the collapse of the German army and the end of the war without the support she had always provided. In the immediate wake of the war the city was threatened by the annexationist ambitions of Marshal Foch and a separatist movement of local politicians and journalists who advocated a Rhenish Republic. Adenauer, whose attitude toward such a new state, Williams writes, "fluctuated in inverse proportion to his perception of the French threat," had to maneuver between them, while cultivating the support of the British occupying power. This was a difficult game, and in later years he was often accused of having been a separatist in 1919.

Even more difficult was the task of rebuilding the city to conform to the demands of the postwar settlement. To this the new mayor responded boldly by carrying out an extensive plan that replaced the city's outer fortifications with a "green belt," expanded its port facilities so that Cologne became the main port of exit to the North Sea, built up a vast new industrial area on the right side of the Rhine, and established a new university to compete with Bonn. Important parts of this master plan were bitterly opposed by special interests and successfully carried through only by the mayor's patience and sense of timing and by the ingenuity in devising expedient solutions that was to become the mark of his career after 1945.

These political gifts were powerless to influence the horrendous inflation that overwhelmed Germany in 1923 as a consequence of the reparations crisis, the French invasion of the Ruhr, and the national government's resort to a policy of passive resistance. While the savings of the German middle class were wiped out, Adenauer concentrated on seeing that his city continued to receive the basic necessities of life. This he did by making deals with friends in the business world to procure coal and food supplies and by negotiating with the British occupation authorities to ensure that they reached the city. It is clear that (not for the last time) he concealed much of what he was doing from the public eye and even from the city council. Williams writes that he "acted in public almost as a dictator," but adds that the task he had set himself was, on the whole, accomplished.

Almost from the beginning of his term, Adenauer was a national as well as a local figure. In 1921 and again in 1926, the moderate conservative Center Party put his name forward as a possible candidate for the chancellorship, although he failed to be nominated the first time, Williams writes, because his demands for authority were excessive and offended all of the parties involved, the second time because the Socialists and Gustav Stresemann's German People's Party refused to support him. Between 1921 and 1933, however, Adenauer was president of the Prussian State Council, the upper house of the parliament of Germany's largest state, and this gave him an excellent opportunity to keep in touch with national affairs.

Even so, most of his energies were concentrated on Cologne, and here, after the problems of the inflation period were overcome, he enjoyed five years of relative relaxation and productive work. This was followed, however, by the Great Depression in 1930, which not only involved Cologne in new financial difficulties as a consequence of having to repay short-term dollar loans and of the sharply rising bill for welfare payments but also wiped out Adenauer's considerable personal wealth because of bad investments. Forced to appeal to Berlin for aid for his city, he had to deal with a new chancellor, Heinrich Brüning, and the two, Williams writes, although sharing membership in the Center Party, did not much take to each other. Brüning in any case was bent on a policy of retrenchment that made no provision for cities that were seeking handouts. Adenauer did not get the aid he sought. Instead, as Cologne's fiscal problems worsened, he found himself confronted with a serious diminution of his local support, for in the Reichstag elections of September 1930, the main beneficiary was the hitherto underestimated National Socialist Party, which now launched an all-out attack on the mayor, concentrating on his contacts with the Jewish community in Cologne, including his support for the emigration of German Jews to Palestine. This onslaught continued without let-up until Adolf Hitler became Chancellor in January 1933, after which Adenauer was stripped of his office and driven into retirement.

Williams makes clear that Adenauer did not understand Hitler, having always regarded communism as the real threat to the kind of Germany he believed in. Indeed, in December 1932, in the last days of the Weimar Republic, he wrote a letter to the head of the Center Party saying that the most urgent issue was to see that "entry of the National Socialists into the Reich government [was] resolved in a positive sense." Williams writes:

> As President of the Prussian Staatsrat, Adenauer was prepared to encourage the formation of a Nazi-led Prussian government, headed by Göring, as a testing ground for a Nazi-led Reich government, headed by Hitler.

Whatever his motives (Williams suggests that he was concerned about his personal financial difficulties and was prepared to support any political combination that would let him keep his job), the scales soon fell from his eyes. Once Hitler was in power, the essential brutality of his policies revealed itself and Adenauer recognized it for what it was. He realized also that his prominence probably put his life in danger and resolved to live as unobtrusively as possible, foreswearing all political activity. In particular, as the years passed, he had no contacts with the resistance movement. When Carl Goerdeler, the former mayor of Leipzig and an active conspirator against Hitler, sought to enroll him, he refused to see him. It was clear enough, nevertheless, that he was on somebody's blacklist, for he was twice arrested by the Gestapo for brief periods, in 1935 and again, with his second wife, in 1944, after the bomb plot.

Politics continued to be much on his mind during these twelve years of personal abstention from it. Williams has a fascinating passage in which he describes Adenauer studying the papal encyclicals *Rerum Novarum* and *Quadragesimo Anno*, which defined the attitude of the Roman Catholic Church toward the social and political questions of the day. Adenauer, he writes, was seeking a theoretical and authoritative underpinning for the practical policies that he intended to espouse in the future. It is clear also that, particularly during the years of Hitler's war, he spent a lot of time thinking about Germany's future, which he was the first to realize must be governed by different principles and policies than in the past.

II

Despite his advanced age, therefore, he resumed his life in public affairs as soon as the occupying powers authorized a new beginning for party politics in Western Germany. After some hesitation, the Western Allies made it clear that they favored him over the courageous but doctrinaire Socialist Kurt Schumacher, the leader of the Social Democratic Party (SPD). More important in advancing his new political career, in Adenauer's own opinion, was the alliance that he negotiated between his own Christian Democratic Union (CDU) and the more conservative Christian Social Union (CSU) of Bavaria, for it was this coalition that won the parliamentary elections of 1949 and made his chancellorship possible.[1]

In his first years as head of the government, he left problems of economic policy to his colleague Ludwig Erhard, whose plan for a free market economy was registering its first successes, while he concentrated on foreign affairs. From the beginning his policy was revolutionary, for he was convinced that the old Europe of national states was no longer relevant to the needs and hopes of the postwar generation and that there could be no European great powers in the old sense of the word. His goal was the integration of Western Europe, and during his first visit to the United States in 1953 he made this clear at a luncheon at the National Press Club, when he said:

> Every historical epoch has its own tasks. In Europe every single rational argument points toward a united advance at the end of which there will one day be the United States of Europe. No one has better understood this than the young people of our continent.

In the years between 1949 and 1954 Adenauer held before the German people the vision of a new European order, which would be founded on the twin pillars of the European Coal and Steel Community and a European Defense Community with German membership. That this captured the imagination of the electorate is attested by the magnitude of Adenauer's victory in the elections of 1953, in which, with a turnout of nearly 86 percent of the electorate, the CDU/CSU won 45.2 percent of the vote to 28.8 percent for the SPD. The campaign was marred by the kind of vicious personal attacks on his opponents that were becoming increasingly characteristic of the chancellor's political style, including, on this occasion, his entirely uncorroborated charge that two prominent Socialist leaders had been aided by a 10,000 Deutschmark subvention from the German Democratic Republic. Such tactics were hardly necessary to assure the result. Nor was the unprecedented intervention by US Secretary of State John Foster Dulles, who, concerned by the outbreak of the Korean War, and believing that Adenauer would be readier than his Socialist opponent to supply a troop contingent for the Western forces, said at a press conference that a defeat for Adenauer "would have catastrophic consequences for the prospects for German unification and the restoration of sovereignty."

Adenauer's hope of European integration suffered a serious setback in 1954, when the French Assembly refused to approve of the European Defense Community. This left the chancellor greatly embittered, and in a conversation overheard by a reporter of *Der Spiegel* he expressed the fear that the French rejection would lead to a revival of nationalism and militarism in Germany. Not only was his view exaggerated, but the British and American governments persuaded the French government to agree to the admission of West Germany to NATO as a member with full sovereign rights. This would, in other circumstances, have been regarded as a diplomatic triumph of the first order, and a Swiss newspaper pointed out that, when one considered the state of Germany in 1949, it was almost impossible to believe what had been accomplished since then and that no more remarkable feat of statecraft could be imagined than Adenauer's transformation of his country "into a partner no longer dictated to but wooed—and all this by means of a consistently pro-Allied policy."[2] But to many Germans these accomplishments threatened to postpone national unification indefinitely and to impose on West Germany military costs that were excessive.

During the Bundestag debate on the ratification of the NATO treaty, Adenauer sought to persuade his critics that a policy of strength based on rearmament and the Western tie would eventually persuade the Soviets that reunification was inevitable. This was farsighted but injudicious; when the chancellor went to Moscow in 1955, he found that his hosts were contemptuous when he tried to raise the question. Indeed, in order to assure the release of ten thousand prisoners of war still held by the Russians, Adenauer had to agree to the formal establishment of diplomatic relations between the Federal Republic and the Soviet Union, an agreement that annoyed his allies because it augured an eventual recognition of the German Democratic Republic.

That this was no idle fear became apparent in the wake of the Suez and Hungarian crises of 1956, which in different ways showed the Western powers to be inept and ineffectual. This heartened the Soviets to make a grab at Berlin, and in November 1958 Nikita Khrushchev sent a note to London, Paris, and Washington informing them that Berlin's four-power status had come to an end and that a new status for the city must be negotiated within six months or the Soviet Union would conclude a separate treaty with the German Democratic Republic. Khrushchev's ultimatum brought about a crisis that was to last until 1962 and that was to show Adenauer both at his worst and at his best. During its course he came to distrust all of his allies, often on wholly insufficient grounds. He was sure that Dulles, in his last days, wanted a nuclear war, that Harold Macmillan was "stupid" and too amenable to Soviet blandishments, that John Kennedy, whom he called "a cross between a junior naval person and a Roman Catholic boy scout," was not keeping him informed of his exchanges with Moscow. In the end he convinced himself that only Charles de Gaulle could be trusted, and in January 1963 he concluded a treaty with the French leader that he henceforth regarded as the best guarantee of the future of Europe.

That Berlin was not lost during this difficult period was owing to a number of complicated factors. One of them was De Gaulle's unwavering refusal to negotiate under the pressure of ultimatums, which prevented the Western powers from agreeing on a policy of concessions to the Soviet Union. Much also depended on the actions of Khrushchev: his breaking up of the summit of 1960, which might have given him most of what he wanted in Berlin, including control of the city by the East German regime; his decision in August 1961 to settle for half of what he wanted by authorizing the building of the Berlin

Wall; and his subsequent mistake in abandoning a strategy concentrated on Germany and becoming involved in the Cuban missile adventure.

Yet if these were the determinative factors, Adenauer's role was far from unimportant. As Williams's account makes clear, he contributed to the final result of maintaining control of West Berlin by stubborn opposition to and detailed criticism of all Allied plans for meeting the Soviets halfway, by the production of elaborate but generally impractical solutions of his own, consideration of which slowed down the negotiations, and perhaps also by hints that he might meet with Khrushchev himself if worse came to worst, which would have greatly alarmed his allies.

III

Meanwhile, Adenauer continued to dominate the domestic scene; the national elections of 1957 were a greater success for him than those of 1953. Thanks to an economy that was growing at a rate of 7 percent a year and an enormously popular reform increasing old-age pensions, the turnout measured 87 percent, and the CDU/CSU polled 50.2 percent of the total. It was the first time that a single party had won an outright majority in German electoral history, and Williams writes that "at the age of eighty-one [Adenauer] was almost the uncrowned king of Germany."

This, however, was his last triumph. The elections of 1961 came immediately after the building of the Wall, to which the chancellor's reaction was inappropriate in manner and disastrous in result. In sharp contrast to his opponent Willy Brandt, he refused to go to Berlin to make a public protest against the Soviet action and continued to campaign as if nothing extraordinary had happened, meanwhile making offensive personal attacks upon Brandt that were much resented in the country. In the elections of September 17, 1961, the CDU/CSU vote fell sharply, and its majority was lost. Forming a new government proved to be difficult, and before it was accomplished the chancellor had to promise the leader of his Free Democratic allies that he would step down in two years' time or at least before the next elections in 1965.

All the available evidence indicates that he hoped to find a way of circumventing this promise. But in October 1962, the journal *Der Spiegel* published an article revealing some of the details of a secret NATO staff exercise showing that civil defense arrangements would be inadequate in case of war; and Adenauer's defense minister, Franz Josef Strauss, backed by the chancellor, foolishly brought charges of treason against its editors. The convolutions of this affair, which outraged the country and left the cabinet in ruins, lasted until April, but the result was that on the 23rd of that month the CDU/CSU parliamentary group in effect dismissed Adenauer from office by choosing Ludwig Erhard as his successor.

This had to be done, as Williams writes. With every succeeding year the Old Man had become increasingly unreliable and disingenuous. But what was to be remembered as his political allies let him go was that Konrad Adenauer had made the party that dismissed him the dominant force in German politics and, more important, that his long tenure of office had provided the West Germans with a sense of continuity and stability as well as the time to become used to democratic institutions and to learn how to make them work. The title of Williams's excellent book is fully justified.

Part Two

Culture

7

Great Scots!

I

When one thinks of Scotland, the first thing that is apt to come to mind is the violence and turbulence that characterized it during most of its history. It is at once a saga of kings and desperate men—Duncan meanly slaughtered in the keep of his host and vassal Macbeth; Robert Bruce stabbing his rival the Red Comyn in the church at Dumfries; the Earl of Moray, Mary Stuart's ambitious half-brother, shot from ambush in 1570 by a member of the Hamilton family in the streets of Linlithgow; the harassment of the Covenanters, groups of Presbyterians who took oaths to defend Scotland against English Anglicanism, in the notorious Killing Time of Charles II. It is also a tale of feckless gallantry and lost causes, in which victories like Bannockburn, where in 1314 a Scottish army led by Bruce defeated an English army twice its size, were always outnumbered by crushing setbacks like Flodden in 1513 and Culloden in 1746, in both of which the English inflicted devastating defeats.[1]

Review of *How the Scots Invented the Modern World*, by Arthur Herman, *The New York Review of Books*, September 26, 2002, pp. 71–72. Reprinted with permission from *The New York Review of Books*. Copyright © 2002, NYREV, Inc.

Arthur Herman, a former professor of history at Georgetown University, is not unaware of this melancholy record, but his attention is fixed on another story and another Scotland. He is intent on demonstrating how the inhabitants of a land that in 1700 was Europe's poorest independent country created the basic ideals of modern life, which he equates with democracy, technology, and capitalism, and how starting in the eighteenth century those ideals transformed their own culture and society and the lands to which they traveled. Herman's exuberant title, which will strike some readers as intended only to shock, is in fact meant quite seriously, and his book is a well-argued tribute to Scottish creative imagination and energy.

He starts by reminding us of modern Scotland's debt to the Reformation. It had been the ambition of the sixteenth-century religious reformer John Knox to turn the Scots into God's chosen people and Scotland into the new Jerusalem, and something of that spirit survived, in secular form, in the Scottish Enlightenment of the eighteenth century. Knox's Presbyterian Church, moreover, had the most democratic system of church government in Europe, and the National Covenant of 1638, signed in protest against Charles I's prayer book, was an early version of democracy in action.

Equally important was Knox's call in 1560 for a national system of education, which was elaborated by a number of statutes in the course of the next century, notably the Scottish Parliament's "Act for Setting Schools" in 1696. By the beginning of the eighteenth century Scotland had become Europe's first literate society, with a male literacy rate 25 percent higher than that of England. Herman writes that "despite its relative poverty and small population, Scottish culture had a built-in bias toward reading, learning and education in general. In no other European country did education count for so much, or enjoy so broad a base." This was notable in the case of Scotland's universities, which were distinguished enough to draw students from across Protestant Europe. Because of their relatively low fees and the swelling tide of literacy, they became centers of popular education as well as of academic learning.

Scotland was well prepared, then, for the takeoff into the modern age before objective circumstances made that possible. The union with England in 1707 was not universally popular in Scotland and its economic advantages were slow in making themselves felt. The challenges of the last Stuarts to the English monarchy in 1715 and 1745 were formidable distractions, and it was not until after the defeat at Culloden in 1746 that cultural questions could supplant the preoccupation with politics. But by then the Scottish Enlightenment was free to begin its destined work, which was nothing less, Herman writes, than "a massive reordering of human knowledge," the transformation "of every branch of learning—literature and the arts; the social sciences; biology, chemistry, geology, and the other physical and natural sciences—into a series of organized disciplines that could be taught and passed on to posterity."

The great figures of the Enlightenment were teachers and university professors, clergymen and lawyers, all driven by a profound didactic purpose. The professor and divine Francis Hutcheson, the jurist Lord Kames, the philosopher David Hume, and the economist Adam Smith—to whom Herman gives pride of place among them—all broke with the austere fundamentalism of Knox's Kirk (church) and the supposed immutability of divine providence. Instead, they placed human beings at the center of things, human beings seen as individuals with their private interests and frailties and limited rationality, and as the products of historical and social change.

Kames demonstrated that the development of human communities passed through four distinct phases and that the way people thought and acted was dependent upon whether they were occupied in hunting and fishing, or in pastoral and nomadic activities, or in agriculture, or in commerce. After that, the writing of history could never be the same again. And social analysis and indeed the science of government were profoundly different after Hume' argument, as Herman puts it, that

> self-interest is *all* there is. The overriding guiding force in all our actions is not our reason, or our sense of obligation toward others, or any innate moral sense—all these are simply formed out of habit and experience—but the most basic human passion of all, the desire for self-gratification. It is the one thing human beings have in common. It is also the necessary starting point of any system of morality, and of any system of government.

It was Adam Smith's appreciation of this view, Herman writes, and the courage with which he confronted and analyzed the tension between what human beings ought to be and what they really are, rather than his role as high priest of modern capitalism, that made him one of the great modern thinkers.

The Scottish Enlightenment had two centers, Edinburgh and Glasgow. Unlike London and Paris, the only cities that could compete with it as an intellectual capital, Edinburgh's cultural life was not dominated by state or aristocracy, but by its intellectuals and men of letters. It was a remarkably democratic society, in which there were no intellectual taboos and virtually all ideas could be debated freely. Herman writes that it was "like a gigantic think tank or artists colony, except that unlike most modern think tanks, it was not cut off from everyday life."

Edinburgh was, even so, more artistic and literary and more intellectual in the abstract sense than Glasgow, which was truer to older attitudes, including a deep-seated Calvinist fundamentalism. Glasgow was also practical and innovative and intent upon how things were made and how to get things done. If Adam Smith and his friends were at home in the intellectual hurlyburly of Edinburgh, Glasgow was the natural habitat for James Watt, whose experiments with steam, Herman says, "created the work engine of the Industrial Revolution." He adds:

> The version of technology we live with most closely resembles the one that Scots such as James Watt organized and perfected. It rests on certain basic principles that the Scottish Enlightenment enshrined: common sense, experience as our best source of knowledge, and arriving at scientific laws by testing general hypotheses through individual experiment and trial and error.

This gave capitalism its modern face and, among other things, created the classic industrial city. By 1801 Glasgow was Scotland's biggest metropolis, with textiles, iron-working, and ship-building the driving forces of economic and demographic growth, and a population that was to increase from 77,000 to nearly 275,000 in the next forty years.

II

How the fruits of the Enlightenment were carried beyond Scotland's borders, Herman describes in the second half of his book. He begins with North America, whose Scottish ties go back to James I's plans for a Scottish colony in Nova Scotia and were strengthened by the millions of Scots-Irish immigrants who arrived between then and the break with

Britain in the eighteenth century. These were Scottish people who had settled in Ireland and became convinced they would do better in the New World.

Herman makes no claim that Scots won the American Revolution, but he insists that Scottish ideas had a crucial part in the formation and early development of the Republic. He makes much of the work of John Witherspoon, the minister from the town of Paisley, west of Glasgow, who became president of Princeton University in 1768. During his twenty-six-year tenure he numbered among his students a future president of the United States (Madison), a vice-president (Aaron Burr), six members of the Continental Congress, nine cabinet officers, twenty-one senators, thirty-nine congressmen, three Supreme Court justices, twelve governors, thirty-three state and federal court judges, and thirteen college presidents. Witherspoon exposed all of these to the ideas of the Scottish Enlightenment. James Madison in particular fell deeply under the influence of David Hume (not entirely to Witherspoon's pleasure, since Hume was a self-confessed atheist), and Hume's ideas are apparent in the tenth of the Federalist Papers, the key to the new constitution, in which Madison argued that countervailing public interests—federal, state, executive, legislative, economic—would guarantee private liberty.

Scots also had a central part in the reform of the British constitutional system at the beginning of the nineteenth century. The loss of America and the defeat at the hands of France and Spain had a demoralizing effect in England, complicated by political factionalism, mutiny in the navy, and a suspension of payments by the Bank of England. The country was saved from more of the same by a virtual invasion of Scottish ideas, writers, inventors, and politicians.

Chief among the forces for change was Dugald Stewart, professor of moral philosophy at the University of Edinburgh, who, Herman writes, influenced "the mind of Europe and the English-speaking world to a degree no Scotsman ever equalled before or since." It was Stewart who gave wide circulation to the ideas of Adam Smith, making *The Wealth of Nations* into the classic source of modern economic theory. Even more important was the liberal optimism that informed his call for basic political reform in Britain. Undeterred by the fear induced by the violence of the French Revolution, he insisted that Britain—a land in which only one man in twenty had the vote—needed a revolution of its own, since "a modern society deserved a modern political system based on liberty, property and the rule of law." The persistence with which Stewart hammered away at this theme prepared the way for the victory of the Reform Bill in 1832 in which two other Scots had important parts— Henry Brougham, an eloquent member of the board of the widely influential *Edinburgh Review*, and Thomas Babington Macaulay, the son of an abolitionist in Inverary. In the debate in the House of Commons that determined the fate of the reform, Macaulay's was the most persuasive voice as he warned members: "The time is short. If this bill should be rejected, I pray to God that none of those who concur in rejecting it ever remember their votes with unavailing remorse, amidst the wreck of laws, the confusion of ranks, the spoliation of property, and the dissolution of social order."

The passage of the Reform Bill, which increased the British electorate by 50 percent and distributed seats in Parliament more fairly, prepared the way for the triumphs of the Victorian Age and the creation of the new British Empire, which eventually covered nearly one fifth of the earth's surface and included a quarter of its population, an empire on which it was said that "the sun never sets." A new book calls it "the Scottish Empire,"[2] and if this is a bit far-fetched it is not greatly so, for certainly Scots were active in India, the Far East, the Pacific, and the later holdings in Africa and the Middle East. Benjamin Disraeli once said, "It has been my lot to have found myself in many distant lands. I have never been in one without finding a Scotchman who was not at the head of the poll."

Critics of the Scots were apt to say that their frequent religiosity merely disguised a desire for gain and that they were driven by the principle "Keep the Sabbath and anything else you can lay your hands on."[3] This is unfair. The historian John Mackenzie has written:

> Perhaps the most extraordinary contribution of the Scots to Empire was the fact that, from the eighteenth century on, they were slotted into international intellectual networks. They became the botanists and foresters of Empire. They had almost complete command of medical establishments until at least the middle of the nineteenth century, when the supremacy of the Scottish universities in this and other fields began to fade. They were the engineers and builders of

imperialism, the creators of infrastructure and the suppliers and runners of railways. They largely carried all the new disciplines of tropical medicine, microbiology, entomology and veterinary science to a global stage from the late nineteenth century.[4]

Nor should this be surprising. While they sent a proportion of their population overseas that was matched only by the Irish, the Norwegians, and the southern Italians, the Scots alone had an advanced industrial and agricultural economy, and this was reflected in their diverse activities overseas.

During the nineteenth century Scotland was conspicuously free from the nationalism that marked other peoples like the Irish, the Italians, the Hungarians, the Greeks, and the inhabitants of Turkey's Balkan provinces. The differences that had marked the first stages of the union with England had been ironed out, and the Scots had neither political nor economic reasons to seek independence. That changed, however, after World War I and the subsequent decline of the Empire, and the 1920s were years of industrial depression in the Lowlands and continued depopulation of the Highlands. The failure of both the Tories and the Labour Party to remedy this situation now made increasing numbers of Scots begin to think of home rule, and in 1928 a disgruntled group of these seceded from the Labour Party and formed their own national party, the SNP.

It was a long time before the new party was strong enough to make much difference in Scottish politics. It had been preceded by a strong wave of cultural nationalism inspired by the desire to end the miserable state into which Scottish literature had fallen since the days of Burns and Walter Scott. Writers such as Cunningham Graham, Eric Linklater, Neill Gunn, Compton Mackenzie, and most of all, Hugh MacDiarmid (Christopher Murray Grieve), who was to write the long poem *A Drunk Man Looks at the Thistle*, were intent on inspiring a literary renaissance that would restore the glories of the pre-Reformation poets Henrysoun, Dunbar, and Gawin Douglas. These intellectuals were drawn to the SNP when it appeared. Their political ideas, however, like MacDiarmid's flirtation with fascism, his admiration of Lenin, and his "struggle . . . to show what Scotland micht hae hed instead / O this preposterous Presbyterian breed,"[5] frightened away potential voters who wanted a party that was douce and canny, as a Glaswegian might say. They got

such a party when some of the nationalist-minded intellectuals turned
to other fields and were replaced by a leadership that one caustic critic
said was "as exciting and imaginative as the Russian *nomenklatura* of the
Brezhnev era."[6] The SNP then grew steadily and emerged as a mass
political party in the late 1960s and early 1970s as a result of the continued failure of the Labour and Tory parties to offer a solution to Scotland's sense of decline.

Today Scotland has a parliament of its own for the first time in nearly three hundred years, as well as a new Parliament House, a growing
computer industry, and a prosperous service sector economy. Its sense
of independence is enhanced by the fact that it is being wooed by the
European Union to become a member. Not so long ago I received a
clipping from an unidentified German paper showing three babes in
swaddling clothes; one of them is female, and commenting, "In 2035
they will rule Europe: a Scottish finance minister, a French minister of
culture, an Italian minister of nutrition." Herman does not appear to be
enthusiastic about an increasingly independent Scotland and seems to
feel that Scotland under home rule may forget the great lessons of the
Enlightenment. He writes: "The great insight of the Scottish school was
that politics offers only limited solutions to life's intractable problems;
by surrendering her sovereignty the first time in 1707, Scotland gained
more than she lost. She has to be careful that, in trying to regain that
sovereignty, she does not reverse that process."

Frederick the Great and the Prussian Style

It is an honor and a pleasure to have been invited to come back to my favorite city to address this distinguished association. One way to express my appreciation would be perhaps, at the very outset, to reassure those among you who may know that I began my career as a historian of military affairs that I do not intend this evening to talk about the art of war. In the nineteenth century, this might have been a not inappropriate theme for a meeting of the Verband deutscher Kunsthistoriker [Union of German Art Historians], for in those days there were theorists of the aesthetics of war, who would gravely debate such things as whether Frederick II's victory at Leuthen could be compared—from the standpoint of the economy with which material forces were employed to achieve defined objectives according to a preconceived plan—with other historical clashes of arms, like Arbela, Marathon, Lützen, and Austerlitz, which were considered to be "beautiful battles."

A lecture delivered to the Verband deutscher Kunsthistoriker, Berlin, October 2, 1986. Published by permission of the estate of Gordon A. Craig and the Department of Special Collections, Stanford University Libraries. Translations from German sources are by Carolyn Halladay and Donald Abenheim. The volume editors have supplied the endnotes for this lecture.

The time for such enthusiasms has, I think, passed, and rightly so.

When I was a young man, I found myself at the dinner table one evening with a general in the U.S. Army named Clarence R. Huebner, who had commanded the First Division, Big Red One as it was called, in the Normandy landing of 1944. Trying to make conversation, I said, "General, who do you think was the best American commander in the European theater in World War II?," expecting him to name either George Patton or Omar Bradley. Instead, he answered promptly, "Courtney S. Hodges!" a general who was not widely known.

"Why Hodges?" I asked. "Because," Huebner answered, "I once saw him move a whole division around ninety degrees, practically leap-frogging the battalions over each other. It was the most beautiful thing I ever saw!" Even at the time, I found this a curiously Olympian view of battle, completely detached from the cursing columns and stalled tanks and the noise and the death that accompany strategic maneuver, taking delight in pattern rather than reality. It didn't strike me as anything I wanted to pursue and, in view of what has been happening in the field of warfare since 1945, my view hasn't changed. So I'll spare you any reference to the aesthetics of war or related military topics.

Instead, I'd like to talk about some sins committed in the name of history and the history of art, with particular reference to Arthur Moeller van den Bruck's brilliant book of 1914, *Der preußische Stil* [*The Prussian Style*],[1] to other works inspired by it, and to one particular way of representing the Prussian style pictorially. Inevitably, the man to whom today's papers have been devoted will play an important role in these remarks (Moeller considered him so central to his argument that he placed a photograph of his head from the equestrian statue of Christian Daniel Rauck on the dust-jacket of his book); and at their end I shall have to consider whether he, or for that matter Prussia, merited the treatment accorded to them by those who designed the styles that they were compelled to wear.

Although Moeller van den Bruck was a descendant on his father's side from a long line of Protestant pastors and Prussian soldiers, and although it had been expected that he would follow a military career, it was only in 1916 that he fulfilled that expectation by enlisting and going to the eastern front. Before that time, he had applied himself with remarkable assiduity to the study of art and literature, producing in the course of twelve years an 800-page history of German literature since Nietzsche, an eight-volume series of biographical essays called *Die Deutschen*, a study of contemporary culture and its leaders entitled *Die Zeitgenossen* [*The Contemporaries*], a survey of Italian art from the Etruscans to his own time (*Italienische Schönheit* [*Italian Beauty*]), and a magnificent edition of Dostoevsky in 23 volumes, a writer whom he may have been said to have discovered for Germany. It was in the introductions to the separate volumes of this edition, and in *Die Zeitgenossen*, that Moeller first clearly articulated the cultural pessimism that made him the most eloquent voice among those end-of-century critics who railed against the materialism, conformity and artistic poverty of their age, against the soulless capitalism that they believed stifled individuality and independence, against modern science, which was its handmaiden, and against bourgeois liberalism, synonymous in their view with everything that was flabby and corrupt, which was its dominant voice.

Moeller's sense that the prevailing style of the pre-1914 age was degenerate and doom-laden found its confirmation in the coming of the war; but that conflict also appeared to him to be a challenge to Germans to rediscover themselves, and his book *Der preußische Stil* was an attempt to show them the way.

In his introduction to the first edition of the book, Hans Schwarz, later director of the Moeller van den Bruck Archives, explained how the idea for the book burst upon its author, how he was standing one day beside Schinkel's Hauptwache[2] on Unter den Linden when it suddenly occurred to him that the building represented a style of architecture, an artistic form, a spirit, a philosophy, and a way of life just as independent and self-sufficient as the classicism of Italy and the ancient world, a style in its own right, a "Prussian style" that could not be fully understood by relating it to similar structures in other places and times, but only by reference to German and Prussian history. Prussia, Moeller realized, meant the beginning of a new period in German history and the Prussian style was the last great style to develop in Europe. It was also Germany's hope for a future of independence and honor, and Moeller made his belief that this was true clear and unequivocal by taking as a motto for this book the words: "Prussia is the greatest colonizing act of Germandom, just as Germany will be the greatest political act of Prussianism."

It is clear from this that the word "style" in Moeller's title was meant to have a comprehensive rather than a narrow meaning and that the book was intended less as a history of art than as a political essay, indeed, a political manifesto. There was, to be sure, much about architecture and sculpture in it—about the fortresses of the Teutonic Knights, about *Backsteingotik* [Gothic Architecture Built in Brick] as a reflection of the sturdy virtues of those who built it, about the baroque, which in Andreas Schlüter's hands had assumed almost Roman qualities, about the plain *Zopf* style of the time of Frederick William I and the rococo, which was somehow nobler in Prussia just as the baroque was simpler, and about Langhans's Brandenburger Gate as a visual translation of Ludwig Gleim's line "Berlin sei Sparta!" ["Berlin be Sparta!"]. Indeed, all of this—and particularly what Moeller had to say about this transition from the rococo style of Frederick II's early years to the classicism of his last—was essential to his argument. Even so, his message was a political one. Moeller saw the history of his country as a conflict between two principles: on the one hand, the German, whose origin was myth, "and out of myth grew romanticism, which accompanied our history in the old Reich for a millennium or more, until it finally overshadowed it," and, on the other, the Prussian "without myth," given to reality rather than dreams, simple austere, practical, with the energy "that now has allowed us for the first time to accomplish things in the world, instead of losing our way again and again."[3] The essence of the Prussian spirit was its *Sachlichkeit* ["objectivity," in the sense of realism], and this was epitomized in all of the manifestations of Prussian life and history—its colonization of the eastern lands, the Great Elector's foreign policy, the architecture of Königsberg and Potsdam and the *forum Fridericianum*, the state-building of Frederick William I, whom he called "der Nurpreuße, der Urpreuße" [the only Prussian, the original Prussian] and, above all, the life and achievements of Frederick II.

Of this ruler, Moeller wrote passionately:

> Spirit and blood achieved what a crown and a name alone could not: following Frederick the Great's example, one felt Prussian in Prussia, just as one felt *fritzish* [Frederickian] in Germany—and that because Prussianism was a living philosophy, a certain theory of morality and objectivity. It had always existed in the sterile tracts of

northern Germany, of course, but Frederick the Great brought it to political prominence, evident to and accepted by all.

Prussianism lived in the glory of the king, in the renown of a hundred battlefields, in the image of his unconquerable army. Foreigners felt it; poets sang of it; even in the work of non-Prussians, it became momentously fruitful. And as it rippled outward there arose over all of Germany for the first time something like hope for the renewal of the empire's glory.[4]

Moeller's description of Prussianism and Germanness as antithetical principles, his argument that the former was a necessary corrective to the German tendency to succumb to romanticism and *Innerlichkeit* [inwardness], and his eulogy of Frederick as the embodiment of the Prussian style in politics were not, of course, new. The historian Heinrich von Treitschke, fearing that what he called "the cowardly and short-sighted [attitude of average Germans] in politics" would not sustain the national unity achieved by Prussian arms and statecraft in 1870, had sought to strengthen identification with the new Empire by literally inventing a historical tradition for it. In the first volume of his *Deutsche Geschichte*, which appeared in 1879, he strongly implied that German history began only with the rise of Prussia in the seventeenth and eighteenth centuries and achieved its first triumphant realization when Frederick II, whose dominant characteristic, Treitschke wrote, was his "relentlessly fierce veracity," strode "in proud liberty . . . right through the great powers . . . and the Germans were compelled to believe once more in the wonder of heroism."[5]

Similarly, Friedrich Nietzsche, in a remarkable passage on Frederick William I and Frederick II in *Jenseits von Gut und Böse* [*Beyond Good and Evil*] in 1885, spoke of how the father "knew what Germany was missing, a deficit a hundred times more dreadful and urgent than, say, the lack of culture and social graces . . . Germany lacked *men!*" and how the son supplied the felt want with "the skepticism of bold masculinity, which is closely related to the genius for war and for conquest, which made its first appearance in Germany in the figure of Frederick the Great"—a realism which, "as a continuing Frederickianism elevated to the most spiritual level," was able, "gradually and despite all romanticism in music and philosophy" to manifest itself in German behavior in such things as "intrepidity of gaze, as the courage and rigor of analysis, as the tenacious will to undertake dangerous journeys of discovery and spiritualized expeditions to the North Pole under bleak and foreboding skies."[6]

Both Treitschke and Nietzsche saw in the Prussian style or spirit a possible means of sustaining the imperfect creation of 1870/71. Writing from a later perspective, Moeller van den Bruck argued that the opposite had taken place, that, in assuming the leadership of Germany, Prussia had lost its own soul.

> The collapse of this so strict, purely spiritual culture—which until then had gone along with both style as well as conception—only took place with the foundation of the empire: Prussia was sacrificed to Germany. The disintegration began with the self-alienation, with the complete failure to recognize [Prussia's] native values—and destruction followed. Now Prussia denied its past, which had been its pride and in which it appeared no longer to take pride: its de-Prussification had begun.[7]

In the years that followed, the values of the *Gründerzeit* [that is, commercialization and pomp] had supplanted Prussian virtues; German romanticism had blunted the edge of Prussian realism; liberalism with its spineless tolerance and sentimentality had become universally triumphant. Symptomatic of the Germanization of Prussia was the architectural degeneration of Berlin, where the triumphs of Schlüter, Nering, Gilly and Schinkel had been forced to give way to buildings designed to impress by their monumentality and the garish flamboyance of their decoration, and where the lack of planning had turned a manly and dignified town into a sprawling metropolis without soul or character.

And yet, Moeller wrote, in a chapter written at the end of the war, this was not the end. The war had shaken people into an awareness both of what had been lost and what the consequences of that loss had been. The defeat must compel them to return to the foundation of their vitality.

> Fate had decided against Prussia. *Aber Preußen muß sein* [But Prussia must be]. There have often been great lulls in Prussian history. Once—from Hubertusburg to Jena—a great exhaustion followed the exertion [of war against Napoleon]. *Aber Preußen muß sein.* Similarly, Prussia will overcome the disintegration of the world war, just

as Germany will overcome it. Germany cannot do without Prussia because it cannot do without Prussianism. Prussianism—that is, the will to the state and the recognition of the historical existence as a political existence, in which we, as political men, must act. *Preußen muß sein.*[8]

Here, the Prussian style has been transformed into the spirit of resistance to the domestic and international order that resulted from the war, and for the rest of his life Moeller worked tirelessly for the new revolution in which "the old Prussia in a modern form" would overthrow the post-war system and usher in a new empire—*das Dritte Reich*, he was to call it in 1923—of incomparable strength and grandeur.

In the prevailing mood of disenchantment and disorientation that followed the collapse of 1918, Moeller's ideas had a profound effect upon the thinking of young intellectuals of the nationalistic right, upon the neo-conservatives who gathered in the Juni-Club, like Paul Fechter, Rudolf Pechel, Walter Schotte, and Otto Strasser, and upon the contributors to Eduard Stadler's *Das Gewissen*, a journal that became increasingly violent in its attacks upon the new parliamentary democracy and insistent upon a radical change of the political system. *Der preußische Stil* was probably not without effect upon Walter von Molo's best selling biography *Fridericus*; it supplied the title and the basic theme to Wilhelm Stapel's *Preußen muß sein!*; and Oswald Spengler's powerful essay *Preußentum und Sozialismus* could not have been written without it.

Spengler not only used the term "der preußische Stil" but did so in the same way that Moeller had, defining it as "a collective feeling not of rest but of work," as "a high ethic . . . not of success, but of the task," as "an attitude toward life, an instinct, a couldn't-be-otherwise," which had found its most perfect embodiment in the achievements of Frederick William I and Frederick II and was now Germany's only hope of salvation. The dissonance that Moeller found between *Preußentum* and *Deutschtum*, Spengler accepted and turned into a harsh dichotomy between Prussian resistance and German willingness to accept the values and political forms of the victors of 1918. Prussianism (and Socialism, which was practically the same thing, Spengler argued, as long as one remembered that the great Hohenzollerns and not Marx were its fathers) was the "unflinchingly liberal Michel [the German everyman]" in the German soul. In a passage reminiscent of Moeller's attacks upon romanticism, Spengler wrote:

> Michel-ism is the sum of our inabilities, the fundamental discontent with superior realities, which demand service and regard, criticism at the wrong time, rest at the wrong time, the hunt for ideals instead of rash acts, rash acts instead of careful consideration, the "*Volk*" as a mass of grumblers, the assembly of the people's representatives as a beer table of the highest order. It is all English character, but in German caricature.[9]

And it must all be swept away. In a peroration that both betrayed the narrowness of his conception of the Prussian style and pointed towards the tragic consequences of his kind of thinking, Spengler wrote:

> We need no blather about culture and cosmopolitanism and the spiritual mission of the Germans. We need toughness, we need skepticism, we need a class of lordly personalities. . . . Power, power, and once again power. Plans and thoughts are nothing without power. The path to power is prescribed: the valuable parts of the German working class in combination with the best bearers of the old Prussian sense of state . . . both welded together by the unity of their sense of duty; by the awareness of a great undertaking; by the will to obey in order to rule [and] to die in order to triumph; by the strength to make colossal sacrifices in order to achieve what we were born to [achieve], what we are, and what would not exist without us.[10]

These words, we remember almost with a shock, were written in 1919. It is easy to see why the bookstores would display a handsome new edition of *Preußentum und Sozialismus* in their windows after Hitler's seizure of power, as I was to discover as a student in Munich in 1935.

All of this re-styling of Prussianism to suit the political purposes of the radical right had limited powers of penetration; it reached the ears of intellectuals but had little or no effect upon the masses. The opposite was true of another treatment of Prussianism, this time by film. Even before Moeller and Spengler had written their essays, the first of the films about Frederick II had appeared—*Der alte Fritz* of 1898, followed by three others before 1914—and after 1918 Prussia was trump in the cinema, with thirteen Frederick films during the Weimar period. Kurt Tucholsky wrote:

Fridericus Rex, unser König und Herr,
Der rief uns noch einmal in das Kino daher.
Zweitausend Meter lang ist der ganze Quark—
Und jeder Parkettplatz, der kostet sechzehn Mark—

[Fridericus Rex, our king and master,
He summoned us once more into the cinema.
The cheesy junk runs for two thousand meters
And every seat costs sixteen marks—]

With six more after 1933, and with dozens of other films on Prussian themes: the *Freiheitskrieg* [war of liberation against Napoleon, 1813–15], the storming of the Düppeler Schanzen [1864], the French War of 1870, the life of Queen Luise (three films) and that of Bismarck (the same number), and many more.

Certain aspects of these productions are worth noticing. In the first place, the Prussia portrayed was idealized rather than realistic and, because styled for the mass audience, stereotypical, that is, filled with images and themes that would be readily recognizable. The filmmakers were not, as historians, either critical or energetic. On Frederick, they found most of what they thought they needed in the *Geschichte Friedrichs des Grossen* of the *Kunsthistoriker* [art historian] Franz Kugler, written in 1840 to commemorate the hundredth anniversary of Frederick's accession to the Prussian throne, a book whose simple and charming style, patriotic tone, anecdotal method, and reverential approach to its subject commended it to a wide readership. The first comprehensive treatment of Frederick's life and times, Kugler's book had the additional advantage of being illustrated by 400 woodcuts by Adolf Menzel and, although the old Schadow[11] had criticized these as "Kritzeleien" [scrawlings] and had denied that they were "true reflections of those old days," the combination of text and illustration fixed a series of images in the popular consciousness that were somehow transmitted from generation to generation and proved to be indelible. This greatly facilitated the filmmakers' work and increased its impact. In the Frederick films, whole scenes were literally cinematographic versions of Menzel's woodcuts or—one thinks of the climactic scene in Gustav Ucicky's *Das Flötenkonzert von Sanssouci*—of his paintings.

In the second place, the films were highly selective in their treatment of Prussian history, avoiding, for the most part, any treatment of economic and social problems and restricting references to politics and morality to pictorial disquisitions on the State as the end of all human endeavor and the paramount duty of serving it. As presented on the screen, Prussian history seemed to be largely concerned with putting on uniforms and marching off to fight purely defensive wars against forbidding odds. As for Frederick, his screen life was limited for the most part to altercations with his father and winning the Seven Years' War.

In the third place, with the passing of the years the films became increasingly political and ideological in tone. It is true that Arzen von Czerépi's four-part *Fridericus Rex*, produced by UFA in 1922–1923, was, while eminently pleasing to monarchists and militarists, designed more to appeal to a general nostalgia for the good old days than to deliver a specific political message. Even so, the tendency to portray Prussia, for dramatic effect, as an almost mythic land of great men and great triumphs could only invite comparisons with the problem-ridden parliamentary republic that were invidious, and such comparisons became deliberate after Alfred Hugenberg, the leader of the German National People's Party, purchased UFA in 1928. From that time on, the company's Prussian films took on a pronounced nationalistic, antidemocratic coloration that deepened as the country was overwhelmed by the depression in 1930. The Prussian style now became authoritarian with a vengeance. The clear message of Ucicky's *Das Flötenkonzert von Sanssouci* (1930) was that in critical times a country would do well to put its faith in a strong leader; this was repeated in more transparent form in Carl Fröhlich's *Der Choral von Leuthen* (1933), a glorification of war in which Frederick had become a charismatic figure who stood above reason and whose commands, which often appeared to be irrational to his subordinates, were nevertheless obeyed by them out of blind faith in the leader.

It has been observed—perhaps for the first time by Siegfried Kracauer—that the protagonists of these and other Prussian films of the years 1930–1933 began to talk in the commanding tones and drastic formulations of the leader of the Nazi movement. Worse was to come. Once that movement had seized power, they tended to acquire Hitlerian mannerisms and opinions as well. In Hans Steinhoff's *Der alte und der junge König* (1935), Frederick William I burns books; in Veit Harlan's *Der große König* (1942), Frederick II says, "To doubt victory is high treason!"

In the end, art revenged itself upon its manipulators, as the cinematographic Prussian style subverted reality in the minds of those who had been using it for their political purposes. Wilhelm van Kampen has pointed to the irony of the fact that—and I quote him—"Just as the Führer was magically made for his followers, with the help of the Frederick myth, into a towering figure, onto which all hopes and desires were projected, this same Führer, with his irrational need for validation, relied on the same historical example as an irrefutable holy message." In the last days in the bunker, Adolf Hitler was obsessed by the presence of Frederick, and had Joseph Goebbels read to him from Carlyle's history, and waited for the miracle of the House of Brandenburg to come again.

But let us leave these fantasies and return to what I said at the outset about sins committed in the name of history, for it is clear, I hope, that that is what I have been talking about. Was not everything that Moeller van den Bruck and the members of the Juni-Club and Wilhelm Stapel and Oswald Spengler and the UFA *Regisseure* [director] had to say about Prussia and Prussianism a distortion? And was not this so because it included nothing about the infinite variety of Prussia, or (aside from Moeller's highly politicized treatment) about Prussian creativity, or about the critical spirit in Prussian thought, or about Prussian humanism, or about Prussian wit, or (after so much about the power and rights of the State) about Prussian theories of limiting the State, or (after so much about Prussian obedience) about Prussian disobedience?

Should we not question the validity of any definition of the Prussian style that does not take some account of the qualities and achievements and idiosyncrasies, even eccentricities, of people like Johann Gottfried Herder (a cosmopolitan in spirit but Prussian enough to note with a mixture of pride and contempt, in a letter to Johann Caspar Lavater, that "all the princes are affecting the gaping aquiline expression of the bird in Potsdam") and Gotthold Ephraim Lessing? Of Friedrich Nicolai, who once wrote, "Criticism is the only assistant who, in exposing our imperfections, at the same time arouses in us the craving for higher perfection," and his friend, the Jew of Berlin, Moses Mendelssohn? Of

Wilhelm von Humboldt, the humanist, educator and political thinker, and his brother Alexander, who knew that there were vast worlds beyond Prussia? Of Staatsminister vom Stein, who loved and hated Prussia in almost equal measure, and E. T. A. Hoffmann, who served the State punctiliously and parodied it without mercy? Of Rahel Varnhagen, and Bettina von Arnim, who sent unpalatable truths to her sovereign, who disregarded them? Of the Prussian lieutenants August Willich and Friedrich Engels, who threw down their commissions and went and fought for the Badenese Revolution, and Wilhelm Rüstow, who did the same and served with Garibaldi in Sicily? Of Adolf Glassbrenner, who wrote, "Don't burden your mind with useless knowledge. . . . For almost everything beyond the basics is high treason!" and Kurt Tucholsky, who inherited his wit and critical incisiveness? Of Ferdinand Lassalle, and Lily Braun, and Otto Braun? Of the Marwitz who was jailed by Staatsminister Hardenberg for protesting to King Frederick William III against government infringement of the privilege of his class, and the other Marwitz who disobeyed Frederick II's order to destroy Schloß Hubertusburg, was cashiered, and had written on his gravestone the words "Chose disgrace, where obedience did not bring honor"?

And what about Frederick, the chief victim of the distortions of the Moellers and the Spenglers and the filmmakers? What are we to do for him? Perhaps, in the first place, we should insist that he was never as one-dimensional as they liked to make him, that, like the Prussia he helped to make, he was more diverse, more self-contradictory than they could afford to admit. In his great biography of Frederick, the late Theodor Schieder called him a "rätselhafte Doppelnatur" [puzzling dual nature]. The deeper one penetrates into the details of his domestic policy, Schieder wrote, the clearer it is that "its highest value was the promotion of state power"; and yet the rationalization of the institutions that he felt would enhance state power had another side. As *Staatsvernunft*, as *Staatsräson*, it was also an element of the *Aufklärung*, and Frederick never entirely got over his youthful idealistic belief that "State rationality must serve such higher purposes as justice, humanity, and happiness." This impulse doubtless weakened with time and was overborne by political considerations and Frederick's deepening pessimism. Even so, Frederick never became a heedless *Realpolitiker*—here

Schieder is surely right—and he never became the irrationalist and *Vabanquespieler* of the late UFA films. He was always the philosopher who reflected upon his actions and for whom "the power in which he dealt was always a problem of thought."

In the second place, we should allow someone whose Prussian credentials are impeccable to serve as a kind of counsel for the defense for the real Frederick against the one invented by the ideological stylists of the early decades of this century; and we could find no one who would fill this role better than the novelist Theodor Fontane, who was proud to call himself an *"in der Wolle gefärbter Preuße* [dyed-in-the-wool Prussian]." Towards Frederick, Fontane's attitude was always critical, and the protagonist of his novel *Der Stechlin* says that there was too much *Befehlscharakter* [command character] and too little tolerance for freedom and self-determination in his system of governance. Even so, Fontane never ceased to admire the King for demanding as much from himself, in the way of labor and sacrifice, as he did from his subjects.

In *Wanderungen durch die Mark Brandenburg* [*Walks through the Mark Brandenburg*], there is a long quotation from the memoirs of Friedrich August Ludwig von der Marwitz,[12] describing Frederick coming into Berlin in May 1785 and riding, at the head of his suite of generals and adjutants, from the Hallesches Tor to the Palais of Princess Amalie. "The whole bastion," Marwitz wrote, "and the Wilhelmstraße were pressed full of people, all the windows occupied, all heads bare, everywhere the deepest silence and on every face an expression of respect and confidence, as if in the rightful ruler of all fates. . . . Through this reverent silence sounded only the hoof beats of the horses and the cries of the Berlin street urchins, who danced before him, cheered, threw their hats in the air, or sprang to his side and wiped the dust from his boots."

A scene made for the cinema, and often screened—the weary hero returning home from another punishing victory over the Russians or the French. Only, as Fontane realized, it was 1785, and the wars lay twenty years back, and much hard, unexciting, necessary work had been done since then, from which Frederick's subjects had benefited. When he used the Marwitz passage in his novel *Vor dem Sturm* [*Before the Storm*], Fontane gave it a different accent. He wrote:

No pomp, no cannons, no fifes and drums—just a 73-year-old man, poorly dressed and covered in dust, returned from his laborious day's work. But everyone knew, that in forty-five years, not one day of this labor was missed, and reverence, admiration, pride, and confidence stirred in every breast as soon as they caught sight of the duty and toil of this man.

It was this Frederick rather than the god of battles whom Fontane admired. He detested the Prussian style of his own age, which seemed bent upon inflating Prussian virtues for the sake of using them to justify special privilege and upon inventing a Frederick myth that could be used against all of the progressive forces of the time. He dismissed all that as *Borußismus.*[13] But there was never any question in his mind that the *"Mann der Pflicht und der Arbeit"* [man of duty and toil] merited the attribute of historical greatness. In May 1898, Fontane wrote to Friedrich Paulsen about William Ewart Gladstone, who had just died. "What everyone is saying about Gladstone these days reminds me again of the great king; in the end, only he is great who advances humanity a few kilometers."

9

Frederick the Great and Moses Mendelssohn: Thoughts on Jewish Emancipation

Historians are fond of calling attention to anniversaries, and it is a double anniversary that supplies the occasion for these remarks, for next year will be the 200th anniversary of the deaths of both Moses Mendelssohn, who died on 4th January 1786, and of Frederick II of Prussia, who died on 17th August of that year.

One may object, of course, that this coincidence is a poor excuse for lumping together such disparate personalities, but, in truth, Moses Mendelssohn and Frederick were not so different as all that. To be sure, one was a King and the other was not; but, despite that salient discrepancy, there were striking similarities between them. In both cases, for example, their adolescence and early manhood were troubled and painful, with much deprivation, much drudgery over unrewarding tasks, and a considerable amount of physical and psychological torment.

This paper was delivered by the author in New York on December 28, 1985, at a function of the Leo Baeck Institute on the 100th meeting of the American Historical Association. It was published in *The Yearbook of the Leo Baeck Institute* 32 (1987): 3–10. Reprinted by permission of Oxford University Press.

Frederick, of course, never had to worry about where his next meal was coming from, as Mendelssohn sometimes did; but then Mendelssohn never had to suffer the anguish of having to watch his closest friend being beheaded and of having subsequently to sit for weeks in confinement, waiting to learn whether he would suffer the same fate.[1]

Both men overcame the difficulties of their early lives by means of strict discipline and prodigious intellectual labors; both became voracious readers of systematic works on philosophy, theology, politics and—in Frederick's case—military science, as well as dramatic works and epic verse; and both, using models that they found in their reading, trained themselves to write about serious subjects with clarity, grace and authority. Writing seems, indeed, to have become for them a psychological necessity, in which they sought perspective and perhaps reassurance in times of doubt and danger; Mendelssohn's pen was always his friend and comforter, while Frederick, after his defeat at Kolin in 1757, not only wrote floods of letters and analyses of recent operations and reflections on how his conduct of battle might be improved, but told his correspondents that misfortune had reawakened his desire to write poetry.[2] So too, after the murderous fight at Hochkirch in 1758, the King noted, "You will often find me engrossed in reading and writing. I need this diversion at a time when I am preoccupied with gloomy thoughts."[3] Wilhelm Dilthey was perhaps guilty of exaggeration when he described Frederick as one of the four great writers of his age, the others being Voltaire, Diderot and Lessing,[4] but the King's histories of his own time are still accorded respect for their substance as well as their style. As for Mendelssohn, who wrote in a language that he had had to acquire painfully in his first years in Berlin, his works were praised by such discerning critics as Nicolai, Kant, and Hamann.

Even the accomplishments of their mature years are, while different in nature, comparable in grandeur.

By the sheer force of his personality, Frederick—against forbidding odds and the armed opposition of all his neighbors—transformed a relatively poor and heterogeneous collection of territories into a great European power and made it at the same time not only the newest but also the most modern state in Europe, a land of unlimited opportunities that served as a magnet for talented young men in all parts of Germany. Mendelssohn's achievement was no less a victory of personality.

In a society that regarded Jews with contempt and suspicion, he showed by his own example how mistaken stereotypical German views of the Jews really were. To his own people, he demonstrated—as Hans I. Bach has written—that "the transition from the secluded life of medieval Jewry to participation in Western civilization could be achieved without loss of faith. . . . Without his example, the emancipation of the Jews, the freedom to take their place as valued citizens of the Western world, could never have been contemplated."[5]

Finally, both Mendelssohn and Frederick were leading representatives of the Enlightenment, that proud and self-confident movement of the eighteenth century which based itself on the faith that human reason was capable not only of determining the universal laws of nature but also of refashioning the world and freeing it from the burden of superstition, prejudice, outmoded institutions and injustice, and which expressed this in an ambitious program of secularism, humanity, cosmopolitanism, and freedom in all of its forms.

About the legitimacy of Mendelssohn's credentials as an *Aufklärer*, there is no question. His biographer Alexander Altmann has described his almost herculean labors during his first Berlin years to acquire the languages necessary to study the work of the great *philosophes*, of his laborious reading of Locke's *Essay Concerning Human Understanding*, which he had to translate word by word from an edition in Latin, and of the formative influence upon his thinking of Leibniz, Shaftesbury, and Wolff.[6] Accustomed by his training in Jewish doctrine to believe in the efficacy of reason, its compatibility with the Law, and the merits of tolerance, he had no difficulty in making the ideals of the *Aufklärung* his own, and all of his subsequent activities and works, from his correspondence with Lessing and Nicolai and Kant to his collaboration with Christian Wilhelm von Dohm, the author of the treatise *On the Civic Improvement of the Jews*, testify to his abiding faith in reason, his love of humanity, his belief in the intrinsic goodness and unity of human nature, and his willingness to be modern at the expense of the traditional and the Orthodox.

More problematical is Frederick's right to be considered as a true *Aufklärer*. The friend of Voltaire, the ruler who sometimes styled himself the *philosophe de Sans Souci*, was in the end repudiated by his fellow philosophers as a recreant and traitor to the cause, and Rousseau was speaking for the majority of them when he wrote in 1758 that he was an "admirer of the talents of the King of Prussia, but in no way his partisan," adding, "I can neither esteem nor love a man without principles, who tramples on all international law, who does not love virtue but considers it as a bait with which to amuse fools, and who began his Machiavellianism by refuting Machiavelli."[7] In our own time, Peter Gay has written that Frederick, like Catherine of Russia, "forced [himself] on a movement to whose ideals [his] policy owed little."[8]

It is possible that these judgments are too severe. What most people know about Frederick's treatise against Machiavelli, which was written in 1739, is that it was followed almost immediately by his unprovoked assault upon the territories of Empress Maria Theresa, the so-called rape of Silesia. But no one who reads the *Anti-Machiavel*, or the work that preceded it, the *Considerations sur l'état présent du corps politique de l'Europe* of 1737–1738, can remain entirely unimpressed by the strong strain of idealism that runs through them. When Frederick declares in the former work that politics should be regarded not as a storehouse of cunning artifices and tricks, but as the totality of the wisdom of princes; when he writes that their task should be to ban falsehood and intrigue from international affairs and to promote the welfare of their subjects; when, in place of Machiavelli's hero Cesare di Borgia, he sets up Fénélon's Télémaque as a model for rulers and as the embodiment of goodness, justice and restraint, there is no reason to believe, simply because his later actions did not conform to his professions, that he was being deliberately insincere. Even as he wrote, he was painfully aware that, once he assumed the throne, he would be confronted with the dilemma that is posed for every responsible political leader by the contrast between the world as it is and the world as it should be. Even in his fulminations against Machiavelli, he did not ignore the Florentine's warning that a prince's freedom of action was circumscribed by necessity—that of maintaining his realm against jealous and unscrupulous foes—and that his best-designed plans were at the mercy of fortune's whims, and that in such circumstances his greatest resource was *virtú*. But Frederick's definition of *virtú* was *"Qui dit la vertu, dit la raison."*[9]

This definition should be remembered in any evaluation of Frederick's work as a ruler. There is no doubt that the deeper one penetrates the details of his internal policy the clearer it becomes that its chief aim was the enhancement of the power of the State. Yet the reforms that he made to accomplish that purpose—the decree of tolerance, the abolition of torture, the reform of the legal system, the economic and colonization projects, the measures to improve the efficiency of the State administration—were part of a rational process, an application of *Staatsvernunft* or Reason of State, which was, of course, a salient feature of the politics of the Enlightenment. What could be more characteristic of the spirit of the Enlightenment than Frederick's insistence in his *Political Testament* of 1752 that "a well-conducted government ought to have a system as coherent as a system of philosophy"?[10]

Moreover, Reason of State was not entirely incompatible with the idealism that had found expression in the *Anti-Machiavel*. In the latest biography of Frederick, Theodor Schieder has written that the King never got over his youthful belief that *Staatsvernunft* must serve not purely utilitarian ends, but "the higher goals of justice, humanity, and happiness."[11] It is not difficult to find passages in both the *Testament* of 1752 and that of 1768 that support this view, as do some of the major reforms, notably the encouragement of the formulation of rules of war as a means of introducing a measure of restraint to the century's intermittent blood-letting. This impulse doubtless weakened with time and was overborne by political considerations and by Frederick's deepening cynicism. Even so, he never became a heedless *Realpolitiker*. He was always the philosopher who reflected upon his actions and for whom, as Schieder says, "the power with which he worked was always an intellectual problem."[12]

Having said all this, one must nevertheless admit that most of Frederick's statements about "the higher goals of justice, humanity, and happiness" suffered from their abstract quality. Otto Hintze's view that the *Political Testaments* in part reflect French and American theories of the rights of the individual is not persuasive. Frederick was not accustomed to thinking of individuals and their specific needs, and his comments about his subjects as human beings were not infrequently atrabilious. As a ruler and reformer, he tended rather to think in terms of functional groupings with specific roles in society, and this necessarily diminished the humanitarian content of his reforms, while negating his professed desire to promote justice. No better example of this can be found than his attitude towards his Jewish subjects.

In eighteenth-century Prussia, the Jews were a small—there were only 333 Jewish families resident in Berlin in 1743, with a total Jewish population of less than 2,000—under-privileged, over-taxed minority that was tolerated for its economic usefulness but was often an object of abuse and mistreatment. Their rights of residence and movement were, except in the case of a small elite of *Generalprivilegierten*, restricted, and they were subject to expulsion from their places of domicile at the caprice of local authorities. They were excluded from the public service; they could not belong to guilds; they were forbidden to engage in certain trades, to open barbers' shops, for example, to sell spirits, baked goods, fish, meat and milk products; and they were taxed mercilessly and, as Henri Brunschwig has written, on every possible occasion, when travelling, when marrying, when buying a house, taxed for the right to remain in the city, taxed whenever they left it, taxed for the privilege of being excluded from the armed forces, and so forth. The story is an old one and does not bear repeating. The civic disabilities of the Jews seemed to most of the *philosophes* to cry for correction, although it should be noted that there was a certain ambivalence in their attitude, since the Jewish religion seemed to them to be even more benighted and obscurantist than that of the various Christian sects. Hence Voltaire's mixed feelings about the Jews.[13]

There was, however, no ambivalence about the feelings of the philosopher king. His ordinance of 1750 divided Jews into four categories, defined their rights, and placed all matters concerning them under the control of the General Directory, but it in no way improved their condition. Frederick recognized them as an economic resource that could be tapped when needed (when the *Königliche Porzellanmanufaktur* needed shoring up, for example, he decreed that Jews must buy large amounts of its products on set occasions), but otherwise regarded them with a distaste bordering on contempt. In the *Political Testament* of 1752, in the section on religious denominations, he wrote:

> The Jews are the most dangerous of all these sects because they do damage to trade of Christians and because they are unusable as far as the State is concerned. We need this people in order to maintain a certain amount of trade with Poland, but one must prevent their

numbers from growing and must limit them not only to a fixed number of families but also to a fixed number of individuals. One must also restrict their business activities, preventing them from engaging in wholesale trade, for they should only be retailers.[14]

Sixteen years later, in the *Testament* of 1768, he showed that his views had not changed. In the section on "future plans," he wrote:

We have too many Jews in the cities. On the borders of Poland they are necessary, because in that land only the Jews are traders. As soon as a town is distant from Poland, the Jews become harmful because of the usury they practice, the smuggling that goes through their hands, and the thousand rascalities that work to the disadvantage of *Bürger* and of Christian merchants. I have never persecuted the members of this sect, or anyone else. However, I think it wise to watch that their number does not increase too greatly.[15]

On 16th April 1786, four months before his death, Frederick granted an interview to Count Gabriel Honoré de Mirabeau.[16] The French reformer was interested in two subjects: Frederick's views of Christian Wilhelm von Dohm's treatise *On the Civic Improvement of the Jews*, and his reasons for failing to encourage or even recognize native German literature, which was already, in the works of Klopstock, Lessing and the young Goethe, showing a vitality equal to that of the French literature that Frederick preferred. We do not know what Frederick said on the first point, but it is unlikely that he confessed to being moved by Dohm's arguments, and it is possible that he gave an answer similar to the one he gave to Mirabeau's second question: "What could I have done for German writers that equaled the advantage I granted them by *not* bothering about them and *not* reading their books?"

Frederick's aversion to the Jews was unalloyed by any appreciation of the achievements of the most brilliant members of the Jewish community. Long after Moses Mendelssohn had become one of the best known inhabitants of Berlin, with a reputation as a philosopher that extended well beyond the borders of Frederick's kingdom—indeed, long after he had become a friend of the King's confidant the Marquis d'Argens and a consultant on appointments to the minister of education, Karl von Zedlitz—the King acted as if he did not exist. It was only with difficulty that Mendelssohn, in 1763, received the royal *Schutzprivilegium* that entitled him to maintain a residence of his own, and in 1779, when he tried to have it extended to his children, Frederick refused.[17]

In February 1771, the Royal Academy in Berlin voted to propose to the King that Mendelssohn be appointed to fill a vacancy in its philosophical section, and Friedrich Nicolai wrote jubilantly to Lessing: "Our friend Moses was elected a regular member of the Academy . . . last Thursday. True, the King's confirmation has not yet been received from Potsdam, but no one doubts it."[18] Nicolai, who admired Frederick as extravagantly as he did Mendelssohn, can be forgiven for believing that the philosopher of Sans Souci would recognize a kindred spirit in the author of the *Phaedon*. But the King left the Academy's proposals unanswered, and after an uncomfortable pause the academicians lost heart and submitted another list of candidates, which did not include Mendelssohn's name.

Mendelssohn did receive an invitation to Sans Souci in September 1771, when a cabinet minister from Saxony, Baron Thomas von Fritsche, who was visiting Frederick, expressed a desire to meet the Jewish philosopher, and the King undertook to make this possible. Mendelssohn was summoned to appear in Potsdam on 30th September, which coincided with the festival of Shemini Atseret, during which travel is not permitted. A council of experts on the Law, meeting with the Chief Rabbi of Berlin, decided that, because of the special circumstances, a dispensation was in order, and Mendelssohn went off to Potsdam.[19] The visit aroused enough public attention to persuade the Berlin artist Daniel Chodowiecki to commemorate it in a fine print that shows the diminutive philosopher handing his papers over to a lieutenant of the *Garde du Corps* while a grenadier with shouldered musket and bayonet towers above him.[20] Conspicuous by its absence from Chodowiecki's print is the figure of the King, but then he was absent from the interview, too. In fact, the two men never met, and it may be just as well, for it is difficult to see what they could have talked about.

The slights that he suffered at the King's hand, Mendelssohn bore with equanimity. He was not immune to the force of Frederick's personality or insensitive to his great talents. In 1757, after the battle of Leuthen, he composed a sermon praising the King that was read in the Berlin synagogue, and in 1760, in a review of Frederick's *Poésies diverses* for Nicolai's *Literaturbriefe*, he wrote that it would be difficult to find

another poet who combined so much philosophy, sublimity of sentiment, psychological insight, felicity of imagery, tenderness of feeling,
and naturalness of language, adding mildly that it was a pity that he
wrote in French rather than in German and that he borrowed so heavily from a philosopher as shallow as Epicurus.[21] Frederick's failure to
ratify his election to the Academy disappointed him, but he comforted
himself with the reflection that he had at least been recognized as worthy of election by his peers. Mendelssohn was not given to recrimina-
tion, nor did he ever associate himself with Lessing's not infrequent
sneers about the lack of real freedom in Prussia. He was too conscious
of what he himself had been able to accomplish, despite the humblest
of beginnings and the most discouraging of odds, to be cast down by
minor setbacks. And he was too much a man of the Enlightenment to
doubt that reason would in the end triumph over prejudice and injustice and inequality. His experience and his faith in the *Aufklärung*
formed the basis of his belief in the emancipation of his people, and his
example and his own optimism encouraged generations of German
Jews to believe as he did that complete integration in German society
was possible by means of moral growth and self-improvement, or —if
you will—by *Bildung*.

It would be easy to argue that Frederick's deepening cynicism and
his growing conviction that power and human folly between them did
more to determine the course of history than reason was more realistic
than Mendelssohn's faith in the future. The influence of the Enlightenment in Germany was never as great as Mendelssohn believed. It was
confined to the large urban centers, and particularly to Berlin, and even
there it affected only the middle class and part of the nobility. The
masses knew nothing of the writings of the *philosophes* or Lessing's faith
in the education of the human race,[22] or Dohm's *Civic Improvement of the
Jews*. Their minds were still moved by old prejudices; they lived in a
world governed by passion rather than rationality, by myth and symbol
rather than the printed word. Through the very process of their emancipation, the Jews were alienated from the common people, and their
faith in *Bildung* was not sufficient to integrate them even with those
classes that shared it with them. When Frederick and Mendelssohn
died in 1786, the intellectual atmosphere was already changing in Germany; with the coming of the French Revolution and the advent of

Napoleon, the Enlightenment shriveled before the triumphant on-slaught of romantic nationalism and Teutomania, which proved to be long-lived and, for Jewish emancipation, ominous. As George L. Mosse has pointed out in his Efroysom Lectures, as a result of all this the more the Jews came to resemble the Germans the more they were re-jected by them.[23]

To leave it at that, however, would be to do an injustice to Mendels-sohn. Surely the world of reason that he envisioned was a nobler goal than the world of power that Frederick and his successors accepted. And—leaving that aside—who would argue that Mendelssohn's faith in the ability of his people to integrate themselves into German society was misplaced? Can it not be said that, despite the ultimate rejection and the horrors of the Holocaust, the rich contribution that German Jews made to their country's culture—to German art and literature and music and science—is powerful testimony to the contrary? In any case, the record is not complete; history did not end in 1945. Mendelssohn's faith in reason and humanity, his confidence in the inevitability of the full emancipation of his people, have not lost their power to inspire and, indeed, as Hans Bach has written, "still form the basis of the con-tinued existence of the Jews, in the Jewish State of Israel as well as in the Dispersion."[24]

10

The Magic Circle

In June 1849, in the last days of the revolutionary German National Assembly, the vice-president, Gabriel Riesser, one of its seven Jewish members, addressed the body during a debate on civil rights. Speaking of the inequality from which he and his fellows suffered, he brought thunderous applause from his audience when he cried:

> We are not immigrants—we were born here—and so we cannot claim any other home: either we are Germans or we have no homeland. Whoever disputes my claim to this my German fatherland disputes my right to my own thoughts, my feelings, my language— the very air I breathe. Therefore, I must defend myself against him as I would against a murderer.

Riesser was one of a long line of assimilated German Jews whose story is told in *The Pity of It All*, Amos Elon's impressive new book, Jews who worshiped German culture and civilization, which they claimed as their own, and who were preoccupied and tormented by the resultant duality. Their enterprise ended badly, but Elon does not be-

lieve that this had to be so; nor does he agree with those writers who
have seen an inexorable pattern in German history, preordained in Lu-
ther's time and culminating with the Holocaust. "According to this
theory," he writes, "the Jews were doomed from the outset, their fate as
immutable as a law of nature. Such absolute certainties have eluded
me." Instead, he sees only a series of ups and downs and unforeseeable
contingencies, and he reminds us at the outset that even Hitler, who
wrote the story's final chapter, was a kind of accident, who confounded
the intentions of those who put him in power.[1]

In the nineteenth century, German Jews who worried about their
identity had no dearth of models to inspire them. Preeminent among
them was Moses Mendelssohn, who came to Berlin in 1743 at the age
of fourteen as a student of the Talmud and who could neither write
nor speak the German language. As a student of Berlin's chief rabbi,
and later as tutor to the son of a wealthy silk merchant, Mendelssohn
taught himself not only German, but Latin, Greek, English, and
French, while at the same time beginning a systematic study of the ancient classics and such modern writers as Spinoza, Newton, Montes-
quieu, and Rousseau. He met and became close friends with Gotthold
Ephraim Lessing and the Berlin publisher Friedrich Nicolai, and with
their encouragement began to write works of philosophic-aesthetic
criticism, the most famous of which, *Phaidon, or The Immortality of the
Soul in Three Dialogues*, an adaptation of Plato's dialogue on that subject,
became the most widely read book in Germany and made him a European celebrity.

As his book about the Rothschilds has demonstrated,[2] Elon has a
special affinity for the period in which Mendelssohn's reputation grew,
and his account of the philosopher's relations with his contemporaries
is as amusing as it is rich in detail. Understandably, Mendelssohn's
company was sought by other intellectuals, and it was not long before
the Prussian Academy of Sciences elected him as a member. That body,
however, was a kind of private preserve of King Frederick the Great,
and his whims decided who was allowed to enter it. The King vetoed
the proposal to admit Mendelssohn, although he never explained why
he had done so. The Academy's president, the French mathematician
Pierre-Louis Maupertuis, was probably correct when he said that Mendelssohn possessed all of the qualifications for membership except a

foreskin. No one dared to suggest, at least not publicly, that Mendelssohn's stature was enhanced by the King's silence.

Mendelssohn was also the target of people intent upon self-gratification. The Zurich deacon Johann Caspar Lavater, a popular disseminator of the pseudoscience physiognomy, concluded after studying engravings of Mendelssohn's features, which he considered to be unusually noble, that the philosopher was ready for conversion to Christianity and began a public campaign to persuade him to take that step. Despite considerable pressure from well-intentioned zealots, Mendelssohn refused to be cozened into accepting a religion that he privately considered to be filled with dogmas that contradicted reason. "On this occasion," he wrote, "I declare myself a Jew. I shall always remain a Jew."

Parenthetically, it may be noted that many of Mendelssohn's fellow Jews did convert, mostly for secular reasons, in order to enhance their social status or facilitate marriage, or to avoid legal restrictions on professional or academic position. Elon points out that "before conversion most converts were nonpracticing Jews; after conversion, they were nonpracticing Christians."

Mendelssohn's friendship with Lessing—which was celebrated in Lessing's play *Nathan der Weise*, with its plea for a common humanity—and with other leading intellectuals of his age inspired German Jews throughout the nineteenth century and stirred in them the hope of a similar acceptance. They drew comfort also from the stature of Heinrich Heine. Elon writes of him that no other writer was ever so German and so Jewish and so ambivalent and ironic about being both. And as time went on they were heartened by the intellectual and artistic accomplishments and the wide social acceptance of other German Jews—one thinks of the composer Felix Mendelssohn-Bartholdy and the now forgotten novelist Berthold Auerbach, who was read throughout Europe and compared by Turgenev with Dickens. The transformation of the German Jews from a handful of ill-treated peddlers and cattle-dealers scattered through the German states into an industrious bourgeoisie whose share in the country's social and intellectual product belied the fact that they never made up more than one percent of the population was certainly due in some part to the fact that they had such models.

Their political emancipation was delayed by the prevailing division of the country. The political agitations of the 1830s were largely devoid of result, but the nationwide revolution of 1848 was different and, despite its failure to achieve its announced goals, it proved to be a crucial turning point for German Jews, strengthening their sense, Elon writes, of finally becoming Germans. The revolutionary year increased the number of Jews who became involved in politics and brought them together with other liberal parties, increasing the pressure for civil rights. The process of emancipation was completed as a result of Prussia's unification of the German states in 1871, which was followed by a formal emancipation law that abolished all restrictions on civil and political rights derived from religious differences.

The Jews were for the most part elated by this recognition of their equality. The more perceptive of them soon recognized, however, that, equal or not, they had not gained everything they wanted, and could not do so as long as they were regarded as being different from other people. This was what Heine's friend Ludwig Börne called "the Jewish misère." "It's a miracle!" Börne wrote:

> I've gone through it a thousand times but each time I experience it as something new. Some reproach me for being a Jew; others forgive me for being one; there are even those who commend me for the same—but there's no one able to put this fact out of his mind. They all seem bound by the spell of this magic Jewish circle, from which none are able to escape.

In the years after unification Germany could boast not only of its military and economic prowess but of its unrivaled educational system, its scientific and research facilities, and its rich cultural life. The Jewish contribution to all this was prodigious, and Elon ruminates on the reasons why. Was it "self-conscious marginality" or "the stimulus of suffering and blows," he asks, or "the interplay of challenge and response" or "tribal pressure"? The simplest explanation was that generations of hard-working merchants and businessmen and what Heinrich von Treitschke called "pants-selling Jew boys" had sons who were not content with these occupations and turned to higher education in order to escape them and seek careers in the sciences and the arts. Albert Einstein once said that the proverbial industry of the younger generation made it appear that they had spent the last two thousand years preparing for university entrance examinations.

The result was an explosion of talent that contributed powerfully to the expansion of the sciences—one historian has identified thirty-nine leading German-Jewish scientists born before 1880, nine of whom, including Einstein and Paul Ehrlich, won Nobel Prizes—and of journalism, publishing, the theater, and the arts. This became so noticeable that a young German journalist named Moritz Goldstein wrote an article in 1912 claiming that Jews now controlled German culture and that "we are administering the spiritual property of a nation that denies our right and our ability to do so." Elon demonstrates that this was a grossly inflated claim and that most of the country's leading lights in the arts and literature were non-Jews—the brothers Mann, Gerhart Hauptmann, the poets Rilke and Stefan George, the composers Wagner and Strauss, to mention only a few. Even so, Goldstein's article was widely read and debated, and, what was worse, widely believed, and this contributed to the never insignificant and now growing anti-Semitism in the country.

Compared with other European countries, Germany had generally been considered as the one in which Jewish assimilation and acculturation had the best chances of success. In contrast, Russia was a land of pogroms; France was paralyzed by anti-Jewish feeling during the Dreyfus case; and as late as 1900 the British imposed rigorous limits on Jewish immigration, and in 1916 denied a scholarship at All Souls to Lewis Namier because of his "Polish-Jewish origins." In the last quarter of the nineteenth century, however, this situation began to change as German politics began to be affected by what might be called scapegoating, that is, a tendency to put the blame upon Jews for occurrences and ailments in public life over which they had no control.

The first example of this came during the economic crash of 1873, which was due essentially to the overheating of the economy under the impact of the French reparations payments for the recent war and complicated by the Reichstag's failure to heed the liberal Eduard Lasker's warnings about corrupt dealings between parliamentarians and the railroad tycoon Bethel Strousberg. As a result, tens of thousands of middle-class and aristocratic families lost their fortunes. In the search for culprits that ensued, the fact that both the villain Strousberg and the well-intentioned Lasker were Jews, as were a good many stockbrokers, gave the victims a convincing explanation for losses that had been due to their own credulity and loosed upon the land an anti-Semitism more extreme than anything the country had seen since the Middle Ages.

In the years that followed this found expression in the sermons of the court chaplain Adolf Stöcker, who insisted that "if we wish to hold fast to our German national character, we must get rid of the poisonous Jewish drop in our blood," and in an article in the *Preußische Jahrbücher* by the historian Heinrich von Treitschke, in which he declared that "the Jews are our national misfortune." Although neither man was a racist and both argued for Jewish conversion to Christianity, they gave a spurious respectability to the more extreme forms of anti-Semitism. The end of the economic troubles in the 1890s and the return of prosperity alleviated this situation. Stöcker's political activities came to an end when Emperor William II became annoyed with them and demoted his chaplain, while Treitschke's position was roundly attacked by his colleagues, led by Theodor Mommsen. After that, attacks upon Jews became infrequent, and things returned to normal.

This was only temporary, however, and in the course of World War I scapegoating returned in a more extreme form. German Jews responded to the coming of the conflict with enthusiasm. Even longtime critics of the regime like the popular German-Jewish journalist Maximilian Harden (whose original name was Witkowsky) became superpatriots overnight. The linguist Victor Klemperer, usually a discerning man, was moved to wish the worst of misfortunes upon England, while writing in his diary, "We, we Germans, are a truly chosen people." The war, it was widely believed, would finally consummate the German-Jewish symbiosis.

When the tide of battle turned, however, and the strategy of attrition began to wear down the spirit of both the army and the home front, complaints began to be heard that the prolongation of the war was owing to the fact that rich Jews hadn't yet made enough money from it and that the army's strength was weakened by large numbers of Jewish draft-dodgers. Pressure was put upon the War Ministry to determine the number of Jews serving at the front as compared with those at the rear. In October 1916, by which time, Elon reminds us, three thousand Jews had already died on the battlefield and more than seven thousand had been decorated, it complied.

The fact that a so-called "Jewish census" was being taken had a devastating effect upon German Jews in the army. Its findings were never released publicly, although distorted versions were leaked to right-wing circles. In consequence, as defeat came to Germany in 1918, the theory that the Jews were in some large part responsible for it became firmly embedded in the German consciousness.

Elon's account of the final act of this tortured drama could hardly be improved on. The Weimar Republic began, he writes, in a flurry of hope, and this was justified by its intellectual achievements. Nowhere in modern Europe did arts, sciences, and advanced thought flourish as they did in Germany. "In literature, music, film, theater, and design," he writes, "Weimar evoked a marvelous sense of the new, the vanguard admired to this day," and in all this German Jews played a leading part. But, culture aside, Weimar was a disaster. As Alfred Döblin once wrote, it was a republic without proper "instructions for use."

The government was handicapped from the outset by the lost war, the revolution that put an end to the monarchy, and the crippling peace treaty that was imposed by the Allies. It was fatally wounded by the horrendous inflation caused by its attempt to escape the financial demands of the treaty and finally dispatched when the Great Depression ended its last hopes of recovery. Weimar was from the beginning a republic without republicans, for the members of the middle-class democratic parties soon gravitated to the extreme right and left. And it was a republic with only two great leaders, one of whom, Gustav Stresemann, died in 1930 on the eve of a fateful crisis that only he might have mastered, while the other, Walther Rathenau, who hoped to reconcile Germany with its former enemies, was assassinated in 1922, presumably for the crime of being a Jew and daring to serve as foreign minister.

For an untold number of Germans, the republic was a *Judenrepublik*. Everything that was disliked about it was blamed on the Jews. Indeed, Elon writes, "every unresolved problem and all the world's evils from the crucifixion of Christ to capitalism, Communism, syphilis, and the lost war were projected onto a tiny minority representing 0.9 percent of the population." It is true, of course, that not everyone who made such allegations really believed them, but after 1930 there was a man waiting in the wings who was determined to use them for his own purposes and who would know how to do so.

Even in the last days German Jews did not waver in their insistence that they were Germans. Some of them may have taken comfort in something Heine had written long ago:

The marriage that I have had with our dear Frau Germania, the beautiful bear-skinner, has never been a happy one. I still remember well several beautiful moonlit nights when she pressed me tenderly to her great bosom with the virtuous nipples. But these sentimental nights could be counted on one's fingers and toward morning a peevish yawning coolness always intervened and the endless nagging began. And in the end we lived separated in bed and board. But it never came to a real divorce. The stone mason who has to decorate our last resting place with an inscription will have to reckon with no objection if he engraves there the words, "Here lies a German writer."[3]

11

On the German Historical Consciousness

When I received the invitation to address this distinguished society, I accepted it with pleasure, tempered, I must admit, once I had learned the subject that had been given me, with trepidation. It is challenging enough for a foreigner to talk to a German audience about German history; but it requires a high degree of temerity for him to venture opinions about something as portentous and problematical as *das deutsche Geschichtsbewußtsein* [the German historical consciousness]. And for an Anglo-Saxon, the problem is compounded by his own national bias or, if you will, his native lack of qualification for discourse on this theme, for in his own country consciousness of history (which is the closest that English can come to giving a sense of *Geschichtsbewußtsein*) is neither portentous nor problematical.

Let me make this point clearer by means of a homely example. Some of you, during the course of the summer [1984], may have attended the Olympic Games in Los Angeles, and others, I dare say,

---

A lecture delivered before the Bremer Tabak-Collegium in the Berlin Reichstag, December 1984. It is published here with the permission of the estate of Gordon A. Craig and the Department of Special Collections, Stanford University Libraries. Translations from German sources are by Carolyn Halladay.

watched them on television. You may recall that, in the opening ceremonies, after the welcoming speeches and the lighting of the Olympic
flame, the floor of the stadium was suddenly filled with hundreds of
dancers who formed a gigantic outline of the United States of America,
following which other dancers, dressed as cowboys and farmers, advanced across it in covered wagons and, when they had reached its
western limits, proceeded to build a church and a town hall and other
buildings representing the coming of civilization to the wilderness and,
this work being accomplished, held a shivaree and danced a hoedown.
A foreign guest, leaving the stadium after this extravaganza, was heard
to murmur, "Only the Americans would think of doing something like
that!" and his tone indicated that he was referring to a combination of
grandiosity and *Kitsch*. But surely that spectacle can also be taken as an
example of American historical consciousness.

It is often said that Americans don't know much about their history.
But, as the stage managers of that Olympic show knew perfectly well,
they do respond positively to some historical memories. They remember and are proud of the fact that their forefathers brought forth upon
the American continent a new nation conceived in liberty and dedicated to the proposition that all men are created equal and that that nation
survived the trials of a wearing civil war and then went on to conquer
the continent and to unite it from coast to coast. Without much understanding of the political and philosophical principles that animated the
founding fathers, they have a curiously intimate relationship with them,
particularly with Washington and Jefferson and Franklin, as they do
with the two great antagonists of the civil war and that greater man, the
emancipator and reconciler, and as they do with the pioneers who won
the west. One need only watch the hordes of schoolchildren who swarm
down the steps of the Capitol in Washington and stream past the equestrian statue of Grant, sitting calm and indomitable at the head of the
Mall, on their way to the Washington Monument or the Lincoln Memorial—one need only mingle with the crowds that stand before the
majestic Pioneers Memorial in Salt Lake City—to have a sense of the
strength and essentially uncomplicated nature of the American connection with the past, a historical consciousness that has, incidentally, been
able to reconcile and transcend the divisions and defeats and injustices
and cruelties that can be found on the darker pages of our history.

The British attitude toward the past is less simple than the American but certainly no more problematical. The Englishman's greatest pride is that his country was the first to establish the rule of law on the basis of representative government, and Thomas Babington Macaulay put this in words in 1848, when he wrote:

> All around us, the world is convulsed by the agonies of great nations. Governments which lately seemed likely to stand during ages have been on a sudden shaken and overthrown. . . . Meanwhile, in our island, the regular course of government has never been for a day interrupted. . . . We have order in the midst of anarchy.[1]

But the British have an unbridled delight in the whole of their past, and in celebrating their greatest achievement they place it, by means of ceremonial and pageantry, within a broader historical frame. The Queen, in her royal coach, escorted by the Yeomen of the Guard in their sixteenth-century uniforms, proceeds to Westminster, where from a throne in the House of Lords she reveals her desires for the new year to her Commoners, standing humbly before her. The fact that her words have been written for her by a committee of the Commons and that neither she nor her Lords have any power to affect the disposition of their recommendations is passed over in silence, for the fictional aspects of the ceremony make it more effective as spectacle and, indeed, invest the occasion with a heightened sense of legitimacy and continuity.

The British are skilled in using the rich habiliments of their past to clothe the often uncomfortable outlines of their present, and they take such pleasure in this that there are no impassable barriers for them between present and past. They live easily in their history and take sustenance from it. Thus, when the former trade union leader Ernest Bevin became Foreign Secretary in the Labour Government of 1945, he had no difficulty in adjusting to the traditions of that office. He read the papers of Castlereagh and Palmerston with interest and pleasure and once said to Dean Acheson, "Old Salisbury. Y' know, 'e 'ad a lot o' sense." Acheson commented, "He talked about them as slightly older people whom he knew with affectionate respect. In listening to him, one felt strongly the continuity and integrity of English history."[2]

Even the French, despite the divisiveness that has marked their past, are capable of finding in their history communality and inspiration.

Charles De Gaulle, to whom France was "both a fact, a product of history, and a value, derived from and embodied in her culture" was able to communicate this feeling to his countrymen, who responded eagerly to his insistence that there was only one history of France and that therefore there was no need to define a French identity but only the necessity of saving and proclaiming it. "Old France," he wrote, "burdened by history, bruised by wars and revolutions, relentlessly going back and forth from grandeur to decline, but straightened, century after century, by the genius of renovation, . . . made, for example, enterprise, combat, always the star of History."[3] What some of us are inclined to describe as the arrogance of the French is really the assurance that comes from this kind of historical consciousness.

In contrast to their western neighbors, the Germans never seem to have had an easy relationship with their past. At times, they have complained about its lack of richness, as Goethe did frequently in his conversations with Eckermann, comparing it unfavorably with British history as a source of inspiration to contemporary writers.[4] At times they have cursed the negative effects of its long record of disunity upon the patriotic feelings of young people, as Leopold von Ranke did in an early speech in 1818, in which he said:

> Who has foretold for us the course of our way? Religious sectarianism drives the lad to madness just as soon as he begins to think; no great aspiration arises that could capture his imagination, and win his heart, and drive him, as the vital principle of his life. There is nothing that could remind him vividly of the Fatherland . . . everything is mute and dead—O, tell me where should the German lad [find] the guiding principle of the deed, the love of his Fatherland, the firm, certain spirit?[5]

More usually, however, they have tended to idealize the past and to use it as the basis for their visions of the future, discerning in their enhanced view of the First Reich the outlines of the wonderful Third Reich that would one day fulfill all of their ill-defined longings. This was an enterprise of which the present was usually the victim. How, asked Heinrich Heine in 1837, can foreigners possibly understand "the emotional ways of a people that has only a yesterday and a tomorrow, but no today—that continually recalls the past and continually foretells the future, but no longer knows how to grasp the present, either in love or politics?"[6] Whatever may be said about the former (and to attempt to deal with it would force me to exceed the proper limits of these remarks), it is clear enough that the kind of consciousness that Heine was describing had as its political corollary such a preference for ideal solutions at the expense of realities, such an imperfect command of the requirements of actual situations, that the western world was confirmed in its already long-held suspicion that the Germans were by nature unpolitical animals. "The vagaries of German policy," the *Times* of London said in 1860, "are such that we cannot pretend to follow them. It is useless to look for profundity where, in all likelihood, there is only pedantry, or for a tangible object in what may be only a desire to carry out some dreamy historical notion."[7]

A member of the *Nationalverein* [German National Union] in the 1860s might have answered the *Times* leader-writer by arguing that, given the divided state of Germany and the obvious material and moral disadvantages that it suffered in comparison with the national states of the west, to dream of unity was a necessary part of the process of changing the unloved present—that, in fact, it was wholly right and proper that (in Richard Wagner's phrase) "in his longing for German glory the German can usually dream of nothing else but something similar to the restoration of the Roman Empire."[8] But of course it wasn't the dreamers who effected the changes of 1866 and 1870, nor did the dreamers approve of the methods used and the results achieved. After all, the dream of national unity, insofar as it was achieved at all, came about as a result of the first German partition, the separation of Austria from the rest of Germany.

Indeed, with the creation of the new Reich in 1871, the problem of establishing a healthy relationship between the present and the past became more complicated and created real problems of identification for significant parts of the population. For the Reich could be called neither a new creation nor a product of history. Its title evoked the memory of the medieval Empire while its structure excluded some of that Empire's most illustrious provinces. In form and substance it was a repudiation of the old Germanic Confederation, but it allowed some of its members privileges similar to those they had enjoyed in that organization. It looked superficially like an actualization of the plan of unity devised in the Frankfurt Assembly in 1848–49, but this was emphatically denied by its architects. No wonder that this worried some Germans. Konstantin Frantz felt that the disregard shown for history in the writing of the new constitution would turn out to be a grave psychological burden, writing:

> It is clear that a country containing such varied elements as does Germany—which on all sides has grown intertwined with its neighbors, bordering as it does on six different nationalities; moreover a country that has lived through an incomparable history, granted the diversity of political formations as well as the internal heft of events—that such a country should of necessity achieve its own peculiar constitution.

But what had in effect happened? The new constitution was based on a slavish imitation of foreign models. What, after all, was the true uniqueness of Germany's historical development? It had always been more than an ordinary state. It was "the special honor and special calling of Germany to fulfill for European development the task of forming the living connection between the law of states and the law of nations." Now that tradition had, through impatience and ignorance, been sacrificed on the altar of modernity.[9]

I shall not apologize for having cited Frantz at such length, because his attack upon the new political circumstances had a high significance. It showed that the creation of the Reich in 1871 had not corrected the old disjunction between past and present in the German historical consciousness, and it was an early instance of a tendency that was to reach its height during the Weimar Republic, of using history to mount attacks upon the existing state form. In its own time, it was important because, even though it was drowned out by the chorus of Bismarck adulators, its sentiments were shared, in whole or in part, as Theodor Schieder has pointed out, by many conservatives and Catholics, by a significant portion of the liberal community, by minority groups, and by many intellectuals.[10] It was the potentially divisive effects of this resistance to what seemed to many people to be too sharp a break with the past that led Heinrich von Treitschke to attempt to legitimize the new creation by means of history—that is, by writing a history of Germany that would show that the events of 1866 and 1870 grew naturally out of Germany's past and were, in fact, as he said in 1871, proof of "the divine *Vernunft* [reason] that compels us Germans to become one people."[11]

Treitschke's attempt to accomplish this was ultimately unpersuasive, as he himself seemed to realize, for the later volumes of the *Deutsche Geschichte* were increasingly shrill and dogmatic and included passages in which the historian seemed to be hunting for enemies of the state with a fervor equal to that of the Chancellor whom he now idolized. Meanwhile, Treitschke's lectures on politics at the University of Berlin seemed to indicate that he was incapable of legitimizing the Reich except in terms of power and future triumphs. This was the fate of other attempts to find legitimacy through historical theory. In the new Reich, the ruling establishment (Prussian bureaucracy, army, East Elbian *Junkertum*) had a different historical perspective from that of the Reichstag and the south German states or the economic centers of the country, and against all of these stood a rapidly growing deracinated industrial proletariat that had no tradition at all. The result, as Helmuth Plessner has written, was a "contest of views, an inner particularism."[12] This was always a debilitating element in German society before 1914, and in the end it could only be overcome by the State's plunging into frenetic and ill-considered competition with other Great Powers, with ultimately disastrous results.

Symptomatic of the Reich's *Bewußtseinsproblem* was the difficulty of finding any agreement on the question of national symbols. With respect to national monuments, the contrast with the United States was dramatically sharp: in Germany, the heterogeneity of their style and symbolism was evidence of the imperfect development of a truly national consciousness. Thomas Nipperdey writes:

> The multiplicity of living governmental, cultural, historical, and political traditions in Germany, as well as the conflict over tradition, meant that until nearly the end of the century, no event and no person, no allegory and no compendium of great Germans unequivocally attained the stature of a national symbol.

And, at the end of the period, even such relatively successful representations of national concentration as the *Völkerschlachtdenkmal* [Monument to the Battle of the Nations] in Leipzig and the Schaudt-Lederer Bismarck memorial in Hamburg were ambivalent in the message they conveyed. "The heroic mood of monuments of this type" Nipperdey writes, "manifests a sense of the internal and external precariousness of the nation, which corresponded to the experiences of unsuccessful international and class politics. Even in the quiet intrepidness of the Bismarck memorials, national feeling has not yet achieved a calm, balanced position."[13]

None of these problems was solved in the Weimar Republic, where indeed the gap between idea and reality became wider and the relationship between past and present more difficult. The Bismarck Reich, challenged in its own time by backward-looking historical projections, now appeared in idealized form as the embodiment of all the virtues that the republic seemed to its enemies to lack. In making this comparison, historians played a leading role, for in the great majority they regarded the coming of the republic as an event without legitimacy. Those who, like Johannes Ziekursch, Ludwig Bergsträsser and Veit Valentin, argued that the republic was a final realization of a German liberal-democratic tradition that had been suppressed or retarded by Bismarck, had far less effect upon informed opinion than those who repudiated its constitution as an amalgam of western ideas or who contrasted its foreign difficulties with Bismarck's foreign triumphs. In his widely read *Philosophie der Politik* (1921), Otto Westphal declared that the revolution of 1918 was "the hour in which German self-alienation took shape, [wrought] of the receipt of spiritual and political ideas from abroad";[14] this was the same historian who, ten years later, discovered that the National Socialist program was a resumption of the ideas of 1871, that Bismarck and Hitler were ideological kin, and that Nazism was a "transubstantiation" of the idea of Prussia.[15]

To the widespread public resentment of the Versailles Treaty and the failure to understand the limitations imposed upon Weimar foreign policy, the historians made their contribution by constantly invoking the memory of more glorious days. Thus, in his *Heidelberger Antrittsvorlesung*, Gerhard Ritter declared that it had been "the historical role of the monarchy, through the deeds of the army [and] through great outward successes, to lead the state out of the stuffy, tight internal battles into the clear mountain air of grand history."[16] Thus, the Bismarck biographer Erich Marcks, on the fiftieth anniversary of the *Reichsgründung*, carrying the role of *laudator temporis acti* to an embarrassing extreme, apostrophized the past by declaring:

It lay in the bright sun and now is shrouded in thick clouds, but the

Alps remain the Alps. And moreover, the past is our one certain possession. We have neither the desire nor the inclination to let it be stolen from us. Of this possession, we create strength and solace, pride and love and hope. We find in it what is lacking in our day: greatness.[17]

This rhetorical breast-beating could not entirely conceal the poverty of positive content in Marcks's address, which did little more than counsel escaping into history as the best way of evading the responsibilities of the present. But rhetoric is not unimportant, and in this case it had wide public resonance. Not that historians alone were guilty of this sort of thing. The whole intellectual ragtag and bobtail of the right—the Moeller van den Brucks and the Spenglers and their followers—used spurious historical examples to support their *Zukunftvisionen* [visions of the future]. The agrarian romantics, the *"los von Berlin"* ["out of Berlin!"] demagogues, the late followers of De la Garde and Langbehn and Riehl, attacked the modernity of the republic as a degenerate falling off from a golden age that had been free of industrialism and unthreatened by *Mechanisierung, Demokratisierung* and *Vermassung* [industrialization, democratization, and massification] and implied that it was still possible to return to the truly German values of that admittedly ill-defined earlier time.[18]

In view of all this, Rudolf von Thadden is surely justified in writing that Hitler's triumph came about, not because there was too little *Geschichtsbewußtsein* in Germany, but rather because a faulty understanding of history prevailed and because misleading *Geschichtsbilder* [images of the past] dominated the thinking of contemporaries.[19] This was by no means the sole reason for the Nazi *Machtübernahme* [seizure of power], but it certainly contributed powerfully to the erosion of the republic's legitimacy.

I suppose it can be said that the *deutsche Geschichtsbewußtsein* was one of the notable victims of the destructive career of Adolf Hitler and its ghastly dénouement. If this was the end result of German national development, many people must have asked themselves, then we had better live without memory and orient our lives in accordance with other than historical values. From the traumatic effects of the Nazi experience, many results flowed: the general approval of Konrad Adenauer's statement that the Germans of the West wished to escape from the narrowness of national existence into the wholeness of the European consciousness; the almost obsessive concentration on the tasks of reconstruction and economic growth; the decline in the number of university students who wished to study history; the tendency of schools to reduce the historical content of curricula to the advantage of subjects like sociology; the growing tendency to believe that political problems are amenable to technocratic solutions without regard for historical experience; and much else. Most of these tendencies, however, lasted for only a generation. The European movement died as quickly as faith in technocracy; the limits of consumerism as *Lebensphilosophie* were soon reached; the eternal *ricorso* asserted itself; and soon Germany was thinking about history again, and the foreign press was filled with stories about a new German search for national identity.

What can be said about the contemporary state of *das deutsche Geschichtsbewußtsein*? For a foreigner it would not be seemly to be oracular. Let me merely make three observations that are based on the impressions one gets from seeing Germany from the outside.

[First observation]

I have been reading Botho Strauß's novel *Der junge Mann*, in which there is a scene in which the tyrant Belsazar dies suddenly, and death takes from him "not only gaze and breath; it robbed him in one stroke of esteem and commemoration, indeed, even of history." Outside his castle, society breathes the now clean air and hopes in the morning to find its way back to sobriety, to clear thinking, to a better conscience. It doesn't succeed. "And thus it remained. It remained for many, many years, overall and without exception; and many are even of the opinion that until this very day, this strong and beautiful land has not fully awakened from its Belsazar night."[20]

Before we dismiss this as an example of poetic license, should we not ask ourselves whether there is not an uncomfortable degree of truth in it? No one can complain that German writers have neglected Adolf Hitler, but certainly much of what has been written—and particularly the part that has attracted most public attention—has been trivial or sensational; and, as the Aschaffenburg conference of 1978 indicated, there is still no real consensus among scholars about Hitler's role or even about his culpability for the great crimes of his regime. The general feeling of shared guilt that was part of the atmosphere of the first years after 1945 has understandably diminished; but one of the unfortunate psychological results of the reception in this country of the "Holocaust" film[21] was a doubtless largely subconscious feeling of "There! We have admitted to ourselves that he did dreadful things. Now we can forget him." But of course he hasn't been forgotten. Instead, we have been witnessing since 1980 a wave of new interest in the mythic and cultic side of National Socialism and its psychic-pornographic fascination. In a recent book called *Kitsch und Tod* [*Kitsch and Death*], the Israeli writer Saul Friedlander has noted this trend and commented:

> Nazism has disappeared, but the obsession it represents for the contemporary imagination—as well as the birth of a new discourse that ceaselessly elaborates and reinterprets it—necessarily confronts us with this ultimate question: Is such attention fixed on the past only a gratuitous reverie, the attraction of spectacle, exorcism, or the result of a need to understand; or is it, again and still, an expression of profound fears and, on the part of some, mute yearnings as well?[22]

These are troubling questions, and they suggest, at the very least, the need for more systematic attention in both university research and school instruction to the *real* history of the rise, triumph and consequences of National Socialism, lest reality be once more subverted by fictitious and sentimental notions. It is clear, moreover, as Hans Mommsen had pointed out, that this must be a continuous rather than a sporadic process.[23]

[Second Observation]

A connected aspect of the contemporary *Geschichtsbewußtsein* is the continued habit of using historical examples or analogies to criticize or censor contemporary practices or institutions, sometimes with dubious appropriateness. It was, of course, natural in the post-Hitler trauma to view anything that seemed to be connected, however remotely, with the Nazi experience with suspicion, but this was sometimes carried to extremes. One remembers the difficulties that Theodor Heuß had in convincing his colleagues on the Parliamentary Council that drafted the Basic Law that their memory of how the Nazis had abused power should not lead them to deprive the new government of authority and that their eagerness to break with the past should not prevent them from adopting older institutional forms that had proved their usefulness.[24] Other examples of the too heavy hand of the past could certainly be found: for example, the suspicion that has, from the beginning of its career, hung over the *Bundeswehr* [Federal Defense Force].

One is aware, of course, of the malevolent influence of militarism in modern times; but one remembers also that militarism is a civilian rather than a military failing. One is aware of the great harm done in German history by transgressions of their proper sphere by politically-minded soldiers; but one remembers that this was very much on the minds of those who established the *Bundeswehr* in the years from 1950 to 1955. With deliberation and circumspection, and with an eye to the political and sociological factors that had made the *Reichswehr* [the German Army from 1919 to 1935] an essentially undemocratic force during the Weimar years, those men drafted concrete measures to prevent the recurrence of the historical civil-military problem and to create a force that would be, not "a collection of robots and functionaries with weapons," but rather an organization of *Staatsbürger in Uniform* [citizens in uniform]. To an outsider, it would appear that they were successful: that in the almost thirty years of its existence the *Bundeswehr* has demonstrated its loyalty to the democratic order, while becoming the most effective component in the NATO battleline. Yet it is still so much a target of suspicion that it dare not hold its ceremonies in public. The question naturally arises: On the basis of which history do you make judgments? At what point do you begin to weigh your knowledge of what has happened in your own time against your memory of what happened in former times?

[Third observation]

Finally, in the ongoing discussion about German national identity, there are uncomfortable hints of the old German tendency to prefer the ideal to the actual and to prefer *Zukunftsvisionen* to the realities of European life. One would sometimes suppose, listening to the more unbuttoned critics of the NATO connection, that the alliance is another Versailles Treaty and that, if only Germany could be liberated from it, it could be a truly independent power once more and stand up for its own interest. I will confess that, as a critic of some aspects of the Reagan foreign policy, I have often stated publicly that the *Bundesrepublik* should be a bit more assertive in alliance politics that it has always been in the past. But there is a great distance between that and the apparent willingness of some participants in this discussion to throw the baby out with the bathwater. Since Bismarck's time, German governments and the German public have frequently shown themselves to be impatient with his reminder that diplomacy is the art of the possible and his lesson that nothing is more difficult, or more necessary, than a balanced assessment of interest. In most cases, their impatience has had unfortunate, and in some cases tragic, consequences.

When I was invited to give this talk, it struck me that anything that I might say had already been said better in two texts: the first, Nietzsche's *Vom Nutzen und Nachteil der Historie für das Leben* [*On the Advantage and Disadvantage of History for Life*], in which the author argues that people must learn to forget history; the second, the conclusion of the third book of Heine's *Zur Geschichte der Religion und Philosophie in Deutschland* [*On the History of Religion and Philosophy in Germany*], where the author, addressing the French, tells of hearing a "junger Altdeutscher" [a young old-German, that is, a young chauvinist] in Göttingen say that Germany must have revenge for the French execution of Conradin von Hohenstaufen in Naples and adds, "You have certainly long ago forgotten it. We, however, forget nothing."[25]

I imagine that the first text is derived from the second. Nietzsche did not, of course, mean that all history should be forgotten. He merely wanted to prevent the German memory from stifling the energies and potentialities of contemporary society. What he called for was "kritische Geschichte" [critical history], by which he meant the ability, after painful inquiry and sober judgment, to decide what in history was relevant, and what was not relevant, to the needs of the society in which one lived. His advice was, of course, not taken by the society for which he wrote, which was unfortunate for it, for it might have provided the basis for a sounder relationship with the past than it was to enjoy then or for three-quarters of a century to come. We should not make the same mistake. In our search for a *Geschichtsbewußtsein* that will sustain our society and hearten it to master the perplexities that confront it, we should all ponder Nietzsche's words:

> For the individual as well as for the nation, everything depends on
> the fact that one can, at the proper time, forget as well as remember

at the right time. It depends on one feeling, with strong instincts, when it is necessary to perceive historically and when, unhistorically. . . . The unhistoric and the historic are equally important for the health of the individual, the nation, and a culture.[26]

12

Irony and Rage in the German Social Novel: Theodor Fontane and Heinrich Mann

I

It has often been noted that, in contrast to the situation in Britain and France, the national literature of Germany was not, in the nineteenth century, rich in works of social realism or authors who combined high aesthetic standards with gifts of political and social analysis. There were no Thackerays and Stendhals, or Flauberts and Dickenses, among the prose writers in the decades before unification, and indeed, the German writers who made any pretense of dealing with contemporary and social subjects before 1870—Jean Paul, E. T. A. Hoffmann, Karl Immermann, Gustav Freytag—rarely ventured beyond the realm of the idyllic or the fantastic or the parochial. Their works seldom awaken any shock of recognition among non-German readers and in general have an antiquarian flavor that may be charming but is usually remote from the realities of the modern world.

Reprinted from *Essays on Culture and Society in Modern Germany*, edited by Gary D. Stark and Beda Karl Lackner, by permission of the Texas A&M University Press. Copyright © 1982 by the University of Texas at Arlington. All rights reserved.

The explanation often given for this is that Germany was, in two senses, a retarded nation. Long after the Western countries had become powerful nation-states, Germany had continued to be fragmented into dozens of separate political entities, and the resultant lack of a cultural capital like London or Paris, where artists might gather and exchange ideas, had led necessarily to a narrowness of focus, a provincial perspective, and a lack of that urbanity which characterized the literature of the West.[1] Moreover, the effects of political disunity upon economic development, the relative slowness of industrial growth and of the rise of a strong middle class, and the late arrival of such concomitant features of industrial society as urbanization, the proletarianization of the lower classes, and the disintegration of inherited social categories and values deprived German writers of the kinds of themes that challenged their colleagues in countries that were more advanced economically.

There is much to be said for this explanation, but it is not entirely satisfactory, else how would we account for the fact that, even after 1871, when the formation of the empire put an end to Germany's political divisions and the country experienced a surge of economic development that transformed it within a generation into one of Europe's leading industrial producers, German writers still, on the whole, avoided social and political themes? It was not until the 1880s, with the coming of the naturalist movement, that writers and dramatists showed any appreciable interest in such subjects as social justice, sexual discrimination, and the plight of the poor; and, even when they did so, their attention lacked persistence and was often disingenuous, for they tended to concentrate on prostitution, the more lurid aspects of urban crime, and other subjects that were calculated to titillate the palate of the middle-class reading public.[2] In the underlying values of society, the naturalists had little interest, and in its politics none; and by the end of the 1890s, when the vogue of naturalism was past, Germany's writers were little more concerned with serious problems of contemporary life than in the period before 1871. There was a good deal of talk in artistic circles in the 1880s about the need for German writers to emulate the work of Emile Zola and to write sociological novels—this was the stock-in-trade of Michael Georg Conrad and the group in Munich that founded the journal *Die Gesellschaft* in 1885[3]—but, in fact, few German imitators appeared.

The causes of this lack of social engagement must be sought, therefore, not in the slowness of the country's political and economic development but in German views of the proper function of literature. It
had long been a strongly rooted prejudice that writers worthy of respect, true *Dichter*, should concern themselves with transcendental
themes and spiritual values, that the problems and politics of contemporary society were no business of theirs, and that anyone who persisted in dealing with such questions was automatically deprived of his
artistic status and relegated to the company of mere scribblers or
Literaten.[4]

Erich Auerbach has suggested that this odd differentiation owes
much to the towering figure of Goethe, whose interest in the actualities
of social development was minimal, who found such things as the
growth of industry and the increasing evidence of social mobility dis-
tasteful, and whose own novels were set in static social contexts, the
actual conditions of life serving merely as immobile backgrounds
against which the drama of Goethe's own ideological growth unfolded.
To the emerging modern structure of life Goethe paid little attention,
and such was his authority, Auerbach suggests, that his exclusive concentration on individuality and ideas came to be regarded as the criteri-
on of art as opposed to mere literature.[5] Whether or not Goethe is really responsible for this is less important than the fact that the double
standard prevailed. It is notable that Heinrich Heine, a writer of whom
one would think any nation in the world would be proud, has never
received his due recognition in the land of his birth, in part because
political and social criticism was never far below the surface of anything he wrote. This confirmed bias against present-mindedness has
doubtless served as a warning to countless writers with aspirations to
lasting fame. In our own century, Thomas Mann, who proved that he
was capable of writing superb social novels, seemed uncomfortable in
this genre and once confessed, "Social problems are my weak point
[although] this puts me to some extent at odds with my art form itself,
the novel, which is propitious to the examination of social problems.
But the lure of . . . individuality and metaphysics simply happens to be
ever so much stronger in me. . . . I am German. . . . The Zolaesque
streak in me is feeble."[6]

The inhibition imposed by literary tradition was reinforced by a concern for what the reading public would tolerate. Authors like to be read; and German authors after 1871 could not but be aware that a reading public that had made Heinrich von Treitschke's *German History* (*Deutsche Geschichte im XIX Jahrhundert*, 1879–94) a bestseller was hardly likely to welcome books that criticized the social foundations or political practice of the new Reich of which they were so proud. The educated middle class of the Bismarckian and Wilhelmine period was excessively preoccupied with its own social status and prestige, which were its substitutes for the political power that it did not possess; its jealous regard for its position, which it felt was threatened by the rising class of technicians and functionaries, made it vulnerable to a process of ideological feudalization and robbed it of its intellectual independence.[7] Increasingly more conservative as the period advanced, this *Bildungsbürgertum* expected from the authors of its books entertainment or moral elevation. It did not want to be told by them that there were things in its world that ought to be put right and that it was responsible to correct them; and it had the power to make its disapproval felt. It took a determined writer to disregard this.

There were, nevertheless, writers who did disregard it. Some of them were undistinguished artists and have been forgotten. Who today reads the novels of Friedrich Spielhagen (1829–1911) and Max Kretzer (1854–1941) and Paul Lindau (1839–1919)? But two, at least, were writers of distinction whose works are still extant in standard editions, in paperback and in cinematographic form. Theodor Fontane and Heinrich Mann were both writers who had less respect for the literary conventions of their own country than for models they found abroad; for Fontane, a descendant of French Huguenots on both sides of his family, was an admirer of Sir Walter Scott and an imitator of Thackeray, while Heinrich Mann, the son of Lübeck patricians, found Voltaire a more congenial spirit than Goethe and was a follower of Balzac and Flaubert.[8] Both shared a scorn for self-proclaimed *Dichter* who struck priestly attitudes and discoursed of ideas without social content, and both strove, in imitation of their Western models, to write—in the spirit of Trollope's title—about "the way we live now." Both were fascinated by the way in which the circumstances of the founding of the new Reich and its tumultuous development affected the values of German society and the attitudes of the different classes, and both were concerned with society's growing indifference to social injustice. Finally, both strove, although in different ways, to warn their fellow citizens of the dangers to which their country was prone; and, if their admonitions fell on deaf ears, this was doubtless due partly to the methods they employed, but even more to the persistence of the evils they detected and to their society's self-satisfaction and imperviousness to criticism.

II

Theodor Fontane (1819–98) did not begin to write novels until after the founding of the German Empire. His first experiment in that form, the historical novel *Before the Storm* (*Vor dem Sturm*), appeared in 1878, a few months before the publication of the first volume of Treitschke's *German History*, a work that was intended to create a historical tradition for the new nation by identifying Germany with Prussia. There were doubtless many readers who thought that Fontane's book was guided by the same purpose, for he was already known as the author of highly popular ballads, many of which glorified the Prussian past, as well as of a series of historically colored travel sketches called *Wanderings through Mark Brandenburg* (*Wanderungen durch die Mark Brandenburg*, 1862–82) and stirring accounts of the three wars of unification, and his new book also had a Prussian theme. In fact, the two books were significantly different. Treitschke began the first volume of his *German History* by advancing the thesis that Prussia (and hence Germany) was the creation of its rulers and by writing a eulogy of the Hohenzollerns from the Great Elector to Frederick the Great. Fontane's novel was not about the court but about society; it was the author's first attempt to emulate Thackeray by writing a panoramic account of typical people in typical circumstances at a particular moment in history. The moment chosen was 1813, the year of the Prussian rising against Napoleon, an event that Fontane believed—and had the protagonist of his last novel say— was infinitely more to be praised than the achievements that Treitschke admired, because "everything that happened had less of a command character and had more freedom and self-determination."[9]

In his very first novel, the 59-year-old writer therefore gave some indication of the direction in which his future work would lead him. He was interested in the familiar rather than the heroic aspects of life (to use a phrase of Thackeray's),[10] in the thoughts and activities of ordinary people; he was concerned about the degree of freedom and voluntarism that existed in a society; and he had a differentiated view of Prussia's past and its contribution to contemporary German society.

The last point is worth dwelling upon. Until the end of his life, Fontane considered himself to be a "dyed-in-the-wool Prussian"[11] and continued to admire the qualities of duty and dedication that had enabled his country to survive the great crises of the seventeenth and eighteenth centuries. But as early as 1848, as correspondent for a Dresden newspaper, he had written that "Prussia is a lie" and had criticized it as a police state in terms as uncompromising as those that Heine had used in his polemical poem "Germany, a Winter's Tale";[12] and, although this radicalism had faded in the years that followed, he remained uncomfortably aware that the Prussian legacy to a united Germany would always be ambiguous. In the very year of unification, in a curiously veiled passage in one of his war books, he spoke of the spirit of Potsdam as consisting of "an unholy amalgamation . . . of absolutism, militarism, and philistinism" and said that "a breath of unfreedom, of artificiality, of the contrived . . . blows through it all and oppresses any soul that has a greater need to breathe freely than to get in line."[13] And in the same work, speaking of the young Prussian lieutenants and assessors who were moving into occupied Alsace after the victory over France (and perhaps reflecting that Germany had been conquered by Prussia just as France had), he spoke of the dubious blessing of being ruled by "careerists, adventurers, the restless, and the ambitious."[14]

In the twenty years that followed the publication of *Before the Storm*, Fontane published fourteen novels. Through them runs a steady stream of careerists and adventurers and restless and ambitious men, beginning with Rittmeister von Schach in Fontane's second and last historical novel, *Schach von Wuthenow* (1883), including Landrat von Instetten and Major von Crampas in what is perhaps Fontane's greatest novel of society, *Effi Briest* (1895), and ending with Ministerialassessor von Rex and the mill owner von Gundermann in his last novel, *Der Stechlin* (1899). Hans-Heinrich Reuter has pointed out that there are other Prussians in these novels of admirable character and attractive temperament—the general in *Die Poggenpuhls* (1896), Effi's father in *Effi Briest*, Dubslav in *Der Stechlin*—but these are, with one conspicuous exception to be mentioned in a moment, men of advanced years who represent a dying generation.[15] It is the others, who in Fontane's stories are as ruthless in their dealings with their fellows as the young officials whom Fontane saw moving into Alsace, who represent the new Prussia that he detested and feared.

He feared it most of all, perhaps, because in the new Reich Prussianism had acquired an ideological weight that led many people to regard it as a superior form of culture.[16] Fontane always took an ironical view of this idea, for it was his conviction that the values that had sustained Prussia and had made it, for a time, a progressive element in German history were now in the process of atrophying and were, in their genuine form, hardly recognized any longer by those people who boasted most loudly of being Prussian. Nothing illustrates the soundness of his suspicion better than the reception accorded his novel *Trials and Tribulations (Irrungen, Wirrungen)* when it began to appear in the *Vossische Zeitung* in 1887. This is the story of a happy love affair between a young nobleman and a daughter of the people; both know that, because of the norms of society, it cannot last, and they are reconciled to this. The heroine of the novel, Lene Nimptsch, is one of Fontane's most fully realized creations, and she is also perhaps the most positively Prussian, as her lover recognizes when he says that her character is one of "simplicity, truthfulness, and naturalness" and that "she has her heart in the right place and a strong feeling for duty, right, and order."[17] Nevertheless, during the serial publication of the book, the *Vossische Zeitung* was bombarded with letters from members of the Prussian aristocracy demanding to know when "this dreadful whore's story" was going to be terminated.[18]

The disintegration of values took several forms. It was, for one thing, clear to Fontane that the military virtues that had characterized the Prussian upper classes were in the process of degenerating into a blend of arrogance and braggadocio that, communicated to the general public, assumed the form of a dangerous kind of militarism. When he published his first novel, Fontane wrote to his publisher that "it struck a blow for religion, morality, and the fatherland, but was full of hatred against the 'blue cornflower' [the Prussian national flower] and against 'With God for King and Fatherland'—that is, against the windy spouting and caricature of that trinity."[19] On another occasion he noted that if people insisted on decorating their lapels on every military anniversary, they ought to find something better than the "stupid" cornflower, something "with red trouser stripes" (the sartorial distinction of the General Staff).[20] In his novels, references to the pervasive militarism of society are numerous. In *Frau Jenny Treibel* (1892), Fontane caricatures the kind of person, all too numerous in Bismarckian and Wilhelmine Germany, who believed that the attainment of an officer's commission in the army reserve made him a superior being, whose opinions had more weight than those of mere civilians;[21] and, in *The Adulteress* (*L'Adultera*, 1882), Melanie van Straaten, reading the visiting card of a caller, says, "Lieutenant in the Reserve of the Fifth Dragoon Regiment. . . . Abhorrent, these everlasting lieutenants! There are no human beings any more!"[22]

One of the worst aspects of this progressive militarization of society was that it tended, in Fontane's view, to spread formalistic and artificial ethical concepts and taboos that had deleterious social effects. Thus, the old military concept of honor had, in civilian life, been translated into a cruel and unnatural code of etiquette that imprisoned the upper classes in a moral straitjacket. As early as 1883, Fontane hit out at this in his novel *Schach von Wuthenow*, which tells the story of a young officer who kills himself because he is forced by considerations of military honor to take a course of action that he fears will lead to a degree of social ridicule that he will not be able to tolerate. After the young man's death, Fontane's spokesman in the novel, a staff captain named von Bülow, says:

> I have belonged to this army long enough to know that "honor" is its every third word. A dancer is charming "on my honor"; yes, I have even had money-lenders recommended and introduced to me as superb "on my honor." And this constant talking about honor, about a false honor, has confused the concept and made real honor dead. . . . To this cult of false honor, which is nothing but vanity and perverseness, Schach has succumbed, and better men than he will do the same. Remember what I say. . . . When the Ming dynasty was coming to its end, and the victorious Manchu armies had already penetrated into the palace gardens of Peking, messengers and envoys continually appeared to announce victory after victory to the Emperor because it was contrary to "the tone" of good society and the court to speak of defeats. Oh, this good tone! An hour later

an empire was in fragments and a throne overturned! And why? Because all affectation leads to lies, and lies to death.[23]

Fontane's most extended treatment of the tyranny of honor comes in *Effi Briest*, after Effi's husband, the Prussian bureaucrat von Instetten, discovers that, six and a half years earlier, his wife had an affair with a Major von Crampas. Although he knows that she has had no relations with Crampas since that time and although he dearly loves her, Instetten challenges the major to a duel and kills him, then drives Effi from his home and takes her child away from her. As an intelligent man, he is well aware that his conduct is not rational, but, in order to render his doubts ineffectual, he tells a close friend, Baron von Wüllersdorf, of the affair, thus making it, as he sees it, impossible for him not to go forward with his drastic course of action. In what has been called "the greatest conversation scene in the German novel,"[24] Instetten says:

> We're not isolated individuals, we belong to society, and we must continually take society into account; we are dependent upon it. If one could live in isolation, I could let this go; I would then be bearing a burden that I had agreed to accept. . . . But with people living all together, something has evolved that exists here and now, and we've become accustomed to judging everything in accordance with its rules, other people and ourselves as well. And to violate that doesn't work. Society would scorn us and, in the end, we would scorn ourselves and not be able to stand it, and would shoot a bullet through our heads.

In any case, he adds, there's no keeping the secret now. He has to go ahead. If he does not, then some day, when someone has suffered an affront, and he suggests that allowances should be made because no real harm has been done, he will see a smile pass, or start to pass, over Wüllersdorf's face and will imagine him thinking, "Good old Instetten! He's never been able to discover anything that smells too strong for him!" Wüllersdorf, who has been trying to dissuade him, now strikes his guns. "I think it's dreadful that you're right," he says, "but you *are* right. . . . The world is how it is, and things go, not the way we want them to, but the way others want them to. All that high-flown stuff about a judgment of God is, of course, rubbish, and we don't want any of it. On the other hand, our cult of honor is a form of idolatry, and yet we must submit to it, as long as the idol is allowed to stand."[25]

Fontane's view that the Prussian aristocracy had submitted to a kind of totemism convinced him that it was fast losing its originality, spontaneity, and moral energy and was ceasing to be a vital force in German life, a conviction that he expressed in the novel *Die Poggenpuhls.* But it had meanwhile corrupted other sections of society, the educational establishment and the clergy, which repeated and sanctified its prejudices, and the once self-reliant middle class. In the days when, as he said, to be a *Bürger* meant to possess three qualities, "property, respect for the law, and the feeling of freedom that flows from the first two," Fontane had high hopes for the middle class, and in 1865 could say that its dominance of German life would be beneficial.[26] But that was before its political energy had been sapped by its final defeat in the constitutional struggle in Prussia and its moral instincts eroded by the easy affluence of the first years of unification. The portraits of the *Besitzbürgertum* (propertied middle class) that Fontane gives us in his novels are increasingly unflattering and show that he reprobated their materialism less than their attempts, at any cost, to effect a symbiotic relationship with the aristocracy.

In *The Adulteress* the parvenuism of the new bourgeoisie is symbolized in the acquisitive instinct of van Straaten, a typical entrepreneur of the *Gründerjahre* ("founding years" of the Reich) with pretensions to culture that he satisfies by buying copies of great paintings. In *Frau Jenny Treibel,* Counselor of Commerce Treibel prefers to copy the politics of the aristocratic classes and becomes a candidate for a conservative seat in a rural district, while cultivating decayed gentlewomen to help his cause. One of them is bewildered by his ambitions and lectures him on the politics of social stratification. "Aristocratic estate owners are agrarian conservatives," she tells him. "Professors belong to the National Liberal party; and industrialists are Progressives. Become a Progressive! What do you want with a royal order? If I were in your place I would go in for municipal politics and seek bourgeois distinction!"[27] This is not the kind of advice Treibel wants, or his wife Jenny, as ruthless a social climber as Proust's Madame Verdurin. As a friend says, Jenny "really imagines that she has a sensitive heart and a feeling for higher things, but she has a heart only for the ponderable, for everything that can be weighed and that pays interest."[28] Finally, in *Der*

Stechlin, Fontane shows us, in the figure of the mill owner von Gundermann, the kind of person who has squandered so much of himself to acquire an aristocratic title that he has forfeited all respect and is generally regarded as a mean-spirited intriguer and sycophant. "Gundermann is a bourgeois and a parvenu," someone says, "therefore just about the worst thing that anyone can be."[29]

It was the effect of all this on social relations that most concerned Fontane. As early as January, 1878, in a letter to Mathilde von Rohr, he wrote: "When I look around me in society, I encounter in the upper strata of our people, among the aristocracy, the officials, the dignitaries, the artists, and the scholars, a merely moderate decency. They are narrow, covetous, dogmatic, without a sense of form and propriety; they want to take and not to give; they respect the appearance of honor rather than honor itself; and, to an unbelievable extent, they lack nobility of mind, generosity, and the gift of forgiveness and sacrifice. They are self-seeking, hard, and unloving."[30] A society whose upper classes were like this was unlikely to have much understanding of, or sympathy for, its most vulnerable members.

It has often been pointed out that Fontane's range of social vision was limited and that he did not write, for example, about the problems of the poor. This is true enough, but he did pay more attention than most of his·contemporaries to another and larger group of victims of society—namely, women, who are the main characters of all but the first and last of his novels.[31] This was not because he held theoretical or doctrinaire views on the subject of women's rights, although he knew, of course, that this was becoming the subject of lively debate, and he was acquainted with August Bebel's widely read *Woman and Socialism* (*Die Frau und der Sozialismus*), which was published in 1883. Rather, his observations of German life convinced him that the current condition of women was a distressing commentary on the moral state of the country.

Fontane's reaction to the protests against the serialization of *Trials and Tribulations* illustrates his approach to the problem. He wrote to his son: "We are up to our ears in all sorts of conventional lies and should be ashamed of the hypocrisy we practice and the rigged game we are playing. Are there, apart from a few afternoon preachers into whose souls I should not like to peer, any educated and decent people who are *really* morally outraged over a seamstress who is having an unsanctioned love affair? I don't know any. . . . The attitude of a few papers, whose yield of illegitimate children well exceeds a dozen (the chief editor having the lion's share) and which are now pleased to teach me morality, is revolting!"[32] It was these hypocrisies that he sought to attack in his novels, exposing that double standard of morality which tolerated infidelity and sexual license on the part of males (in *Stine* [1890], for example) but outlawed women who acted similarly (in *The Adulteress*, for example, and *Effi Briest*). In two of his most interesting but least read stories, *Quitt* (1891) and *Cécile* (1887), and also in *Effi Briest*, he dealt with the tendency in upper-class society to educate women only in such things as would make them attractive to men and secure them good marriages, a practice he found shameful and degrading, since it deprived women of the opportunity for full development of their talents and depersonalized or reified them by turning them into commodities in the male market or, as in the case of *Cécile*, into odalisques.

Finally, in his books about women, Fontane challenged the basic assumptions of a society that was male dominated and could read with complacency the views of people like Arthur Schopenhauer, Friedrich Hebbel, and Richard Wagner, who regarded women as an inferior species. In the relationship between Melanie and Rubehn in *The Adulteress*, Stine and Waldemar in *Stine*, Lene and Botho in *Trials and Tribulations*, and Mathilde and Hugo in *Mathilde Möhring* (1891), it is the woman who is the stronger partner, the more resilient under the pressures of society, and in every sense the educator of the man. It has been said of Mathilde Möhring that none of Fontane's other women possesses as many qualities, positive and ambiguous, that point to the future—that Mathilde, indeed, seems to the modern reader more a twentieth-century than a nineteenth-century woman.[33] If that is true, it is also true that she reflects the basic predicament of women in Wilhelmine society, for she is allowed to profit from the fruits of intellectual energy and social and political skills only as long as her husband is present to take credit for them. After his death, she is forced to return to the position out of which she lifted him. Nevertheless, she remains undefeated.

Having said all this about Fontane as a critic of his society, one must admit that the cultural and educational establishment of Fontane's own time was almost completely impervious to his strictures, apparently finding it impossible to regard the man who had written *Wanderings through Mark Brandenburg* as anything but a loyal subject, true to king, nobility, and the existing social order. It was only after the publication of his correspondence that it was realized that this was far from being the case, and this caused a small revolution in German studies.[34] That this is so, and that the reading public of Fontane's time read his stories with no deeper discomfort than an occasional twinge of moral outrage over his frankness in dealing with the relations between the sexes, gives some substance to the charges of critics like Georg Lukács who have written that, with all his social sensitivity, Fontane never sought to explain the basic causes of the ills he revealed or to suggest any solutions for them. In novels like *Effi Briest*, Lukács has written, Fontane was really predicting that the Bismarckian Prussia-Germany was headed for another Jena. But "it was really a passive, a skeptical pessimistic prophecy. The forces of German renewal lay outside his literary horizon."[35]

This last sentence is perhaps not wholly fair. Fontane's weakness, if that is what it was, was not so much a matter of lack of analytical depth as it was of choice. He believed that it was the function of the novelist not to tell his readers what to do but, rather, to explain to them the way things are. "The task of the modern novel," he once said, "seems to me to be that of portraying a life, a society, a circle of people who are an undistorted reflection of the life we lead."[36] If one can do that, with the intensity, clarity, perspicuity, comprehension, and feeling that are demanded of the artist, then readers should be able to understand their society and their lives better. Whether they will want to change them is really up to them.

Fontane's critical mode was one of detachment, ambiguity, and irony. It is no accident that there is more conversation than action in his books, for conversation is the ideal medium for expressing the differences of view and of perception of reality that we find in real life. As a private individual, Fontane might feel, as he said in a letter in 1898, that "everything that is interesting is to be found in the fourth estate. The bourgeoisie is frightful, and the aristocracy and clerics are old fashioned. . . . The new, the better world begins with the fourth estate. . . . The workers have attacked everything in a new way; they have not only new goals but new methods of attaining them."[37] But he did not say this unambiguously in his novels. In *Der Stechlin*, the pastor Lorenzen says: "A new world is coming. I believe a better and happier one. Or, if not happier, at least a time with more oxygen in the air, a time when we can breathe more freely." But he gives no reasons for this optimism. A little later in the book, old Stechlin says, "Our whole social system, which prejudice rates so high, is more or less barbarism," but he does not reveal any prescription for changing this.[38] There is hardly a major political issue that was canvassed during the Bismarckian and Wilhelmine years that does not surface in a conversation in one or another of Fontane's novels, but it is never discussed at length and is often dismissed with that ironical humor that is the hallmark of *Frau Jenny Treibel* and *Der Stechlin* without having afforded any clear indication of what the author thinks.

Robert Minder has lamented this failure to speak out and has written that, if only Fontane had been as forthright in his novels as he was, for example, in his letter to his friend Friedländer on April 5, 1897, when he shrewdly criticized the character and policies of William II and declared that the East Elbian aristocracy was Germany's misfortune,[39] the empire would have had, "along with Nietzsche and Wagner, an epic-writer of world rank."[40] This may be true. But it seems likely that Fontane chose his ironic and detached method with an eye to his audience, knowing its self-satisfaction and unresponsiveness to criticism and hoping that, if he helped it to understand what was happening to German society, he might at least trouble its complacency and stimulate doubt.

III

If Fontane was a gentle critic, as one American historian has called him,[41] Heinrich Mann (1871–1950) was just the opposite. Born in Lübeck in the year of unification, the eldest son of a merchant in grain who became a senator of the Hanseatic town in 1877, he showed his preference for the arts rather than for commerce at an early age and was making his first experiments in verse and prose before he was fifteen. His first literary hero was Heinrich Heine, and he may have derived some of his gift of satire and his rage over the crimes committed in the name of authority from that great enemy of social injustice. From Heine, too, it was an easy step to French culture, to Stendhal and Balzac and, from them, to Flaubert and Zola, who taught him, as he later wrote, that "the novel should not only portray; it should make things better."[42]

Fontane he also read at an early age and with mounting admiration, describing him in 1890 as "my favorite among the moderns . . . a brilliant critic without prejudices and . . . a novelist of pace and skill," although at that time his great predecessor's poetry, particularly the ballads, seems to have appealed to him more than the stories.[43] It may very well have been Fontane's influence, combined with that of Stendhal, that led Mann at the age of twenty-five to decide that he wanted to write novels about contemporary life in Germany, because, as he remembered later, he felt that German society no longer knew itself and was dissolving into fragments. He later wrote: "Do you think that democracy can grow [in Germany] without the portrayal of society? In terms of the future, it is the only thing that has any significance or meaning—not 'timelessness,' which is today still the highest aim [of literature]." Stendhal's novels, he added, were not "timeless" in the German sense of the word; "they portrayed their time with absolute critical sensitivity."[44] When Mann wrote his first novel in 1900, a story of Berlin life called *The Land of Cockaigne* (*Im Schlaraffenland*), the influence of Stendhal's *Lucien Leuwen* was apparent, as was that of de Maupassant's *Bel Ami*; and to an even greater extent this first experiment could be described as a direct descendant of Fontane's *Frau Jenny Treibel*.

Indeed, Fontane's study of bourgeois life and social parvenuism influenced both Heinrich Mann's first work and the novel *Buddenbrooks*, written by his younger brother Thomas a year later.[45] *Buddenbrooks*, Thomas Mann's only real novel of society, tells of the rise and decline of a bourgeois family in a middle-sized city, whose fortune was founded, as was that of Fontane's Treibels, in the *Gründerjahre* immediately after the consummation of German unification. *The Land of Cockaigne* describes a new generation of parvenus that has consolidated its social position in the first years of the reign of William II and shows every sign of continuing to flourish. If its tone was sharper and its attacks upon the tuft-hunting proclivities of the bourgeoisie more savage than that of Fontane's novel, where the author regarded the social machinations of his protagonist with a degree of ironic affection, this was because Heinrich Mann recognized in the kind of people represented in his novel by the Türkheimer family a new and dangerous force. These parvenus were not like those who, a generation earlier, had sought status by means of social and cultural collaboration with the aristocratic classes and who had generally been fobbed off with meaningless trifles. They resembled neither the effete bourgeois intellectuals who were to become the subject of Mann's novel of Munich life, *The Hunt for Love* (*Die Jagd nach Liebe*, 1904), nor the Austrian liberal bourgeoisie whose frustrations are described in Carl Schorske's book about *fin-de-siècle* Vienna.[46] The Türkheimers represented the new power of finance capital, which threatened to be the solvent of all forms of status and all the values that held society together.

The Land of Cockaigne, in other words, was really about power, and it marked the beginnings of Heinrich Mann's fascination with the dimensions assumed by this problem in Wilhelmine society, with the growing obsession with power, and with the infinite ability of power to corrupt. In contrast to Fontane, who was inclined to believe that the working classes might be immune to the ills that he saw afflicting the aristocracy and the working classes, Mann made no such distinction. In each of his three great social novels, representatives of all classes are shown as equally vulnerable to the seductions of power and equally unrepentant when their ambitions are defeated. *The Land of Cockaigne* is a kind of distorted *Bildungsroman* about an ambitious young man from the country named Andreas Zumsee. He is advised by a journalist of his acquaintance that, if he wants to make his way to fortune and fame, he must attach himself to the Türkheimers and become part of their system. This adviser says:

> Türkheimer is, in fact, a reasonably enlightened man. He even recognizes that the communism that is so popular today represents a contemporary need. Provided, of course, it is a sound communism that stays within appropriate bounds. . . . But the family has many branches and extends, on the one side, even to princely personages who are accustomed to plant trees here and there in the Türkheimer garden. . . . And, at the other end, it reaches to people like us, who, if we show skill and agility, can pick this or that fifty-mark note out of the air.[47]

Zumsee is easy to persuade. He becomes an attendant lord at the court of these flashy but powerful parvenus, has a giddy series of preferments, and then makes a mistake and is cast aside. He has by then, however, been so completely corrupted by the system that he is incapable of resentment against his former patrons. At the end of the book, as he watches them driving down the Leipziger Straße, swollen with new commercial successes in eastern Europe, "stupid, profligate, and happy," and learns that Türkheimer has just received a decoration from the Crown, Andreas feels only anger at the inadequacy of his own social adroitness; he has, he says, "cravings that cannot be stilled and an endless regret."[48]

Heinrich Mann's second important novel is better known to Western audiences than any of his other works because, in 1931, it was made into a popular motion picture called *The Blue Angel*, starring Marlene Dietrich and Emil Jannings and directed by Joseph von Sternberg. A powerful study of sadism, the film tells the story of a martinet schoolmaster who is destroyed by an infatuation for a cabaret performer, to whom he sacrifices his career and his social position.[49] But the film has little of the analytical incisiveness and bite of the novel, *Professor Unrat*, which was published in 1905 and was less a story about sexual attraction than it was about power and its affinity with anarchy.

In *Professor Unrat*, and, indeed, in his later trilogy about the Wilhelmine Reich, Mann was in a sense writing a commentary on Nietzsche's statement in *The Twilight of the Idols* that obsession with power deprives a society of the vital energies that it needs to sustain civilization.[50] The schoolmaster Rath (or, as he is called by his students, Unrat, or garbage) has no interest in his calling as a teacher or in the world of scholarship. He is wholly possessed with the idea of the power that his position gives him over his charges and, by extension, over society in general. He hates everyone with whom he comes into contact because he senses that he is not respected:

> He went among these people unesteemed and even ridiculed, but in his own consciousness he belonged to those who ruled. No banker and no monarch had a greater share in power or was more interested in maintaining the existing order than Unrat. He was zealous in behalf of all authorities and raged in the secrecy of his study against the workers, who, had they attained their goals, would probably have seen to it that Unrat too was better paid. He warned young teachers . . . against the baleful disease of the modern spirit that was

shaking the pillars of order. He wanted those foundations to be strong: an influential church, a reliable army, strict obedience and sound morals. . . . As a tyrant, he knew how one controlled slaves: how the mob, the enemy, the fifty thousand refractory students who afflicted him were to be tamed.[51]

When this monster of rectitude and adulator of authority fell in love with the singer Rosa Gründlich and was dismissed from his post and accused of spreading a pestilence among right-thinking people by his example, the notion of his being able to do such a thing, the prospect of revenging himself by poisoning society, had an exciting effect upon him;[52] he proceeded, with the assistance of his paramour's attractions, to debauch the town by running a combination of gambling hall and bordello for the very people who condemned him. "In the midst of those who rushed, by way of the tables, towards bankruptcy, disgrace, and the gallows," Mann writes, "Unrat, with his knock-knees and impassive mien, was like an old schoolmaster whose class had fallen into a dissolute frenzy and who, from behind his eyeglasses, was taking note of the ringleaders so as to be able later to ruin their character references. They had dared to set themselves up against the power of the ruler; very well, he would loose them from restraint so that they could beat each others' ribs in and break each others' necks. Out of the tyrant, the anarchist had finally emerged."[53]

Moreover, as an anarchist, gloating over his success in disclosing what lay beneath the respectability of the town's leading citizens, Unrat made an important discovery—namely, that what is ordinarily called morality is merely a form of stupidity or philistinism, used by the powerful and cynical to maintain their control over those who think that they cannot do without it. It has no real depth or strength and can be stripped away by the clever practitioner of power, who knows how to arouse and mobilize the baser impulses for his own purposes.[54] We are reminded of Fontane's definition of the spirit of Potsdam as "an unholy amalgamation . . . of absolutism, militarism, and philistinism"; but Mann's insight had a disturbing forward thrust and was a chilling premonition of things to come in Germany.

So, finally, was the so-called Empire (*Kaiserreich*) trilogy, which Mann intended to be the crowning achievement of his preoccupation with the social novel. Theodor Fontane had never tried to deal directly in his novels with the real stuff of politics, with the struggles of the parties, the political influence of agriculture, industry, and high finance, the relationship between interest groups and foreign policy, and the whole complicated web of relationships between the activities of government and the life of ordinary people. Heinrich Mann conceived the daring notion of dealing with all of this in three novels, whose action was set in the years from 1890 to 1914. It seems clear that he was inspired by the example of Zola's novels about the end of the Second French Empire; and, like Zola, he sought to add verisimilitude to his account by having his characters move against the background of real events, like the workers' riots in Berlin in 1892, the debate on the military law in 1893 and the dissolution of the Reichstag, the court scandals of the late 1890s, the beginning of the naval agitation, the *Daily Telegraph* affair of 1908, and the gathering tension before 1914. This did not always work well.

The first and most successful of the three novels was *The Man of Straw (Der Untertan)*, finished in 1914 but not published until four years later. In the broadest sense, this is the story of the defeat in a small town of what is left of the liberal tradition of 1848 by special interests and political jobbery in the form of an alliance between a new "Kaiser's party" and an unprincipled local Social Democratic organization. Within this framework Mann has set the young careerist Diederich Hessling, who, by modeling himself in speech and manner, and as far as possible in appearance, upon the young emperor, by making undeviating loyalty to him a personal attribute and a weapon against his rivals and enemies, and by disregarding considerations of professional integrity and human decency, tramples his way to eminence in his community. The second novel, *The Poor (Die Armen)*, written during the war and published contemporaneously with *The Man of Straw*, continues Hessling's career, focusing now upon his direction of a gigantic industrial complex and upon the unscrupulous methods that he uses to keep his workers at minimal wages, to exploit them by making them live in company quarters and eat company food, to use strikebreakers and spies to defeat their attempts to organize, and to discredit their leaders, and describing how, when the workers are finally goaded into rising against him, vigorous government intervention frustrates them and leaves him with undiminished power. The conclusion of the trilogy, *The Head (Der Kopf)*, published in 1925, is a *roman à clef* in which the protagonist, a humanist with the improbable name of Claudius Terra, seeks to defeat the dangerous policies of figures who resemble Bülow, Tirpitz, and Bethmann Hollweg in the decade before the war.

Only the first of these novels can be considered a successful work of art, and even it seems hardly to merit the praise lavished on it by Kurt Tucholsky and other left-wing intellectuals during the Weimar period.[55] Even so, it is a powerful indictment of a society that seemed increasingly to be composed of the tyrannical and the servile, a system that rested upon brutality and Byzantinism and seemed to be inspired by a secret death wish, which is hinted at in the paean to power that comes to Diederich's mind as he sees the emperor riding through the Brandenburger Gate: "The Power that rides over us and whose hooves we kiss. . . . Against which we are powerless, because we all love It. Which we have in our blood, because we have submission in our blood. . . . Living in It, sharing in It, showing no mercy toward those who are further from It, and triumphing even as It smashes us; for thus does It vindicate our love for It!"[56]

Despite Mann's relentless insistence upon the moral obliquity of nearly every character whom he presents to our gaze, the socialist leader being shown to be as self-seeking as the protagonist, the book has undeniable satirical power. The burlesque association of Diederich's oratorical style with that of his royal master is well sustained, and the passages dealing with Diederich's university career, his membership in the New Teuton fraternity, and his interruption of his honeymoon to follow the emperor to Rome are rich in comic invention.

In the novels that follow, these qualities are sadly diminished. If *The Poor* was intended to be another *Germinal*, it fell far short of the mark, for Mann's workers lack the elemental savagery of Zola's, and their leaders hover between tortured indecisiveness and Germanic sentimentality. Mann's hatred of the system that he was portraying was beginning to make him forget the requirements of his craft, and sometimes the motivation of his characters—Diederich's decision, for example, that to expose his son to the risk of murder was an acceptable price to pay for eliminating the chief labor agitator—was contrived and improbable.

Yet Mann's powers of social analysis remained as acute as ever. His treatment of the activities of the Pan-German League in *The Head* has the realistic sharpness of his earlier treatment of the theme of money and power in *The Land of Cockaigne* and was perhaps a sign of concern that this danger had not been eliminated with the fall of the empire, a feeling also expressed in his powerful novella *Kobes*, which appeared in the same year as *The Head* and was inspired by the role of the magnate Hugo Stinnes in Weimar politics. But his method of presentation was now departing from the realism that Theodor Fontane had insisted should be the novelist's principal concern. Perhaps because he wanted his books to change things rather than merely describe them, Mann was resorting increasingly to exaggeration, and his language was beginning to resemble that of the expressionists in its passion and intensity. After reading *The Poor*, his admirer Arthur Schnitzler wrote to him: "The realities that you present in all their shattering power strike me at times as being distorted into caricature and often as being elevated into symbols, without it generally being clear to me what principle determines these distortions and enhancements. . . . Certain oversimplifications, which I think I find not so much in the action as in the willful, precipitate stylistic execution that you have chosen this time, have distressed me—perhaps because it's almost as if I were watching you distrust your own genius."[57]

This was shrewd enough, although, if Mann was beginning to have doubts, they were less about his own gifts than about the importance and usefulness of what he was doing. The reading audience that had tolerated Fontane's irony had no similar patience with Mann's rage. The social novels after *The Man of Straw* were not successful; indeed, Mann never again had a significant success until he wrote his great historical novels about Henry IV of France, and that happened when he was in exile from his own country. Years later he reflected upon the reasons for the failure of his earlier books and wrote to a friend, "What I had to suffer for was my feeling for public life. It alienated people in Germany at the time I began writing, despite Fontane, who was there." Later on, he added, he was rejected for his foresight. "I wrote in advance of what would actually become of Germany. People blamed me for it, as if I had been the one who caused it."[58]

IV

In 1955 Gottfried Benn addressed himself in a public lecture to the question, Should writers improve life? and concluded that they couldn't and shouldn't try to do so.[59] This was not surprising, coming from a writer whose lack of political responsibility was such that he had actually accepted the presidency of the Literature Section of the Prussian Academy of Arts in 1933, after Heinrich Mann had been forced from that post by Nazi pressure and had left the Academy, along with his brother, Käthe Kollwitz, Ricarda Huch, and other distinguished artists.[60] Benn's view was a restatement of the traditional German attitude that *Dichtung* was a sphere unto itself, elevated above the crass realities of ordinary existence.

Both Fontane and Heinrich Mann rejected that view of literature, Fontane with jocularities, Mann with bitter reflection on *la trahison des clercs*.[61] Both tried to change their worlds by using art to illumine the problems of their time, and both failed, for reasons that we have noted. But their failure was at least an honorable one, and it was by no means complete. By rejecting the inherited convention of the novel, they showed German writers the way to break out of the provincialism that had for long years denied them a hearing outside their own country; and, by demonstrating that it was possible to combine great art with social engagement, they set a standard for the writers of contemporary Germany to follow, one that is being followed to an extent that would have been inconceivable before 1945. This was no mean achievement, and it is certainly no accident that their memories are green and their readers numerous in both parts of Germany today and that there are constant reruns, not only of *The Blue Angel* but also of Wolfgang Staudte's film of *The Man of Straw*, made in the German Democratic Republic in 1951, and of Rainer Werner Fassbinder's much-admired recent production of *Effi Briest*.

13

The Good, the Bad, and the Bourgeois

I

In the first half of the nineteenth century, the curriculum of Rugby School in England was dominated, as was true of other public schools, by instruction in Greek and Latin. In addition, however, all students from the first to the sixth grade read history, both ancient and modern, which was interlarded with generous portions of Herodotus, Thucydides, Xenophon, and Livy. Dr. Thomas Arnold, the famous headmaster of Rugby, once gave the rationale for this by saying, "The history of Greece and Rome is not an idle inquiry about remote ages and forgotten institutions but a living picture of things present, fitted not so much for the curiosity of the scholar, as for the instruction of the statesman and citizen."[1]

History was central to Victorian education as a means of forming character and preparing students for the challenges of the times, and this

Review of *Thinking with History: Explorations in the Passage to Modernism*, by Carl E. Schorske; *Pleasure Wars: The Bourgeois Experience: Victoria to Freud*, by Peter Gay; and *My German Question: Growing Up in Nazi Berlin*, by Peter Gay: *The New York Review of Books*, August 13, 1998, pp. 8–12. Reprinted with permission from *The New York Review of Books*. Copyright © 1998, NYREV, Inc.

was not the only field in which it was accorded a respect that has no equal in our own age. Because it seemed to express and validate the hopes and ambitions of the rising middle class and its belief in progress—after all, what Englishman would deny that he lived in a land where freedom broadened from precedent to precedent, and what citizen of the Bismarckian Reich that he was a beneficiary of history's law of natural selection?—its influence was apparent in all fields of human thought and activity. This was true of the arts as well as the sciences. Historical painting remained popular throughout the century, and the historical novel had a vogue that was never enjoyed by the more analytical novels of society. Indeed, Leopold von Ranke, the most famous practitioner of *Quellenkritik*, always insisted that history was more an art than a science and cited Scott's *Quentin Durward* as the ideal model of historical narration.[2]

In architecture, too, history found important expression. In an absorbing chapter in his new book on the ascendancy and eclipse of historicist culture in the nineteenth century, Carl E. Schorske writes of how the post-1848 tension between the crown and the liberal elite in Vienna was moderated by the construction of the Ringstrasse and how the different architectural styles of the principal buildings along this thoroughfare served as a kind of visual mastering of a difficult past. Crucial to this, he argues, was the construction of the Kunsthistorisches Museum and its positioning between the Rathaus and Parliament of the ascendant liberals and the monumental dynastic buildings of the Hofburg, so that it served as a bonding element between the monarch and the new elite. Schorske points out that the most visible symbol of the implied political compromise was the statue of the Empress Maria Theresa that stands in the center of the museum square, surrounded by the leading figures of her reign. These included not only her soldiers and diplomats, but representatives of the Enlightenment like the reformer Joseph Sonnenfels, who abolished torture, and Gerard van Swieten, who modernized the university, and great artists like Gluck, Haydn, and the young Mozart. He adds:

> The Empress's caring, motherly figure contrasts strongly with the two military heroes whom Francis Joseph had chosen in the 1850's as focal statues of the Heldenplatz across the Ring. She stands in contrast, as well, to the figure whom the liberals chose to place be-

fore their Parliament: Pallas Athene. Lacking any heroes of their own in Austrian history, the liberals had turned to classical culture for an appropriate symbol.

Historicist architecture served other than political ends. It helped to alleviate the shock that the progress of industrialism and modernization inflicted on conservative sensibilities. Anyone who has traveled by train from Berlin to Hamburg will have been struck as he passes Potsdam by the imposing Turkish mosque on the banks of the Havel. This is the so-called waterworks of Sans Souci, built in 1841–1842 to pump water from the Havel to the royal fountains, and its impressive exterior is intended to conceal the Borsig steam engine that makes it work, as its minaret is designed to disguise the fact that it is really a chimney.

In cities across Europe, it was believed that such byproducts of the new industrialism as factories and railroad bridges would be less offensive and threatening if their stark utilitarianism was hidden beneath a style drawn from an earlier age. Schorske writes:

> In London even the railway stations struck archaic poses: Euston Station sought in its façade escape to ancient Greece, St. Pancras to the Middle Ages, Paddington to the Renaissance. This Victorian historicism expressed the incapacity of city dwellers either to accept the present or to conceive the future except as a resurrection of the past.

Among intellectuals, the counsel of history was constantly invoked in debates about the shape of the future and the preservation of values in an age of change. Schorske describes how conservative thinkers like Coleridge and Disraeli sought an answer to the growing greed and individualism of modern society in the revival of ideas of community rooted in the religion-centered Middle Ages, and how Wagner and William Morris, at different stages of their careers, found in Nordic mythology the model of healthy community existence. Similarly, during the days when Germany was under the domination of Napoleon and seemed to have no future, Johann Gottlieb Fichte invoked the memory of the medieval German city, which he regarded as a pure creation of the *Volk*, as "the nation's youthful dream of its future deeds," and his eloquent championing of this model of communitarian morality provided new standards for the later criticisms of the nineteenth-century city as a center of capitalist individualism. Thus, also, Jacob Burckhardt, returning to Basel after the publication of his *Civilization of the Renaissance in Italy*, and sensing that the neohumanistic values that had inspired the patricians of his native city-state were threatened by democracy and industrialism, abandoned scholarly research and took upon himself a staggering burden of public lectures designed to teach his fellow citizens how to understand history through contemplation and reflection, acting, as Schorske writes, like Nietzsche before him, as "a kind of home missionary whose vocation was to develop cosmopolitan *Bildung* in allegiance to the local scene."

The ascendancy of history in the consciousness of Europeans began to wane in the second half of the nineteenth century. This had something to do with the decline of faith in progress, as intractable political and social problems multiplied and the counsels of tradition seemed increasingly bootless. Schorske places the turning point in the 1850s and writes:

> No agreement yet exists on the great sea change in our culture ushered in by Baudelaire and the French Impressionists, and given philosophical formulation by Nietzsche. We know only that the pioneers of this change explicitly challenged the validity of traditional morality, social thought and art. The primacy of reason in man, the rational structure of nature, and the meaningfulness of history were brought before the bar of personal psychological experience for judgment.

This is a good working definition of modernism, and it is a pity that Schorske does not discuss the movement in its European setting (we hear nothing more, unfortunately, about Baudelaire, and little about Nietzsche), confining himself to a series of essays on individual expressions of modernist consciousness in Vienna which elaborate on themes already discussed in his previous book on that city.[3] Still, we have no reason to complain about this. Schorske knows a great deal about Vienna, and the essays in this section are original and penetrating, particularly those on Mahler and Freud.

The rise of modernism in Vienna was conditioned by the breakdown, at the end of the 1870s, of the political ascendancy of the Liberal Party and the rise of new forms of mass politics. This shook the confidence of the liberal elite and weakened the cohesion of its cultural tradition, that synthesis of aesthetic cultivation inherited from the baroque and of rationalist political and academic dedication inherited from the Enlightenment which Schorske calls the union of Grace and the Word. Tolerance of opposing points of view became less frequent, the search for culprits on whom to blame the disarray of the times became more common, the tie between generations broke down.

Indeed, the evolution of modernism was marked by a series of Oedipal revolts by the sons against the fathers. The first came in the wake of the expulsion of Austria from Germany after the defeat by Prussia in 1866 and the subsequent economic crash of 1873, with its revelations of speculation and corruption in high places. *Die Jungen* in the universities called for a thoroughgoing regeneration of Austrian society and a new German nationalism (the critic Hermann Bahr recalls telling his astonished father, "Liberalism is finished. A new age is dawning. Make way for us!"), finding their models in ancient Greek culture and in Germanic myth as preached by Richard Wagner. This tendency did not last long, for the nationalist movement was superseded by the rising force of anti-Semitism, and those among its leaders who were Jewish— Bahr, Theodor Herzl, Gustav Mahler, Viktor Adler, Sigmund Freud, Heinrich Friedjung—were expelled. Their successors—the *Jung-Wien* movement of the 1880s, and the Secession of the turn of the century— were not interested in remaking society after ancient models, for they no longer, in Schorske's words, "did their thinking with history."

Jung-Wien espoused the "modern" (a word used only in deprecation by Wagnerians) as a form of existence and a sensibility different from all that had gone before, one detached from history. Although they still used the reportorium of history as a source of images, they ceased to regard history as a meaningful succession of states from which the present derived its purpose and its place in human destiny.

This was true also in architecture. Otto Wagner, a leading social critic of the Ringstrasse style, argued in an influential book that its architects, instead of answering modern needs, had been unduly influenced by the quite different requirements of earlier civilizations. What was essential now, he argued, was a public architectural style that would be consistent with the new building materials and technologies of the present age and expressive of its democratic, commercial, practical character. In the private rather than the public sphere, the Secessionists called for an architecture based on what Schorske calls "a new, meta-historical beauty" that would seek to adapt buildings to the personalities of their owners, and thereby—somewhat mysteriously, one might think—help to brake the dissolution of the ego in modern society, which was one of their principal concerns. At the same time, a bitter opponent of the Secession, Adolf Loos, who in 1898 described Ringstrasse Vienna as a "Potemkin city" whose façades hid a world of sordidness and squalor and hypocrisy, took the puritanical view that art and aesthetics, like history, should have nothing to do with architecture at all, which was merely a business of meeting practical needs in the most economical way.

The break with history was not, however, always so sharp and irrevocable as in the case of *Die Jungen*, and this becomes very clear as Schorske turns to the careers of the two greatest Viennese modernists. His portrait of Gustav Mahler, who once wrote of himself that he was "thrice homeless, as a native of Bohemia among Austrians, as an Austrian among Germans and as a Jew throughout the world," emphasizes Mahler's ability to understand and identify not only with the rich tradition of Austria's past but with the warring cultures of her present. His path to modernism was marked by his widening of the classical idiom when he introduced vernacular popular elements from the musical practice of his Bohemian background, by a growing sensitivity to psychological states and to the power of the instinctual that was the result of his membership in the Wagnerian counterculture of the late 1870s, and then by a belief in art as a surrogate for life that resulted from his association with the Secession at the end of the century. Yet, as Schorske writes, "if as a composer Mahler affirmed in music a nonhomogeneous, contradiction-ridden modern world no longer easily contained in historically given forms, in his career as a conductor [as director of the Court Opera], he devoted himself to the preservation of the musical tradition."

In the case of Freud, the founding father of the most influential of Vienna's contributions to modernism, psychoanalysis, the stubborn persistence of his interest in history is even more remarkable. As a young man in the great age of modern liberalism, Freud was an ardent student of history, both classical and modern, but when he turned his interest to the psyche and the unconscious, and was working through the problems raised by his path-breaking work *The Interpretation of*

Dreams, his historical interest went into eclipse. But it never died completely, and in a masterful tracing of the influence of other cultures upon Freud's reflections about his own psyche, Schorske shows how it revived. Central to this was the triumph of National Socialism, which reinforced his most dire psychoanalytic forebodings about the return of repressed collective aggression and forced him to reconsider his own Jewish identity. His reflections culminated in *Moses and Monotheism*, his last major work, which, in a homecoming both to the Jewish culture of his fathers and to the universal liberalism of his early social environment, sought to hearten those who were struggling to save civilization from the new barbarians. In this work, Schorske writes, he not only resumed thinking with history but became a historicist himself:

> Once again in the aging Freud, historicism was serving as a model to confront the uncongenial present with an assignment for the future, as historicism had so often done in the nineteenth century.

II

Modernism, so prominent in Schorske's essays, is also a central theme in Peter Gay's new book, although its effect upon historical thinking does not concern him directly. *Pleasure Wars* is about the artistic and cultural tastes of the bourgeoisie, and Gay is well aware that most of its members stayed apart from modernism. The continued appeal of best-selling novels, light musical entertainment, and sentimental or religious paintings at the end of the century as opposed to the works approved by the avant-garde is enough to confirm this. So is the fact that in architecture, a favorite stamping ground of modernists, even those bourgeois with some pretensions to artistic taste seemed happy enough to leave them in abeyance when their own architectural arrangements were involved. Their desires usually went no further than "vague notions about beauty, practical requirements like a well appointed kitchen, and the longing for a small garden, [which] struck modernists as singularly unaesthetic."

Even so, it would be a mistake on the basis of this to deprecate the cultural ambitions and attainments of the bourgeoisie as a whole. Nor does Gay allow us to do so, suggesting that it would be prudent to be guided instead by the youthful Walter Gropius's answer to the question about his favorite color. Gropius replied, "*Bunt*—multicolored."

Pleasure Wars is the fifth and concluding volume in Peter Gay's grand investigation of the bourgeois experience and consciousness in the nineteenth century, an enterprise requiring a daring and breadth of knowledge possessed by few other contemporary historians, and one which he has carried to its term with inexhaustible energy and patience and an exuberance of spirit that has enabled him to rise above the sometimes niggling charges of his critics. The previous volumes have dealt with the role of sensuality and sexuality in the bourgeois experience, with love and its varied expressions, with forms of aggression and destruction and their repression, and with the exploration of the inner self through art and literature. All have been original in the choice of the materials used to elaborate their themes, often provocative in their conclusions, and always highly readable. This is true also of the final volume.

The idea that the bourgeoisie is bereft of interest in matters of art and the higher culture dates back to the time when the rising middle class was contesting the political and social dominance of the crown and the aristocracy. The mercantile origins of the new class led its opponents to attribute to it an insensitivity to any feeling for finer things, a prejudice that found expression, for example, in German student songs of the eighteenth century, which expressed good-humored contempt for the citizens of university towns, who were referred to as *Philister*, or unenlightened, uncultured people. Goethe's Werther found more true feeling in the ordinary people than in the *Bürger* who considered themselves their betters, and his creator told Eckermann in 1830 that it was the narrow-mindedness of the *Philister* that had driven Byron to his death.

As the bourgeois age came into its own, this opinion hardened, reaching its extreme form in the fulminations of people like the critic Georg Brandes, who once wrote: "One can never sufficiently imagine the philistinism of the Danish middle class, its impenetrable resistance to enlightenment and clarity, its cowardice and stupidity," and Gustave Flaubert, who delighted in attacking the bourgeoisie as *épiciers* (grocers). Flaubert, Gay writes, considered them to be "commonplace, cowardly, colorless, censorious, sentimental, devious, . . . materialistic from head to toe, and bereft of all sense for the exotic, the adventurous, the extraordinary," and he once wrote to George Sand, "Axiom: Hatred of

Bourgeois is the beginning of all virtue."

Were these opinions, as Gay seems to suggest by the emphasis he places upon them, too exaggerated to be credible? Probably not. So judicious a writer as Matthew Arnold once wrote: "Philistinism!—We have not the expression in English. Perhaps we have not the word because we have so much of the thing."[4] He went on to say that intellectual curiosity was not well-regarded in his country, the very word "curiosity" always conveying "a certain notion of frivolous and unedifying activity," and that Liberal politicians as eminent as John Bright made a practice of flouting at the friends and preachers of culture, as if they were sure of the approval of their middle-class constituents.[5] In most of Europe the teachers in the schools that taught the children of the middle ranges of the bourgeoisie resembled Dickens's Thomas Gradgrind of Coketown in their belief that facts were more important than fancy. In his important report on the school systems of France, Germany, Italy, and Switzerland, Arnold noted in the 1860s that few schools, even in France, exemplified the French ideal of *la grande culture*, and many of them preferred to serve more practical ends, like the Swiss schools, which were guided by "a spirit of intelligent industrialism," that saw instruction and the intelligence it produced as "valuable commodities."[6]

In these circumstances, the arts were apt to be *terra incognita* for most of the bourgeoisie, and artists widely regarded as people whose lives were irregular and whose activities were offensive, if not subversive. This explains, at least partially, the shocked indignation aroused in the general public by the paintings of the Impressionists and other schools that departed from the standards set by state-supported galleries. It also helps to explain the wide approval that Hitler's antagonism to modern art enjoyed among ordinary Germans. In this context the difficulties experienced by the National Endowment of the Arts in receiving federal funding in the United States might also be mentioned.

In the absence of statistical evidence, it is difficult to reach an entirely satisfactory conclusion to the difficult question of bourgeois attitudes toward culture, and Gay is certainly justified in insisting that there were more members of the bourgeoisie with active cultural interests than Flaubert would allow; he cites Baudelaire's opinion that it might be a good idea to stop using the word "bourgeois" as an epithet, since so many of the maligned class were natural friends of the arts and others would like to be.[7]

Gratification of this last desire, however, was always determined by financial considerations. In a fascinating chapter called "The Political Economy of Art," a phrase borrowed from Ruskin, Gay points out that members of the petty bourgeoisie had to spend a disproportionate amount of their barely adequate salaries on keeping up appearances, that is, in distinguishing themselves from the working class, and that this left little scope for internal improvement. The middle reaches of the bourgeoisie—teachers, lesser officials, reasonably thriving merchants and professionals—were better off, but not sufficiently so to frequent theaters and concert halls or travel to museums that were not situated in their home towns. Even so, the cultivation of music at home, the eager purchase of cheap reproductions of famous paintings, the use of Baedekers on occasional trips, and, now and then, a bit of extravagance to buy works of art or attend concerts are proof of significant cultural interest on the part of ordinary bourgeois. Gay tells us of a middle-grade court official who attended one of the sensational concerts that Paganini gave in crowded and stifling halls in Vienna in 1828 and wrote later, "It cost me a lot of money. I was dripping with sweat, but I heard him, and in order to get an idea of his playing, one must hear him."

The spirit that guided this persistent music lover sometimes took collective form. In 1848, a group of Manchester merchants and manufacturers, led by a prosperous calico printer named Hermann Leo, invited Charles Hallé, the concert pianist and friend of Liszt and George Sand, to come to Manchester and, in Leo's words, "stir the dormant taste for art." Hallé did precisely that. Manchester already had respectable musical institutions, although not of a professional standard. Hallé remade its orchestra and, in decades of inspired leadership, "dragg[ed] the taste of its middle classes away from the seductions of the easy and the conventional" by a judicious mixture of the familiar and the new, introducing his audience for the first time to Berlioz and to Brahms's Third Symphony. Since Manchester had no opera house, he presented concert performances of the third acts of Wagner's *Lohengrin* and *Tannhäuser*. His experiments were supported with mounting enthusiasm by his middle-class patrons. In another, quite different city, Munich, the support of culture was largely the province of the crown, but independent groups of bourgeois businessmen often stimulated innovations in musical repertory and art exhibitions.

Gay makes the important point that the raising of standards of taste was not a natural process but often a matter of indoctrination. Many bourgeois did not know what they liked or what they should like, and here they needed someone to explain the importance of individual works of art and their deeper meaning. That function was performed by critics and, although many of those who posed as such spent most of their time pandering to popular taste—Gay remarks that "the lower reaches of French criticism were a slum"—the nineteenth century was fortunate in having others, like Charles Augustin Sainte-Beuve and Théophile Thoré, who considered it a privilege and a deep responsibility to act as arbiters of taste.

Lord Acton once said that an honest historian was unlikely to have friends. In his long career Sainte-Beuve proved that this also applied to critics, but he never allowed his independence of judgment to be compromised as he pursued his goal of seeking to "renew Art and liberate it from certain conventional rules." As for Thoré, the haunter of museums who first established the reputation of Vermeer, he was an uncompromising realist who labored to disabuse his readers of the idea that themes drawn from antiquity and mythology were the only proper ones for paintings and to persuade them that in any case beauty was the only true standard of judgment.

Gay acknowledges that it is difficult to say with any assurance whom the Victorian critics educated and with what result. Yet the fact that Matthew Arnold's authority as a critic of politics and literature extended well into our own time suggests that he was not unheard in his own, and the very volume of abuse directed at Sainte-Beuve surely indicated a fear that his *Causeries du lundi* were having too much influence upon their readers. It would be equally difficult to determine how many people had their knowledge and appreciation of art improved by the donations made by Victorian collectors to museums and galleries, and, in a book about the taste of the bourgeoisie, it is surely more profitable to concentrate on what an extraordinary number of these collectors there were. Gay gives us a catalog of businessmen with no artistic credentials who, out of idleness or self-gratification or the sudden awakening of aesthetic inspiration or the desire to fulfill an old love, decided to begin systematically purchasing paintings and sculpture. He writes about the American sugar tycoon Henry Havemeyer, whose wife persuaded him to begin collecting Courbet nudes, and the German industrialist Eduard Arnold, who after making millions from coal mines, gratified a lifelong interest in art by beginning to collect contemporary painters, first Lenbach, Böcklin, and Feuerbach and then the French Impressionists, building a collection that included five Manets and several Renoirs, Monets, Pissarros, Sisleys, and Cézannes. As donors to public museums, bourgeois collectors like these performed the role that governments had played in the eighteenth century as educators of the public taste.

As modernism reached its high point in Europe, Gay writes, "the best publicized avant-garde performances remained an alien country to most of the bourgeoisie." Even so, much had changed, thanks to the success of Sainte-Beuve and his fellows in liberating art and literature from the tyranny of received opinion. Gay believes that "for the most part it was the commitment, or the conversion, of cultivated bourgeoisie to the unconventional that would make the principle difference in the rise and triumph of modernism." At the same time, it is worth noting that many of the bourgeois who had learned to throw off old prejudices and appreciate new forms of art had acquired the zeal and belligerence that often goes with the acquisition of a new religion. Charles Rosen and Henry Zerner have written that "the trouble with nineteenth-century art is that it seems to have been almost impossible to be an interesting painter without creating some controversy."[8] In the age of modernism the pleasure wars that resulted were no longer waged between artists and *Philister* alone. Bourgeois warriors were embattled on all fronts.

III

Both Carl Schorske and Peter Gay have been strongly influenced in their historical work by the personality and thought of Sigmund Freud, and, in a statement in *Pleasure Wars* with which Schorske would certainly agree, Gay says that it is to Freud that he owes his "continuing sensitivity to the impact of social, political, economic realities on the mind." This common debt is apparent when they write about their own lives, as Schorske does in a short essay in *Thinking With History* and Gay in his little book *My German Question: Growing Up in Nazi Berlin*.

Schorske's essay, the larger part of which is an account of his teaching career at Wesleyan, Berkeley, and Princeton, will be of particular interest to readers who were themselves members of the academic community during the crises and cultural changes of the post-1945 years, a period of ardent reformers, and the 1960s, the time of rebellion of the frustrated and the defiant. Some of them will doubtless recognize their own experience in his account of how his psyche and his values and commitments were shaped by his discovery of Nietzsche and, later, by what he calls "the sudden blaze of interest in Sigmund Freud"; others will be struck by his acknowledgment that the development of the self is always subject to the dictates of the intractable external world and is often a circular process. At the end of this essay, Schorske writes:

> Preparing this account . . . made me realize all too clearly that I have not moved very far from the issues that arose in my formative years, when, under the pressures of history, the value claims of intellectual culture and the structure of social power first appeared in a complex interaction that has never ceased to engage me.

In Peter Gay's book, the external pressures upon the self are more insistent and menacing, for he describes the experience of growing up in Berlin as a child of a liberal and largely assimilated Jewish family in the first six years of Hitler's dictatorship and what the lasting effects of this experience were. In telling it, Gay, who escaped with his family to the United States in 1939, betrays a recurring exasperation with the many people who are apparently convinced that any Jew who did not leave Germany immediately after Hitler's accession was either a fool or a coward, and who underestimate the forces, both material and psychological, that militated against emigration, as well as (and this is often forgotten) the impossibility of predicting, at any time before 1938, what the Nazis intended to do about the Jews when the Nazis did not know themselves. "After spending years of pondering this matter," Gay writes, "I remain convinced that our critics have never quite understood our dilemmas in the 1930s; most of them never even took the trouble to understand them."

Gay's family had a fortunate existence compared with most Jews in Berlin. His father was a self-made man, "a striving bourgeois" and "faithful partisan of the German Social Democratic Party," whose business (which had to do with persuading specialty and department stores to sell mass-produced versions of high-priced articles that he selected) paradoxically flourished in the early Nazi years. Because he was a decorated war veteran, Peter was able to attend a Gymnasium of his choice, and his teachers treated him well. Thanks to his father's contacts, he was able to witness the 1936 Olympics and a championship soccer final between England and Germany, which he calls the greatest experience of his youth. He had no experience of bullying or terrorism that others had to suffer. Nevertheless, he writes, "even the most fortunate Jew who lived under Hitler has never completely shaken off that experience," and for adolescents like himself, he suggests, it may have been particularly hard, even when no brutality was involved, since they

> had to come to terms with their hormones amid massive slanders of their "race" and mounting threats to their survival, threats which were in themselves, not so subtly, offenses to their manhood or conviction of desirability . . . that must have disturbed and delayed our sexual development in troubling ways.

The time of brutality was not long delayed, and the attacks on the Jews in Vienna that followed the *Anschluss* were the prelude to the orgy of violence in Berlin on *Reichskristallnacht*, during which Gay's granduncle's shop on the Olivaerplatz was completely devastated. Gay's family now began to seek a way of leaving Germany, in a world in which there were many professions of sympathy for the Jews but very little willingness to take them in. Once again they were fortunate and made their way via Cuba to the United States. But the young Peter Joachim Israel Fröhlich brought to his new home a deep hatred for the Germany he left, a feeling that he repressed for years, refusing to talk about the Berlin that had been his childhood home and never visiting it until 1961. Not the least interesting part of his moving book, a book that he says is the "story of a poisoning and how I dealt with it," is the account of his personal *Vergangenheitsbewältigung*—the process by which he came to terms with his own past.

14

The End of the Golden Age

I

The last four years of the reign of William II of Germany—that is, those that stretched from the outbreak of the First World War until the Emperor's abdication—were of such tragic weight and consequence that they have tended to obscure the twenty-six years that preceded them. As a result, when these are studied at all it is generally only for the clues they yield to the catastrophe that was to follow. This is an unfortunate distortion, for seen in its own right the period from 1888 to 1914 was characterized by a degree of institutional stability, technological progress, and economic prosperity that Germany as a whole was not to enjoy again until the last years of the twentieth century, as well as by a cultural and intellectual eminence second only to that of the classical age of the years between 1770 and 1830.

That earlier time had been the age of the Kantian revolution in philosophy and the poetic and dramatic triumphs of Goethe and Schiller and Hölderlin, accomplishments which, because unchallenged by anything comparable in the sphere of politics, had won for Germany a reputation as the land of *Dichter und Denker*. In contrast, the second "age

Review of *Einstein's German World*, by Fritz Stern, *The New York Review of Books*, November 4, 1999, pp. 13–16. Reprinted with permission from *The New York Review of Books*. Copyright © 1999, NYREV, Inc.

of genius," as it was sometimes called, was dominated by natural scientists. The reign of William II witnessed tremendous progress in biological and virological research, which was facilitated by the foundation of great new research institutes financed by industry and the state, and was a golden age of physics which culminated in 1915 with Einstein's general theory of relativity. It was a time of great discoveries like tuberculin, and salvarsan, the "magic bullet" against syphilis, and the X-ray. And it was above all a time when science enjoyed an unblemished public renown, and scientists applied themselves to their calling with a disciplined zeal that reflected their belief that they were serving the cause of human progress. In 1911, when the Kaiser Wilhelm Society was founded, the chemist Emil Fischer declared, in a tribute to Paul Ehrlich, the discoverer of chemotherapy, that the future did not lie in the conquest of colonial empires; rather "chemistry and with it, more generally, all of natural science is the true land of boundless opportunities."

This faith in science was not unalloyed, and as it became more organized and more specialized, doubts emerged. Max Weber was not alone in fearing that the traditional centers of scientific inquiry, the universities, were becoming "state capitalist enterprises," managed for purposes external to learning for its own sake, and that freedom of inquiry was beginning to give way to the production of knowledge useful to the state for technical and economic reasons, if not for purposes of legitimating state authority.[1] And others remembered Nietzsche's concern over the heedless pace of modern science ("as if science were a factory and every minute's delay would bring punishment after it") and his troubled question, "What will become of science if it doesn't have time for culture? . . . Whence, where, why all science if it does not lead to culture? Perhaps to barbarity?"[2] These doubts, from which the early years of the period were relatively free, increased in number as Germany moved toward war and totalitarianism.

To introduce readers to the role of science and scientists in this critical period in German history, Fritz Stern, Seth Low Professor of History Emeritus at Columbia University, is uniquely qualified. He was born in 1926 in Breslau, where his father, a doctor, was a friend of the chemist Fritz Haber, who became his godfather, and one of his cousins was on intimate terms with Einstein. He has long been convinced that the German question, in all its guises, has had a decisive and tragic influence on the history of the world. It was perhaps inevitable that, after completing his great work on Bismarck and his banker Bleichröder and, particularly, his penetrating study of the romantic cultural pessimism that so colored rightist political thinking in Germany in the 1890s and during the Weimar Republic,[3] Stern should have begun to wonder about the ethos and sense of commitment of the great scientists of whom he had heard so much in his youth, the role of personality in their careers, the special pressures exerted upon them by official responsibilities or by government policy, and, since so many of them were Jews, how that fact affected their lives and work. These are the essential themes of his new book, and what he has to say about them is based upon intensive research on three continents.

It should not be surprising that the Jewish question is so central to this book. Stern rejects the thesis propounded by Daniel Goldhagen in his book *Hitler's Willing Executioners* that, with respect to the Jews, almost all Germans had an eliminationist cast of mind, and in a persuasive chapter points out that this is unproved and so inclusive as to be historically unprovable. That anti-Jewish prejudice existed in many forms is, however, undeniable, and Stern suggests that it had a certain seductive force for Germans, allowing them to believe in their own superiority while regarding specific traits—ruthless ambition, dogged self-assertion, a desire for power and money—as typically Jewish. This tendency was not, of course, restricted to Germany. When Einstein was being considered for a post at the University of Zürich, a faculty report asked his patron for more information about his character, since "Herr Dr. Einstein is an Israelite and since precisely to the Israelites among scholars are ascribed (in numerous cases not entirely without cause) all kinds of unpleasant peculiarities of character, such as intrusiveness, impudence, and a shopkeeper's mentality in the perception of their academic position."

This did not, however, prevent Einstein from getting the position. So also in the case of Paul Ehrlich, who, as Stern points out in a penetrating chapter on his work, suffered many slights and hindrances because of his Jewishness but was sustained by moral and practical support from colleagues and superiors like the famous internist Theodor Frerichs, once Bismarck's personal physician, Robert Koch, the discoverer of tuberculin, and Friedrich Althoff, a department head in the Prussian Ministry of Education from 1882 to 1907, whose ambition, Stern writes, "was to make Prussia's universities and research centers the best in the world, even against the will of opinionated professors with their insistence on autonomy, and in the teeth of prevailing religious biases."

In the same way, Max Planck, the father of the quantum theory, spent much of his time and energy continuing Althoff's work and, when the bad times came under Hitler, did what he could to defend Jewish scientists against attacks by the Nazis. In general, Stern feels that at its higher levels German science was distinguished by harmonious creativity, and that, although prejudice continued to be widespread in the country, by and large the achievements of Jews were recognized as an immeasurable boon to the nation, to German industry, and to Germany's international prestige, a fact to which the Emperor himself, a notorious anti-Semite, was not insensible. Even so, Jewish success was won at great psychic cost.

II

The careers of Fritz Haber and Albert Einstein, which are the subject of Stern's central chapter, illustrate this. The two men met for the first time in 1911 at a scientific conference in Karlsruhe. Both were already famous, Haber for his discovery of the fixation of nitrogen from the air, an achievement of great importance for German industry after it had been made practical by the Haber-Bosch process, which is still used today, Einstein for the extraordinary papers of 1905 that changed the prevailing view of the nature of the universe. As head of the Kaiser Wilhelm Institute of Physical Chemistry and Electrochemistry in Berlin, Haber had a major part in bringing Einstein to the capital in 1914, and the two men became intimate friends from the beginning, when Haber acted as adviser and go-between during the collapse of Einstein's first marriage.

Despite strong differences of character and personality—Einstein always the theorist and *Einzelgänger*, or loner, Haber the organizer and promoter, devoted to strengthening the ties between scientific progress and practical life—they shared one thing that made them friends until Haber's death. Stern writes:

Both cherished the scientific ethos, even if their ambitions and professional paths diverged; both were autodidacts; both had known early, daunting failures. They both had a sense of their calling and an austere view of their profession. They would have understood Freud's assessment in 1910: "Science betokens the most complete renunciation of the pleasure-principle of which our minds are capable."

Their dedication and the intensity of their labors took a toll on their health and, in each case, destroyed the happiness of their married life. Haber's first wife wrote in 1909 of his "smothering assertiveness for his purpose [i.e., of pursuing science] in the home and in the marriage," adding "All of Fritz's other human qualities except this one [the will to work] are close to shrinking and he is, so to speak, prematurely old."

Einstein, when he was working on the mathematical foundations of what was to become the general theory of relativity, wrote to his divorced cousin Elsa, with whom he was in love but whom he later renounced, "In the last half year I have worked more strenuously than ever before in my life and a few weeks ago I now finally solved the problem. . . . Now I have to give myself some peace or I shall go *kaput* right away."

Both Haber and Einstein were Jews who did not practice their religion. Haber, indeed, as if hoping to keep at a minimum any negative effect that his Jewishness might have upon his career, converted to Christianity in 1892 when he was twenty-four, although he was never a churchgoer and most of his friends continued to be Jewish. In his life religious ardor was replaced by an intense German patriotism and a desire to serve the state, which sometimes took excessive and unfortunate forms. In contrast, Einstein, except for a brief moment of "deep religiosity" in his youth, seemed to be indifferent to religion, which he regarded as a form of "the foolish faith in authority" that was inimical to truth. It would never have occurred to him to seek to advance his career by anything as self-serving as conversion, and, in any case, he scorned the zeal with which German Jews pursued assimilation. He had a deep admiration for German education and classical culture, but was insensible to anything like national feeling.

As Stern shows, this became clear after the outbreak of war. To the national enthusiasm of the days of August 1914, Einstein was completely immune. He regarded the conflict from the beginning as something insane and suicidal and wrote to a friend, "In a time like this one sees what a wretched animal species we belong to." From the beginning he was inclined to blame the Germans more than the Allies for the catastrophe that had ripped the civilized world apart, writing to his fellow pacifist Romain Rolland that the German victory of 1870 had left the country with

> a religious faith in power which found in [Heinrich von] Treitschke an appropriate, not an exaggerated, expression. This religion dominates the minds of almost all of the cultured elite; it [has] almost completely extruded the ideals of the Goethe-Schiller era.

Despite his commitment to science, he had the gloomiest of forebodings about its future, and in a moment of bitterness he wrote: "Our entire much-praised technological progress, and civilization generally, could be compared to an ax in the hand of a pathological criminal."

While Einstein sought to escape from World War I by concentrating on his own work, Haber responded to the crisis with patriotic enthusiasm. Along with Paul Ehrlich and Max Planck, he was one of the signers of the Manifesto of the 93, a declaration that asserted Germany's innocence in causing the war and denied that its troops had committed atrocities. This was a sign of his impulsive love of country, as well as of his political näiveté, for the manifesto alienated the very neutralist opinion that it was supposed to impress.

In more practical matters Haber could be adroit. He became the most important organizer of science in wartime Germany, educating the German military to the necessity of developing alternate sources for raw materials the nation had once imported and transforming his institute in Berlin, Stern writes, into a kind of Manhattan Project for the production of the nitric acid and the synthetic saltpeter that were indispensable for explosives and fertilizers. At the end of the war, the war minister wrote to him:

> Germany was not destined to emerge victoriously from this war. That it did not succumb already in the first few months to the superiority of its enemies in munitions, dynamite and other chemical compounds of nitrogen is in the first place due to you. . . . Your brilliant successes will always live in history and remain unforgotten.

What was unforgotten rather, especially among Germany's antagonists, was that Haber had been the proponent of the use of poison gas
as a weapon and the one whose researches made it feasible. He later
claimed that he had done so in the hope of bringing the war to a quick
conclusion and in the belief that gas was a more humane weapon than
artillery bombardment. But no one who had suffered the horror of a
gas attack was persuaded by these arguments and at the war's end his
name was on the Allied list of war criminals to be extradited for trial. It
did not come to that, but when the fighting stopped, Haber, whose
wife had committed suicide during the war, and who himself had
worked relentlessly for four years, was close to a nervous breakdown.

To Einstein, meanwhile, the defeat of Germany came as a liberation
from the weight of militarism; he was relatively optimistic about the
future of the new Weimar Republic and wrote happily, "I am enjoying
the reputation of an unblemished Socialist." Indeed, as Stern makes
clear, he was one of the beleaguered republic's strongest assets, for in
1919 observations of the solar eclipse confirmed the theory of relativity
and he became an international celebrity. In the years that followed, his
frequent visits abroad helped to reduce anti-German feeling by focusing attention on the eminence of German culture and science, and they
were encouraged by the German government for that reason. Well
aware that his discoveries were repudiated in many quarters in Germany because of professional jealousy or anti-Jewish prejudice, Einstein
remarked with his usual acerbic humor, "Funny people, these Germans. I am a stinking flower for them and still they keep putting me in
their buttonholes."

Despite their differences over wartime policy, Haber and Einstein
remained fast friends, and in the postwar years Haber was constantly
vigilant lest Einstein be lured away by one of the offers that frequently
came his way and persuasive in arguing that this would represent a national disaster. Together, they worked energetically and with some degree of success to improve international scientific cooperation and to
reduce the postwar tendency in the West to exclude Germany from
scientific conferences. Meanwhile, Haber became the driving force behind the founding of the Emergency Committee for German Science,
which was designed to raise funds for basic scientific research, not easy
in a time of runaway inflation and accomplished only at the risk of giv-

ing private industry excessive influence over the direction of policy. As patriotic as ever, Haber was worried about the effects of the disarmament clauses of the Versailles Treaty on Germany's independence and renewed his contacts with the military; he may have been involved in secret deliberations about poison gas and about armed collaboration between Germany and the Soviet Union. His own institute, meanwhile, was experimenting with pesticides and had developed the poison gas called Zyklon B, of whose future use he could have had no intimation.

Nor could he have known how quickly and radically his life was to change. His hectic existence had left him no time for political reflection. He may have felt vaguely that an authoritarian government of the type favored by General Kurt von Schleicher would be better than Weimar's fumbling party system. But he had no conception of what it would be like for Germany to fall into the hands of Hitler. He was to learn within days of the Enabling Act of March 1933 when a new law was promulgated for the "Restoration of the Civil Service" that required the dismissal of all non-Aryan civil servants. Because of his war service, Haber could have stayed on as director of his institute, but only by tolerating the dismissal of men who had been his trusted colleagues. He would not accept that humiliating condition and sent in his resignation, which was accepted immediately and, as he noted with bitterness, aroused no objections, least of all from industrial firms like I. G. Farben that had profited so richly from his work. Characteristically, he sought to enlist aid for the dismissed scientists and in May 1933 wrote Einstein, who had by this time left Germany. Einstein responded generously, but could not resist the wounding, if apt, remark: "I can conceive of your inner conflicts. It is something like having to give up a theory on which one has worked one's whole life. It is not the same for me because I never believed in it in the least."

III

In Stern's study of Einstein's German world, which included so much genius and ambiguity and tragedy, he has included portraits of two other remarkable figures. Walter Rathenau, the son of the founder of AEG, the great electrical concern, was basically driven by the desire for recognition—as an industrialist and financier like his father, as an intellectual whose writings about the spiritual condition of his country were taken seriously, and ultimately as a political leader in time of crisis. But he was well aware that his Jewishness stood in the way of his ambitions. He wrote in 1911,

> In the youth of every German Jew, there comes a moment which he remembers with pain as long as he lives: when he becomes for the first time fully conscious of the fact that he has entered the world as a second-class citizen, and that no amount of ability or merit can rid him of that status.

Unlike Fritz Haber, however, he did not consider the possibility of alleviating his condition by converting to Christianity, which he felt would be a form of opportunistic capitulation. He was determined to realize his ambitions on his own terms or not at all, not entirely aware, perhaps, that this defiance would alienate more people than it impressed and increase the hazards he would have to face.

Once the war came in 1914, Rathenau was appalled, as Fritz Haber had been, by the lack of preparations made by the military to conduct it effectively, and he kept pointing the failures out to the War Ministry until its officials reluctantly authorized him to make a statistical survey of the supply situation and to establish a central authority to control distribution of materials. This was the War Raw Materials Section of the War Ministry, which he directed until April 1915 and which probably staved off critical shortages that could have stopped the German war machine in its tracks. His resignation may have been prompted by disappointment at not having received a ministerial post; but the lack of amicable relations with his military colleagues may also have played a part, and he complained privately that the fact that as a private citizen and a Jew he had volunteered to serve the state was resented both by those who considered the state their own domain and by the Jews as well.

The fact was that Rathenau had a talent for alienating people by his propensity for giving advice, which was all the more annoying because it was right. The two books that he wrote in the last years of the war—*Days to Come* and *To Germany's Youth*—were systematic analyses of the social weaknesses—not least the rigid bureaucracies—that Germany had to overcome if it were to recover from the effects of the war; but they were written in a cloying and pretentious style, crammed with quotations and recondite allusions, that led many people to dismiss their author as an overeducated windbag. When the Weimar Republic began its short and troubled career, Rathenau's patriotism impelled him to seek an opportunity to serve it, and his economic talents qualified him for high office, but few people seemed to want him as a colleague. It was not until 1920 that he was asked to serve as a member of the German delegation to the Spa Conference on reparations. Some hoped that his knowledge of economics might persuade the Allies to moderate the reparations clauses of the Versailles Treaty, but that possibility was vitiated by the presence on the German delegation of General von Seeckt in full uniform and the fulminations of the industrialist Hugo Stinnes, who wanted to pay no reparations at all and resented Rathenau, who he said possessed a *"fremdrassige Seele"* (soul of an alien race), for seeking a compromise.

Rathenau's political moderation had, however, impressed Joseph Wirth of the Center Party, who became chancellor in 1921 and persuaded Rathenau to join his cabinet, first as minister of reconstruction and then, fatally, as foreign minister in 1922. The Wirth-Rathenau policy called for fulfillment of the treaty terms, in the hope of persuading the Allies of Germany's sincerity and eventually gaining a reduction of reparations. It was not a popular policy, and the choice of Rathenau to implement it was probably a mistake, for his technical abilities were offset by a fertility of imagination that made it easier for him to devise new schemes than to stick with established ones. He was also excessively sensitive to snubs. At the economic conference organized by Lloyd George at Genoa in 1922, Rathenau became so nervous at being excluded from private talks in the prime minister's villa that he allowed the Soviet delegation to persuade him to go off with them to Rapallo, where he signed a special pact of friendship and collaboration with the Soviet Union. The announcement of this had the effect of a bombshell, ending the Genoa talks without result, hardening France's intransigence with respect to reparations, and probably making inevitable its invasion of the Ruhr in January 1923.

But this was not the reason for his undoing. Einstein, who was interested in Rathenau's personality and was a shrewd critic of his talents and weaknesses, had urged him not to take the post of foreign minister because it would be considered a Jewish provocation. This was prescient. Rathenau's acceptance of the post was regarded as an outrage by apoplectic patrioteers of the right, and after Rapallo he was accused of treason by Karl Helfferich of the Nationalist Party. He was warned that his life was in danger, but he refused to take elementary measures of security. Pride and stubbornness were not the least of this complicated man's qualities. They did not help him now, for he was murdered by rightist thugs on June 24, 1922, as he was driving to his office.

If Rathenau was always motivated by private ambition, the driving force in Chaim Weizmann's life was the vision of a Jewish homeland in which—as Stern writes—"the best qualities of his people could be nurtured, in which men and women would make a barren land fruitful, unfettered at last from ancient hatreds and oppressions that had left such deep wounds and insecurities." Born near Pinsk in 1874, he grew up in Germany, Switzerland, and England, where, like many Jews of his time, he was drawn to the natural sciences and became a first-rate chemist; he might have dedicated his life to the laboratory had not Zionism absorbed most of his thought and energies. For this cause he possessed the requisite gifts: utter dedication and diplomatic gifts of the first order, including great personal charm. These made him, in the words of David Ben-Gurion, "the greatest Jewish emissary to the Gentile world," able to appeal to the liberal imagination in England and the United States, and to awaken a sense that Zionism was a noble cause.

Nor were his gifts as a scientist unimportant. During World War I he developed a new method of producing acetone, a vital ingredient in the manufacture of heavy artillery, and this gave him a standing with the British government and led to friendship with people like Lloyd George, Balfour, Winston Churchill, and Jan Smuts. Stern describes with great skill how this led to the Balfour Declaration of November 1917, which transformed Zionism from a dream to a practical possibility, and what happened later, when Britain's support of the homeland idea was compromised by the decline of its position in the Middle East and its growing conviction that it was necessary to appease the Arabs. Stern is particularly successful in describing how Weizmann was increasingly caught up in quarrels of different Jewish factions, ranging from assimilated Jews, who were indifferent to the idea of a homeland and believed that it militated against their own interests, to the moderate and radical wings of the Zionist movement. One of his most vocal critics was Einstein, who supported the Zionist cause but warned him against "nationalism à la prussienne," adding that if a way was not found to cooperate with the Arabs, "we deserve the fate that will befall us." This advice Weizmann did not find helpful, and he commented that Einstein seemed "to be acquiring the psychology of a *prima donna* who is beginning to lose her voice"; but what Einstein said was truer than he was willing to admit.

Throughout his life he had relied on moral persuasion to achieve his objectives. But in the years after 1933 that proved to be less effective, and when Weizmann urged the British government to agree to allow Jewish refugees from National Socialism to go to Palestine, he was balked by the British White Paper of 1939. Similarly, in 1945 and 1946, when the Jewish underground resorted to terrorism against the British forces in Palestine, he was powerless to prevent a course of action that he recognized as an offense against practical reason. Even when he went to Washington in 1948 to plead for the immediate recognition of the state of Israel, his success, which marked the culmination of his career, was at best a tentative one. Although he was elected the first president of the new republic, he had little influence over its policy during the cycle of violence and war that jeopardized its existence in the years that followed.

Something like the growing dissonance that Weizmann felt between himself and his times was common to most of the prominent members of what Stern has called Einstein's German world. This was true of Walter Rathenau, who had believed that a policy of accommodation with the West would alleviate Germany's postwar condition but discovered, at the cost of his life, that his country recognized force as the only legitimate solution; and it was equally so for Paul Ehrlich and Fritz Haber and Max Planck, who idealized the life of science but learned that it could be lived only at the expense of shameful compromise with the world of politics and prejudice. Only Einstein himself seemed immune to the pain that this discovery brought, but then Einstein had never expected much of the human race in any case and so was not surprised.

15

Politics and Literature

Fourteen years had passed since the defeat and collapse of the Nazi regime when Günter Grass's novel *Die Blechtrommel (The Tin Drum)* appeared to spectacular success in 1959.[1] But the past still cast a dark shadow over German life and politics. In the West, the conservative government of Konrad Adenauer had provided the country with continuity and political stability since the founding of the Federal Republic in 1949; yet, the chancellor was frequently criticized by the right as well as the left. Some of his appointments to political office often struck observers as influenced by a desire to rehabilitate former Nazis, and his decision to yield to the pressure of the Western Powers and rearm the country was regarded by the Socialists, the university community, and some of the churches as opening the door to a return of the militarism that had played such a baleful role in German history, while also making all prospects for the reunification of the country more difficult. The currency reform of 1948 had sparked a remarkable economic recovery,

"Politics and Literature," by Gordon A. Craig, reprinted by permission of the publisher from *A New History of German Literature*, David W. Wellbery, Editor-in-Chief, Judith Ryan, General Editor, pp. 871–75, Cambridge, Mass.: The Belknap Press of Harvard University Press, Copyright © 2004 by the President and Fellows of Harvard College.

but one of the principal effects of this *Wirtschaftswunder* (economic miracle) was to blunt the memory of the past and encourage people to turn a blind eye to the activities of neo-Nazi elements and the National Democratic Party, which gained considerable strength in the 1960s. Finally, the now aged chancellor's refusal to yield to those in his party who wished him to retire in favor of a more vigorous leader spread an air of disenchantment over the country; new ideas and initiatives were postponed, and government authority suffered in consequence. Grass's novel was informed by all of these circumstances and tendencies.

Born in the Free State of Danzig in 1927, Grass witnessed the growth of National Socialism in the city after 1935 and its takeover by Germany in 1939. He served in the German army in 1944–1945, and after war's end he worked as a stonemason before studying art in Düsseldorf and becoming a practicing artist. In politics, he was a committed Social Democrat from an early age and took an active interest in the issues of the day. In the years 1954 to 1955, he played a prominent role in agitations against rearmament, a position to which he held after he became one of Germany's most famous novelists. From the beginning, he was critical of those writers who had remained silent in face of the worst Nazi outrages, as he was of those ordinary Germans who accepted anything that was described as a matter of civic duty. In January 1967, in a speech to young people in Gelsenkirchen, he recalled the words of the governor of Berlin after Prussia's defeat by Napoleon's army at Jena in 1806, "The king has lost a battle; calm is the foremost civic duty" ("Der König hat eine Bataille verloren, Ruhe ist die erste Bürgerpflicht"). Germany, he said, would never become a democracy unless its citizens abandoned their propensity for order and adopted disquiet and agitation *(Unruhe)* as their primary obligation on important issues that affected the well-being of their society. By natural inclination, Grass tended to be a disturber of the peace.

When he became a practicing artist, Grass understandably turned to Group 47, a loose association of writers who believed that social activism was a legitimate part of their calling and were generally critical of the values of their time. Fritz Raddatz tells us that in the early years of his connection with this group, Grass was so impecunious that he had to sell his drawings and lithographs to other members so he could pay for travel expenses to the meetings. He also produced self-illustrated volumes of comic verse and several short plays that aroused attention for their brutal explicitness of language and the absurdity of their themes. But he was primarily interested in writing a contemporary novel. After several failed drafts and an unfinished verse epic about a bricklayer who becomes alienated by the affluent society and chains himself to a pillar, whence he issues manifestos like a modern stylite, Grass finally succeeded. At a meeting of Group 47 in Großholzleute in 1958, Grass read two chapters of the almost finished *Blechtrommel* and was awarded the highly coveted Group 47 Prize. Publication by Luchterhand followed one year later.

Hans Magnus Enzensberger has called *Die Blechtrommel* "a *Wilhelm Meister* drummed out on tin." This is apt, since Grass's theme is essentially that of growth, on three different levels: its leading character, whose physical growth is halted in 1927, when he is three years old, and does not resume until 1945; Nazism in Danzig; and democracy in western Germany during the occupation years and the first years of the Federal Republic, a development that is viewed with some skepticism.

Grass's approach is that of the *Schelmenroman,* the picaresque novel that describes the fantastic adventures of a hero with extraordinary gifts. During most of *Blechtrommel,* Oskar Matzerath, the son of a German grocer (although he suspects that his real father may be Jan Bronsky, an official in the Polish post office), looks and behaves like a child of three. His constant companion is a tin drum, which serves as his means of communication with the outside world and also as an instrument for awakening memories. His voice is capable of breaking glass from a great distance and with formidable accuracy, a gift he uses in self-defense and as an anarchic weapon against authority. Since he is unable to adjust to a regular school routine, his formal education is limited to what he gleans from a collection of loose pages torn from Goethe's *Die Wahlverwandtschaften (Elective Affinities)* and an illustrated, highly pornographic book about Rasputin. This combination endows his reflections on life with critical rationality as well as an unconquerable prurience. Thus armed, and with a proclivity for finding himself in situations of historical significance and violent issue, Oskar witnesses and recalls the tragic events of Danzig under Nazi rule.

In the early postwar period, German novelists who dealt with Nazism found it difficult to do so without resort to a highly metaphysical and symbolic approach. This was true of Elisabeth Langgässer *(Das unerlöschliche Siegel,* 1946; and *Märkische Argonautenfahrt,* 1950) as well as Hermann Kasack *(Die Stadt hinter dem Strom,* 1947), whose books were often moving but lacked immediacy or any urgent sense of the way in which German society had been corrupted by the Nazis. This was true also of Thomas Mann, who, perhaps because he spent most of the years of the Hitler dictatorship in the United States, chose in his great novel *Doktor Faustus* (1947) to demonize the movement, with the result that, as Michael Hamburger put it, he "paid a paradoxical tribute to its perverse appeal." The writers of Group 47, by contrast, were resolved to dissolve this nimbus of mystery and fate and to present Nazism in its everyday dress. Grass was certainly the most effective in doing this. *Die Blechtrommel* contains nothing that is either heroic or diabolical about the Nazis. They are bogus strongmen, whose banal rituals and mindless brutality would have been intolerable had the German middle class been able to distinguish between the trappings and the responsibilities of power and had they not been so deferential to the shouted commands of those in uniform.

Representative of these compliant masses is Oskar's father, who is portrayed proudly piecing together his uniform, first the cap, "which he liked to wear even in fine weather with the 'storm strap' in place, scraping his skin," then the brown shirt, and finally "the shit-brown riding britches and high boots." In this array, he attends the Sunday demonstrations of the party on the Maiwiese (the same demonstration whose martial order Oskar disrupts by inspired beating of his drum in three-quarter time). The older Matzerath, Oskar tells us, was uncompromising about his attendance at these events even in the worst of weather and refused to carry an umbrella while in uniform. "Duty is duty, and schnaps is schnaps!" he said.

It was the incorrigible romanticism and the hidden resentments of people like Matzerath that made them responsive to the appeals of Nazism. And it was their confused conviction that duty has its own imperatives regardless of its object that transformed them into brutes who could convince themselves that they were doing something admirable and noble when they are—as in *Blechtrommel*—breaking up a Jewish toy-merchant's shop and defecating on his rugs or ordering the machine gunning of a group of nuns on an outing at the beach.

The Nazis were sustained, moreover, by a collective stupidity that was ready to believe in the patently impossible. In an eloquent passage that reveals his creator's anger at the established churches for encouraging this foolish faith, Oskar says:

> An entire credulous nation believed, there's faith for you, in Santa Claus. But Santa Claus was really the gasman. I believe—such is my faith—that it smells of walnuts and almonds. But it smelled of gas. . . . Credulous souls . . . believed in the only-saving gas company which symbolizes destiny with its rising and falling gas meters and staged an Advent at bargain prices. Many to be sure believed in the Christmas this Advent seemed to announce, but the sole survivors of these strenuous holidays were those for whom no almonds or walnuts were left—although everyone had supposed there would be plenty for all.

Oskar's life and adventures as an adolescent are set against a historically accurate, and sometimes remarkably circumstantial, account of the rise and fall of National Socialism in Danzig. He witnesses the first agitations of the movement, the growth of anti-Semitism and its violent eruption in November 1938, the Nazi assault on the Polish post office which ended with the conquest of the city and touched off the war against Poland, the impact of the Second World War on the populace, and the Russian bombardment and occupation. Oskar's involvement in these events is often accidental and generally accompanied by the death of people close to him, for which he bears varying degrees of responsibility. Sigismund Markus, the supplier of his drums, dies in his shop on *Reichskristallnacht;* Oskar's Polish uncle, who is probably his real father, doing him a service, becomes involved against his will in the defense of the Polish post office and is shot by the Nazis after its surrender; during Oskar's visit to the Atlantic Wall, his diminutive sweetheart is killed by a bomb at the beginning of the Allied invasion when she goes to get a cup of coffee that he has refused to fetch; a youth gang called the Dusters, of which he becomes the leader during the disintegration of Nazi Danzig, is betrayed to the police, and all of its members, except for Oskar, are condemned to death; and his German father is shot by the Russians as he tries to swallow his Nazi badge and chokes because Oskar has left its clasp undone when he handed it to him. After this last debacle, Oskar, as if driven by a compelling desire to lead a normal existence, begins to grow again and moves with the remaining members of his family to the West.

He works for a time as a stonemason (as Grass did himself), and later as an artist's model and a jazz musician. However, his erotic adventures, which are as complicated in his new existence as they were in the old, lead to his being charged with murder and placed in an institution. On the eve of his thirtieth birthday, he is proved innocent of the charge and released. Now of almost normal size, he is free to plan a new career. As he looks to the future, however, he is seized by nameless foreboding and memories of sins committed in the past.

> Always somewhere behind me, the Black Witch.
> Now ahead of me, too, facing me, Black.
> Black words, black coat, black money.
> But if children sing, they sing no longer:
> Where's the Witch, black as pitch?
> Here's the black, wicked Witch.
> Ha! ha! ha!

Oskar, like his creator, is doubtful about the stability of Western society. Too many of its citizens complain about how much healthier German society would have been, how gloriously the arts and sciences would have flourished, if only there had been no currency reform and everyday existence had remained what it was in the worst days of the occupation. This tendency, which Oskar calls the "romanticism of lost opportunities," does not prevent them from indulging in the worst excesses of an affluent society, becoming self-absorbed and insensitive to the needs of others. For a time, Oskar is a musician at the Onion Cellar, a nightclub where the customers pay exorbitant sums for the right to cut up onions so they can weep again and give vent to their pent-up feelings of guilt. Even worse is the uncertainty many people feel about the legitimacy of the new order and the incompleteness of their mental liberation from the old. On a midnight excursion, Oskar and a friend become involved with two ominous-looking types in green hats, who are dragging a third man between them and, on being challenged, confess that they are seeking a quiet place where they can kill him. They produce an official order of execution dated October 1939 as justification. Nothing that Oskar and his friend say about the peace settlement and the new government can dissuade them; one of the green hats points out that their arguments are without juridical foundation, since the peace treaty was never signed or even drawn up. "I vote for Adenauer just the same as you do," one of them says. "But this execution order is still valid; we've consulted the highest authorities. We are simply doing our duty and the best thing you can do is to run along."

The reception of *Die Blechtrommel* was remarkable for the extremes of opinion it elicited. Praise of the vitality of Grass's style, his extraordinary poetic gifts, and the genius of his power of invention predominated, but many critics seemed worried about his burlesque attacks on organized religion, his de-romanticized treatment of relations between the sexes and the exuberant detail with which he described them, and the savage, often sadistic, inventiveness of his prose when he was writing about things that had been held sacred by the pre-war generation.

Grass might have responded to those who decried the bluntness of his language that they were rather missing the point and forgetting the fateful role language played in creating National Socialism, propagating its doctrines, and concealing its crimes. In his novel *Hundejahre (Dog Years)*, Grass launched a devastating attack on the bureaucrats, soldiers, philosophers (particularly Martin Heidegger and his followers), professors, and churchmen who manipulated and corrupted the German tongue during the Nazi period. He held the conviction that the German language had to be purged of this debasement to make it worthy of serving the new German democracy. The prose of *Die Blechtrommel*, its frankness, its explicitness, its outrageous humor, and its insistence on calling a spade a spade, marks the beginning of Grass's important contribution to the cleansing process.

16

Berlin: The Hauptstadt, Back Where It Belongs

In 1840 the Prussian writer Willibald Alexis published a three-volume historical novel, *The Roland of Berlin*, set in the fifteenth century. It told the story of a heroic Bürgermeister who fought to protect the liberties of his city against the depredations of an ambitious ruler, the Hohenzollern elector of Brandenburg, Frederick II, known as Irontooth. It is a stirring story, and Alexis, a writer of pronounced liberal convictions intent on creating a myth for his own time, invested his fifteenth-century Berliners with political virtues that they had probably never possessed and with a degree of success that they had certainly never attained. For in real life Irontooth, when he encountered the burghers' opposition to his curtailment of civil rights and his determination to build a palace on the island between the two arms of the Spree, crushed the nascent revolt without difficulty and threw the statue of the fabled Roland, traditional symbol of town rights, into the river. The Hohenzollern remained supreme in Berlin and surrounding Brandenburg-Prussia for the next 470 years, until the day in November 1918 when Emperor William II abdicated and fled to Holland.

Reprinted by permission of *Foreign Affairs*, 77: 4 (July/August 1998). Copyright © 1998 by the Council on Foreign Relations, Inc.: www.ForeignAffairs.com.

Hohenzollern Berlin

The long, uninterrupted Hohenzollern tenure is the most important fact in Berlin's history. It ended the disorder under the robber barons in the half-century that preceded Irontooth's conquest of the city in 1440 and avoided the internecine strife of other German states, caused by disputes over succession and challenges to constituted authority.

From the beginning the Hohenzollern were proud of their capital, their *Hauptstadt*, and served it well. The first electors, for example, set out to attract new trades and expand commerce, introducing paved streets and a more efficient water system and establishing schools for the education of their civil servants, like the Berlinische Gymnasium zum Grauen Kloster, which would one day number Otto von Bismarck among its pupils. The Great Elector (ruled 1640–88) built a canal linking the Spree and the Oder and opened his lands to the Huguenots driven from France, who had a positive and permanent effect on Berlin's economy and culture.

Most of the Hohenzollern were instinctively aware that the prestige of a great state depends to some extent on the attention it pays to the appearance of its capital city and the energy with which it promotes arts and letters. Thus the Great Elector's son Frederick, who became the first king of Prussia in 1701, remodeled the royal palace in ornate Baroque style and, just across the Spree, built a handsome armory, the Zeughaus, which is today being given a new, less martial appearance by the American architect I. M. Pei. Frederick's wife, Sophie Charlotte, turned the royal residence into a center of the arts, where her guests engaged in discussion with distinguished scholars like Pufendorf and Leibniz and listened to chamber music and the first opera ever heard in Berlin. Meanwhile, the court was itself an active promoter of Enlightenment thinking.

Even more energetic in these respects were Frederick the Great (ruled 1740–86) and his successors at the end of the eighteenth century, who continued the embellishment of the city by building at the head of Unter den Linden the opera house, the royal library, and the palace of Prince Henry, which housed the university when it was founded in 1809. At the foot of the great boulevard rose Karl Gotthard Langhans's Brandenburg Gate with the dramatic quadriva by Gottfried Schadow, architectural triumphs of which any city would be proud.

The Hohenzollern expected much of their subjects and for the most part got it. Berliners were profoundly influenced by the dynamism, the ability to surmount crisis, and the orientation toward the future that characterized their rulers, not only in the city's early history but during the remarkable economic expansion that began in 1830, transforming Berlin into a world city and the capital of the German empire. They tended to be energetic, ebullient, colorful in their speech, sentimental, quick at repartee, more often than not optimistic, and courageous in time of trouble.

The nineteenth-century writer Theodor Fontane, who spent most of his life in the city, often criticized the *Berliner Schnauze* (loudmouthedness) and provinciality of his fellow citizens. He once wrote that the Berliner was "an egoistic narrow small-towner. The city grows and grows, the millionaires increase tenfold, but a certain pettiness persists that expresses itself in the belief that mother's dumplings are the best." Even so, Fontane wrote in 1853, one should not forget the Berliner's sound moral sense, belief in equality, and readiness to sacrifice. In 1813, during the war of liberation from Napoleonic rule, Berlin had not only supplied several regiments of the line to the allied armies but had also sent 10,000 volunteers—out of a population of only 180,000—to the front.

The strong-minded Berliners regarded their rulers, at least until the growth of the Social Democratic party at the end of the nineteenth century, with a mixture of loyalty, gratitude, and affection. This is understandable in the case of heroic figures like the Great Elector, whose victory over the Swedes in 1675 was hailed by Berliners as a promise of security and new hope, and Frederick the Great, who saved the state by sheer determination during the Seven Years' War, and William I (ruled 1861–88), who was Bismarck's sometimes grumbling partner in the creation of the new German Reich.

But the people felt the same toward the eccentric and the less obviously successful members of the dynasty. These included Frederick William IV, who had the misfortune to be on the throne when the revolution of 1848 swept over Germany. Though an indecisive leader in a crisis, he was a great wit whose jokes were repeated with appreciation throughout the city. As for the melancholic Frederick William III, the death of his wife, the beautiful and brave Queen Luise, won him universal sympathy during his long reign, from 1797 to 1840. Berliners even accorded affection to the formidable Frederick William I (ruled 1713–40), although his appearances in the streets of Berlin sometimes made his subjects run away. The monarch would chase after them, belabor them with his stick, and demand to know why they had fled. If they admitted being afraid of him, he would redouble his blows and shout, "You should love me, love me!"

On the whole, they did, and this sympathetic tie between the Hohenzollern and the inhabitants of their capital continued until the last days of Emperor William II, when it became clear to all but the most inveterate royalists among his subjects that he was unwilling to share the fate his irresponsibility had brought down upon them.

"Get out of Berlin!"

For a long time before the collapse of 1918, Germans outside the capital resisted Berlin's mystique and its claims to primacy. It was what he considered to be the pretentiousness of the city and its inhabitants that led the Göttingen physicist and writer of aphorisms Georg Christoph Lichtenberg to write in the 1770s, "I should like to be king of Prussia for a single day so that I could give the Berliner what they deserve." Goethe visited Berlin only once, in May 1778, and was not impressed. Later he called it a prosaic city, bereft of any demonic qualities—a curious remark from one who spent his life in a town as unexciting as Weimar. As for Gotthold Ephraim Lessing, friend of such leading luminaries of the Enlightenment as Friedrich Nicolai and Moses Mendelssohn, he became disenchanted with the city when he failed to secure the post of royal librarian and his play *Minna von Barnhelm* fell afoul of the censor. He left town in high dudgeon, and later wrote:

> How can one feel well in Berlin? Everything there makes one's gorge rise. Don't talk to me of your freedom of thought and publication in Berlin. It consists only of the freedom to publish as many idiotic attacks on religion as one wants—a freedom of which any honest man would be ashamed to avail himself.
>
> But just let anyone try to write about other things in Berlin. . . . Let him attempt to speak the truth to the distinguished rabble at court, to stand up for the rights of the subject, and—as now happens in France and Denmark—raise his voice against despotism,

and you will realize which country, up to the present day, is the most enslaved in Europe.

Those holding such views became more vocal after the failure of the revolutions of 1848, when Prussian troops became the main agent in suppressing the risings in Baden and Saxony and in ending the possibility that Frankfurt am Main might become the capital of a democratic— or at least a liberal—Germany. Criticisms were heard even more frequency after the Prussian victories over Austria and France and Berlin's elevation as the *Hauptstadt* of the new Reich in 1871.

On the subject of the new capital, the political publicist Konstantin Frantz was scathing. He had already denounced the constitution of the empire because, in his view, it failed to reflect German history and was a mere amalgam of foreign forms and ideas. In words that reflected the growing concern of many Berliners themselves about the increase in the number of Jewish residents in the city (45,000 in 1880, at a time when there were only 51,000 in all of France and only 46,000 in England), Frantz wrote that the Hohenzollern city was better suited to be the capital of a Jewish Reich than a German one:

> One meets here in all areas of public life the arrogant Jew . . . the flea-market and marts-of-trade and stock-market Jew, the press and literature Jew, the parliamentary Jew, the theater and music Jew, the culture and humanity Jew, and—what is unique to Berlin—the city government Jew. Almost half of Berlin's city councillors . . . are Jews . . . and hand in hand with their kept press and stock-market, they actually control the whole city government.

Frantz's sentiments were shared by a gallimaufry of anti-urban romantics, including Paul Lagarde and Julius Langbehn, who idealized the Germanness of peasant life and regarded the city as a threat to German community and culture, a hotbed of cosmopolitanism and vice. The poet Rainer Maria Rilke in his *Book of Hours* portrayed the city as a rotten center of materialism and depravity, whose inhabitants

> name their snails' slime progress . . .
> and are conscious of themselves and
> sparkle like whores
> and make louder noises with metal
> and glass.

To writers like these, and many of their readers, the slogan "Los von

Berlin!"—"Get out of Berlin!"—was congenial.

German critics of Berlin were, however, greatly outnumbered by non-Berliners fascinated by the big city and irresistibly drawn by the apparently unlimited possibilities it offered the clever, the energetic, and the courageous. The dispatches from Berlin to the *Breslauer Zeitung* in the 1890s by the theater critic Alfred Kerr help explain the hold the great city had over the popular imagination as the new century approached. Kerr described the capital's educational and scientific eminence, the wonders of its industrial invention, its theater, the most daring and modern in the world. Even in its everyday life, Kerr showed, Berlin was exciting—its scandals and crimes, its smart cafés, a parade to celebrate the anniversary of the birth of William I, a congress on women's rights, a trade fair that mounted a replica of Old Berlin complete with buildings, shops, and costumed natives. The very air of the city, nervous, endlessly quivering, smelled of the future.

Such attractions, and the authority that came from historical continuity, were enough to protect Berlin not only from the unrealistic mouthings of the anti-urban romantics of the nineteenth century but from the threat to the city's primacy posed by the crisis that followed the Great War and the revolution of 1918.

"Weimar" Berlin

Three times this century the question has presented itself: is it appropriate that the capital of Germany be a city that is inevitably associated with the most tragic episodes in Germany's recent past?

In its first elucidation after the fall of the Hohenzollern, the challenge to Berlin as the *Hauptstadt* arose from the fact that the surviving German state was a democratic republic, defined as such in the first article of the constitution proclaimed in August 1919. Many of the drafters of this constitution felt the provincial center of Weimar would be a more fitting capital for the new Germany; after all, it had been the home of Goethe and of Schiller, who had tried to teach Germans that greatness should be measured not in terms of power, but of moral conviction and dedication to freedom. On the other hand, was not Berlin the preeminent symbol of the united Germany that Bismarck had created, and would not the choice of any other *Hauptstadt* be tantamount to accepting the diminished status that the Allies at Versailles appeared to be imposing on Germany for all time? One did not have to stay long in Weimar to understand that it would never be a place where, as Fontane said of Berlin, everything that happened or did not happen impinged on world events. The parliamentarians of that day refused to repudiate history for the sake of a democratic gesture, and Berlin remained the capital.

This identification of the Hohenzollern capital with the nation took another political form. It now became the basic assumption of the politics of extremism, both left and right, that whoever took Berlin ruled Germany. Spartakus Week and the Kapp Putsch of 1920 were the first attempts to prove this, and one might have thought that the results would have been discouraging, since both were defeated essentially by action from the provinces. But these failures in no way diminished the symbolic importance of Berlin in the eyes of adherents of revolutionary movements. To capture Hamburg or Dresden or Munich, they all agreed, would be to register at best an inconclusive triumph. Thus the anti-republican conspiracy that centered in the paramilitary forces in Küstrin in September 1923 put its hopes in a direct thrust at Berlin. Thus also, the conservative forces who planned later that year to bring down the Stresemann government and replace it with a quasi-military dictatorship counted on diversions taking place in other cities but always regarded Berlin as the center of the action. Adolf Hitler, whose hijacking of that enterprise led to the failed putsch in Munich in November, did not think differently.

Hitler's Berlin

Originally, Hitler's Nazi movement had been strongly rural. Many of its first leaders had been members of the *Artamanenbewegung*, a youth movement concerned about urbanization and the flight from the land, whose program foreshadowed the *Blut und Boden* ideology of Walther Darré. Darré himself, Hitler's Reich Peasant Leader after 1933, called for an open attack on big-city culture, capitalism, and Jews and a return from the pluralistic to the organic state, restoring the vital connection between land and people.

Hitler was not inclined to encourage such prejudices by giving them concrete form. To be sure, he never liked Berlin or Berliners any more than they liked him. Proud of what he fancied his own artistic talents, he was unimpressed by the grandeur of the capital and often said that it should be rebuilt by southerners. As for the Berliners, he did not enjoy their wit or their audacity in lampooning him and his comrades in satire (Kurt Tucholsky's pretend schoolboy essay, "Goethe and Hitler," for example) and music hall song, as in the popular "I Wonder What Adolf Has in Store for Us?" with its gibes at the provincialism of National Socialism. But Hitler recognized Berlin as the only possible capital and resolved that it would be his. He would have nothing to do with the slogan "Los von Berlin!" and adopted another one coined by the pre-war agricultural romanticist Leonhard, "Bestürmt wird nun die schwarze Stadt!" ("Now will the Black City be stormed!").

That explains why in 1926, after the Nazi movement had recovered from the debacle of the Munich putsch and resumed its march to power, Hitler appointed Joseph Goebbels the *Gauleiter*, or administrative district leader, of Berlin, giving him the mission of conquering the city. Goebbels never actually succeeded in that, but he revived the fortunes of the Berlin Nazi party and its fighting arm, the Stormtroopers. Goebbels was clever enough at propaganda to contribute powerfully to Berlin's political turbulence in the years of the Great Depression, including the breakdown of morale among workers for the city's public services. His dramatic slogans, his carefully planned street battles with communists touched off by provocative invasions of working-class districts, his campaign of calumniation against police officials—these and other Goebbels inspirations put the Nazis on the map in Berlin.

In January 1933, when Hitler was appointed chancellor, it was Goebbels who turned the event into a grandiose torchlight spectacle, with massed brown-clad columns marching jubilantly under banners accompanied by military music down Unter den Linden, along the Wilhelmstrasse, and past the Reich Chancellery. Goebbels well knew the effect this symbolic capture of Berlin would have on the country, preparing it psychologically to accept the real conquest of Germany that was to come in the months ahead.

Any prejudices Hitler might have had against Berlin disappeared once he became its ruler. As Alexandra Richie writes in her new history of the city, *Faust's Metropolis*, the creation of a new Berlin more beautiful than Paris, more splendid than Vienna, more powerful than ancient Rome, was fundamental to his vision of the future. What we know now about the monstrous plans hatched in his brain and that of his favorite architect, Albert Speer, gives us no reason to believe that he would ever have succeeded in clothing his dream with reality. In the event, his chance to do so was spoiled by his overarching political ambitions and the war they unleashed. Berlin was smashed to bits by Allied bombs and its remnants divided among four conquerors who undertook to govern the city and the country jointly through an Interallied Control Council and a military *Kommandatura* in the divided capital.

Four-Power Berlin

The summer of 1945 marked the first time since1806, when Napoleon entered the city after the Prussian defeat at Jena, that Berlin was subject to foreign rule. It was not an arrangement designed to last long. The old maxim that whoever ruled Berlin ruled Germany, which had animated the German communist party in the Weimar years just as it had the Nazis, determined the policy of the city's new Soviet patron. From the start, the Soviets put difficulties in the way of the administration of the western sectors by sporadic interference with the Western powers' access to the city, which depended on Soviet cooperation since all roads ran through their zone of occupation. Importing food and fuel was always problematical, and when political activity resumed in the city, the Soviet occupation authorities attempted to suppress its free expression.

The failure of this policy of pinpricks to produce effective results goaded the Soviets in 1948 to blockade the city. This coup was in the end defeated by an Allied airlift of supplies to Berlin's western districts and by the patience and fortitude of the Berliners, led by their inspiring mayor, Ernst Reuter. This was a startling setback for the Soviet Union, but not a definitive one, as would be demonstrated by the menacing Khrushchev note of 1958 and the long emergency that followed, culminating with the building of the Berlin Wall on August 13, 1961, and ending only when the Cuban missile crisis was resolved in October 1962.

The behavior of Berliners during the blockade transformed their image in the West from beaten and despised foes into allies in a deepening Cold War. The narrowness of the victory, however, the awareness that the threat might be resumed, and the hardening of the line that now divided Europe cast doubt on the advisability of making the riven city the capital of West Germany.

Thus when the Western allies merged their zones of occupation and began the process that produced the Federal Republic of Germany in western Germany in May 1949, the parliamentary council that approved the new republic's basic law chose, by a vote of 33 to 29, to make the Rhineland town of Bonn the provisional capital until such time as the reunification of the country would allow a return to Berlin. In September the Soviets responded by proclaiming the German Democratic Republic in their communist zone. Contravening the provisions of the Potsdam Agreement for Four Power administration of Berlin, the Soviet Union gave theoretical control of the eastern part of Berlin to the GDR, which promptly established its capital in the urban district of Pankow.

Both provisional capitals found themselves preoccupied with history, ever the fate of Eastern Europe. Bonn had no history of its own to speak of, except as the birthplace of Ludwig van Beethoven and the town from which Carl Schurz set out on his exploits during the revolution of 1848. At first this seemed an advantage, since the western parliamentarians could do their work without constant reminders of the unhappy past in the form of ruined buildings. As time passed, it became less of one. Without a real past, or the physical appearance that a real past would have produced, Bonn had nothing with which to combat the growing crisis of identity engendered by the National Socialist experience and the blockage it represented to historical continuity. This was all too apparent in 1986–87, in the protracted and muddled *Historikerstreit*, or controversy of the historians, when adversaries exchanged charges of obsession with guilt for Nazi crimes and of blindness to the need for a new patriotism in teaching history to a new German generation.

East Berlin, on the other hand, was confronted daily by too much history in visible form, all of it ideologically offensive to communist principles. The communist leadership reacted violently and injudiciously by striking out at the Hohenzollern. In 1950–51 they blew up the royal castle, the finest example of North German Baroque architecture in the city and the residence of the Prussian margraves, electors, and kings from 1470 to 1918. The building had been badly damaged during the heavy Allied air bombardment of February 3, 1945, but its walls were strong and it could have been reconstructed had the communists not wished to make a political statement.

They followed this up with the removal from the middle of Unter den Linden of the equestrian statue of Frederick the Great and the expulsion from the Opernplatz of statues of Blücher, Gneisenau, and Scharnhorst, heroes of the wars against Napoleon. Not content with this, the communists carried their campaign against historical memory far outside the city, transforming the castle of Frederick William III and Queen Luise in Paretz into an institute for animal husbandry and reducing to farmland the park in which the queen had loved to wander, and in Schönhausen destroying the birthplace of William I's loyal servant Otto von Bismarck.

All this frenetic activity was pointless, for its propaganda value was negligible and it did nothing to establish historical legitimacy for the communist regime. Where the castle had stood there was now a waste space that the communists did not have the wit to fill until the 1970s— and then with buildings of socialist monumentality so ugly that they only emphasized what had been lost.

In 1981, when the West German government sponsored a highly praised and well-attended exhibition on Prussia in the Gropius Bau, abutting the western side of the Wall, communist authorities abruptly reversed their policy of indiscriminate destruction. Fearing that the Federal Republic would succeed in appropriating the best of the Prussian tradition for its own purposes, the Pankow regime began to encourage its historians to write on Prussian themes. The statues of the military heroes were returned to their former places, and one day pedestrians on Unter den Linden discovered, to their pleasant surprise, that old Fritz was back too.

Bonn and Berlin

The relationship between Berlin and Bonn grew increasingly strained during the Cold War. The first chancellor of the Federal Republic, Konrad Adenauer, had always hated Berlin, whose inhabitants he regarded as un-German, if not indeed Asiatic. He waited nearly a year after his election before visiting Berlin, and he invariably placed a low value on the outpost-city's importance to the future of a free Germany.

When in the 1950s the American secretary of state, John Foster Dulles, intimated that circumstances might require the risk of nuclear war to protect Western interests, Adenauer protested, "For God's sake! Not over Berlin!"

The average West German did not share this visceral distaste, and indeed was likely to admire Berliners for their courage during the blockade and during the workers' uprising in East Berlin on June 17, 1953. As time passed, however, and the hedonism induced by the *Wirtschaftswunder* (economic miracle) spread, it was accompanied by a growing desire for quiet times and a subconscious irritation with Berlin, which always seemed to be causing crises. Even in quiet times, it appeared, Berlin required inordinate subsidies to assure its existence. For their part, West Berliner had a growing feeling that the Germany that they described by the dismissive word *Drüben* ("over there") had no appreciation of, or sympathy for, their problems. The cooling of relations became worse when, after the long Berlin crisis of the 1950s and 1960s, Bonn politicians became interested in *Ostpolitik*, the policy of seeking accommodation with the regime in the GDR and the other governments of Eastern Europe in the interests of European peace. German unification ceased to be a top priority, and as far as Berlin was concerned, Bonn seemed intent only on doing nothing that would encourage another June 17, 1953. Both Bonn and Berlin registered complete surprise when the GDR collapsed like a house of cards in 1989, and German unification came about virtually overnight.

For the third time in the century the question of the *Hauptstadt* arose, although one might have thought the issue had been settled in 1949, with the general assumption that Berlin would become the capital again as soon as reunification was accomplished. But the small town on the Rhine had become a symbol of security and the German tie with the West, whereas Berlin seemed to point in the wrong direction— summoning up memories of the Hohenzollern, the failed Weimar Republic, and all the horrors that followed. The imminent prospect of making good on a promise from dark days for an era too hypothetical even to contemplate now generated agitation in the West.

The influential editor of the Hamburg weekly *Die Zeit*, Countess Marion Dönhoff, wrote in May 1990,

The legacy of Berlin as the seat of Nazi power makes it unsuitable to be the capital of a democratic Germany anxious to bed itself down in a unified Europe. The decision to make Berlin the capital would send out a false signal. It could tempt Germans, even without their intending it, to embark on the path to becoming a nation-state instead of keeping the European goal in mind.

More extreme supporters of Bonn sought to blacken Prussia's and Berlin's reputation by making them responsible for all the crimes of the past, conveniently forgetting Prussia's historical reputation for religious tolerance and openness to refugees from other lands. They overlooked as well the fact that National Socialism had sprung from the provinces rather than Berlin, and that the most spectacular instances of resistance to the Nazis, as to the communists, had taken place in the capital.

Not to return to Berlin would amount to a permanent affront to the five *Länder*, or states, of the former GDR, whose incorporation into a democratic united Germany was a matter of highest priority. That aside, the strongest argument for returning the capital to Berlin came from reflecting on the alternative. Willy Brandt, the former mayor of Berlin and the former chancellor of West Germany, made the point in a remark that aroused much resentment: "It would never have occurred to anyone in France to remain in relatively idyllic Vichy once foreign power no longer prevented a return to the Seine." The implication was that nations of the first rank have an obligation to history, their own self-respect, and their subjects to ensure that their capital cities are characterized over the changing epochs by dignity and grace and vital force.

Of those qualities, Bonn had none. The pleasant town on the Rhine was, as the historian Michael Stürmer said, "a shamefaced capital of a shamefaced state. . . . Now, however, the time has come, in matters of symbols, style and architecture, to make up for what for forty years seemed superfluous because of the German past and the European future." That recompense would become possible only in Berlin.

The *Hauptstadt* controversy at the turn of the 1990s was long and acrimonious, culminating in a protracted debate in the Bundestag on June 20, 1991, after which the deputies voted, 337 to 320, for the return to Berlin. The closeness of the vote was doubtless due in part to worry about the costs of the move and to calculations by government officials who had bought homes in Bonn of the personal losses they would suffer from a swift fall in property values. But more important was the way in which it reflected fears that were not, and perhaps could not be, given rational expression. For the most striking feature of this important decision was that it was accompanied by so little enthusiasm and rejoicing and by so many nameless fears. This puzzled Germany's allies. At an academic conference in Tutzing in March 1993 on the theme of *Angst*, the mode word of the moment, Henri Ménudier, a professor at the Sorbonne, said that no one in France was afraid the shift of Germany's capital would invite a reversion to National Socialism. Rather, there was growing concern about what appeared to be a collective neurosis in Germany, a subconscious preparation for a catastrophic end, which would make the unified nation incapable of facing up to a crisis.

This was, of course, an exaggeration. As Germany prepared for its change of capital at the century's end, *Angst* was replaced by vigorous search for the best way to remodel the public face of Berlin so that it could represent both its past and its future as the capital of a democratic republic in a united Europe.

In his impressive book, *Capital Dilemma*, Michael Z. Wise describes how politics and ideology impinge upon architecture. He stresses that Berlin will not become the sole locus of political power in Germany. Several ministries will stay behind in Bonn, the president and federal chancellor will retain offices there, and the Bundesbank will remain in Frankfurt, the supreme constitutional court in Karlsruhe, and the Federal Crime Agency in Wiesbaden. In short, in its new incarnation Berlin will become the "capital of a kind of polycentric republic corresponding to an age when national decisions are often taken in consultation with other European Union countries, and ministers conduct their work today in Berlin, tomorrow in London, and the next in Madrid."

None of this diminishes the pride that the robust, idiosyncratic, irreverent Berliners now feel in the return of the German capital to where, in their opinion, it belongs. The dawning century seems to bring a sort of corroboration to their mysterious local belief that "in God's eyes, everyone is really a Berliner."

Part Three

War

17

Prussian Soldiers Against Militarism: Corvin, Willich, Engels, Rüstow

I

Among the many opponents of militarism in the nineteenth century were a not insignificant number of Prussian officers, often descendants of military families, who resigned their commissions because of a deep revulsion against the nature and traditions of the military system. The best known examples are Heinrich von Kleist at the beginning of the century and Fritz von Unruh at its close, whose departure from the army marked in both cases the beginning of notable literary careers. But there were many others who left the Prussian service to pledge allegiance to other more revolutionary flags, becoming, indeed, *condottieri* of the barricades, volunteers in a struggle to overthrow the kind of system that they had left.

This was, in a certain sense, true also of Unruh, although not of Kleist, whose patriotism and hatred of his country's enemies proved to

Sincere thanks go to Alina Bolous of the Bundeszentrale für politische Bildung for her kind assistance to the volume editors and publisher in researching the rights history of this essay. This English-language version is the original version of the essay, and it appears with the permission of the Department of Special Collections, Stanford University Libraries, and the estate of Gordon A. Craig.

be stronger, in the end, than his animus against the army. Member of a family that had supplied the Prussian crown with eighteen generals and two field marshals since the Thirty Years War, Kleist entered the army in 1792, at the age of fifteen, as an officer candidate in the King's Regiment of Guards, served competently in the field during the Rhine campaign of 1793–95, and was subsequently promoted to lieutenant. By 1799, he had discovered that the soldier's art was intolerable to him, that the "marvels of military discipline" were "the subject of [his] heartiest contempt" and that, "when the whole regiment performed its marvels, it seemed . . . a living monument of tyranny." Feeling "martyred by two diametrically opposed principles, so that [he] was always doubtful whether [he] had to act as a human being or as an officer, for to combine the duties of both [was] impossible in the present condition of armies,"[1] Kleist handed in his papers. And yet, after 1806, when Napoleon Bonaparte bestrode Europe like a colossus, all of his militant instincts were aroused, duty pulled him in the opposite direction, he became a patriot and a nationalist, a propagandist for a national rising in 1809, the editor of a newspaper that he hoped would "promote the national cause in every way,"[2] the author of the "*vaterländisches Drama*" *Prinz Friedrich von Hamburg*, and finally, as a result of his own petition, a Prussian lieutenant again, although only briefly, since active service was aborted by his suicide.

Fritz von Unruh was more consistent in his anti-militarism. The descendant of ancient Silesian nobility and the son of a Prussian general, he followed family tradition and, after attending a cadet school in Plön, became a cavalry officer. His disillusionment with the army was as abrupt as Kleist's and was expressed in 1911 in his drama *Offiziere*, which portrayed the emptiness and frivolity of casino life and the way in which, in Unruh's opinion, the vital powers of young men were consumed in meaningless routines. A second play, *Louis Ferdinand, Prinz von Preussen*, written in 1913, echoed the concern shown in Kleist's greatest drama (and in Theodor Fontane's powerful novel *Schach von Wuthenau*) over the debilitating moral effects of outworn traditions and false conceptions of honor in the Prussian military system and over their predictable results. By the time this work was published, Unruh had resigned his commission and, although the outbreak of the Great War

brought him back to the colors as a front officer, the conflict confirmed him in his hatred of militarism and its natural product, war.

In all of his post-war writings and speeches—particularly the prose
work *Opfergang*, which described what soldiers of all ranks had to put up
with during the dreadful bloodletting of Verdun, and his dramatic trilogy *Ein Geschlecht*, which told of the effects of the war and its aftermath
upon German society as seen in the fate of a single family—Unruh
fought against the ideas and institutions that had produced the debacle
of 1914, and after 1933, when his country submitted to a political
movement which he sensed would soon plunge Europe into another
ghastly conflict, he continued his private campaign from abroad.[3] The
passion and constancy of his crusade against war is illustrated by the
"speech to the Germans" that he delivered in the Paulskirche in Frankfurt am Main on 18 May 1948, the hundredth anniversary of the opening of Germany's first National Assembly. In this address, Unruh called
on his countrymen to return to the ideals of the democratic leaders of
1848 and described militarism as the chief obstacle to that goal, citing
the slogan of Frederick William IV's reactionary camarilla, "Gegen
Demokraten helfen nur Soldaten" [Only soldiers can counter demo-
crats].[4]

In point of fact, the antithesis suggested by that contemptuous
phrase was not as sharp and irremediable as Unruh suggested. Indeed,
in the heavy fighting that took place in Germany in 1848, the democratic forces were often led by trained soldiers who fought with a skill
and tenacity that won reluctant admiration from the Prussian officers
on the other side. These military pioneers of the revolution, as they
have been called, were all animated by a hatred of the Prussian military
system that was as deep as Unruh's was later to be. Because some of
them also had strong feelings about the necessity of replacing the professional standing army by a radically different kind of military force,
their careers and ideas are still worth examining.

II

Certainly one of the most colorful of these military rebels was Otto
von Corvin-Wierzbitski, who was, like Kleist and Unruh, the descendant of military forbears, his grandfather having been a Prussian general
and his father a *Rittmeister* of dragoons who fought in the campaign of

1806. Corvin was admitted to the cadet school in Potsdam in 1824 and seems to have enjoyed this military apprenticeship to the full, writing later that his three years in Potsdam were "the happiest in my life."[5] This initial enthusiasm began to wane, however, when, after three more years as a cadet in Berlin, he was commissioned and, in 1830, assigned to the 36. Infantry Regiment. The boredom of peacetime service, first in the *Bundesfestung* at Mainz and subsequently in the fortress town of Saarlouis, Corvin's awareness of the ruinous effects of the gambling, the drinking and the debt that it engendered among his comrades,[6] the restrictive nature of the army's social codes, which made it difficult for young officers to marry, and his growing perception of the arbitrary nature of military justice soon made him determined to escape from what he called "lackluster misery"[7] and "slavery in leather gaiters,"[8] and in 1835 he left the army to seek fame and fortune as a writer.

This decision Corvin later attributed to a growth of political maturity. It had gradually dawned upon him, he wrote, that his commission as an officer which enjoined him to be "loyal, true and obedient to the King and his royal house and to serve them by day and night, on water and land," said nothing about either the State or the people, and the more he thought of this the more convinced he became that the proper relationship between the prince and his subjects had been subverted, in such a way as to deprive the people of their rights. His reading of history taught him that "the instrument" through which this change had been effected was the "standing army, and that it was still being used as the means of maintaining this unnatural condition."[9] This was a situation that could only be corrected by the overthrow of the existing political system and the establishment of a new one with democratic military institutions. As Germany entered the turbulent fifth decade of the century, there was hope that this would not be delayed indefinitely. Meanwhile, Corvin wrote in his memoirs, "I made it my life's task to do everything I could to make the German people desirous and capable of united and energetic action when the expected revolution came. . . . Since it was not time to draw the sword, I determined until then to fight with my pen."[10]

Corvin never became a distinguished or even very influential political journalist, and as soon as popular risings began in the spring of 1848 to challenge established authority he was quick to abandon his new career and plunge into the struggle for a German republic. He was in Paris in February 1848 and participated in the fighting that drove Louis Philippe from the throne. Then, as the shock wave from that event began to be felt in Germany, he joined the German Legion, a volunteer force that the poet Georg Herwegh formed in the French capital, and served as its chief of staff in its abortive invasion of Baden in April 1848.

Corvin's memoirs include one of the most circumstantial and fair-minded accounts that we possess of that ill-starred adventure, revealing among other things that it was not as quixotic as conservative German opinion made it out to be after its failure. Herwegh was, to be sure, not the ideal leader for such an enterprise: the power of his rhetoric was greater than his attention to provisioning and arming his followers, and his despotic nature could not tolerate objective criticism of his grandiose ambitions.[11] But no one could fault his courage and, if in the end he was unsuccessful, this was largely due, Corvin makes clear, to the failure of the French republican government to provide sufficient financial and material support, and enough weapons, to make a drive into Germany effective; to the petty jealousies and professional incompetence of Herwegh's military commanders, the former Prussian lieutenants Börnstedt, and Löwenfels and the former Austrian artillerist Karl Börnstein;[12] and to the curious disinclination of Friedrich Hecker, the leader of the Badenese, to accept the Legion as an ally.

Herwegh's forces were never strong enough to do what Corvin thought they should have done, to cross the Rhine at Mannheim and advance on Frankfurt with the intention of revolutionizing the countryside in support of the National Assembly or, alternatively, to strike northwards into Prussian territory and, using Corvin's local knowledge, to capture the fortress of Saarlouis;[13] but they might have made a positive contribution to the democratic cause if they could have effected a timely junction with the republican columns of Hecker, Gustav Struve, and Franz Sigel in southern Baden. This was prevented by Hecker's reluctance to alienate local opinion by inviting into Germany the French anarchists who, he falsely believed, constituted the bulk of Herwegh's forces. Despite two dangerous missions into Baden by Herwegh's wife Emma, Hecker could not be persuaded to coordinate the movements of his forces with the advance of the Legion.[14] As a result, by the time the Legion crossed the Rhine at Großkembs, Hecker's column had already been defeated at Kandern and the forces led by Struve and Sigel were being decisively repulsed before Freiburg. There was consequently nothing that Corvin, who was now the effective military commander of Herwegh's tiny army, could do except to try to avoid battle until his forces could cross the Rhine again and take refuge in Switzerland. He almost succeeded in doing this, but the Legion was finally caught at Niederdossenbach by a superior force of Württemberg infantry and, despite courageous resistance and a gallant but costly flanking movement by the former Prussian lieutenant Reinhard von Schimmelpfennig's *Sensenmänner*, a detachment armed only with scythes mounted on pikes, was defeated and its members forced to flee in disorder.[15]

After the collapse of the Badenese revolution of 1848, Corvin removed to Berlin, where he helped edit a radical newspaper. But there were soon new opportunities to indulge his martial talents, for the Prussian King Frederick William IV's repudiation in April 1849 of the crown that the National Assembly offered him aroused a widespread determination to defend the Frankfurt constitution, and this soon assumed militant forms in Saxony, the Palatinate, and Baden. As the Prussian army mobilized to suppress this recrudescence of the revolutionary spirit of 1848, Corvin made his way to Karlsruhe and then to Mannheim, where he organized a *Volkswehr* and successfully defended the town against the first Prussian attacks.[16] This proved to be an illusory victory, for the insurrectionary forces in the Palatinate were too disorganized and ill-armed to withstand the Prussian corps advancing southward from the Rhine province. As they gave way, the Prussians got across the Rhine at Germersheim, outflanked the Badenese on the Neckar, and, in conjunction with a second Prussian corps and Bavarian auxiliaries that attacked across that stream, imposed a crushing defeat upon their forces at Waghäusel on 21 June. Corvin was ordered by the commander of the Badenese revolutionary army, the Polish patriot Ludvik Mieroslawski, to pull out of Mannheim and join the main force, which was regrouping along the Murg River. The rapidity of the Prussian advance, however, broke that line before it was firmly established and, as the fighting swept southward, Corvin was cut off in the fortress of Rastatt.[17]

During the three and a half weeks in which this last center of Badenese resistance held out, Corvin served as chief of staff to the fortress commander G. N. Tiedemann, with authority over all operational
aspects of the defense, as well as over the employment and general welfare of the six-thousand-man garrison.[18] As it became clear, moreover,
that relief could not be hoped for and that food and medical supplies
were running out, he played an important role in negotiating the surrender of the fortress city to General-lieutenant Graf von der Groeben,
the commander of the besieging Prussian force. His prominence almost caused him to share the fate of the eighteen democrats whom the
vengeful Prussians shot out of hand when the fortress gates were
opened. He was, indeed, tried by military court and sentenced to death,
but this verdict was commuted on technical grounds (he was no longer
a Prussian subject) to ten years imprisonment in a Badenese prison in
Bruchsal, six of which he served. This effectively ended his career as a
soldier, although not his interest in military affairs, for during the
American Civil War he was a correspondent for English and continental papers.[19]

Temperamentally akin to Corvin, and with equally strong political
convictions, was another former Prussian lieutenant who distinguished
himself in the Badenese revolution. This was August Willich, the son of
an East Prussian *Landrat*, who was a companion of Corvin's during his
cadet years but remained longer in the service, becoming a first lieutenant in 1840 and receiving the command of an artillery brigade. Subsequently, however, he joined a group of officers with pronounced socialist and communist views and, because of this, was dismissed from
the service in 1847. To support himself, he took up the trade of car-
pentry, while at the same time becoming a member of the Bund der
Kommunisten. In March 1848, he was one of the leaders of the democratic demonstrations in Cologne; a month later he was in Konstanz
when Hecker, Struve, and Sigel decided to attempt to republicanize
Baden; and he was Hecker's chief lieutenant during his march from
Konstanz to Kandern. A man who never stood on ceremony (his habit
of addressing everyone in the second person singular had the same
startling effect upon the rank-conscious as the rebellious students' habit of calling their professors "du" in the late 1960s), Willich was a
thruster whose own indifference to danger had the effect of inspiring

troops to act beyond the call of duty. He felt hampered by Hecker's desire to avoid bloodshed whenever possible and later reproached him for missing opportunities to inflict heavy damage on the enemy in the days before the luckless firefight at Kandern.

That defeat did not discourage Willich as much as it did his chief, who decided to emigrate to the United States and wrote to Emma Herwegh in November 1848 that, in view of the defeat of popular hopes in Germany, the best course was "to hunt buffalo with Co-manches, Sacs and Fox Indians and to enjoy being rid of civilization."[20] In contrast, Willich withdrew only as far as Straßburg, where he re-cruited and trained a column of militant workers, called the Besançon Company, which he apparently intended to lead to Italy to help in the fight against Austria;[21] simultaneously, he was a member of a group of communists and radical democrats who drafted new projects for revo-lutionizing Germany. Gustav Struve's premature *Putsch* in September 1848 made all of these cloudy plans worthless, and Willich was forced to contain his lust for combat until May 1849, when the so-called *Reichsverfassungskampagne* began. His Besançon Company was the most effective of the units fighting in the Palatinate and formed the rear guard in the desperate effort to prevent the Prussians from getting across the Rhine. When they nevertheless did so, Willich detached his forces, joined Mieroslawski's army as it fell back from the Neckar, and fought a series of holding actions—at Ubstadt, Bruchsal and Durlach, along the Murg River, and finally in the hilly terrain south of Rastatt—until effective resistance was broken and he was forced to lead his re-maining troops across the Swiss border.[22] Subsequently, he made his way to London, where he became a member of the Central Committee of the reconstituted Bund der Kommunisten, only to be expelled in 1850 for following an anti-Marxist *Putschist* line. He emigrated to the United States in 1853, became a citizen and, like other veterans of the Baden campaigns, fought on the Union side in the Civil War, attaining general's rank.[23]

The proletarian complexion of Willich's company during the cam-paign of 1849 had the effect of attracting to it, whether from romantic or ideological motives, a number of middle-class intellectuals. Among them was the former Bonn professor and friend of Jakob Burckhardt, Gottfried Kinkel, whose act of enrolling in its ranks changed his life profoundly, for he was wounded at Durlach and captured by the Prussians, sentenced to life imprisonment in Spandau, whence he was released in a dramatic rescue organized by his former student Karl Schurz, forced to spend years of exile in England, and finally, in 1866, saved from more of this when he received a professorship of art and archaeology at the Polytechnic University in Zürich (a post to which Georg Herwegh had hoped to be appointed), subsequently spending the rest of his life in that city.[24] A more famous middle-class recruit was Friedrich Engels, who served as Willich's adjutant from the fighting along the Neckar to the line of last resistance at Lörrach in July.

Engels was no stranger to the art of soldiering, for in 1840–41 he had interrupted his apprentice training in mercantile affairs to go to Berlin, where he served as a one-year volunteer in the Guards Foot Artillery of the Prussian Army, thus obtaining a reserve commission that he held until 1860, when he was drummed out of the *Landwehr* as a deserter.[25] It has generally been assumed that his real reason for going to the Prussian capital was to share in the intellectual excitement that prevailed there and that he took his military duties lightly,[26] but it is possible that his year in the service appealed subconsciously both to his robust nature and to his active intelligence. Certainly in 1849, when he arrived in Kaiserslautern as a correspondent for the *Neue Rheinische Zeitung* just as the Prussians began their invasion of the Palatinate, he reacted enthusiastically to the opportunity of joining in the fighting. "Since I did not want to sacrifice the chance of enjoying a bit of war college (*ein Stück Kriegsschule*)," he wrote later, "and since in any case the *Neue Rheinische Zeitung* must also *honoris causa* be represented in the Palatinate-Badenese army, I buckled on my battle sword and went to Willich."[27]

Engels's service as adjutant was by no means a sinecure. He went on missions across enemy lines and commanded volunteer units that fought beside the Besançon Company, and he was frequently exposed to fire. He wrote to Karl Marx in July, 1849, "I was in four fire-fights, of which two were significant, particularly the one at Rastatt, and I discovered that the much-praised courage in battle is the most ordinary characteristic that one can have."[28] The conduct of the campaign, however, moved him to reflections upon the nature of revolutionary war. A confirmed enemy of the professional military caste (he was, almost without exception, scornful of the leaders on both sides in the fighting), he was strengthened in this prejudice by the sometimes overweening behavior of the former revolutionary officers when they went into exile. "That the great warriors Willich, Schimmelpfenning and Sigel are spending more and more time together is a good thing," he wrote Marx. "It is very good to be made aware of the spirit of the officer corps . . . and of the officers mess and to see how this cliquism is just as strong among the officers group in emigration as it is in the glorious fighting army. We want to show these gentlemen in due course the significance of civilian clothes. And all this shows me that I can do nothing better than to continue my military studies, so that at least one person from civilian life can stand up to them in questions of theory."[29] This decision, as we shall see, had important consequences.

Another oppositional Prussian lieutenant who might, had circumstances not prevented it, have fought with Corvin, Willich, and Engels in the Badenese revolution was Friedrich Wilhelm Rüstow, the descendant of Pomeranian forbears, whose father had been the commander of an infantry company in the wars of 1806 and 1813. Fascinated at an early age by military affairs, Rüstow broke off his legal studies at Heidelberg to join the Prussian army as a *Gardepionere* in 1838. Two years later, after attending artillery and engineering school, he received his officer's commission. From the beginning, he was a prolific writer on technical and administrative subjects, with pronounced ideas of his own about the necessity of basic reform of the military constitution and, as time passed, his views became steadily more democratic and nationalistic. He was soon in trouble with his superiors because of his book *Der Krieg der Zukunft. Einige Wörter an die junge Generation* [The War of the Future: Some Words for the Younger Generation], which was written in 1848 under an assumed name and which argued for the raising of a people's army, and his appeal to the Prussian National Assembly to support democratic officers and to prevent the army from becoming a reactionary tool involved him in a series of hearings and courts martial. After the defiant publication of his *Deutsche Militärstaat vor und während der Revolution* [The German Military State Before and During the Revolution] (1850), which attacked the standing army for being the inveterate foe of liberty and for having suppressed legitimate democratic aspirations in the recent fighting,[30] he was charged with high treason and sentenced to the loss of his commission and fortress detention for a period of 31½ years, with ten further years of police surveillance. Rüstow actually served six months of this horrendous sentence in the fortress at Posen, but, in July 1850, as he was about to be transferred to another prison, he escaped and, dressed as a woman and with two companions, made his way by carriage and train to Switzerland.[31]

The cultural life of Zürich, where Rüstow settled, was dominated throughout the 50s by a remarkable group of victims of the revolutions in Germany and Italy, such people as Richard Wagner, the architect Gottfried Semper, the historian Theodor Mommsen, and the archaeologist Herman Köchly, all of whom had been involved in the agitations in Saxony, the aestheticist Friedrich Theodor Vischer, a refugee from Baden, and Francesco de Sanctis, the historian and philosopher of literature, who had been on the barricades in Naples. Rüstow became friends with Georg and Emma Herwegh, who also lived in Zürich, and with the group of Mazzinian émigrés, like Fillippo de Boni, who frequented their household and filled it with optimistic talk of new risings that would complete the work started in 1848. He earned his living by his pen and, after 1852, by his work as a teacher at the University and, later, at the Polytechnic. With Hermann Köchly, he collaborated on a bilingual edition of Greek military writers, a history of the Greek military system, and a very successful edition, with commentary, of Caesar's *Gallic War*. He became a Swiss citizen in 1853 and shortly thereafter established contact with the new federal army, lecturing to its officers and writing historical and technical studies, including a handbook on tactics, a history of the infantry, and treatises on general staff functions, that were useful to it.

This hectic literary activity was apparently not enough to satisfy what Gustav Mayer called the "desperado" side of Rüstow's nature,[32] and when Garibaldi began his campaign in Sicily in May 1860 he proved susceptible to Emma Herwegh's suggestion that he put his talents at the disposal of the Italian patriot. Filippo de Boni made the necessary arrangements, and Rüstow went to Genoa in June, where he became chief of staff of a division and was asked by Mazzini to plan an attack upon the Papal States. This was cancelled because of urgent needs in the south, and Rüstow went to Sicily, where he served as

Garibaldi's chief of staff and, later, in the fighting at Salerno, Naples, and on the Volturno line, commander of the Milan Brigade. He was a competent and audacious leader, having three horses shot under him on the Volturno front, but the campaign was over all too quickly, and Garibaldi's willingness to hand the fruits of his victories over to the Piedmontese, whom Rüstow regarded as the Prussians of Italy, left him without an occupation, and he returned to Zürich in a restless and discontented mood.[33]

It is not surprising then that, when the Kingdom of Prussia became involved in the protracted constitutional struggle caused by liberal opposition to the King's plans to reform the army, Rüstow should have begun to indulge in expansive but impractical plans for exploiting it. On the one hand, he bombarded Rudolf von Bennigsen, the head of the *Nationalverein*, with detailed plans for the recruiting of a volunteer army, which would be built up on the basis of local *Turnvereine* and would exert pressure for a democratic federal union.[34] At the same time, after meeting Ferdinand Lassalle and his friend Countess Sophie von Hatzfeldt during their visit to the Herweghs in Zürich in 1861, he began to formulate plans with them for an attack upon Austria by a mixed Italian-German force under Garibaldi's command that might spread to Germany and give Lassalle an opportunity to play tribune in a popular rising against reaction.[35]

Nothing came of all this. Bennigsen did not encourage Rüstow, and the Italian plan (which may have been inspired in part by Emma Herwegh's love of Italy and even more by Rüstow's passion for Sophie) faded away after Garibaldi's rash attempt to take Rome in 1862 and his defeat at Aspromonte. The love affair with Countess von Hatzfeldt did not survive Lassalle's death in 1864, for she blamed Rüstow for having encouraged him to fight the duel in which he was killed, and opportunities to create the kind of Germany of which Rüstow had dreamed died after the Prussian victory over Austria in 1866. Rüstow's last years were productive in a literary and professional sense (he became a colonel in the Swiss Army and chief of the historical and statistical section of its General Staff), but were darkened by a feeling of unfulfillment. He left the army in 1875 and, three years later, took his own life.

III

Between 1848 and 1863, the military systems of four of the Great Powers were challenged by irregular forces inspired by national and democratic ideals and led by trained officers who had gone over to the revolutionaries. Initially, this had a disconcerting effect upon the old military establishments, which had little experience in dealing with barricade fighters and were not always sure of the reliability of their own forces when they were in combat against their fellow countrymen. Engels attributed both the large number of troops used by the Prussians in the Baden campaign and the ponderous and at times timorous nature of their tactics to their fear lest even a limited success by the rebels touch off a widespread defection on the part Prussian *Landwehr* units.[36]

In the end, the old system prevailed. The *beaux sabreurs* who had joined the revolution in the hope of changing society and its military institutions were forced to admit, not only that they had failed, but that the outcome of the wars of the 60s had made it unlikely that they would have another chance. The military systems that Corvin and Willich and Engels and Rüstow had challended were stronger by far in 1866 than they had been in 1848 and seemed now, indeed, invulnerable to change. It was no accident that, as if anticipating this, so many of the former officers who had fought unsuccessfully in Baden to overthrow a reactionary system concluded, during the American Civil War, that their talents would be more effectively employed in fighting to preserve a democratic one. Thus, Hecker, Sigel, Willich, Schimmelpfenning, Blenker, Wedemeyer, Schurz and many other veterans of the Badenese insurrection volunteered for service in the Union Army during the American Civil War.[37]

Rüstow and Engels, however, remained undiscouraged. The former had, to be sure, considered going to America and in 1861 actually asked Garibaldi for a letter to Abraham Lincoln, recommending him for a command, but he never used it, perhaps because he was too committed to his plans for action in Germany and Austria.[38] When these evaporated, he concentrated on the task of making the citizen army of his adopted country as effective a fighting force as any in Europe. The 1860s saw the publication of his treatises on the theory of small wars and the doctrine of the fire-fight, as well as a book on tactics. The following decade was marked by a renewed effort on his part to improve the efficiency of the Swiss General Staff. How great a debt that body owed to his earlier works on staff organization and functions can be judged from its recently published official history;[39] now he dedicated himself, in his lectures at the staff school in Thuner and in maneuvers and staff rides, to improving its performance and was particularly vigilant in watching over its selection process, insisting that it be rigorously democratic and that candidates with wealth and social position not be given preference over more talented officers, as was sometimes true in other systems.[40]

Rüstow never wavered in his belief that well-organized and well-trained milita forces—citizen armies—were more efficient than standing armies, which were, in his view, resistant to change and innovation, and he remained convinced that democracy and standing armies were incompatible. His views on these subjects had continuing influence, on the one hand on later advocates of the militia idea, like Jean Jaurès, and on the other later students of the art of war like Hans Delbrück, who admitted that his choice of a career owed much to his reading of Rüstow and whose doctrine of the reciprocal relationship between a state's civil and military institutions, elaborated on in his *Geschichte der Kriegskunst* [History of the Art of War], was an extension of Rüstow's ideas on the subject.[41] There is some reason, therefore, for regarding Rüstow as the most important nineteenth-century critic of war and its institutions after Clausewitz.

Or perhaps one should say the most important bourgeois critic, for Friedrich Engels had remained true to his resolve in 1851 to make a serious study of war, with results that both amused and impressed his party comrades, who nicknamed him "the General," and also, because of the acuity of his analyses of specific military events, won the respect of other military observers. In the socialist movement, Engels's achievement was to establish the importance of war in the revolutionary process and the vital necessity of studying it, not only because, as Marx once wrote to his collaborator, "the whole history of the structure of middle-class society is clearly summarized in the history of armies,"[42] but because only a realistic appraisal of the nature of modern war and the capabilities of modern armies could prevent the revolutionary movement from indulging in illusory hopes and costly adventures. Temperamentally, Engels always remained the man who was ready at any moment to saddle up for "that great duel to the death between bourgeoisie and proletariat;"[43] intellectually, he was consistently opposed to those party members, like Willich in the 50s, who agitated for new *Putsches*, because he realized, as he wrote at the end of his career, that "the fighting methods of 1848 are obsolete today in every respect. . . . The time is past for revolutions carried through by small minorities at the head of the unconscious masses. When it gets to be a matter of the complete transformation of the social organization, the masses themselves must participate, [and] must understand what is at stake."[44]

But when would the time be propitious for that transformation and how was it to be effected? Engels was as convinced as Rüstow that militarism, in the form of the standing army, was the real obstacle to successful revolution, although he rejected Rüstow's faith in the militia principle as a means of correcting this.[45] Instead, with his deep consciousness of the interdependence of economic, diplomatic, psychological and military factors in history, he predicted that militarism would itself create the opportunity for the proletariat to seize power and transform society. In 1878, in his *Anti-Dühring*, he wrote of how the Prussian victory over France had stimulated a heightened competition in armaments among the Great Powers which would invite new conflicts among them. And then, looking to the future, he wrote:

The army has become the chief end of the state and an end in itself; the peoples are there only to deliver and feed soldiers. Militarism is ruling and engorging Europe. But this militarism also carries in itself the seeds of its own downfall. The competition of the individual States forces them, on the one hand, to spend more every year on army, navy, weaponry, etc., and, on the other hand, to apply universal service ever more strictly, and thus in the end to train the whole people in the use of weapons, so that it is made capable at a given moment of asserting its will against the ruling military establishment. And this moment will occur as soon as the mass of the people—rural and urban workers and peasants—has one will. At that point, the prince's army will be transformed into a people's army, the machine will refuse to work, and militarism will collapse in the dialectic of its own development. What the bourgeois democracy could not accomplish in 1848, precisely because it was bourgeois and not proletarian, namely, to give the working masses a will that accords with its class position—that socialism will accomplish without fail. And that will mean the disruption of militarism, and with it of all standing armies, from inside out.[46]

This was a chilling and not inaccurate vision of the future, for in the years before 1918 militarism did evolve along the lines that Engels suggested. But it proved in the end to be more resilient than he had supposed, and in this respect he was no wiser than the Prussian soldiers who had hoped to overthrow it by direct assault.

18

The Political Leader as Strategist

The proper role of the political leader in the direction of a nation's war effort is difficult to establish in theory. Clausewitz's statement that "policy is the guiding intelligence and war only the instrument. . . . No other possibility exists, then, than to subordinate the military point of view to the political," though of great theoretical significance, is of little use to anyone trying to formulate rules for decision making in twentieth-century warfare or to delineate responsibility for the determination of strategy.[1] If, as David Fraser has argued, "the art of strategy is to determine the aim, which is or should be political; to derive from that aim a series of military objectives to be achieved; to assess these objectives as to the military requirements they create, and the preconditions which the achievement of each is likely to necessitate; to measure available and potential resources against the requirements and to chart from this process a coherent pattern of priorities and a rational course of action," the difficult question is how much of the deriving and assessing and measuring and charting falls within the political leader's purview and how much of it becomes a military function.[2] It is clear

This essay originally appeared in *Makers of Modern Strategy from Machiavelli to the Nuclear Age*, edited by Peter Paret, © 1986 Princeton University Press. Reprinted by permission of Princeton University Press.

that this cannot be answered by any categorical formulation, even one that is invested with the authority of Clausewitz's name.

Much the same can be said of the relationship between civilian and military authority at that moment in the process of war in which strategy is translated into operations. Sir Edward Spears has written with some asperity:

> The picture [of] . . . civilians examining plans and maps and working out the meaning of the vast number of orders based on these, issued by Army Groups and Armies to artillery of every description, to the air force, the cavalry, infantry, tanks, etc. is ridiculous. . . . Only one possessed of that most dangerous of disqualifications, an amateur's half-knowledge, would [suggest] that statesmen, innocent of all military training, [were] capable . . . of estimating such things as the firepower on their own side and the power of resistance of the enemy, the weight of the shock of the attacking infantry and its tactical dispositions, without any knowledge of the ground, of assimilating in fact . . . the highly technical staff-work which represented many weeks of study by highly trained professionals."[3]

This is all very well, but one feels that it is overstated. All operations have political consequences. They can increase or diminish a nation's ability to achieve its goals; they can commit it unwisely to new and unforeseen objectives; they can, by failure of calculation or execution, discourage its allies or bring new support to the side of the enemy. If excessive meddling in operational planning and decision making by political leaders can have disruptive consequences, inability or unwillingness on their part to exercise critical control over such plans and decisions runs the risk of placing in military hands powers that can jeopardize the national security for which the political leadership has ultimate responsibility. Here too, then, it is difficult to frame a theoretical definition of appropriate roles that is not so general as to be meaningless.

In practice, these questions have been resolved by the interplay of such factors as the nature of the political system, the efficiency and prestige of the military establishment, and the character and personality of the political leader. In the two world wars of this century, the last of these has been the most important.

I

The case of Germany's first chancellor in the Great War, Theobald von Bethmann Hollweg, may serve as an extreme but by no means unique illustration of the difficulties that confronted the political leaders of all belligerent states in 1914. As soon as hostilities commenced, he found himself in a situation in which nearly all the political parties, the business community, a high proportion of the university professoriate, the bulk of the middle class, and significant portions of the working class were desirous of the most ambitious kind of territorial expansion and were sure that the war would make this possible. Simultaneously, he had to deal with a military establishment that had greater freedom from political control and a higher degree of public veneration than any similar body in the world.

Judged from the standpoint of intelligence and administrative talent, Bethmann was certainly the best of Bismarck's successors, but he was also, as Gerhard Ritter has pointed out, "an intellectual who lacked a wholly secure instinct for power, . . . who did not enjoy possessing it, and who [held on to office, only because he] regarded this as an iron responsibility in the service of the national state and the traditions of the Prussian-German monarchy."[4] He was not a fighter, the kind of robust man of will who follows his own objectives without scruple or distraction. His natural diffidence disarmed him when he was opposed by arrogance and self-confidence, and in moments of crisis he was apt to be overcome by fatalism.

It is therefore not surprising that in August 1914 Bethmann allowed himself to be over-impressed by the technical arguments of the soldiers and swept into a war that he had, in any case, convinced himself was all but inevitable. He had had no share in devising the strategical plan for the war, and he does not seem to have questioned openly its basic assumptions, that a massive enveloping movement in the West would knock France out of the war in six weeks and discourage the British from further participation, and that the bulk of German forces could then be turned eastward to relieve the Austrian holding operation and destroy the Russian advance.

What has to be said for Bethmann, however, is that, after the strategy of the First High Command had failed and the long stalemate in the

trenches began, he strove valiantly to submit the war to rational control
and to direct it to achievable ends. For a time it looked as if he might be
successful. He denied Chief of Staff Falkenhayn's demands to be consulted on all matters of foreign policy that might conceivably affect
operations in the field, a patent attempt to broaden the powers of the
military at the expense of the chancellor. He won a signal victory over
Tirpitz and the admirals in 1915, preventing the introduction of unlimited submarine warfare at that time. He used all of his persuasive powers to prevent the emperor from falling completely under the sway of
the military and, until 1917, was not ineffective in this effort.

He was less effective with respect to the annexationists, whose ambitions he considered to be unrealistic and dangerous, since they
threatened to broaden the scope of the war to a point where any peace
by negotiation would become impossible. In the end, he became so
concerned about this that he resorted to tactics that helped to undermine his own position. He conceived the idea of using the authority of
the military against the expansionist lobbies, of finding a general who
would support his own moderate course and would be popular enough
to force the annexationists into line. He decided that he must persuade
the emperor to dismiss Falkenhayn—whose popular support had
seeped away during the wasting Verdun campaign—and to bring in
Hindenburg, the hero of Tannenberg, in his place. In an audience with
William II in July 1916, he said flatly that Hindenburg must be made
supreme commander at once. "This is a matter that involves the fate of
the Hohenzollern dynasty. With Hindenburg he could make a compromise peace, without him he could not."[5] A few weeks later, the emperor agreed, and the change was made.

This proved to be a grave miscalculation. Hindenburg did not want
a compromise peace, and neither did his first general quartermaster
Erich Ludendorff, who proved to be more rabid about territorial acquisition than the annexationists themselves. Moreover, the chiefs of the
new Supreme Command were not as easily barred from intervention in
political decisions as Falkenhayn had been. Before long, they were
claiming and obtaining the right to be heard on all matters of high policy and were themselves urging courses of action that could not help
but prolong and broaden the war. In November 1916, Ludendorff successfully defeated the possibility of a negotiated peace with Russia by

insisting that military needs required the creation of a satellite Kingdom of Poland out of Russian lands occupied by German troops since 1914, a decision that led to the fall of the peace party in St. Petersburg and kept the Russians in the war for another year. And not content with that, the Supreme Command, in the spring of 1917, called for the immediate inception of unlimited submarine warfare.

Bethmann had fought staunchly against the expansion of submarine operations in 1915. This time his resistance was weaker, and in the end he yielded. His reasons for doing so show the dilemma of the civilian statesman in wartime in all its cruelty. In the crucial Crown Council, Bethmann was surrounded by naval experts who brandished statistical tables and technical charts, all of which proved that to loose the submarines would bring victory in a given number of months. He was not an intellectually arrogant man and, before this massive uniformed assurance, he could not help but doubt his own instincts. He gradually convinced himself that the Admiralty might, after all, be right and gave way. This was doubtless an act of weakness, but Ritter has a point when he writes that it would have taken a person of wholly extraordinary will and self-confidence to oppose a course of action that was demanded by all of the responsible military leaders, as well as by the emperor, the Reichstag majority, and most politically aware Germans, including the Social Democrats.[6]

Bethmann's capitulation on this issue was not enough to satisfy either the Supreme Command, who were irritated at the chancellor's presumption in opposing their views on a matter of national security, or the annexationists, who knew that he still hoped for a compromise, and hence a "soft," peace. In the months that followed, these forces allied and launched an elaborate campaign against Bethmann's "flabbiness," insisting that the successful prosecution of the war would be impossible unless he were dropped. Their intrigues were successful, and the man who had striven to keep the war within rational limits was hounded from office. The striking thing about his fall is not the way in which it was accomplished but rather the fact that no voice was raised in his behalf. It was not only the soldiers and the business interests that brought Bethmann down. Such future leaders of Weimar democracy as Matthias Erzberger and Gustav Stresemann actively participated in the dirty maneuvers that effected his dismissal; the Reichstag majority gave its approval, the Socialists were mute, and public opinion in general greeted the event with satisfaction, apparently convinced that Hindenburg and Ludendorff would bring them the total victory that they craved.

In a striking corroboration of Clausewitz's insight that the successful prosecution of war depends upon the proper coordination of political leadership, armed forces, and the passions of the people, it was the disarticulation of these forces that defeated Bethmann. The combination of military self-confidence and public heedlessness nullified all attempts to coordinate Germany's political and military strategies rationally and to direct its operational planning to achievable ends. The result was a stubborn prolongation of the war that caused millions of needless casualties, an ill-conceived offensive in 1918 that the country did not have the resources to support, and, in the end, defeat and revolution.

II

Although the British are supposed to be politically more sophisticated than the Germans and more firmly set against vesting authority in the military, the difference is hardly supported by their experience in the First World War. Indeed, it can be fairly said that the country's first wartime prime minister never tried as hard as Bethmann Hollweg did to see that war was used as an instrument of policy and that the great strategical issues remained under the control of the political leadership.

H. H. Asquith was a gifted parliamentarian and a superb party leader, but he had neither the knowledge nor the energy to be a great war minister. A. J. P. Taylor has said of him that he "did not understand the great issues which the conduct of the war provoked. Though resolved on victory, he supposed that the only contribution that statesmen could make was to keep out of the way, while free enterprise supplied the arms with which generals would win the battles."[7] This was a curious attitude for a British statesman to take, for Great Britain was a sea power and, at war against predominantly land powers, it had strategical options, the choice between which could not, or should not, be made by the military alone. Asquith's diffidence about taking a firm line himself meant that the basic decisions that would affect the nature, locus, length, and financial and human cost of the conflict, and the future of the British Empire, would not be made logically and responsibly. Rather they would be haggled over in various ministries, committees, and staffs; compromise solutions would be found that pleased no one and proved to be ineffective (like the Dardanelles plan, which failed for lack of conviction, energy, and resources), and ultimately the country would drift into a strategical posture from which it was impossible to withdraw, whether it was rationally supportable or not.

This is pretty much what happened under Asquith's lax leadership in the first two years of the war. After much strategical backing and filling, and the unhappy Dardanelles affair, the leadership of the army passed into the firm control of Douglas Haig and William Robertson, a combination that proved to be almost as impervious to civilian supervision as the Hindenburg-Ludendorff team and which imposed a set of strategical concepts upon the country that were very nearly as fatal in their results as those of their German counterparts. Both Haig and Robertson were "westerners"—that is, they believed that the war could be won only by killing Germans in Flanders, and they were prepared to accept the heavy loss in British casualties that this would entail. Under their leadership, the war became not one of movement but of attrition. As Roy Jenkins has written in his biography of Asquith, and his words are a judgment and a criticism of his subject, "In these circumstances, the job of the politician ceased to be that of looking for strategical alternatives and became concentrated upon supplying men and munitions for the slaughter"[8] Unless one regards the bloodletting that went on at the Somme or at Arras as a rational use of war for an intelligible end (and it is difficult to do so), then one is forced to conclude that the prime minister had given up the effort to keep the war within the limits of reason long before Bethmann had done so, and that he had surrendered his proper functions to the soldiers, first to Kitchener, later to the duumvirate Robertson-Haig.

Asquith was a shrewd politician, and it was probably his knowledge of the currents of public opinion, rather than personal lethargy, that inspired this abdication. A few days before the outbreak of the war, he had written disdainfully in his diary: "There were large crowds perambulating the streets and cheering the King at Buckingham Palace, and one could hear the distant roaring as late as 1 or 1:30 in the morning.

War or anything that seems likely to lead to war is always popular with the London mob. . . . How one loathes such levity!"[9]

Once the war had started, the passions of the mob became more inflamed, and Asquith probably felt that any attempt to assert himself in strategical questions would meet with popular disapproval and lead to a governmental crisis. And, in any case, how could one really prove that the soldiers were wrong in their estimates of military possibilities? It was all so difficult to get at! On the first day of the battle of the Somme in July 1916, more than 1,000 officers and 20,000 men were killed, fatally wounded, or reported missing, and over 1,300 officers and 34,000 other ranks were wounded. Before the battle was over, the British had suffered 420,000 casualties. These were impressive and daunting figures. Yet, when the government remonstrated with the commander in chief in France, Haig gave them the kind of answer that has been heard from many commanders on many occasions since 1916 and is always difficult for politicians to deal with. The Somme battle, he pointed out, had relieved pressure on other parts of the Allied line and had diverted enemy resources from other fronts. At the same time, by proving that Britain could mount an offensive in the main theater of war and drive the cream of German troops from their positions, it had had important psychological effects and had fortified the will to victory. Most important, the attacks had used up 30 percent of the enemy's divisions so that, in another six weeks, he "should be hard put to it to find men. . . . The maintenance of a steady offensive pressure will result eventually in his complete overthrow."[10] Who was to deny the validity of these confident assertions? Confronted with them, Asquith simply lapsed into tacit acquiescence.

His successor as prime minister, David Lloyd George, had stronger convictions about strategy and a greater desire to bring logical direction to the war effort, but he suffered from the same fear of public disapproval or disavowal if he were to be too outspoken. He argued with the soldiers. He told Robertson, "I will not drive thousands to slaughter like cattle. For three years we have been promised victory in France and Belgium. What is there to show for this ceaseless battery? We must strike again at a soft front!"[11] When the army command nevertheless planned new offensives in Flanders, he muttered about "wild military speculation," "insane enterprises," and "muddy and muddle-headed ventures," but he did not try to forbid the soldiers to go on squandering the nation's resources, nor did he urge their recall. As Leon Wolff has written, he knew all too well that "were Haig to be summarily dismissed, Robertson would quit in sympathy, and the entire country, Parliament, even the War Cabinet would hit the ceiling. Firing Haig would also imply that the Empire was losing the war, would encourage the enemy, and was certain to strike a heavy blow at Allied morale."[12] With these thoughts in mind, and that of his own political future, Lloyd George did not insist too much, and the killing went on.

In these circumstances, the idea of seeking a peace by negotiation got as short shrift in Britain as it did in Germany. In 1916, when Lord Lansdowne sent a memorandum to the cabinet, urging a vigorous search for opportunities for negotiation, Asquith was less interested in following up the idea than he was in preventing it from being leaked to the soldiers or the general public. A year later, Lansdowne took a more direct approach and made his proposal public in a letter to the *Daily Telegraph*. It was received, in the words of his biographer, with "a flood of invective and an incredible mass of abusive correspondence which, though largely incoherent, was marked by a violence rare in English political life."[13] The *Times,* then owned by Lord Northcliffe, denounced Lansdowne with a quite exceptional lack of moderation, and the Rothermere and Hulton press chimed in to castigate his letter as "craven," "inept," and "inopportune." Before this flood of denunciation, neither the Lloyd George government nor the Opposition had any desire to make the cause of negotiation its own. As in Germany, the soldiers, having already smothered the issue of strategical alternatives, were allowed to carry the war in France to the ultimate in irrationality, with consequences hardly less drastic than those suffered by the enemy.

III

The experience of French political leaders came close in the first years of the Great War to duplicating that of their counterparts in Germany and Britain, and in the critical year 1917 France provided a quintessential illustration of civilian diffidence and capitulation before military expert opinion. In the last year of the war, however, the political leadership reasserted its authority, and, as a result, France enjoyed a degree of political-military collaboration in the direction of the war that was achieved in neither Britain nor Germany.

France started the war with what amounted to a military dictatorship, for reasons noted by Jere King:

> That France had been no better equipped to meet the problems of a democracy at war was due to a complex of historic circumstances. The great prestige which the military had enjoyed for centuries gave them an advantage over the civilians at the outset of the war. The very idea of the 'sacred union' was chiefly to the benefit of conservatives, of which the military were a most important part. Criticizing the command would have been considered disloyal—if not downright treasonable—during the crucial weeks of August and September 1914. The government and Parliament deferred to the command, thus carrying out popular expectation. A short war was anticipated, and only a temporary overshadowing of the civilian power."[14]

But France also had a revolutionary tradition and an expectation that its generals would be successful or would be replaced. The inconclusive battle of the Marne and the coming of the war of attrition aroused enough doubts about French commanders to prevent the ascendancy of the military chiefs from becoming as pronounced as it was in either Germany or Britain. The emergence of a really successful general, another Napoleon, might have made a difference. Even as late as 1917, the political leaders were cautious in dealing with potential Napoleons, and the generals retained sufficient authority to have their way in operational matters, as was tragically demonstrated in April of that year at a conference in Compiègne. At this meeting the President of the Republic, Raymond Poincaré, the Prime Minister Ribot, and the War Minister Painlevé reviewed the plan of General Nivelle for another great offensive against the German lines. They had no faith in his project. They had the authority to forbid it. Yet they were incapable of pointing out its failings or suggesting alternatives and hence were impotent to block it. Sir Edward Spears has written, "The Cabinet was hobbled by its lack of technical knowledge and fettered by public opinion, which, aware of its ignorance in military matters, would have been intolerant of civil intrusion into the military sphere. [The conference] epitomizes the terrible disability from which democracies, even when fighting for their existence, are unable to free themselves. What this weakness in the supreme direction of the war cost the Allies in lives and money can never be computed."[15]

The disaster that resulted from the conference, however, prevented the French from following the example of the other countries discussed here. The doubts of the civilians were more than justified. In the first ten days of the Nivelle offensive, 34,000 troops died in the field, 90,000 were wounded, of whom a good percentage died, and 20,000 were missing. Before long the whole French army was wracked with mutiny, and public sympathy had turned decisively against the military establishment. In the resultant shakeup, the man who emerged to direct the war effort was Georges Clemenceau.

This odd mixture of cynical condottiere from the parliamentary wars of the 1880s and 1890s and impassioned patriot was no great admirer of the military. Upon assuming office, he made it clear that he regarded war as too serious a matter to be left in the hands of the generals. While having no compunction about making his own views felt in all fields of military administration and on operational questions as well, he treated military ventures into the political realm with brutality. *"Taisez-vous!"* he snapped at Marshal Foch at a meeting of the Supreme War Council in London in March 1918. "I speak for France here!"[16] Clemenceau had all the political skill necessary to rally parliamentary support behind his sometimes willful self-assertiveness, and he acquired (largely from his military aide General Mordacq) the kind of expertise necessary to enable him to speak with authority on questions of strategical and tactical choice, so impressing Lord Alfred Milner with the clarity and force of his views that in March 1918 the British statesman proposed that Clemenceau be made generalissimo of the Allied armies."[17]

The French premier had perhaps too great a sense of his own limitations to encourage this plan, but this in no wise diminished his paramount authority in the direction of the French war effort in 1918. Among the achievements attributed to him by Mordacq are the reorganization of the War Ministry, the abolition of many military sinecures and useless commissions, the selection of new and energetic troop commanders, the reorganization of the general staff on a logical basis, the revitalization of the French structures of command in Italy and

Salonika, and a great expansion of tank and armored car production.[18] More important than any of these, certainly, was his reaction to the shattering impact of the German spring offensive of 1918. The strategical disarray in Allied councils that Ludendorff's hammer blows effected convinced Clemenceau that a continuation of the dual leadership of Pétain and Haig would lead inevitably to the loss of the war. He became the most determined and persuasive advocate of a unified command under Foch, and his success in carrying this through and his insistence, once the momentum of the German offensive began to wane, upon coordinated attacks against the German lines of communication were major contributions to the Allied strategic offensive of July–November 1918.[19]

There is no doubt that the enhanced role of the political leader in directing the war in France was influenced by the fact that public opinion was more volatile and critical than in Germany and Britain, and by the additional fact no French general possessed the charisma of Hindenburg or Haig. But greater than these factors was the accident of personality: it was Clemenceau's willpower that impressed itself upon his contemporaries and commanded their cooperation or obedience.

IV

In the final volume of his war memoirs, David Lloyd George, reflecting upon the general course of civil-military relations in the various belligerent nations, wrote: "Looking back on this devastating war and surveying the part played in it by statesmen and soldiers respectively in its direction, I have come definitely to the conclusion that the former showed too much caution in exerting their authority over the military leaders."[20] That this was far less true in the Second World War will become clear from the three examples that follow, in each of which it is again the accident of personality that supplies the explanation, although the constitutional framework in which authority was exercised was not of negligible importance.

Adolf Hitler, to take our first example, was the supreme political authority in his country, by virtue of his double role as chancellor (an office to which the powers of the former Reichspräsident had been added in August 1934) and uncontested leader of Germany's only political party, the others having been eliminated, with all other potentially dissident elements, in the process of *Gleichschaltung* in the years 1933-1934. His authority over the army was firmly established by the oath of allegiance that all officers and other ranks had, ever since August 1934, made to him personally as leader of the German Reich and Volk and supreme commander of the Wehrmacht, and by the reorganization of the command of the armed forces in February 1938, which established a Supreme Wehrmacht Command (OKW) under his direct authority. In December 1941, Hitler made his command over army operations even more immediate by dismissing General von Brauchitsch as commander in chief of the army (OKH) and taking over his duties, explaining to the OKH chief of staff that "the trifles" of operational leadership were something that "anyone could perform."[21]

In these circumstances, there was no possibility of military domination of the strategical decision-making process. The question became rather whether and how far the Führer could concede to his OKW and OKH operations staffs the role of strategical advisor. It rapidly became apparent that he was little inclined to think in terms of a genuine collaboration. General Alfred Jodl, chief of the OKW operations staff said in a memorandum dictated to his wife during the Nuremberg trials:

> Hitler was willing to have a working staff that translated his decisions into orders which he would then issue as Supreme Commander of the Wehrmacht, but nothing more. The fact that even men like Frederick the Great would have their own thoughts and decisions tested and re-examined against the often contradictory ideas of their generals made no difference to Hitler, who resented any form of counsel regarding the major decisions of the war. He did not care to hear any other points of view; if they were even hinted at, he would break into short-tempered fits of enraged agitation."[22]

Already pronounced before the war (it was after the success of his Rhineland coup in March 1936 that he said, "I go my way with the assurance of a sleep-walker"), Hitler's mystical conviction of his infallibility as the leader of his country's march to world power was enhanced by the successes of his strategy in 1939 and 1940. As Jodl testified,

> The man who succeeded in occupying Norway before the very eyes of the British fleet with its maritime supremacy, and who with numerically inferior forces brought down the feared military power of

France like a house of cards in a campaign of forty days, was no longer willing, after these successes, to listen to military advisers who had previously warned him against such over-extensions of his military power. From that time on, he required of them nothing more than the technical support necessary to implement his decisions, and the smooth functioning of the military organization to carry them out.[23]

In fact, this self-confidence was nothing more than an advanced form of megalomania. Hitler's strategical gifts, once he turned to actual operations, were limited and guided by no realistic assessment of capabilities and costs.

Hitler's grand strategical plan for Germany's future has been well described by Andreas Hillgruber."[24] Limned for the first time in the long-unknown book of 1928, Hitler's dream was to make Germany the dominant world power, first, by the conquest and consolidation of Europe and Russia, preferably with the benevolent neutrality of Great Britain, and then at a later date, after colonial bases had been acquired and a powerful navy built, by a war—perhaps in alliance with Great Britain—against the only power that could still threaten Germany, the United States of America.

Toward the completion of the first stage of this ambitious program, Hitler made remarkable progress in the years from 1933 to 1939, initially by means of a dazzling display of diplomatic virtuosity, by which he succeeded in hiding his real objectives from the Western powers while skillfully exploiting all of their differences and distractions, and then, after the spring of 1938, by an adroit combination of military and political pressures. It is by no means certain that he had exhausted the possibilities of this strategy of mixed means by the fall of 1939, when he seems to have decided that victories won without the direct application of German military might were not satisfying enough. It is evident, however, that once he abandoned the political weapon and chose to seek his objectives by the sword alone, his strategical gifts soon proved inadequate to solve the problems he created for himself.

This became abundantly clear as early as June 1940, that is, at the very moment when General Keitel was hailing the victor over Scandinavia, the Low Countries, and France as "the greatest commander of all times." The OKW chief might more accurately have described his

Führer as a strategical bankrupt, for the fact that Great Britain refused to surrender as France had done disrupted his grand design, and he had no plan for resolving the difficulties that this posed. Field Marshal Erich von Manstein wrote after the war that Hitler was always so confident that his force of will would be able to overcome any possible obstacle to his desires that he forgot that the enemy possesses a will too.[25] Now this awkward truth confronted him for the first time, adding a dimension to the war that he did not understand and could not master. The effect upon his strategy was disturbing and permanent. From now on, it was marked increasingly by impatience, by plans that were ill-conceived, implemented without conviction, and then abandoned, by profligacy in the use of human and material resources, and by an impulsive willfulness that had disastrous results.[26]

The extraordinary lability of Hitler's thinking in the second half of 1940 is indicative of his lack of a clear sense of direction. The plan for an assault on the British Isles was slipshod in conception and the air offensive upon which it depended ill-designed for the objectives it sought to gain. There are indications that Hitler was never very deeply committed to Operation Sea Lion in any case, since, as early as July, he was letting his highest commanders know that the key to ending Britain's participation in the war was Russia, which might have to be destroyed first. In October, when it was clear that the aerial bombardment of Britain was not sufficiently effective, he was off on another tack and was holding conferences with Mussolini, Pétain and Laval, and Franco in an effort to induce them to join in a series of attacks to cut Britain's Mediterranean line of communications completely; and in the same month he was actually considering trying to talk the Russians into an offensive against British holdings in the Middle East. Hitler's staff planners in the OKH had good reason to be bewildered by their master's continual changes of front, since they had, in the course of five months, been ordered to draw up plans for Sea Lion, the capture of Gibraltar, the Azores, and the Canaries, the defense of the Finnish nickel mines, the support of the Italians in North Africa, and the invasion of Russia.[27]

Clarity came at the end of the year, after Foreign Minister Molotov's visit to Berlin in November convinced Hitler that the Nazi-Soviet Pact had outlived its usefulness and that the time had come for the long-desired assault upon the Soviet Union. As the detailed planning for Operation Barbarossa got under way, however, the more prescient of Hitler's staff had some difficulty in understanding what its strategical purpose was to be, and the OKH chief of staff Halder became increasingly fearful, as his diary reveals, lest military objectives be subordinated to ideological ones, and the destruction of the Bolshevik system and the extermination of the Jews take priority over a Clausewitzian strategy of seeking the most expeditious means of weakening the enemy's will to continue the struggle.[28]

That there was reason for such concern became abundantly clear once the attack was begun in June 1941, and the campaigns of 1941 and 1942 in Russia were marked by bitter but unavailing attempts by the soldiers to persuade Hitler to recognize the importance of coherence and consistency. It has been argued that the German armies failed to take Moscow in 1941 because of the delays caused by the campaigns in Yugoslavia and Greece, which were necessary to eliminate a potential danger to the German right flank; but this overlooks the more serious loss of time that was spent between July and September on debates over the missions of the three German army groups in Russia and the question of priority among them. Both Jodl and Halder favored concentrating upon the capture of Moscow, not only because it was the capital of the Soviet Union but because the Russians would defend it with all of their resources and thus provide an opportunity for the destruction of their military strength. Hitler shied away from this solution, insisting at various times that Leningrad was his chief goal or that it was essential to capture the Donets Basin and immobilize the Crimea and end its threat to the Romanian oil fields. He indignantly rejected a Brauchitsch-Halder memorandum of August 18, 1941, in which they argued for an immediate drive on Moscow before the approaching winter made it impossible, and scathingly described the OKH as being filled with minds that were "fossilized" in obsolete theory,[29] an insult that led Halder to suggest to Brauchitsch that they submit their resignations. It was not until September 30, after the southern armies had taken Kiev, that Hitler authorized the advance upon the Soviet capital, and the long delay proved fatal to the enterprise.

The same kind of nervous vacillation characterized Hitler's conduct of the 1942 campaign. Instead of resuming the attack on Moscow, the

Führer declared in April that the principal thrust would be made in the south with the aim of destroying units of the Red Army in the Don Basin and then seizing the oil fields of the Caucasus. Concern over the Reich's shortages of fuel gave some plausibility to this operational plan, but once it was put into effect in late June Hitler again showed his tendency to be diverted by local opportunities and to sacrifice strategical goals for tactical successes. A fateful example of this is provided by his War Directive no. 45 of July 23, which split his southern forces, ordering Army Group B, commanded by General Maximilian von Weichs, to move on the city of Stalingrad, while Army Group A under Field Marshal Wilhelm List—weakened by the loss of two armored divisions that had been detached and sent to Weichs's Sixth Army and most of the Eleventh Army in the Crimea, which had been reassigned to the siege of Leningrad—was expected to cross the lower Don and the Kerch Strait from the Crimea and penetrate the Caucasus.[30]

This was a prescription for disaster. Halder wrote in his diary, "The chronic tendency to underrate enemy capabilities is gradually assuming grotesque proportions and develops into a positive danger. Serious work is becoming impossible here. This so-called leadership is characterized by a pathological reacting to the impressions of the moment."[31] Indeed, Hitler's disposition of his now seriously diminished resources and his choice of objectives were increasingly determined by willfulness and volatility of mood: the names Leningrad and Stalingrad appeared to exercise a baleful attractiveness out of all proportion to their strategical importance; as the Führer's difficulties mounted, his designs became more grandiose and unrealistic; and he became ever more irrational in his reaction to setbacks, squandering resources out of obstinate blindness to facts or for reasons of prestige. The refusal to allow Paulus's Sixth Army to break out of Stalingrad while there was still time to do so and—in another theater of war—the decision to go on reinforcing the bridgehead in Tunisia with troops and equipment long after its fall was predictable were signs of a strategical judgment in disarray.

The decision to declare war upon the United States in December 1941, after the Japanese attack upon Pearl Harbor, is more difficult to explain. A reading of Hitler's speech to the Reichstag on December 10, with its long passages of personal abuse and vituperation of President Franklin Roosevelt, lends some credence to the view that the action was motivated by the Führer's long-bottled-up resentment of Roosevelt's pro-British actions in the Atlantic in 1940 and 1941. A desire to demonstrate solidarity with the Japanese in the hope that they might still be induced to attack the Soviet Far Eastern provinces doubtless played a part also. But it is just as likely that Hitler took this critical step for the sake of the gesture alone and its effect upon the German people and because he knew that it could do no harm: that is, he realized that he must win the war in Russia in 1942, and that if he did so there was nothing that the United States could do to prevent his winning the global mastery that he desired; if he did not, Germany's doom was certain, and deserved.

"Earlier than any other person in the world," Jodl wrote in his Nuremberg memorandum, "Hitler sensed and knew that the war was lost." After the catastrophe at Stalingrad, Rommel's defeat at El Alamein, and the Allied landings at Casablanca, Oran, and Algiers, the momentum of the war had shifted to the enemy's side, and, in Jodl's words, Hitler's "activity as a strategist was essentially ended. From then on, he intervened more and more frequently in operational decisions, often down to matters of tactical detail, in order to impose with unbending will what he thought the generals simply refused to comprehend: that one had to stand or fall, that each voluntary step backwards was an evil in itself."[32] The war now attained the ultimate in irrationality, with Germany's commanding generals reduced, as one of them said, to the status of "highly paid NCOs" and the Führer giving the orders in every sector of every front and insisting that willpower was enough to triumph over superior numbers and equipment.

It was a kind of warfare best characterized in the words of one of Paulus's subordinates in Stalingrad, who described the orders to fight and die in place as "not only a crime from a military point of view but a criminal act as regards our responsibility to the German nation." But then Hitler, to whom the war had always been a personal drama, had never had a very highly developed sense of that kind of responsibility, and perhaps, at bottom, that was his greatest deficiency as a strategist.

V

One could never say the same of Winston Churchill, whose thinking was deeply influenced, in the first place, by his memory of what the losses of the First World War had meant to his country and a determination that the defeat of Hitler should not be won at the same cost and, in the second, by an awareness of the kind of problems that would have to be faced after victory was achieved. In consequence, his strategical ideas had a more emphatically political cast than was true, as we shall see in due course, in the case of his friend and ally in Washington, Franklin Roosevelt.

Of all the political leaders of the major belligerents in the Second World War, Churchill had the greatest experience in war. Commissioned in the 4th Hussars in 1895, he had within eight years seen fighting in Cuba, the northwest frontier of India, the Sudan, and South Africa, either as a combatant or as a war correspondent. Elected to the House of Commons at the age of twenty-five, he made his name first as a cogent critic of military budgets and later as a vigorous advocate at naval construction, the change of heart coinciding with his translation in 1911 from the post of Home Secretary in Asquith's Liberal cabinet to that of First Lord of the Admiralty. During the Great War, he was an energetic First Lord, boldly resorting in 1914 to the use of Britain's amphibious capability to prevent German capture of the Channel ports and, a year later, becoming a powerful champion of the plan to take the Dardanelles and drive Turkey out of the war. When the failure of this operation led to a cabinet shakeup and the loss of his position, he went back to the army and was given command of the 6th Royal Scots Fusiliers, earning the praise of his superiors. He returned reluctantly to Parliament in the spring of 1916 when it became apparent that he could not expect a brigade when Haig became commander in chief.[33] In the last year of the war, Lloyd George appointed him as minister of munitions, over the objections of those who still held him responsible for the failure at the Dardanelles.

This varied experience had two sharply different effects upon Churchill's thinking about war and its management. In the first place, his memory of the unhappy results of the loose and redundant committee system of the Asquith-Kitchener days led him, as soon as he became prime minister in 1940, to introduce structural changes that sharply centralized government operations and had the effect of making him both head of government and supreme commander of the armed forces. Working through a small War Cabinet, he formed under it a Defence Committee (Operations) consisting of the deputy prime minister, the three service ministers and, later, the foreign secretary, with other ministers attending when necessary and the chiefs of staff always present. Within the new Ministry of Defence, whose leadership he also assumed, the chiefs of staff formed a "combined battle headquarters," which met daily in Churchill's presence or that of his deputy defence minister, General Ismay. The minister of defence had direct authority over both the Joint Planning Committee and the Joint Intelligence Committee, as well as over a Joint Planning Staff that was independent of the separate service ministries and met, under Ismay's chairmanship, in the War Cabinet Secretariat. As the war continued, the concentration of power in the hands of Churchill and the chiefs of staff gradually excluded both the War Cabinet and Parliament from any effective role in the formulation of strategy, a fact that occasioned intermittent protests and complaints, which were, however, rendered ineffective by the system's proven efficiency. The coordinated staff planning that it made possible was far superior to anything produced by its American counterpart, as the Americans learned to their discomfiture at the Arcadia, Casablanca, and Trident conferences in 1942 and 1943. Ronald Lewin has written that "the embodiment in Churchill of both political and military authority provided the keystone for a new High Command structure which proved to be the most efficient central system for running a war ever evolved, either in Great Britain or any other country."[34]

For the first two years of Churchill's tenure of power, much of the energies of the chiefs of staff had to be directed toward restraining the impetuosity of the system's creator and toward trying to maintain a tolerable working relationship between him and the commanding generals in the field. For, if the Great War had taught Churchill a good deal about effective organization for the direction of the war effort it had also left him with a low regard for professional soldiers that comported ill with his boundless confidence in his own military judgment and in his talent for strategical and tactical decisions. Since he was also a robust and combative personality who had no patience with the systematic and unexciting aspects of operational command and was further endowed with a powerful imagination that dismayed practitioners who were forced to have a scrupulous regard for the relationship between means and ends, conflict between him and his commanders was inevitable. Field Marshal Archibald Wavell once said that Churchill "never realized the necessity for full equipment before committing troops to battle. I remember his arguing that, because a comparatively small number of mounted Boers had held up a British division in 1899 and 1900, it was unnecessary for the South African Brigade to have much more equipment than rifles before taking the field in 1940. In fact, I found that Winston's tactical ideals had to some extent crystallized in the South African War. His fertile brain was always inventive or receptive of new tactical ideas and weapons, but I do not think that right up to the end he ever understood the administrative side of war; he always accused commanders of organizing 'all tail and no teeth.'"[35]

Because he suspected his generals of lacking enterprise and aggressive spirit, Churchill deluged them with streams of orders, memoranda and directives on matters that were really their business rather than his own. On August 16, 1940, for instance, to the astonishment of Chief of the Imperial General Staff Sir John Dill and Major-General Sir John Kennedy, director of military operations, he sent a directive for the conduct of the campaign in the Middle East that was virtually an operations order including detailed tactical instructions, down to the forward and rear distribution of battalions, and giving minutely detailed orders for the employment of forces[36]—the very kind of supersession of the authority of the field commander to which Hitler was prone in the last stages of the war. He was constantly on the watch for signs of faintheartedness on the part of his generals, and, in April 1941, learning from Kennedy that Wavell had a plan for withdrawal from Egypt if it should be forced upon him, shouted in rage, "Wavell has 400,000 men! If they lose Egypt, blood will flow! I will have firing parties to shoot the generals!" and—when Kennedy protested that every prudent general must have such a plan—"This comes as a flash of lightning to me. I never heard such ideas! War is a contest of wills! It is pure defeatism to speak as you have done!"[37]

There is no doubt that Great Britain was well served by Winston Churchill's indomitable spirit in the grim years of 1940 and 1941, and that his defiance of odds that would have daunted most men not only sustained the courage of his own countrymen but won the admiration and the material support of the people of the United States as well. Even so, his combativeness exacted a price, and his eagerness to get at the enemy wherever an opportunity to do so presented itself led to a serious muddling of priorities. The decision to go to the aid of Greece in March 1941, without any rational estimation of how gravely this would drain the strength of the Middle East Command and how slight the chances of success, seems in retrospect to have been an almost frivolous exercise in gallantry, and Churchill's responsibility for the resultant debacle is not palliated by the fact that Dill and Wavell, against their better judgment, concurred in the decision. And Churchill's later fascination with Rommel, which was doubtless due to his penchant for seeing the conflict in terms of individual combatants, led him to elevate the position of Egypt in Britain's list of strategic priorities from fourth place (after the security of the home islands, Malaya, and the Cape of Good Hope) to second and to declare, in a directive issued without consulting the chiefs of staff, that its loss would be second only to successful invasion and final conquest, a conclusion with which the DMO Kennedy violently disagreed.[38] Nor was this merely the rhetoric of the moment. It influenced Churchill's views on the allocation of resources; it deprived Malaya, in particular, of needed reinforcement; it led to the fall of Singapore, an event that went a long way toward advancing that dissolution of the British Empire over which Churchill had vowed he would not preside.

After Sir Alan Brooke succeeded Dill as CIGS, Churchill's forays into the operational field were gradually limited, for Brooke was more willing than his predecessor to resist notions that he thought were dangerous and was cunning enough to keep from the prime minister's attention matters that he thought might have an excitable effect upon his stormy temperament. "The more you tell that man about the war" he said to Kennedy after radically reducing a minute to Churchill, "the more you hinder the winning of it."[39] At the same time, the entrance of the United States into the war, which took place in the same month as Brooke's appointment, marked the opening of a new phase in which the most important requirement was effective joint strategical planning, and Churchill's response to this challenge was flawed by none of the impulsiveness and lack of measure that he had shown in 1940 and 1941.

Thanks to the special relationship that the prime minister had established with Franklin Roosevelt from the very beginning of the war, which was fostered at the outset by their common interest in naval affairs,[40] a certain amount of contingency planning had been accomplished even before the United States became a belligerent. Thus, Anglo-American staff talks were held in Washington from January 29 to March 29, 1941 to determine "the best methods by which the armed forces of the United States and the British Commonwealth . . . could defeat Germany and the Powers allied with her, should the United States be compelled to resort to war." These ABC-1 talks had been guided by the conclusions of an earlier American memorandum of chief of naval operations Admiral Harold Stark that, in the event of war, the United States would adopt an offensive posture in the Atlantic as an ally of Great Britain and a defensive one in the Pacific.[41]

The American mood after Pearl Harbor, however, aroused concern in Churchill's mind lest this order of priorities be reversed, and he resolved to go to Washington at once "with the strongest team of expert advisers who could be spared . . . to persuade the President and the American Service chiefs that the defeat of Japan would not spell the defeat of Hitler, but that the defeat of Hitler made the finishing off of Japan merely a matter of time and trouble.[42] As it happened, his fears were groundless. At the Arcadia Conference in Washington in January 1942, the concept of "Germany first" was reaffirmed, as was the continuation of a bombing campaign, a blockade, and measures of subversion to weaken Germany until major landings could take place somewhere in western Europe, presumably in 1943. No positive proposals were made for the Pacific beyond the establishment of a supreme command (ABDA) for all allied forces operating in the area from Burma to the China Sea, a plan that soon proved to be unworkable.

On the voyage to America in *Duke of York,* Churchill composed a series of papers that came close to justifying Ismay's statement that "in his grasp of the broad sweep of strategy [he] stood head and shoulders above his professional advisers," and that embodied what came to be the basic assumptions of British strategy for the next two years.[43] He recognized the limited capabilities of the Allies in the immediate future. "Hitler's failures and losses in Russia are the prime facts in the War at this time." The most favorable areas for Anglo-American action were on the Atlantic sea lanes and in the air, to maintain supply lines and inhibit German production, and in the northern African theater. The main offensive action in 1942 should be "the occupation of the whole of the North and West African possessions of France, . . . further control by Britain of the whole North African shore from Tunis to Egypt, thus giving, if the naval situation allows, free passage through the Mediterranean to the Levant and the Suez Canal." Planning should simultaneously be made for landings, in the summer of 1943, in Sicily and Italy, as well as in Scandinavia, the Low Countries, France, and the Balkans, the actual choice of several specific targets to be deferred until later. He made clear his belief that the war could only be won "through the defeat in Europe of the German armies or through internal convulsions in Germany." He envisaged an invasion army of forty armored divisions, covered by command of the sea and superior air power, with their way prepared by an intensive bombing offensive.[44]

This was, in fact, the strategy that was followed by the Allies in 1942 and 1943, although there were, along the way, stormy scenes with the American chiefs of staff, who, after joint consultation with the British in April, thought that they had persuaded them to agree to a cross-Channel invasion in 1943 (and even in 1942, if the Russians seemed on the point of collapse) and who suspected them of reneging and, indeed, of having no stomach for a Western landing. At such moments, Churchill's friendship with the President proved to be invaluable. It was his eloquence in the Washington conference of June 1942 that persuaded Roosevelt that a delayed Channel crossing was preferable to one that failed; it was his persuasion that edged the President toward the acceptance of a North African invasion as a feasible and profitable alternative; and, at Casablanca, it was his skillful portrayal of the offensive possibilities opened by the North African lodgment that won Roosevelt's support for a landing in Sicily and, by extension, in Italy.[45]

In a real sense, then, Churchill's strategical views were determinant of Allied operations in 1942 and 1943 and had the consequence of preventing the implementation of the Overlord plan until the attrition of German strength and the improvement of the shipping situation made it seem feasible to the British Chiefs of Staff. It was not until the Teheran conference of November 1943 that this ascendancy came to an end, when, with Stalin's strong support, the Americans got a firm date for Overlord and for a supporting invasion of southern France (Anvil). Before agreeing to this, Churchill and Brooke were given a clear understanding that operations in Italy would not be curtailed until the other landings took place, since they were the only means of pinning down German divisions that might otherwise be employed in Russia or France, and that Roosevelt's light-hearted promise to Chiang Kai-shek at the first Cairo conference, to launch an amphibious operation against the Andaman Islands in the next few months—Operation Buccaneer, to which, as Brooke said, the British "had not agreed and of whose merits they were not convinced"—was revoked.[46]

The diminution of Churchill's strategical influence in the subsequent period he bore manfully but with mounting foreboding. However great his admiration of the Americans, he was exasperated by their insensitivity to the fact that wars create as many problems as they solve and that the art of grand strategy is to foresee the outlines of the future and be prepared to deal with it. After Stalingrad, when the momentum in the east shifted to the Soviet side, he began to apprehend an excessively large Soviet pressure in postwar Europe and to consider plans for limiting it by border agreements or mutually recognized spheres of influence. Such suggestions were, however, vigorously resisted by Secretary of State Cordell Hull, who had returned from the Foreign Ministers Conference in Moscow in November 1943 convinced that in the future there would "no longer be any need for spheres of influence, for alliances, for balance of power, or for any other of the special arrangements through which, in the unhappy past, the nations strove to safeguard their security or to promote their interests."[47]

Nor was Hull alone in opposing the intrusion of the concepts of the old diplomacy into the pursuit of the war. American soldiers, who were convinced that their preference for the direct rather than the peripheral approach to battle problems showed their adherence to Clausewitz's doctrines, were all too obviously ill-informed about the German theorist's insistence that political considerations can be forgotten in wartime only with peril,[48] as Eisenhower was to prove in April 1945 in refusing to consider an advance on Berlin.[49] As for the President himself—to whom Churchill, in an appeal not to foreclose strategical options, had wired in July 1944, "On a long-term political view, [Stalin] might prefer that the British and Americans should do their share in France in this very hard fighting that is to come, and that East, Middle and Southern Europe should fall naturally into his control"[50]—he was no more open to the idea that strategy had a political side than his secretary of state or his soldiers. In his view, winning the war was the first priority, and politics would come later.

VI

If Franklin D. Roosevelt had been slow in appreciating Hitler's boundless ambitions and if, in consequence, his diplomacy before 1939 had been at best indifferent,[51] his direction of American policy after the outbreak of the European war, while hesitant, tentative, and even contradictory in its tactics, inevitably so in view of his domestic restraints, was masterly in its overall strategy. To the military situation, he responded with vigor and assurance. He had long been interested in naval affairs and geography, and his service as assistant secretary of the navy from 1913 to 1920 had given him confidence in his ability to make decisions about military questions and grand strategy.[52] In July 1939, as the certainty of war became apparent, he had issued a Military Order in his capacity as commander in chief, moving the Joint Board of the Army and Navy, the body that coordinated the strategical plans of the two services, and the Army and Navy Munitions Board, which controlled procurement programs, and the civilian agency in charge of military production into the new Executive Office of the President. This meant that he intended to keep the military power of the United States under his own control, for as members of the Joint Board the chiefs of staff were now responsible directly to him, and the secretaries of war and the navy, Henry L. Stimson and Frank Knox, were largely excluded from the area of strategic decision.

To the British, this was a system of baffling looseness. Sir John Dill wrote to Brooke on January 3, 1942 that the American chiefs of staff never seemed to have regular meetings and, when they did meet, there was no secretariat to record their proceedings. Unlike the British, they had no joint planners or executive planning staff, and their contacts with the President were intermittent and, again, unrecorded. "It seems to me," Dill wrote, "that the whole organization belongs to the days of George Washington, who was made Commander-in-Chief of all the Forces and just did it. Today the President is Commander-in-Chief of all the Forces, but it is not so easy just to do it."[53] The American system was, in fact, more efficient than Dill supposed, but there is no doubt that it was less coordinated than its British counterpart. Franklin Roosevelt always preferred to keep his options open, his thoughts shrouded, and the right of ultimate decision firmly in his own hands and, although in time he became dependent upon General George Catlett Marshall and relied increasingly upon his military judgments, this was less true in the period between his Military Order of July 1939 and Pearl Harbor, during which, Kent Roberts Greenfield has written, "FDR made all his important decisions regarding the use of American military power either independently of his military chiefs, or against their advice, or over their protests."[54]

Even before the outbreak of hostilities in 1939, the President had come to the conclusion that, if war came, the United States would be forced, in its own interest, to support Great Britain. It was his hope that, if it did so vigorously enough, actual military intervention by the country might not be necessary. This strategical concept was implemented by three decisions. The first was Roosevelt's order in November 1938 for the creation of a plant capacity to produce ten thousand combat planes a year, later stepped up, in May 1940, to fifty thousand, to the indignation of the chiefs, who feared that the rearmament of their services would become hopelessly unbalanced. The second was the decision in May-June 1940 to commit the country to all-out assistance to Great Britain, a step revealed to the public for the first time in the President's Charlottesville speech on June 6 and later put in force by means of the destroyers-bases arrangement and the Lend-Lease legislation. This too the army and navy found dangerous, expecting the imminent collapse of Great Britain and preferring a policy of hemispheric defense. The third was the decision in the spring and summer of 1941, against Marshall's strong reservations, to establish garrisons and convoys in the Atlantic and to extend them as far as necessary in order to keep the supply lines to Britain open.[55] These actions and the stubborn refusal on the part of the British government to consider surrender were the crucial factors in disrupting Hitler's grand strategical plan and in forcing him along the desperate course that led to his destruction.

After Pearl Harbor, the President's greatest concern was that popular passions might force a concentration of the American effort upon the war with Japan, thus fatally compromising the strategical assumptions of ABC-1 with which he was in full agreement. This explains the course that he followed in the debates between the American and the British staff planners. Roosevelt was always more skeptical about the possibility of a successful invasion of the European continent from the British Isles in 1943 than he thought it advisable to make clear to his chiefs of staff, and he was, for domestic political reasons, attracted by Churchill's argument about the necessity of engaging the Germans before the end of 1942 and the feasibility of doing so in North Africa. In July 1942, when Marshall, exasperated by what he considered to be British stalling on plans for a cross-Channel operation, joined forces with Admiral Ernest L. King and suggested shifting the major American effort to the Pacific, Roosevelt firmly overruled them, saying tartly that this would be like angry children "picking up their dishes and going home." He ordered Marshall, along with King and his chief civilian advisor Harry Hopkins, to go to London and reach some decision that would bring American ground forces into action against the Germans in 1942, and he gave them a set of orders that allowed them little freedom of action. "Please remember three cardinal principles—speed of decisions on plans, unity of plans, attack combined with defense, but not defense alone. This affects the immediate objective of U.S. ground forces fighting against Germans in 1942. I hope for total agreement within one week of your arrival."[56] Since the British chiefs had already voted firmly against a cross-Channel attempt in 1942, these instructions eventuated in the plan for Operation Torch, the North African landing of November 1942.

Roosevelt's primary motive had been to ensure domestic support for the Allies' grand strategical concept; and this also guided him in two other decisions that were likely, like the support of Torch itself, to postpone a 1943 cross-Channel invasion. The first, to which the President persuaded the British to agree at the Casablanca Conference, was to authorize Admiral King to go on the offensive in the Pacific as opportunities presented themselves; and the second, activated in 1943, was to follow up the German defeat in Tunisia with an invasion of Sicily and Italy. Superb politician that he was, Roosevelt had a remarkable ability to gauge the public mood, and he was aware by 1943 that, although the danger of a groundswell of opinion, orchestrated by the China lobby, in favor of an exclusive emphasis upon the Pacific war was no longer as great as it had been, it had been replaced by another source of concern. There was a growing tendency in the country to regard the war as all but won and a growing irritation that it wasn't completely won.

This new mood was reflected in such things as the threatened strike of the Railway Brotherhoods in December 1943, the widespread resentment against proposed legislation dealing with civilian manpower, the increased pressure for deferment from the armed services, and a tendency on the part of the press to give prominence to news items that discredited the administration of the services. A major part of George Marshall's time was devoted to attempts to check these tendencies by explaining to Congress, the press, and business, labor, and private groups the enormities of the task ahead and the importance of a truly national effort—an assignment that he performed so ably that, when it came time to choose a commander for Overlord, the President felt that he could not do without Marshall in Washington and selected Eisenhower, although the chief of staff had been considered the obvious choice.[57] Concern over the public mood also influenced Roosevelt's strategical choices, persuading him to support Churchill's Italian proposals so that there would be no slack periods in the European conflict and so that there would be demonstrable daily evidence of progress toward final victory.

It was for the same reason that he was little inclined, in the last two years of the war, to share Churchill's worries about the looming Soviet threat and the necessity of agreements about spheres of influence in southeastern Europe and a firm and united stand against Soviet intentions in Poland. He was well aware that such terms as balance of power and spheres of influence were viewed with distrust by most Americans, and that many of them were uninterested in what went on in other countries and unpersuaded that the domestic problems of other peoples were a legitimate source of concern to the United States. He feared that any intimation of cracks in the Grand Alliance would cause a degree of consternation and indignation at home that would be deleterious to the war effort. He was conscious of the fact also that, after Germany was defeated, there would still be the task of defeating Japan, in which it appeared that the collaboration of the Soviet Union would be necessary. Finally, he recognized the strong sentiment in the United

States for a new international system after the war that would secure the hard-won peace. Whether that was to take the form of a Great Power directorate (like the curious Four Policemen plan of which he was so enamored)[58] or would be modeled after the League of Nations, Soviet participation would be indispensable.

In the President's mind, these great goals precluded disputes over boundary lines in Europe or the claims of rival Polish governments. He was, in his airy way, confident that on matters of high import he would be able to handle "Uncle Joe," but he had no intention meanwhile of following the cautionary prescriptions of Winston Churchill. *Realpolitik* must not be allowed to interfere with the winning of the war. The American people would not tolerate that.

VII

These observations began with a quotation from Clausewitz concerning the necessity, in a nation's strategy, of subordinating the military to the political point of view, and it has become clear, from the cases chosen, that the political leaders who were most successful in doing this were Clemenceau, Hitler, Churchill, and Roosevelt. This is such an oddly mixed group that it merely illustrates the fragility of general rules. If we set Clemenceau aside—for he was more an *animateur de la victoire* than one who put any distinctive stamp upon the strategy of the Entente powers—the case of Hitler would seem to prove that the subordination of the military point of view to the political can be just as disastrous in its results as the opposite state of affairs. The case of Franklin Roosevelt, on the other hand, suggests that the legitimate political concerns of the most responsible of war leaders can be contradictory and self-defeating, domestic political considerations making it inexpedient to attend to political issues that have been created by the war itself and that threaten, unless attended to, to render strategy ineffective in the long run.

Even more ambiguous is the example of Winston Churchill, who was both *animateur de la defiance* and a leader with great strategical vision, and who succeeded in mastering his own military establishment and making it an efficient collaborator in the pursuit of his objectives. This was a notable achievement, but an imperfect one. For Churchill was, after all, forced by circumstances to fight side by side with stronger allies, and, in the end, their conflicting strategies for victory and peace defeated his own.

19

The War Against War

The military history of the first half of the nineteenth century was marked by a curious discrepancy between the heightened destructiveness of warfare and the lack of attention paid to means of controlling its human costs. As armies adopted infantry weapons like the breech-loading Dreyse needle gun and the French *chassepot*, whose range and rate of fire greatly exceeded those of previous models, casualties in the field increased in number. It was the rare army, however, that made adequate provision for the care of the wounded. In 1854, the British army went into the Crimean War without a field commissariat, an effective system of supply, a corps of service troops, or an ambulance corps or medical service. After the battle of the Alma it was discovered that there were no splints or bandages on hand, and, in the barracks hospital at Scutari, the spread of cholera, gangrene, and dysentery raged virtually uncontrolled until the Secretary of War persuaded Florence Nightingale, who had administered a sanitarium in London, to organize a corps of nurses and go to the Crimea to prevent a disaster.

Review of *Dunant's Dream: War, Switzerland, and the History of the Red Cross*, by Caroline Moorehead; and *The Good Listener: Helen Bamber, A Life Against Cruelty*, by Neil Belton: *The New York Review of Books*, June 24, 1999, pp. 40–42. Reprinted with permission from *The New York Review of Books*. Copyright © 1999, NYREV, Inc.

In the war that broke out in 1859 between France and Piedmont on the one hand and the Austrian Empire on the other, the situation of the wounded was no less calamitous. The French Emperor Napoleon III, who had taken to the field with his armies, was so shaken by the heavy losses at Solferino on June 24 that, without consulting his ally, he began secret negotiations with the Austrians for peace. After the day of battle 6,000 dead lay in the fields and vineyards around the tower of Solferino, as well as 30,000 wounded, who could not be moved because the retreating Austrians had taken all the carts and horses with them, and who lay without care or water, some in the throes of death and others crazed with pain.

On the evening of the 24th a young Swiss businessman named Henri Dunant came to Solferino, hoping to meet the French emperor and to enlist his aid in behalf of an ailing business he owned in Algeria. He was unsuccessful in this, but he was horrified by the devastation of the battlefield and the hapless condition of its victims, and stayed to do what he could to alleviate their suffering by recruiting women and children in the neighboring villages to take food and water to them, and by organizing a primitive field hospital in a church in Castiglione. Without an adequate supply of bandages, anesthetics, or surgical help, the hospital proved unable to deal with the thousands of casualties who were brought to it, and the scenes that he witnessed there—of wounds becoming gangrened because they were not treated soon enough, of last-minute amputations followed inexorably by death—were etched in Dunant's mind. After he returned home, he recorded them in a book called *A Memory of Solferino*, which was published at his own expense in October 1862 and aroused wide attention, less perhaps because of Dunant's eloquence than because the horrors it described spoke to a widespread feeling of guilt that such things could take place in a century of progress.

From the standpoint of its effect upon posterity, the most important part of Dunant's book was a problem posed in its last pages. Why, he asked, could not societies of volunteers be set up in peacetime so as to be ready to help the wounded when war came? And why could not some international principles be codified to regulate the treatment of the wounded in future wars, neutralizing medical care, for example, and stipulating that friend and foe receive equal treatment? In these suggestions lay the origin of the Red Cross movement. They were taken up by Gustave Moynier, a Swiss lawyer and philanthropist of great energy and organizing talent, who formed a five-man committee, with himself as chairman and Dunant as secretary, to give them more precise form and to solicit international support. The speed with which this was accomplished confounded skeptics. Dunant's ideas fitted naturally with the reforming temper of the nineteenth century and its desire, while accepting war as an indispensable tool of statecraft, to diminish its rigors whenever possible. Within two years the Convention for the Amelioration of the Condition of the Wounded in Armies in the Field was ready for signature and in the next three years it was ratified by twenty-one nations. It specified that all wounded be accorded humane treatment, that medical personnel, whether military or civilian volunteers, should be considered neutral, that anyone helping the wounded should be "respected and remain free," and that medical personnel and supplies should bear, for purposes of ready recognition, a red cross on a white background, in the form of a flag or armband. Meanwhile, national societies for the providing of medical volunteers and other wartime services—soon generally called Red Cross Societies—were multiplying.

Dunant himself, sadly, was prevented from participating in this heady success; he was expelled from his post as secretary of the coordinating committee because of the collapse of his personal fortune, bankruptcy not being lightly regarded in a bankers' city like Geneva. His sense of dedication was undiminished by this blow, and he spent his years in exile giving lectures on the significance of the Geneva Convention and doing what he could to encourage the formation of new national societies. He continued to be regarded widely as the founder of the Red Cross, and in 1901 he was awarded (with Frédéric Passy, who established the International League for Permanent Peace in 1867) the first Nobel Peace Prize.

I

Caroline Moorehead has written the first satisfactory account of how Dunant's idea inspired the creation of the greatest humanitarian movement of modern times. The author, a writer on human rights with a column in *The Independent*, has wisely not tried to be comprehensive; there is little here about Red Cross activity in Africa and South America and during the Vietnam War; the work of the various national Red Cross societies, with the exception of the American one, is not treated in any detail. Instead, she writes, she has chosen "from 130 years of war and natural disasters those conflicts, issues and moral dilemmas which seem to have had the most determining effect upon the growth of the modern Red Cross." The center of her account is the International Committee of the Red Cross, to whose records and files she has been the first historian to have unimpeded access.

Her story is filled with anomalies. In her preface Moorehead points out that what is called the International Committee is really a private Swiss company based in Geneva and governed by twenty-five (originally five) Swiss citizens. Like its numbers, its functions have greatly increased since the days of Dunant and Moynier. It monitors violations of the laws of war as defined in the now amplified Geneva Conventions; it seeks not only to treat the wounded but to improve the conditions of prisoners of war, political detainees, and, increasingly, refugees from war zones. It performs a host of relief and welfare tasks, including visiting prisons, but it does all this without self-advertisement. It employs "delegates"—about eight hundred in 1997, mostly Swiss—who gather information about special problems in places where order has broken down or civil wars are causing breaches of international law, including human rights abuses. But the delegates are prohibited from making their findings public and report only to Geneva, where the committee officials decide what should be done about them. They sometimes choose to make private complaints to governments about their practices, hoping they will improve, and then go on to make public statements if they don't. The International Committee shuns the word "politics" but, Moorehead says, is "one of the shrewdest political actors of our day." It has no enforceable authority, relying upon its considerable moral power.

As the movement has grown, the Committee has, not surprisingly, been criticized for being too parochial, too Swiss, and too unpolitical. On occasion its primacy has been challenged by one or another of the larger national Red Cross societies. Such calls for change have always been beaten off because the International Committee's record of success has made any fundamental change of leadership seem unwise. In 1870, during the Franco-Prussian War, Moynier, the Committee's president, came under attack for not protesting publicly against French violations of the Geneva Convention, and the Prussian chancellor Bismarck threatened to reconsider his own support of the Convention.

Moynier's response, which became standard in the years that followed, was that it was not the Committee's role to act as judge and jury. At the same time he called the attention of his critics to the countless lives spared in the name of the Convention during the fighting, to the Committee's work in protecting and repatriating prisoners of war and channeling relief to distressed areas, and to the fact that Red Cross societies had sent 347 doctors into the field, of whom 46 had died. Meanwhile the Red Cross had succeeded in achieving general recognition of the principle of the neutrality of medical services.

Similarly, during the First World War, when passions ran much higher and when national intolerance of restraints was formidable, Moorehead writes of the International Committee:

> It was universally acknowledged to have transformed the lives of prisoners-of-war, pushing always for more and more concessions; it had transmitted two and a half million letters; it had reunited families scattered by the fighting; it had kept open communication between the different Red Cross societies; its prison visits were now accepted and respected and its reparation schemes were working smoothly; and it continued to act, despite innumerable violations of the Geneva Convention, as a constant moral reminder of the atrocities of war.

Moreover, when the conflict came to an end and Europe was inundated with liberated prisoners of war trying to get home, Red Cross delegates, some of them exhausted from four years of difficult missions, willingly set off to remote parts of Central and Eastern Europe to assist people in situations of anarchy and chaos; and they sent to Geneva meticulous reports about the conditions they found, the means required to facilitate repatriation, and the amount of relief needed to alleviate current distress. It was hard to deny that the Red Cross richly deserved the Nobel Prize that it was awarded in 1917 or that its efforts to preserve the idea of community between the war-wracked nations had been impressive.

In the postwar years, however, everything became more difficult, as democracies and monarchies were supplanted by dictatorships that repudiated previous standards of international law. In the war in Ethiopia that was touched off by Mussolini's attempt to carve out an African empire for himself, the Italians bombed Red Cross ambulances and violated their own adhesion to the 1925 protocol against the use of poison gas by employing it in air raids that made no distinction between soldiers and civilians. Sidney Brown, the English Committee's delegate in Ethiopia, warned that

> if we do not manage to have the Red Cross emblem respected by a country calling itself civilized, we will never be able to do so later if we are ever faced by a war in Europe.

Brown argued that a public stand be taken against an Italian air force that was becoming "more and more murderous" and turning the war into one of extermination. But he soon found that the International Committee, now chaired by Max Huber, a widely respected Zürich judge, believed that public remonstrances would destroy the Committee's reputation for neutrality. When it sent a delegation to Rome in March 1936 to discuss setting up a commission to investigate violations of the Geneva Convention by both sides, the sole result was a bland assurance by Mussolini that he had every intention of respecting the Red Cross emblem; the question of poison gas was never raised.

It was rumored that this anodyne conclusion was a result of a deal between the Italians and the Committee member Carl J. Burckhardt, historian, diplomat, and after 1937 League of Nations Commissioner for Danzig, who was, Moorehead says, "at this point something of a defender of the Fascists, seeing them as a bulwark against Bolshevism." There is, however, nothing certain about such allegations, and it is more likely that the Committee's conduct expressed the victory of tradition over conscience, of its commitment to silence and discretion over its fear of politics. Such traditional inhibitions perhaps also explain why Sidney Brown was now eased out of the Red Cross because of his outspoken fury against the Italians.

The long war in Spain, the International Committee's first experience with the special problems caused by a civil war, did much to redeem some of the doubts raised by the Ethiopian war. It was a conflict, Moorehead says, "of hostages and reprisals, secret detention centers and executions," yet the seventeen Red Cross delegates who monitored every phase of the war managed to visit 75,000 prisoners, exchanged

five million messages between the two Spains, restored thousands of
children separated from their homes by the war to their parents or sent
them abroad to places of safety, and sought stubbornly, but on the
whole successfully, to persuade both sides that international law protected doctors, priests, and civilians and to arrange for the exchange of
hostages.

But the question, first raised in Ethiopia, of taking a moral stand
against the dictators would not go away, and Hitler's genocidal policy
posed it starkly. For years the International Committee had been working to win international assent to a convention forbidding the deporta-
tion of civilians in occupied territory. Now deportations began in all
twelve of the countries occupied by German troops, and the civilians in
question were sent to labor camps or transit camps or concentration
camps where they died from malnutrition, overwork, or brutal treatment. After Hitler's attack on the Soviet Union, Soviet prisoners of war
were added to the list of victims, and after the Wannsee Conference of
January 1942 the destruction of the Jews became an acknowledged objective of German policy.

News of these outrages spread rapidly in Europe. By the beginning
of 1942 the Committee's delegates in Berlin were informing the Geneva office of deaths in camps in Poland, France, Belgium, and Norway,
and the pressure upon it to speak out was becoming irresistible. Many
members and supporters echoed a statement made in 1935 by Edmond
Boissier, one of its delegates, who said, "The ICRC's prestige is not
harmed if, having done all it can to defend a humanitarian cause, it suffers a defeat; on the contrary, the authority is damaged by inaction and
excessive caution."

Yet it was caution that won the day when, on October 14, 1942,
twenty-three members of the Committee met in Geneva to decide
whether or not to launch a public appeal on behalf of the Jews.
Moorehead gives a dramatic account of this meeting, describing how
the proponents of such an action dominated the first hour of the discussion and then, one by one, were overcome by the arguments of their
opponents and finally voted to do nothing. Why, she asks, in a world in
which there was no other group capable of taking a clear stand and in
which its moral revulsion was needed, did the Committee take a decision that would haunt it until the present day?

Part of the reason, she argues, lay in the very Swissness of the International Committee, not only temperamentally (its members being people given more to reasoned debate than to precipitate action) but in material ways. Its membership was completely Swiss; it had 3,500 Swiss citizens working for it; and half of its budget came from the Swiss federal government. Any public action it took was bound to be regarded as reflecting Swiss federal policy, and hence as a breach of neutrality and an unfriendly act against the Axis countries. It might lead the Axis powers to take military action against Switzerland. During a Committee meeting in June, these considerations were raised by Philippe Etter, the president of the Swiss Confederation, who made a unique appearance at a Committee session and who played a central part in the debate.

More important, however, was the feeling, encouraged during the October meeting by the acting chairman Edouard Chapuisat and its most influential member, Carl Burckhardt, that a public appeal might not help the Jews, while it might also hurt the Committee's ability to perform its principal function, that of improving the condition of prisoners of war. After all, Burckhardt argued, part of the world was opposed to the "ideas out of which the Red Cross was born." Was it wise in such uncertain times to make public statements, when work behind the scenes might be more effective?

This argument was persuasive to the committee members. It is hard to deny, however, that whether or not a public appeal would have helped the Jews, failure to make one was a capitulation that tarnished the Committee's reputation. Thus in the 1990s, when the Committee was accused of pro-Nazi behavior during the war on the basis of an unsubstantiated report by the Office of Strategic Services that it had employed German agents, and when charges were made that some of its members had, in their own businesses, profited from the employment of slave laborers in Swiss-owned factories supplying German troops, many people automatically found such accusations credible.

Because of illness, Max Huber, the longtime and much respected president of the International Committee, had not attended the 1942 meeting, but he agreed with its conclusion and was entirely convinced that the Committee should concentrate on its traditional tasks, chief among which was the expansion of the scope of humanitarian law. At the end of the war, Huber's dearest wish was to repair the deficiencies in the Geneva Convention that had been revealed during the conflict; in 1949, thanks to his urging and to much laborious committee and conference work, fifty-five states signed four new Conventions, the first three dealing with protection of the wounded and sick, the ship-wrecked, and prisoners of war, the fourth protecting civilians who have fallen into enemy hands from arbitrary treatment and violence. At the time, Frédéric Siordet, head of the Commission on Delegates, called the additions "a monument to humanity," but some critics wondered whether the conventions were not in fact more applicable to the wars of the past than they would be to the new forms of violence that were becoming prevalent in the postwar world.

Symbolic of the new age was the murder of Count Bernadotte of Sweden in Jerusalem in September 1948. Long active in Red Cross af-fairs and talked of as a future president of the International Committee, Bernadotte was acting as UN mediator between the Arabs and the Jews and planning a new relief program for the refugees in the area. He was returning to his Palestine headquarters when his car was fired on by members of the Stern Gang. From then on, violence increased steadily, with such bloody conflicts as the Korean and Vietnamese wars, the long struggle between Iran and Iraq, and the countless brutalities and expulsions and ethnic cleansings of the 1990s, in which violations of the Geneva Conventions—in the words of Cornelio Sommaruga, pres-ident of the International Committee after 1987—"defied humanitarian reasoning" and resulted in entire populations being "threatened, starved, terrorized, massacred, turned senselessly into refugees."

This woeful story Moorehead tells clearly and with a wealth of mel-ancholy detail, as when she notes that civilians who during World War I made up a bare 10 percent of casualties account for 90 percent in to-day's wars, almost all of whom are women, children, and old people. In Rwanda, between the end of 1994 and the autumn of 1996, the number of unaccompanied children registered by delegates of the International Committee increased from 37,000 to 90,000. Of the International Committee she asks:

> How is it to work when its delegates are refused access to victims or are themselves made targets for armed gangs who do not want wit-nesses to the atrocities they commit? When civilians are slaughtered with disregard for all the recent additions to the Geneva Conven-

tions? When the infrastructure of states collapses as the states themselves collapse, destroyed by marauding warlords? . . . When the nature of modern conflict makes it impossible to tell where war stops
and peace begins?

The answer, she believes, lies in continuing to make the Committee's presence and its experience felt wherever conflict occurs, working
through its delegates in the field and as the ultimate authority on humanitarian law. Despite its setbacks and compromises, the Red Cross
has been faithful to this historical mandate, and its founder Henri Dunant would doubtless be proud to know that in today's chaos along the
Kosovo-Macedonian border its presence, symbolized by the large
crosses on many of the tents dispensing relief to the refugees, is a
promise of hope.

II

One of the most distressing signs of the decline of civilization in our
time has been the willingness of governments to use torture in the
treatment of their prisoners or their domestic enemies. In the nineteenth century this would have been unthinkable, and Victor Hugo was
doubtless acknowledging the universally accepted legacy of the Enlightenment when he said quite matter-of-factly in 1874, "Torture has
ceased to exist." But the coming of the totalitarian states put an end to
that assurance, and in Hitler's and Stalin's camps and prisons it would
have been idle to cite the words of such opponents of torture as the
Italian penal reformer Cesare Beccaria.

The Geneva Convention of 1949 clearly condemned torture, declaring that freedom from this abuse was a fundamental human right, but
almost immediately there was widespread evidence that its provisions
were being flouted. This was true in Algeria in 1957, where General
Massu's paratroops perfected the art of the *gégène*, the application of
electric shocks to the testicles of their prisoners; it was true in Greece
after the colonels' coup of April 1967 (Moorehead writes: "Greece
marked the moment when political detainees became the subject of
worldwide interest and when torture and abuses of human rights really
entered the language of humanitarian law"); and it was true in Israel in
1977, where the International Committee issued one of its rare public
protests after the government did nothing to curb the brutal methods

of its interrogators. The Committee has had its successes in its fight to preserve human dignity against physical abuse, but the problem has remained and is endemic today in half of the nations of the world.

Neil Belton's profound and moving book is essentially a reflection on torture and its effects upon its victims. He calls it "a footnote to the scholarship of an infamous period," the fifty years that have passed since the passage of the Geneva Convention of 1949. But he adds that he has attempted

> to imagine how the extreme violence of our world affected one woman, beginning with the Holocaust, and how she did something creative about it. I have tried to give a stand against cruelty the force of a human story.

Helen Bamber had her first experience with the effects of torture in 1945, at the age of twenty, when she went as a British member of a Jewish Relief Unit to the former Nazi camp at Bergen-Belsen. It was only two months since its capture, and the smell of the burned huts still hung in the air. Still housed in the camp were 12,000 former Jewish prisoners who were unwilling to return to the homes from which they had been driven by the Nazis and who were also forbidden by the administration of the British-occupied zone to go to Palestine. The Jewish Relief Unit's function was to supply these people with food and clothing, to try to find whether they had living relatives, and to aid them in other ways. This involved dealing with their compulsive tendency to talk about their wartime experience, what they had suffered, and what they had lost. Here Helen Bamber—brought up in England as the daughter of a Polish Jewish refugee and not a practicing Jew herself— discovered in herself an unsuspected talent for listening. She said later:

> They would hold you, and it was important that you held them . . . and you would hold onto them and they would tell you their story. Sometimes it was in Yiddish, and although I had learned some, it was as though you really didn't need a language. It took a long time for me to realize that you really couldn't do anything but that you just had to hang onto them and that you had to listen and to *receive* this, as if it belonged partly to you, and in that act of taking and showing that you were available you were playing some useful role.

Throughout her life, Bamber's gift has been a source of comfort to other victims of inhumanity and torture who all too often found that the world they returned to after the war had neither interest in nor understanding of what had been done to them. Belton writes of the satisfaction Bamber derived from her trips north to Berwick-on-Tweed to talk with survivors of the machine-gun battalion of the Northumberland Fusiliers, who were captured at the fall of Singapore in February 1942 and spent the next four years in slavery, suffering the casual brutality of their Japanese captors and a work schedule that Belton calls "a form of slow murder." After their liberation and return to England, they received no official recognition from their government, which seemed to regard them as being responsible for Singapore's loss, and little understanding from their neighbors in Berwick. Bamber was able to penetrate their closed community and encourage some of them to talk freely about their pent-up feelings and their sense of isolation.

As she pondered the lessons of Bergen-Belsen, Bamber became aware of how seductively easy it was to rationalize torture. The Nazi doctors in Belsen used the bodies and minds of their captives for experimental purposes, justifying the pain involved and the not infrequent deaths by boasting about the future benefits that would accrue to medical science. This was a practice that was not confined to totalitarian states, and the use of unwitting patients for the sake of science was not unknown in Britain. While she was working as a medical secretary in St. George's Hospital in Wapping in the 1950s, Bamber met Maurice Pappworth, a doctor who had become an outsider in the closely knit British medical profession because of his propensity for speaking uncomfortable truths. His abiding concern, Belton writes, was "the potential of medicine for cruelty": the unnecessary operations, both the overuse and the denial of drugs, the distress caused by painful procedures that were justified as "research." In the late 1940s, after the Nazi doctors' trials, Pappworth began to collect details of unethical experiments from reports printed in medical journals, and after he met Helen Bamber they compiled an archive of such cases. From this in time came Pappworth's book *Human Guinea Pigs*, which was published in 1967. Pappworth's influence is to be detected also in the Medical Foundation for the Care of Victims of Torture which Bamber established in 1985.

The analogy between medical and political malpractice became close during the cold war years, when would-be dictators did not hesitate to use the most radical means against what they defined as "cancers" in the body politic. Perhaps the most egregious example of such abuses occurred during the coup launched by Augusto Pinochet against the government of Salvador Allende in Chile in September 1973 and the subsequent war of the military against civil society, in which many thousands of people were tortured. Belton writes that more than any other event since the end of the war, the grossly excessive violence that Pinochet used against what he called "the germs" affecting society sealed Helen Bamber's decision to dedicate herself to the struggle against cruelty.

What made the Chilean case particularly obscene to her was that so many respectable people in Chile, in England, and in the United States found it possible to look at the means Pinochet used to achieve his ends without any feeling that they had a moral obligation to intervene. During her years on the board of Amnesty International, as she worked to publicize the growth of cruelty in the world, Bamber said:

> What I find difficult, and always have done, is how easily we become bystanders. A whole structure of power, even in those states that don't themselves torture, seems to find it necessary to support, or at least not to confront, torture states. Rather than put their foot down and say we do not trade, we do not supply, on the contrary, they say we will supply, and then talk about jobs for the boys. I'm putting this in very simplistic terms, but the remedies are available, and they are not used. The legal instruments are there to prevent torture. And states could apply practical pressure, yet nothing is really done by powerful states to stop it.

As in the case of the Northumberland Fusiliers, not enough people are listening to the victims; and as a result more people today live under governments that use torture than under regimes that forbid it.

20

"A Very Strange Machine"

In November 1917, at Cambrai, three hundred British tanks broke through the supposedly impregnable Hindenburg trench system on a front of seven miles and, for a loss of four thousand men, captured eight thousand terrified German prisoners. It was a penetration equal to that which had taken three months and countless deaths to achieve at the Third Battle of Ypres. When the victory bells rang in England at the end of November, tank supporters were sure that they were tolling out an old style of war and sounding in a new one, which would be characterized by deep thrusts and encirclements rather than the bloody paralysis of the trenches.

These prophets were eventually proved correct, but it took a long time. It is true that the tank had an important part in the last year of the Great War—in General Ferdinand Foch's counterattack in the Battle of Soissons on July 18, 1918, for example, and in Sir Henry Rawlinson's rapid advance on the first day of the Battle of Amiens on August 18, 1918, which caused the chaos and panic of what General Erich Luden-

Review of *Tank: The Progress of a Monstrous War Machine*, by Patrick Wright, *The New York Review of Books*, April 25, 2002, pp. 45–46. Reprinted with permission from *The New York Review of Books*. Copyright © 2002, NYREV, Inc.

dorff called the "black day" of the German army. But the predicted tactical revolution was delayed for another twenty years, largely because of the entrenched conservatism of military establishments.

This conservatism took different forms in different countries. As far as Britain is concerned, the reader of Patrick Wright's insightful new book may be inclined to believe that it was chiefly owing to the continued mystique of the cavalry, which seemed to most soldiers to be a truer form of war than anything that could be accomplished by machines. The cavalry, as one soldier explained ruefully, was "the social difficulty," for it had always been "the high class thing to be in." It seems likely also that the zeal of the tank's advocates helped to discredit their arguments.

The most distinguished of these, J.F.C. Fuller, a theorist of rare imagination who was one of the architects of Cambrai, made no secret of his contempt for the uninspired strategy of Field Marshal Haig and for what he called the craven acquiescence of the civilian government in his failure of vision. But Fuller's shrillness and his propensity for political extremism (he was a member of Sir Oswald Mosley's Fascist Party, an early admirer of Hitler and Mussolini, and an ardent anti-Semite) helped to discredit his views and bring his military career to an early end. What postwar tank exercises there were in Britain were badly handled and tended to discourage the cause of mechanization.

This was also true of France, where the voices of the rare supporters of the tank like Charles de Gaulle were drowned out in the postwar years by the Pétainist advocates of defensive war, and also of the United States, where isolationist feeling was so strong that the promising Tank Corps of the war years was dismantled and all tanks were placed under the command of the infantry and trained in traditional infantry tactics. In Italy, the prestige of the Fascist movement made tanks indispensable, if only for their symbolic uses, as platforms for speeches by Il Duce. But the Italians never developed effective tactics for the light Fiat tanks they possessed; they used them in Ethiopia to support infantry in offensive operations even when the terrain was inappropriate, and in the Spanish civil war the Italian tanks, while attracting much press attention, were roundly defeated at the Battle of Guadalajara in April 1937.

It was only in Germany and the Soviet Union that real progress was made toward articulating a new style of war in the interwar period. The terms of the Treaty of Versailles, of course, made it impossible for the Germans to possess tanks, but, as Wright tells us, they soon discovered that much could be learned about them from exercises with motorcycles, sports planes, and armored cars borrowed from the police. As early as 1924 officers like Heinz Guderian were studying Fuller's theories and testing them in such maneuvers. In the Soviet Union, Mikhail Tukhachevsky and Vladimir Triandafillov, both of whom owed more to Fuller than they liked to admit, developed a theory of "deep war" in which tanks would have a major part. Preliminary steps to build up the mechanized Red Army of the future were taken at the Kazan Tank School in the late Twenties, and in the 1936 maneuvers one thousand tanks passed in review.

This progress was dramatically curtailed after the Great Purge of 1937, in which Stalin satisfied an old grudge against Tukhachevsky by eliminating him and his chief followers. The Soviet dictator did not possess the imagination to understand tanks, which he dismissed as products of bourgeois capitalism, and his commissar for defense, Voroshilov, put an end to independent armored operations, although—fortunately for the Soviet Union in the light of what lay ahead—he continued with the production of the prototype of the T-34 tank that was to turn the tide at Stalingrad.

It was therefore the German blitzkrieg, in the fulminating campaigns in Poland, the Low Countries, and France in 1939 and 1940, that changed the face of warfare. The first of these bred the stubborn myth that the Polish war was "an undignified rout with a few deluded lancers charging at tanks," a story spread equally by the German commander Heinz Guderian and the British military historian Basil Liddell Hart. Wright will have none of this. Citing the Polish historian Tadeusz Jurga's decades of work on the campaign, he points out that the Poles actually resisted longer in 1939 than the French did in 1940, and that they mobilized 200,000 troops which, in an operation comparable to the Germans' Ardennes offensive of 1944, forced Hitler's Eighth Army into a tactical retreat. The Poles were defeated not by innocence about the capacities of tanks but by German superiority in numbers, airpower, and armor, and by the devastating speed with which they deployed them. And Germany's other antagonists in the first years of the war had the same experience.

These quick victories, however, had ruinous aftereffects when Hitler's arrogant ambition led him to launch his assault on Russia in June 1941. In the first campaigns in the east, Nazi armor was no less successful than it had been in France, but, as Geoffrey Megargee has pointed out, both Hitler and his generals vastly underestimated the resources at their enemy's disposal and pinned their hopes on a short campaign.[1] This was a fatal error that should have become obvious after the halt before Moscow in December 1941 and became painfully so with the Soviet counterattack at Stalingrad a year later. This so-called Operation Uranus exemplified in certain respects Tukhachevsky's concept of "deep war." Under the command of Colonel General N.F. Vatutin, Soviet armor smashed through the weakened flanks of the German Sixth Army to the north and south of Stalingrad and then came together to encircle that army and parts of the 4th Panzer Army as well. Before the resultant "Operation Ring" was completed in January 1943, German casualties amounted to 209,000 dead and 91,000 captured.

Hitler still made one final attack before the long retreat began. Launched in July 1943, and designed to devastate Soviet forces in Central Russia, the Battle of Kursk has often been called "the biggest tank battle in history," and as it is usually described as pitting fifty German divisions with 3,155 tanks against a Soviet force of over a million men and 3,275 tanks. Wright believes that this description is misleading, and that in reality Kursk was a sequence of four separate battles, climaxing at the railway junction of Prokhorovka, where five hundred German tanks, including some new heavy- model Panthers and sixty-ton Tigers, fought against 793 Soviet machines, mostly T-34s, but including some British Churchills. There are other estimates of the numbers involved, but general agreement that this engagement was an "enormous armoured brawl" which turned Prokhorovka into a graveyard for burned-out Soviet and German machines, as well as the soldiers that manned them. Taken all in all, Kursk marked the end of Germany's strategic control of the war, and, in the words of Soviet Marshal Konev, was "the swan-song of the German armoured force."

What Wright has called the "progress" of the tank did not stop when peace was restored at the end of World War II, for the founding of Israel in 1948 inaugurated a period of warfare with Egypt, Syria, and other Arab states that continued for more than fifty years and involved battles that were at times as large and as violent as those that had occurred on the Soviet–German front. In the Six-Day War of 1967, and again in the October War of 1973, it has been estimated that at least five thousand tanks and perhaps more than six thousand were engaged. Nor were they employed with any less sophistication than in World War II. Israeli commanders like Major Generals Israel Tal, Avraham Adan, and Ariel Sharon were professors of the blitzkrieg, and Tal, at least, was well read in the works of Fuller, Liddell Hart, and Guderian. After Tal's triumphant breakthrough at Rafah in the Six-Day War, Wright tells us that he began, altogether in the spirit of Fuller, to argue that Israel needed "an army that would operate by fast breakthroughs carried out by 'all-tank' brigades, supported by air but not hindered by armoured infantry . . . which should be relegated to 'mopping-up' operations."

Israeli tanks had an important part in ending the feeling of victimization that was caused by the Holocaust, and the brilliance of the Six-Day campaign completed what Wright calls "the transformation of the Jew from the cowering ghetto victim to the victorious armed citizen." But, as in the case of the Nazis, military success also bred overconfidence, in this case, a tendency to believe that "the miserable Arabs" were incapable of mounting or sustaining a serious war effort. For this Israel had to pay a price in October 1973 when, handicapped by late mobilization, it was subjected to combined assaults by Egyptian and Syrian forces, well supplied with Soviet T-54s, T-55s, and brand new T-62s, which came close to driving their outnumbered units from the Golan Heights while simultaneously crossing the Suez Canal and attacking the Bar Lev line.

Contrary to the prevailing doctrine, the Israeli tanks were forced to resort to piecemeal counterattacks against superior forces (on the Golan, 177 Israeli tanks to 1,400 Syrian machines), and the situation became so desperate that ministers in Jerusalem were, according to Wright, discussing the possible use of nuclear weapons. Luckily, when the Israelis were down to their last reserve of seventeen tanks, the Syrians lost heart and began to retreat from the Golan, while simultaneously the Egyptian mistake in leaving the canal's west bank unprotected led to Sharon's counterattack and encirclement of their Third Army, which forced them to sue for peace.

The October War was followed by recriminations and outrage in Israel, forcing the resignation of Prime Minister Golda Meir and a shakeup of the army command and intelligence service. At the same time, because of the heavy armored losses that it suffered in the October campaign, the Israeli Defense Force speeded up the production of a new tank, the Merkava, or Chariot, which General Tal had designed and perfected over the previous ten years. In an interview with Wright that is reproduced in *Tank*, Tal explained that, whereas all tanks represent a triangular reconciliation of three partly contradictory capacities, namely, firepower, mobility, and protection, the Merkava is notable for giving priority to protection above all, with inbuilt safeguards against the danger of fire or exploding munitions, and more effective means of escape for the crew in case the tank is hit. Wright believes that the Merkava Mark III is "as safe as a monstrous killing machine can be: a tank for a small country of four million that, humanitarian considerations aside, must do everything it can to minimize losses among its trained tank forces."

Meanwhile, the popularity of the tank in Israel at large and the sense of being dependent on it remains strong, although the tank evidently cannot protect civilians against suicide attacks. Wright cites a 1994 Claude Lanzmann film about the Israeli Defense Force in which a reservist who was the sole survivor of his tank crew in the October War gives a moving description of the fate of his comrades but then says: "I like tanks very much. I like to drive them. I like to shoot from them. A tank is a very beautiful machine. It is a very strange machine. It's not human at all, but it's very dynamic, very vital."

Less satisfactory than this brilliant discussion of armored warfare in Israel is Wright's concluding chapter about his visit to the US Army Armor Center at Fort Knox and his discussions there with tank specialists. His account of these will not always be easy for the layman to understand, and it is a pity that he did not spend more time explaining the military conviction that a restructuring of the army "to make the most of digital technology . . . would finally disperse what Clausewitz called the fog of war." As for the tank of the future, Wright writes mysteriously that it had been engineered out of the cultural imagination in the second decade of the twentieth century; and it was apparent, eighty years later, that if it was to survive into the twenty-first century as anything other than an obsolete hunk of old steel, it must now be turned back into a "concept."

"Maybe it won't even touch the ground," said one of Wright's interlocutors, "maybe it will ride on an electro-magnetic cushion; . . . maybe its gun will be a laser beam." But there would always be "one platform providing direct and indirect force defense power."

One senses that these ruminations have been overtaken by time, like the reference to Desert Storm having become "the model of future American wars," a sentiment difficult to defend now that it is realized that that operation failed to achieve a satisfactory result and now that members of the current administration are agitating to have it refought. In any case, the tank has survived into the twenty-first century without being reduced to a concept; and another soldier at Fort Knox told Wright that he was perfectly happy with the civilian impression of tanks as "ponderous machines that will squash you. . . . And let me tell you, if you want to get somebody's attention, just put a M1A1 tank on the ground."

Wright's book is an excellent military history of his subject, written in lively prose and with a wealth of unfamiliar detail. He is fascinated also by the mythic cult of the tank and the way in which it has affected the popular imagination, and his book is filled with references to the ways in which countries have come to be known by their tanks (the T-34, the Tiger, the Merkava), and politicians had their destinies affected by them (Boris Yeltsin and Michael Dukakis), and how the tank has symbolized tyranny (Prague in 1968) and been an object of popular defiance (the confrontation in Tiananmen Square between a single individual and a column of tanks in June 1989).

What he has to say on these topics is interesting but not always persuasive. Is the current booming market for SUVs in the United States really powered by the insecurity of drivers? ("It's a jungle out there," according to one writer. "It's Mad Max. People want to kill me, rape me. Give me a big thing like a tank.") Surely the social prestige of owning the biggest car on the block, as well as the ideal soccer mom's vehicle, is a likelier motive.

21

How to Think About the Swiss

In the modern history of Switzerland, the heroic days were those of 1847 and 1848. It was then that the Swiss liberals founded a new nation by defeating an attempted secession of the Catholic cantons in a short but crucial conflict, the *Sonderbundskrieg*, and then by providing the restored union with an effective constitution and the institutions that would help make it work.

No less remarkable than this impressive beginning was the country's ability to defend its independence from external threats during its first vulnerable decade. These were perilous days for the new federal state. The revolutions in Central Europe in 1848 and 1849 posed in its most acute form the problem of reconciling Switzerland's policy of neutrality with its long tradition of providing asylum for political refugees. The

Review of *The Swiss, the Gold, and the Dead: How Swiss Bankers Helped Finance the Nazi War Machine*, by Jean Ziegler; *Hitler's Silent Partners: Swiss Banks, Nazi Gold, and the Pursuit of Justice*, by Isabel Vincent; *Hitler's Secret Bankers: The Myth of Swiss Neutrality During the Holocaust*, by Adam LeBor; and *Movements of Nazi Gold: Uncovering the Trail*, by Sidney Zabludoff: *The New York Review of Books*, June 11, 1998, pp. 36–39. Reprinted with permission of *The New York Review of Books*. Copyright © 1998, NYREV, Inc.

conservative powers of Europe, irritated by the proud independence of the new federal state's foreign policy, seemed on more than one occasion to be searching for a pretext for intervention. From this eventuality Switzerland saved itself by stubbornness and inspired diplomacy, while at the same time giving refuge to the fragments of the defeated revolutionary army in Baden and those who had fought on the barricades of Dresden and Milan. A hundred years later Max Frisch's stern critic of his country's fortunes, Anatole Stiller, was to say of its founders, "In those days they had a blueprint. In those days . . . they rejoiced in tomorrow and the day after. In those days they had a historical present."[1]

The 150th anniversary of the Swiss federal constitution will come in September of this year [1998], but it is to be doubted that it will be quite as self-celebratory an occasion as it would have been in quieter times. Since the beginning of this decade the Swiss government has been buffeted by charges, from domestic and international critics alike, that its conduct during the Second World War systematically betrayed all of the principles laid down and defended by its founding fathers. Specifically, the Swiss authorities are accused of pretending to a status of neutrality which was from the beginning fraudulent, slanted as it was in favor of Germany, and, with respect to the right of asylum, of following a highly selective immigration policy, which in particular discriminated against Jewish refugees; while the Swiss banks are accused of helping finance German aggression by laundering Nazi gold that had been looted from countries throughout Europe.

I

From the beginning of the war the Swiss government was attentive to the desires of its dangerous northern neighbor and, particularly after the fall of France, anxious not to annoy its unpredictable leader. This led it to be deferential in many ways: it yielded to the German insistence on a Swiss blackout that would confuse Allied bombers, for example, and adopted a press policy that forbade the publication of items that might be offensive to the Germans. But these were small things in comparison with its tolerating a policy of financial collaboration between Swiss and German banks that facilitated Germany's military operations and may very well have prolonged the war.

This is the aspect of Swiss behavior that has done the most to cause and sustain the current discussion of Swiss wartime policy, and it is the principal theme of the authors of the four books discussed here: Jean Ziegler, a Socialist member of the Swiss parliament and a longtime opponent of the banking community; Adam LeBor, a correspondent for the London *Times* and *The Jewish Chronicle*, who lives in Budapest; Isabel Vincent, a reporter with the Toronto *Globe and Mail* and the winner of several awards for investigative journalism; and Sidney Zabludoff, an economist who works for the World Jewish Congress. What they have written is complementary and sometimes overlapping. Of the four books Vincent's is the most critical and the one with the widest perspective; she reminds her readers frequently that they would do well to consider the wartime sins of their own governments before rushing to judgment on Switzerland. Ziegler's language is often colored by his feeling of betrayal by his own leaders but, perhaps because of this, his book is the most readable. LeBor is so intent on seeking the big story that he is not always critical enough of his sources, and he sometimes, with headlines like "The Financiers of Genocide," promises more than he delivers; but he makes up for this by what he has to say about cooperation between the Swiss and German intelligence services and about the resistance of individual Swiss officials to their country's immigration policy.

Taken together, these works can read as a kind of commentary on the remark of one of the characters in Gottfried Keller's story "The Little Banner of the Seven Upright Ones," written in 1860. Alluding in general terms to the state of values in the country, this person says, "Luckily there are no terribly rich people among us; wealth is fairly enough divided. But just let fellows with many millions appear, who have political ambitions, and you'll see what mischief they'll get up to!"[2] It was precisely such types, in the guise of bankers with political connections, who, in Ziegler's words,

> fenced and laundered the gold stolen from the central banks of Belgium, Poland, Czechoslovakia, Holland, Luxembourg, Lithuania, Albania, Norway, Italy, and elsewhere. It was they who financed Hitler's wars of conquest. Switzerland, the world's only neutral financial center of truly international standing, accepted Hitler's looted gold throughout the war years in payment for industrial goods or

as bullion that was fenced and laundered and exchanged for foreign currency or traded off in other financial centers under new, "Swiss" identity. But for Switzerland's financial services and the willing fences of Bern, the zealous gnomes, Hitler would not have been able to wage his rapacious wars of conquest. Swiss bankers supplied him with the requisite foreign exchange.

There seems to be no doubt about the essential truth of these accusations. With respect to the activities of the banks, for example, Sidney Zabludoff's circumstantial study of the movement of Nazi gold during the war, commissioned by the World Jewish Congress, proves convincingly that

> Swiss banking institutions played the pivotal role in handling the looted gold sold by the Nazis. They were the initial recipient of $438 million or 85 percent of all gold Germany shipped to foreign locations from March 1938 [the date of the Austrian *Anschluss*] to June 1945. In most cases, this precious metal was shipped from the Reichsbank to its depot account at Swiss National Bank (SNB), with the heaviest flow occurring from the fourth quarter 1941 [after the invasion of the Soviet Union] to the first quarter of 1944.

It all flowed back again in the form of goods and currency that could be used for the benefit of the German military establishment.

To what extent can it be said that this policy enjoyed popular support? There was a wartime saying, quoted by LeBor, that ran: "For six days a week Switzerland works for Nazi Germany, while on the seventh it prays for an Allied victory." This is ungenerous without being inaccurate. It was not only the bankers who profited from the trade with Germany. Many ordinary Swiss citizens earned their wages from making things that Germany needed and paid for in looted gold. Ziegler argues that many of these people did not particularly like what they were doing and that some men and women of all social classes and all cultures and languages opposed the government's policy whenever and however they could, pointing to the Swiss journalists who risked and often sacrificed their careers by defying the official, pro-Hitler censorship of the press.

He may be right, but the fact is that there is no way of estimating accurately the feelings of the Swiss people during the war. As for the Allied governments, they knew of the traffic between Germany and

Switzerland but were unable to prevent it and were aware that complaints might risk the undeniable services that the Swiss government provided them (whether by representing their interests and protecting their nationals in occupied countries, or by acting as a conduit to Berlin and Rome when it was necessary to communicate with them officially, or by turning a blind eye to the activities of Allen Dulles's OSS unit in Bern). The Allies thus found it politically expedient to assume that the Swiss people were on their side. In a speech in 1944 Winston Churchill said:

> Of all the neutrals Switzerland has the greatest right to distinction. She has been the sole international force linking the hideously sundered nations and ourselves. What does it matter whether she has been able to give us the commercial advantages we desire or has given too many to the Germans to keep herself alive? She has been a democratic state, standing for freedom in self-defence among her mountains, and in thought, in spite of race, largely on our side.

In Allied capitals it was recognized also that the Swiss government was not exactly a free agent, and that resistance to Hitler's will, on anything that he considered important, might very well lead to a German invasion of Switzerland. Today, with the memory of Hitler and his *Blitzkriege* far behind us, there is some disposition to assume that the *Führer* wanted hard currency so badly that invasion of Switzerland was out of the question. One of LeBor's sources is quoted as saying that Hitler depended so much on Bern to keep the Nazi war machine rolling that anyone "who even suggested the possibility of invading Switzerland would have been sent to the Russian front." But Ziegler believes that if the Swiss had refused to go along with Hitler's wishes after the fall of France, it "would very probably have suffered the same fate as Austria or Czechoslovakia"; and Vincent reminds us that in 1940 the German army already had a plan for an invasion, Operation Tannenbaum, and in 1943, Himmler was a strong advocate of a military coup. Hitler's reputation for sudden unexpected action (the snatching of Mussolini from the Gran Sasso in 1943 and the strike through the Ardennes in 1944) must have been enough to keep Swiss apprehension alive and to counsel against any change in their policy of financial support.

That Swiss collaboration was tremendously important to the Nazi war effort seems beyond question. Whether it prolonged the war is a plausible but essentially unprovable hypothesis. That the American offensive in Northern Italy ground to a halt along the Rimini-Bologna-Pisa line in April 1944 because the enemy was equipped with vast supplies of arms, ammunition, spare parts, and gasoline transported to it by way of Switzerland, as Ziegler mentions, proves nothing one way or another. Battles are not won by supplies or money alone, and this Clausewitzian truth is probably applicable to the question of the duration of wars. In any case, this is a question that cannot be answered unless we have a lot more information than is currently available.

II

In May 1995, on the fiftieth anniversary of the end of the Second World War, Kaspar Villiger, president of the Swiss federal state and minister of defense, delivered a speech in the Bundeshaus in Bern in which he dilated on Switzerland's behavior during the war and admitted that it was not in accordance with its ideals. Among other things, he spoke of the restrictions placed upon the right of asylum, particularly for Jewish refugees.

> Would Switzerland have been threatened with extinction had it been more definitely receptive to victims of persecution than it was? Was this question, too, affected by anti-Semitic sentiments in our country? Did we always do our utmost for the persecuted and disenfranchised? . . . Fear of Germany, fear of foreignization by mass immigration, and concern lest the anti-Semitism that also existed here receive a political fillip—these sometimes outweighed our tradition of asylum, our humanitarian ideals. We were also prompted by excessive timidity to resolve difficult conflicts of interest at the expense of humanity. In introducing the so-called Jewish stamp [on passports], the Germans were acceding to a Swiss request. That stamp was approved by Switzerland in 1938. An unduly narrow conception of the national interest led us to make the wrong choice.

These admissions, doubtless prompted by the growing domestic and foreign scrutiny of Switzerland's war record, were accompanied by an insistence that all those who had been responsible for immigration policy had acted "solely and exclusively in the interests of the country's welfare as they perceived and saw it," and that to castigate them now would be unjust. However that may be, history will record that, while Switzerland in the course of the war took in 295,000 refugees, including about 25,000 Jews, they turned away 30,000, most of them Jews, in collusion with the Germans and in violation of international law, and that in doing so, knowingly or not, they consigned most of them to death in the extermination camps.

This was a form of collaboration more shameful than the traffic in gold, and there were Swiss officials who risked their careers to protest against it. One of these was Commandant Paul Grueninger, a career police officer in the Saint Gall canton on the Austrian border. In 1938, after the *Anschluss*, when the government closed the frontier to the hordes of Austrian Jews seeking refuge in Switzerland, Grueninger allowed 3,600 of them to enter his country by falsifying their papers. When this was discovered, he was dismissed, tried for forgery and insubordination, and sentenced to the loss of his position and the forfeiture of all retirement and severance payments. Nor was this punishment corrected after the war came to an end. Until his death in 1971, Grueninger remained without a suitable position and was harried by a smear campaign which accused him of having acted for personal profit.

III

Meanwhile, the financial collaboration between Switzerland and Germany continued, unaffected by a January 1943 inter-Allied prohibition of looting and laundering of the treasuries of occupied countries. In 1944, the United States and Great Britain mounted an intelligence effort, Operation Safehaven, to monitor the movement of Nazi gold to Switzerland, but according to Isabel Vincent, this was not very effective because Dulles's OSS unit in Bern showed no enthusiasm for the task and the British, conscious of the fact that they would need the assistance of Swiss banks to get loans on favorable terms in order to rebuild their shattered economy at the war's end, did not wish to alienate them in advance. Even when an American mission headed by Lauchlin Currie negotiated an agreement in March 1945 by which the Swiss undertook to cut off trade with Germany and freeze German assets in return for renewed supplies of the coal whose delivery had been disrupted by the liberation of France, the Swiss dragged their feet in implementing it. One month after it was signed, and one month before the German unconditional surrender, the Swiss accepted three more tons of looted gold. While much of the world was waiting in breathless anticipation for Hitler's imminent fall, the Swiss banks seemed intent only upon squeezing as much profit as possible from the Nazi connection before that should happen.

Nor can it be said that this behavior backfired on them. When, in consequence of proposals made by the Paris Reparations Conference in November and December 1945, Allied and Swiss negotiators met in Washington in February 1946 to discuss the status of German assets in Switzerland, there was some expectation that the Swiss would be made to pay for their collaboration with the defeated enemy. But the shadow of the gathering cold war was already falling over their deliberations, distracting the Allied negotiators and forcing them to think of how they might soon need Swiss assistance against the Soviet Union. The Swiss delegates, on the other hand, led by Walter Stucki, deputy head of the Foreign Ministry, were tough and immovable, arguing that in the recent conflict—in which, they intimated, there had been no moral difference between Germany and its opponents—they had stood above the fray as neutrals, working in accordance with international law. They saw no reason why they should be called upon to share their wartime profits with anyone.

At the beginning of the Washington conference, there had been some talk of forcing the Swiss to hand over all German assets held by their financial institutions as reparations. After sixty-eight days of grinding negotiations, during which, as Ziegler says, Stucki displayed "an astonishing degree of arrogance and self-righteousness," the Allies took what they could get: 250 million Swiss francs ($58.1 million) in full settlement of all claims relating to Switzerland's transactions with the German *Reichsbank*. This sum was, moreover, to be paid not as reparations but as a voluntary contribution to the reconstruction of Europe. To understand what a victory this represented for the Swiss negotiators, we must note that Zabludoff's careful calculations lead him to the conclusion that the amount of looted gold handled by the Swiss during the war period was $275 million. He adds, however:

> If gold forcibly purchased from German citizens during the 1930s is also classified as looted, then the Swiss would have taken in some $375 million in looted gold. All these figures are much greater than

the $58 million in gold the Swiss turned over to the Allies after the war. To understand these numbers in today's prices, they must be multiplied by about 10. Thus, after subtracting its modest postwar payment, according to postwar agreements Switzerland would now be obliged to pay some $2 to $3 billion to compensate for taking in looted gold.

The Washington accord was bitterly attacked by some American politicians. Senator Harley Kilgore had chaired hearings of the Senate Subcommittee on War Mobilization in June 1945 to look into the possibility of Swiss financial institutions bankrolling German rearmament. Long a champion of cracking down on the Swiss, Kilgore now wrote to President Truman that

> justice, decency and plain horse sense require that the allies hold Switzerland responsible for all of the . . . looted gold which they accepted from the Nazis and reject their proposition of settling for 20 cents on the dollar.

It was, as we now know, considerably less than that but, even if that had been known, there was no likelihood that Truman would do anything about it. The US was wracked with strikes, and the Soviets were in northern Iran; Swiss affairs were now in the back pages of the newspapers.

And there they remained for over forty years. Intermittently, the attentive reader might come upon a reference to a smoldering dispute that had not been touched upon in the Washington accord: the question of access to dormant accounts of people, mostly Jews, and many of them victims of the Holocaust, which was being impeded by Swiss bank secrecy regulations and obstructed by Swiss bureaucrats. The Jewish organizations that might have made this a major issue had until very late in the cold war been engrossed by other problems. As one of their representatives said, they had first to deal with the fate of people displaced as a result of their experience in the concentration camps, and then to fight for the state of Israel; and after that came reparations from Germany and other things. "There were always other priorities that took a long time to overcome."

In 1954, the Israeli government urged the Swiss government to deal with the question of dormant accounts, but it was only in 1962 that the banks were authorized to break their rule of secrecy in order to identify unclaimed funds of foreigners persecuted for racial, religious, and political reasons. A subsequent inquiry identified only 961 accounts of this nature, whose contents were returned to their rightful owners. This was clearly unsatisfactory, but nothing was done to correct it.

Switzerland became news again at the beginning of the 1990s for a number of reasons. In the first place, the end of the cold war revivified the movement toward European integration and raised the question of Switzerland's role in the new Europe. In Switzerland this caused a protracted debate between Europeanists and traditionalists. This led Adolf Muschg, one of the country's most distinguished writers, to challenge the viability of neutrality and to call for a return to the vision of 1848, when, he said, Switzerland was

> a model for the continent, which for a while had all the European powers against it, but the wind of history in its favor. Today, the *Musterländchen*, which has become sated, must learn to have a new model, the little Gold-Majesty Switzerland must thoroughly repudiate its consciousness of being a special case in order to become again what it once was—and what it must otherwise become in any case, only without a will of its own and the pride that comes from independent action—an integral part of Europe, jointly sharing its hopes, jointly responsible for its success. That will require of my much blessed country a hard piece of work and the overcoming of a good deal of *Angst*, the *Angst* of those who have much property and a high degree of security.[3]

Despite this appeal, the Swiss people rejected membership in the EC and reaffirmed their neutrality in 1992.

Then came the continent-wide preparations for the celebration of the fiftieth anniversary of the end of World War II, in which the Swiss government initially decided not to participate on the grounds that it had been neutral. This caused much controversy and stimulated, not least of all among local historians—like Jacques Picard, author of an important study called *Die Schweiz und die Juden, 1933–1945*—a critical examination of the nature of Swiss neutrality during the war.

Finally, in September 1995, Edgar Bronfman, president of the World Jewish Congress, decided to take up the cause of Holocaust survivors who had been living behind the Iron Curtain but were now in a position to demand the return of family assets which they believed had been deposited for them in Switzerland by relatives or friends during the Nazi period. Bronfman was authorized by the Israeli Prime Minister Yitzhak Rabin to act on behalf of these putative depositors, and when he was received coolly and unresponsively by the Swiss Bankers Association, he resolved, as he later said, to "get their attention."

This he did by enlisting the services of Senator Alfonse D'Amato, the chairman of the U.S. Senate's Banking Committee, who was quick to see that his sagging political fortunes might be revived if he took up the cause of Holocaust survivors. The senator's dramatic hearings in Washington were marked by excessive sound and fury, by sensational disclosures that sometimes turned out to be neither new nor correctly stated, and by fulminations and extravagant threats to boycott all Swiss banks. But they threw so much unflattering light upon Switzerland's wartime practices that in the end the bankers and the government decided that it would be wise to stop stonewalling and complaining about unfair attacks and to choose instead a strategy of conciliation. They agreed to cooperate with a committee headed by Paul Volcker, former head of the Federal Reserve Board, which would study Swiss banking practices in the Nazi period and audit the records of 450 Swiss banks. They undertook to engage in an energetic search for holders of dormant accounts. And, in a move that astonished many in Europe and elicited words of praise even from Bronfman and D'Amato, they established a fund of 7 billion Swiss francs ($4.7 billion) to support persons in need who had been persecuted for reasons of race, religion, or politics or were otherwise victims of the Holocaust.

Ordinary Swiss citizens were less impressed by this resolution of the dispute. In general, they appear to have been divided. Some took comfort in the feeling that the extensive airing of wartime practices might be good for the country by leading to a disenchantment with neutrality and a willingness to reconsider the question of joining Europe. Others felt that the tactics employed by Bronfman and D'Amato had demeaned the image of Switzerland unfairly and perhaps irretrievably. After the Washington hearings there was a perceptible increase in anti-Semitic incidents in the country, although anti-Semitism was by no means the sole motivation of a widespread sense of outrage. "We were not consulted," the president of the Swiss Federation of Jewish Communities has said, "and this led to all types of distortions. Switzerland may have profited from the war, but it did not knowingly or deliberately profit from the Holocaust. Switzerland was not Auschwitz, yet these accusations make it seem as if the Swiss supported the extermination of Jews."

Recently Hans Schaffner, head of the Swiss Federal Office of War Economy from 1939 to 1946, wrote with some asperity in *The New York Times* of April 6 that the recent charges against Switzerland were not based on any new information. "All the relevant details have been available since 1946," he wrote. "But what is new is the surge of resentment against Switzerland" and, underlying it, the ignorance of Switzerland's wartime services to the West, despite its vulnerability to German attack. On the contentious question of unclaimed deposits in Swiss banks, Schaffner noted that such accounts continued to exist, and that the records are available for inspection, adding, "Other countries, including the United States, simply took the money after a period of time and destroyed the records." As for the talk about reopening the freely negotiated agreement of 1946, Schaffner describes this as nothing short of scandalous.

Detached observers may tend to sympathize with these views and with Isabel Vincent's point that the more strident of Switzerland's recent critics have had a tendency to ignore the beam in their own eyes for the mote in Switzerland's. One does not have to condone Switzerland's wartime behavior to recognize that other nations were also guilty of abuses similar to theirs. As Vincent writes, other neutral and nonbelligerent countries, such as Portugal, Spain, Sweden, Turkey, and Argentina, helped the Nazis launder looted gold and other assets and sold them strategically important goods. It is worth remembering, moreover, that during the war American officials, hiding behind a cloak of moral superiority as their Swiss counterparts hid behind one of neutrality,

> cavalierly overlooked the suffering of millions of Jews. Although they knew about the Final Solution, they chose not to bomb railway lines leading to the death camps. Despite reports of Nazi atrocities against Jews in the Third Reich, the United States, like Switzerland, set up strict quotas on allowing Jewish refugees into the country.

And when it had a chance to work for justice after the war, the United States simply chose not to act.

It comes as no surprise to learn that recent findings in the National Archives in Washington suggest that financial institutions in the United States and Canada helped the Swiss launder Nazi gold during the war and that an inquiry is underway in Canada to determine what part the Bank of Canada may have had in such activities.

Fate and the Führer

In 1950, appalled by the flood of books and articles about National Socialism that was pouring from the printing presses, a German journalist wrote, "He has played a trick on us. This Hitler, I think he'll remain with us until the end of our lives."

Fifty years later, the situation has not changed. It is true that Hitler has failed to go down in history as "the greatest German," as he predicted he would after the completion of Germany's absorption of Czechoslovakia in March 1939, but he has surely become the one most written about, leaving such competitors as Frederick II, Goethe, and Bismarck far behind. In *The Third Reich*, Michael Burleigh writes of "the avalanche of morbid kitsch and populistic trivia" evoked by the mere mention of his name ("surface scratchings about whether Hitler slept with his niece, loved his dog or had plans for the Duke and Duchess of Windsor"), and it is true that this makes up a large part of the total. For-

Review of *Hitler, 1936–1945: Nemesis,* by Ian Kershaw; *The Third Reich: A New History,* by Michael Burleigh; and *The Social History of the Third Reich, 1933–1945,* by Pierre Ayçoberry, translated by Janet Lloyd: *The New York Review of Books,* November 2, 2000, pp. 6–9. Reprinted with permission from *The New York Review of Books.* Copyright © 2000, NYREV, Inc.

tunately it is balanced by works that reveal new information about the Führer's life or see old problems in ways that illuminate and instruct. The three books considered here share those qualities, while differing markedly in content and approach.

I

In the first volume of his biography of Hitler, Ian Kershaw described the early political life of his subject, how he was brought to political power more by chance and the manipulations of others than by his own talents, and how he then, through the weakness of the Western Powers, had a series of diplomatic successes that made Germany once more a power of some consequence.[1] These came to a climax in March 1936, when Hitler, disregarding the warnings of his generals, dispatched troops into the demilitarized Rhineland, destroying the Locarno Treaty of 1925, in which Germany had promised to respect established European borders.

For the mass of the German people, these incidents served to turn Hitler into a statesman of extraordinary talent, and the Führer was not inclined to disagree. As Kershaw tells us at the beginning of his second volume, subtitled "Nemesis," he soon developed new ambitions and, in November 1937, at a meeting with his top commanders, told them that they must be prepared to solve Germany's problem of "living space" sometime between 1943 and 1945, at the expense of Austria and Czechoslovakia. Once more the professional soldiers were overcome by misgivings, but—more by accident than design—the Austrian problem was actually solved to Germany's advantage within four months by the Anschluss, the incorporation of Austria into Germany as the province of Ostmark. Kershaw writes:

> The Anschluss was a watershed for Hitler, and for the Third Reich.
> . . . The overwhelming reception he had encountered on his grandiose procession to Vienna, above all his return to Linz, had made a strong impression on the German Dictator. The intoxication of the crowds made him feel like a god. The rapid improvisation of the Anschluss there and then . . . proved once more—so it seemed to him—that he could do anything he wanted. His instincts were, it seemed to him, always right. The western "powers" were powerless. The doubters and skeptics at home were, as always, revealed as

weak and wrong. There was no one to stand in his way. . . . The Anschluss now suggested to him that the Great Germanic Reich did not have to be a long-term project. He could create it himself. But it had to be soon.

The rest of Kershaw's second volume carries Hitler's assumptions about the Anschluss to their logical conclusions. It is an impressive, detailed, and sobering story, telling as it does of the destruction of an entire continent by the insensate ambition of one man, and if it has an edifying side it is only because nemesis turns out to be fully as efficient as it is claimed to be.

The reader is, indeed, given the impression that he is seeing nemesis in action when Kershaw recalls the story told by Hitler's interpreter, Paul Schmidt. On the eve of the Polish war, Hitler expected that the impact of the Nazi-Soviet Pact would persuade the British to terminate their guarantee of Poland. Instead, as he sat with Ribbentrop on September 3, 1939, awaiting news of the British defection, what he received was an ultimatum from London, demanding an immediate withdrawal of German troops from Polish soil. Hitler turned savagely on his foreign minister. "What now?" he asked. The question was a good one, for from then on, Britain was his greatest problem, limiting his freedom of action and driving him on to other, more disastrous decisions. It was when his later victories over Poland and the Low Countries and France failed in any way to weaken Britain's defiance that he was reduced in June 1941 to declaring war on the Soviet Union as a means of persuasion. He fully expected that this would produce a speedy Soviet defeat that would so discourage the British that they would sue for peace. He could not believe the British would remain in the war to the very end.

The war is Kershaw's grand theme, and Hitler the soldier dominates the action. Kershaw's opinion of his military talents is mixed. That Hitler had an excellent record as a front-line soldier during the First World War is well known, but of course he had no opportunity there to develop the gifts he would need in the Second. In a careful analysis of the campaign against Norway ("the Weser Exercise") in the spring of 1940, Kershaw points out that Hitler was responsible for lack of coordination between branches of the armed forces, for flawed communication between the high command and the navy and, especially, between the army and the Luftwaffe, and for constant interference in the minutiae of controlling operations. Moreover, when things began to go wrong at Narvik in mid-April, he showed signs of panic and bad judgment. General Walter Warlimont later described "the impression of truly terrifying weakness of character on the part of the man who was at the head of the Reich." On the other hand, he showed none of these weaknesses during the campaign against France, where he was one of the strongest voices favoring the daring Ardennes offensive over the more conservative offensive scheme of the army chiefs, which he dismissed as "a cadet's plan."

More important was Hitler's decision to invade the Soviet Union, which, Kershaw writes, "in retrospect . . . seems sheer idiocy." Kershaw points out, however, that in taking this step he was strongly supported by his military commanders, who were convinced that the Soviet forces were ill-equipped and ill-trained and that they would collapse within four months. Whatever may be said of the decision to attack Russia, it was not Hitler's alone, and no one spoke out against it at the time. It can be claimed, moreover, that when the German drive ground to a halt before Moscow in December, and the army commanders called for a retreat, Hitler, by refusing to accede to this, not only remained true to his original decision but saved the invading army from complete dissolution.

Referring to the postwar apologetics of German commanders who tried to leave the impression that they had been forced to comply with the orders of a military bungler, Kershaw writes that the verbatim records of the conferences demonstrate that "Hitler's tactics were frequently neither inherently absurd, nor did they usually stand in crass contradiction to the military advice he was receiving." Where his inadequacies as supreme German warlord became increasingly exposed was in the last stages of the Russian war, when Germany was forced completely on the defensive and the lightning offensives of an earlier period became impossible. It was then that his constant references to his own early career to prove that willpower solved all problems became both tedious and irrelevant, and he exasperated the professional soldiers by dismissing out of hand all attempts to reach a political settlement, arguing that one must only negotiate from strength.

Meanwhile, Germany was gradually turning into a country without any centralized coordinating body and with a head of state largely detached from the machinery of government. As Kershaw points out, the respective spheres of competence of the party and state had never been clearly defined; ad hoc agencies had always proliferated; and the system had for a long time been marked by a high degree of voluntarism in which officials issued orders on their own initiative. Policies that were defined and justified simply as being in accord with the Führer's wishes took on a life and authority of their own. None of this implied any slippage in the Führer's authority, which was supreme when he chose to exert it; but the distribution of power was confusing, and there was a continual erosion of regular patterns of government and a disintegration of anything resembling a coherent system of administration.

As the war advanced, moreover, Germany became a Führer state with an absentee Führer, for after the beginning of the Russian war, Hitler spent most of his time at the front. This inevitably accelerated the disintegration of the machinery of state. Kershaw writes that, out of 445 pieces of legislation in 1941, only 72 were the result of any collaboration among the various ministries. The remaining 373 were produced by individual ministries without wider consultation. Martin Bormann's appointment as party chancellor in May 1941 accentuated this trend, for he saw his responsibility as being merely to channel information to Hitler and to let the *Gauleiter* (district leaders) and the heads of party organizations know of the Führer's decisions and opinions. This did nothing to improve coordination, and Hitler's assumption of supreme command of the army in December 1941 (thereby taking on responsibility for tactics as well as grand strategy, something no other head of state had attempted) meant that questions of politics and economic policy would receive even less attention, particularly as the German army moved toward the disasters of Stalingrad and Kursk.

Hitler never persuaded himself that the defeats he suffered at the hands of the Red Army were deserved. In July 1944, when the details of the failed plot against him began to emerge, he cried in triumph, "Now I finally have the swine who have been sabotaging my work for years. Now I have proof: the entire General Staff is contaminated. . . . Now I know why all my great plans in Russia had to fail in recent years. It was all treason! But for those traitors, we would have won long ago. Here is my justification before history."

There seems no doubt that he believed this, and he showed it by the fearful punishments that he unleashed against everyone involved in the plot. The conspirators had hoped, if successful, to negotiate an end to the war. There would be no further opportunity for that, and the German people consequently had nothing to look forward to but the total destruction of their country. In the nine months that remained of the war, the Allies submitted German cities to relentless raids against which they had virtually no defense; thousands of German troops died in the Ardennes and the Oderbruch, and ordinary citizens suffered acute privations in their daily lives as well as intensified fear and repression at the hands of the regime. It is characteristic of their leader that he had no sympathy with them, but came increasingly to feel that their own lack of faith made them deserve what was happening to them.

II

In the telling of his lamentable story, Kershaw keeps his temper, and his tone is level, analytical, and judicious. This is not always true of Michael Burleigh. A British historian, now professor at Washington and Lee University, he cannot prevent his feelings from showing once in a while. He calls Heinrich Himmler a "moralising little creep" and of Hitler he says on one occasion, "He combined being the worst sort of reductionist scientific bore, forever citing cats and rats, with being a saloon-bar conspiracy theorist, forever banging on about Jews." In stating his purpose, also, Burleigh draws a distinction between Kershaw, who insists that "evil is a theological or philosophical, rather than a historical, concept," and himself by writing forthrightly that his book deals with the

> progressive, and almost total, moral collapse of an advanced industrial society at the heart of Europe, many of whose citizens abandoned the burden of thinking for themselves, in favour of what George Orwell described as the tom-tom beat of a latterday tribalism. They put their faith in evil men promising a great leap into a heroic future, offering a "quick fix" to Germany's local, and modern society's general, problems. The consequences, for Germany, Europe and the wider world were catastrophic, . . . the price of mass stupidity and overweening ambition.

In accounting for the victory of National Socialism in Germany,

Burleigh does not doubt that the humiliations imposed by the Versailles Treaty, the ineffectiveness of the Weimar parties, and the depth of the economic depression were largely responsible. He suggests, however, that only a country with a historical and philosophical culture that was particularly drawn to salvationist rhetoric and mystification would have responded so enthusiastically. However that may be—and Burleigh has some suggestive things to say about such tendencies in a section on the power of sentimentality in National Socialist politics—the surrender, once made, was irretrievable; for the new rulers were quick to supersede the rule of law by arbitrary police terror by which people were subject to being arrested, beaten, and killed without any effective legal protection whatever.

This Burleigh calls the most important departure from civilized values engineered by the Nazi government, and as an example—"the most spectacular legitimisation of the gravest of crimes"—he cites the Law Concerning Measures for the Defense of the State of July 3, 1934, by which Hitler legalized dozens of murders of his own Brownshirt followers that he had ordered days or hours earlier during the so-called Night of the Long Knives. It was because of his leading role in that killing spree that Heinrich Himmler assumed such a dominant role in the movement.

Burleigh is simultaneously repelled by Himmler and fascinated by the way in which he routinely outmaneuvered his enemies and spread the power of the SS in state, party, and army through Germany and the whole of occupied Europe. Because of Himmler's private obsessions, SS values were a combination of puritanism, antipathy toward Christianity, and death-fixated kitsch. Its purpose was absolute loyalty to Adolf Hitler, whose enemies it was sworn to destroy, and it found its highest expression in the wanton lawlessness and sadism of the concentration camps—Dachau, Sachsenhausen, Buchenwald, Flossenburg, and Mauthausen, all built in the 1930s and intended to isolate potential opponents and break their spirits.

In his discussion of the persecution of the Jews, which is one of the most interesting in the book, Burleigh points out that in the beginning most attacks on them were private in origin rather than being initiated by the police. Denunciations of Jews for disloyalty, subversion, and alleged crimes emanated mostly from the lower end of the social scale and were intended to settle deep-seated personal grudges and resentments. Burleigh points out how lethal this kind of name-calling was under a dictatorship. Although such denunciations continued to be made in large numbers, they were soon superseded by state-sponsored anti-Semitism (for example, laws dismissing Jews from the civil service and depriving them, as in the case of the Nuremberg Laws of 1935, of their civil rights) and by bureaucratic chicanery that took the form of petty persecution and the denial of privileges enjoyed by other citizens.

The personal effects of these measures have been described in the now well-known diaries of Victor Klemperer, in which the author systematically records how he was denied the right to use public transportation, to go to the theater, to visit public libraries, to buy cigarettes, and to do scores of other ordinary things.[2] Burleigh cites the case of Albert Herzfeld, the son of a major textile manufacturer, a baptized Protestant, and a veteran of World War I, in which he had served as a lieutenant and won the Iron Cross Second Class. After the war he became a gentleman artist and lived what would have been a comfortable middle-class life had it not been for the Nazis, who systematically deprived him of his civic rights and imposed petty humiliations upon him. His artists club, for example, after sending him congratulations on his seventieth birthday, expelled him eight weeks later, and he was finally forbidden the right to paint at all. In the end, deprived of his home and his wealth, he was sent with his wife to Theresienstadt in 1942, where he died a year later. He remained convinced until the end, however, that the broad German public was "absolutely not anti-Semitic."

The intermittent violence that had marked the persecution of the Jews since 1935 reached its crescendo in the dreadful pogrom of November 1938, and this marked a significant turning point in the history of the Jewish question. (Burleigh believes that to identify this event as the *Reichskristallnacht* is to render harmless what was a murderous and deliberately orchestrated rampage of mindless mobs.) There were no more examples of violence on this scale, perhaps because it was realized that Herzfeld's judgment of public opinion was correct and a repetition of the organized November outrages would backfire. Instead, the SS now began to search for a "total solution" of what it now saw apocalyptically as "the Jewish Question." In Hitler's speeches, moreover, all of his enemies were now translated into Jews, in a conflation of Jews, criminality, communism, and subhumanity, which, Burleigh writes, "apparently legitimised messianic violence." In 1939, on the sixth anniversary of his coming to power, he made his famous and later oft-repeated "prophecy" that

> if international finance Jewry inside and outside Europe again succeeds in precipitating the nations into a world war, the result will not be the Bolshevisation of the earth, and with it the victory of Jewry, but the annihilation of the Jewish race in Europe.

To trace the fulfillment of that promise is not easy. Burleigh writes:

> The mass murder of the Jews evolved, not in a simple, linear way, but as a result of blockages and stoppages, options denied and opportunities seized upon, rather as a deadly virus bypasses the human immune system, until the whole continent bore witness to its malignant presence. The enterprise was so vast and detailed in execution, its victims ranging from complete urban communities to infants hidden in remote haylofts, that it is difficult to convey its terrible scope in any account aspiring to depth let alone geographical comprehensiveness.

He copes with these difficulties ably, although he admits that it is impossible to tell when Hitler decided in his own mind to murder the Jews of Europe. What cleared the way, however, was probably a secret speech he made to fifty high state and party officials in his private apartment at the Reich Chancellery on December 12, 1941, in which he said that it was time to "clear the decks" on the "Jewish Question" without "sentimentality" or "pity." No one who was present at that meeting could have doubted, Burleigh says, that this was incitement to general murder.

It is a significant feature of Burleigh's book that it does not restrict its view to events in Germany proper. So much of the history of the Third Reich played itself out beyond Germany's boundaries that Burleigh has felt it important to make some assessment of its impact there. His treatment is comprehensive and in some cases—Vichy France, for example, and Poland, which he calls "the nightmare scenario among the occupied nations of Europe"—highly original. He is to be praised in particular for the acuity of his discussion of the moral dilemmas posed by relations between the occupiers and the occupied, some of which (sexual relations in particular) had serious postwar repercussions.

For example, a significant number of the French mothers of the more than fifty thousand children fathered by German soldiers were punished after the war for "horizontal collaboration." Perhaps his most important point is that, unlike some occupying powers in history, Napoleonic France, for example, which bequeathed administrative and cultural gifts to the peoples they conquered, the Nazi empire lived and died by violence and—despite the amount of time spent by sophisticated German officers such as Ernst Jünger in the salons of Paris—left nothing of any worth behind, "except perhaps its contemporary function as a secular synonym for human evil."

III

In his unusual analysis of German society during the Third Reich, the French historian Pierre Ayçoberry makes it clear from the outset that speculation about why Germany succumbed to National Socialism and reflection on the role of personality in the Nazi years are subjects that he intends to leave to others. The question that he addresses is more fundamental: "How did people live, survive, or disappear under the Third Reich?"; and his inquiry is focused not on individuals but on groups, classes, elites, occupations, and professions. Nor does he find it necessary to preface his story with a systematic survey of the weaknesses of the Weimar Republic. Instead, he begins abruptly with an account of the element in public life that convinced Germans in 1933 that things were different: namely, the violence introduced by the Nazis as soon as they came to power.

To begin by describing this, he writes,

> is surely to reproduce the perception of contemporaries more faithfully [than other approaches], and it also constitutes a rejection of the excuses that conservatives present *a posteriori* in the name of what appears to be scrupulous historicism,

namely, that between 1933 and 1935 no one could have foreseen what would one day become the crimes of National Socialism. Ayçoberry points out that this ignores the offenses against public order committed by the Nazi storm troopers (SA) from the earliest days of the new regime and the fact that, when the SA's freedom of the streets came to an end on the Night of the Long Knives on June 30, 1934, its outrages were replaced by the more systematic violence of Heinrich Himmler's

SS. If there were people who did not perceive from the beginning that an apparatus of repression made up the very core of the new people's community (*Volksgemeinschaft*), it was, in many cases, because they thought it justifiable and regarded the Socialists and Jews, who were its victims, as troublemakers or marginal members of society.

Violence also had a role in what was called *Gleichschaltung*, the process of compelling society to fall into line with the new regime. In a fascinating chapter, "The Illusions, Collusions, and Disillusions of the Elites," Ayçoberry describes how determination to remain free from party control was compromised, in the case of the most important professions in the country, by conflicting interests and ambitions on the part of their members. Even the leaders of industry, confident that their indispensable role in the achievement of Hitler's goals in rearmament and full employment would prevent them from becoming dependent on the orders of party bosses, were so enamored of the profits of collaboration that, Ayçoberry writes, many of them slid into political submission without fully realizing it. In the case of the army, which had since the lean days of Weimar wanted expansion above all else, it achieved its wishes after 1935 only at the cost of its spiritual cohesion, for the very large number of new officers who swelled its ranks after 1935 came in large part from the Hitler Jugend or the Nazi Party and had loyalties that differed from the traditional ones.

Members of government departments found it easier to comply with party standards or meet party expectations than to take a principled stand against them. Thus, in drafting decrees for the application of Nazi racial laws, jurists were unlikely to call attention to instances where they violated existing statutes; and diplomats, reassured by the fact that their ranks had not been purged, were happy to act as agents of Hitler's revisionism even when they had private misgivings. Professional conscience did not serve as a deterrent to compliance. Forty-three percent of doctors and other members of the medical community, the highest proportion of any profession, joined the party, while 7 to 9 percent actually joined the SS. As for university professors, intimidated early on by book burnings and student demonstrations, they found it expedient to avoid unfashionable views unless they were so distinguished in reputation that they could count on appointments abroad.

In the case of Germany's elites, therefore, *Gleichschaltung* was successful. This was less true of the working class—those who worked in heavy industry, on the land, in service industries, and in small firms. There was no question about the workers' basic loyalty to the regime, which was assured by the success of the government's economic and foreign policies and the popularity of the vacation benefits offered by the program of *Kraft durch Freude* (Strength through Joy). But there was no great enthusiasm about the movement's ideology, and most workers "maintained an ambiguous attitude, now keeping their distance from the official world, now making the most of the advantages that it offered." Ayçoberry points out that workers used the Hitler salute as little as possible, boycotted informers, and sometimes refused to contribute to the party's charitable and welfare programs, forms of resistance that were not intended to bring down the regime but rather "to limit the Nazification in their daily lives."

Similar forms of resistance were to be found among women, whom the party sought to eliminate from positions that they had won in public life and the liberal professions during the Weimar years, and among young people, whose political activity it sought to restrict to party organizations like the Hitler Jugend. Party policy with respect to women was so clearly guided by an outdated sexism that it was widely opposed and quickly backfired. The dismissal of two thousand women teachers, for example, caused staff shortages that had to be repaired by new recruitment campaigns; in the end it was only in the judicial bureaucracy that women were eliminated completely. As for young people, in 1936 half the children and adolescents of Germany and in 1939 one third of them eluded party control by remaining members of the youth organizations of the two Christian churches or by forming independent groups, like the "swing clubs" of Hamburg and Frankfurt. In doing so, many young people wanted to make clear their opposition to the Hitler Jugend and some of them harassed its members.

The radicalization of Nazi policy in 1938 and 1939 did not put a stop to these expressions of internal discontent, and when the country went to war in 1939 Hitler could count on the obedience of the military but less so upon the unconditional support of the civilian population. Despite its early triumphs, moreover, the war showed no signs of coming to an end, and the longer it lasted the greater the burdens that were imposed upon the German people. The cohesion of family units was undermined by the mobilization of fathers, the evacuation of children, and the participation of women and young people in defense tasks. The closing of shops and the evacuation of working forces to the country became a matter of course, and people found themselves cut off from familiar surroundings and acquaintances and ordered continually to move on. Civil society, Ayçoberry writes, "turned into a kind of kicked-in anthill." People were subjected increasingly, moreover, to the rigors of bombing and, in the last stages of the war, to occupation by enemy forces.

Faced with these difficulties, the civilian population showed an admirable ability to cope, and in 1943, for example, although hampered by an increasingly inexperienced and heterogeneous workforce, industry managed to produce five times as many weapons and other military items as in 1939. But the endurance of the common people and their ingenuity in finding ways to survive owed little if anything to the party, which showed hardly any of the spirit of sacrifice that it demanded from others and whose leadership was characterized by cowardice and incompetence. In September 1944, when Hitler created the *Volkssturm*, the people's army, which included many children, he vested its command in the hands of the *Gauleiter*, who were derisively called the "golden pheasants." The results were not heartening. In provinces threatened by the Red Army there was a mass desertion of party cadres, and the *Gauleiter* of Poznan, Breslau, Bremen, and Dresden made catastrophic decisions, in Bremen forcing the population to resist until the very end, thus assuring the destruction of the city, in Dresden refusing to allow the erection of bunkers, thus increasing vulnerability to air raids. Ayçoberry writes:

> When in his last days Hitler accused the German people as a whole of cowardice, it was the ultimate deception designed to cover up the collapse of the party he had created and used to seize power, but which then proved itself useful neither in peace nor war.

23

The Goblin at War

In June 1940, after Germany's defeat of France, Field Marshal Wilhelm Keitel, chief of the Wehrmacht Supreme Command, referred to Adolf Hitler as the *Grösster Feldherr aller Zeiten* (Greatest Warlord of All Times). When the fortunes of war began to wane, Hitler's generals transformed this into the shorter *Gröfaz*, a name suitable for a kobold or goblin.

The derisive intention was plain but not entirely deserved. Certainly in the early years of the war, Hitler possessed great military talents, which included vision and an instinct for exploiting opportunity, as well as leadership qualities, including steadfastness and energy of the first order and an astonishing knack for mastering specialized military literature. The German historian Helmut Heiber has not hesitated to call him "one of the most knowledgeable and versatile technical military specialists of his time," while admitting that these gifts were offset eventually by excessive self-confidence and impulsiveness.

Review of *Hitler Strikes Poland: Blitzkrieg, Ideology, and Atrocity*, by Alexander B. Rossino; *Hitler's Arctic War: The German Campaigns in Norway, Finland, and the USSR, 1940–1945*, by Chris Mann and Christer Jörgensen; and *Hitler and His Generals: Military Conferences, 1942–1945*, edited by Helmut Heiber and David M. Glantz: *New York Review of Books*, December 4 2003, pp. 51–52. Reprinted with permission from *The New York Review of Books*. Copyright © 2003, NYREV, Inc.

I

The years between 1939 and 1941 saw Hitler's energy at its most impressive. The Polish war, starting in August 1939, lasted a scant five weeks; General Heinz Guderian's initial thrust into the Polish Corridor on the German border quickly destroyed a Polish cavalry brigade and three Polish infantry divisions. The revelation of new German weapons and techniques, including well-organized infantry assault teams and systems of air–ground cooperation, astonished the rest of the world and discouraged the British and French from mounting a counterattack in the west, although they still outnumbered the Germans by seventy-six divisions to thirty-two. The Poles collapsed without receiving any foreign assistance and, in what the British and French called "the phony war" that followed, the initiative to take on new enemies was left in Hitler's hands.

Hitler's goals in Poland were not restricted to purely military ones, and once hostilities began Reinhard Heydrich let it be known that the Führer had given him "an extraordinarily radical . . . order" to liquidate the Polish intelligentsia, nobility, clergy, and military elite, as well as leading elements of Polish-Jewish society, an operation that would involve thousands of victims. This order was to be carried out principally by elements of the SS and Gestapo which were called *Einsatzgruppen*, operational groups.

For a time it appeared that this ideological objective might cause serious divisions between the army and the Nazi Party. The idea of a war with Poland had been popular in the armed forces ever since the Versailles Treaty, but neither Hans von Seeckt, chief of the army command in the 1920s, nor his successors had ever sought the kind of social decapitation now being discussed by Hitler and Heydrich. Among others, the prospect deeply worried the chief of counterintelligence, Wilhelm Canaris, who, as Alexander Rossino tells us in *Hitler Strikes Poland*, expressed his concerns to the chief of staff, General Franz Halder.

In retrospect, it seems likely that these objections were motivated less by ethnic or ideological considerations than by fear of losing control of the military situation to the SS. Once reassured by empty promises from Hitler, the generals relaxed, doubtless admitting to themselves that their concern over large-scale repression of civilians was not shared by their underlings in any case. The most striking feature of Rossino's study of the social aspects of the Polish war is its demonstration of how, once the fighting began, the behavior of practically all the German participants became equally uncontrolled and violent. The normal casualties of the war were used to justify retaliation against civilians, and these in turn led to atrocities in which the behavior of army troops was not significantly different from that of the SS. To underline the point, Rossino includes a photograph of a distraught Leni Riefenstahl with members of her film crew watching German troops slaughter Jews at Konskie.

The Polish conflict of 1939 is generally remembered for its role in setting off the Second World War. It also, Rossino notes, marked "a critical place in the history of Nazi Germany's descent into mass murder and genocide." The evolution of German military policy to include genocide did not, as is often believed, begin in 1941. That year merely marked an escalation of the horrors begun in Poland two years earlier.

II

If Hitler had had his way, he would have launched a drive to the west immediately after the fighting stopped in Poland. On October 9, 1939, he informed Keitel and the chiefs of the army, navy, and air force that it was necessary at the earliest possible date "to effect the destruction of the strength of the Western Powers and their capability of resisting still further the political consolidation and continued expansion of the German people in Europe."[1] On the same day he sent them a directive to plan an offensive through Luxembourg, the Low Countries, and Belgium. This caused consternation among the higher commanders and led Generaloberst Wilhelm Ritter von Leeb to protest to Walther von Brauchitsch, the commander in chief of the army, that Hitler's plans were exactly what the French expected and would lead to disaster. In the end, the need to repair equipment disabled in Poland and to replenish stores of ammunition forced the postponement of offensive action until the spring, and when it came it took a quite different form.

For one thing, Hitler became obsessed with the possibility of a British attempt to outflank him by attacking Norway and he launched an attack of his own on Norway to forestall them. In their lively new treatment of the campaign, Chris Mann and Christer Jörgensen point out that it was an impressive demonstration of Hitler's imagination and ability to conduct operations combining land, sea, and air forces, although very costly from a naval point of view. (The price of dominating Norway within forty-eight hours was the sinking of the heavy cruiser *Blücher*, the battle cruiser *Lützow*, and a dozen smaller ships.) Hitler himself called "the Weser Exercise" the most daring undertaking in German military history, and although this may seem an exaggeration there is no doubt that the German success in Norway reinforced the psychological effect of the Polish campaign.

Meanwhile, Hitler conceived the idea of attacking to the west below the line running between Liège and Namur and toward the supposedly impassable Ardennes. This was an idea that had also occurred to Lieutenant General Erich von Manstein, and he and the army chief of staff, Halder, elaborated it into concrete plans for military operations. Launched on May 9, this so-called Plan Orange defeated the Dutch in five days, forced the Belgians to capitulate on May 27, drove a joint Anglo-French force into the sea at Dunkirk, and then bypassed the Maginot Line and forced the French to surrender on June 17.

Hitler's part in this triumph was important but not decisive, since the success was owing in large part to Halder's staff work and his ability to prevent his high-strung commander from panicking at critical moments. When Hitler addressed the Reichstag on July 19 and reviewed the events of the last ten months, however, he took sole credit for the victory. Halder was mentioned only as a useful assistant to Brauchitsch in matters of command, and Manstein's name did not appear at all. This transformation of Hitler into an all-seeing *Feldherr* showed a dangerously inflated sense of self-esteem; equally fateful, because insistent, it betrayed a misunderstanding of the relationship between staff work and operations.

The stubborn refusal of the British to contemplate peace negotiations, let alone surrender, then persuaded the Führer—after Goering's botched air war against England—that the best way of driving the British out of the war was to defeat their strongest potential supporter, the Soviet Union. In June 1941 he attacked Russia along a line that stretched from the Moscow plain to the frozen tundra that lay between Finland and Murmansk. The commander of the northern drive, General Eduard Dietl, the conqueror of Narvik in the Norwegian campaign, had the most serious doubts about the prospects. After preliminary studies, he concluded that

> there has never been a war fought in the far north. . . . The region is unsuited to military operations. There are no roads, and these would have to be constructed before any advance could take place.

Dietl nevertheless pushed on, only in the end to be defeated by a historical irony of the first order. In order to accomplish the tasks necessary to reach Murmansk, he felt he needed more troops and he expected these to come from Norway. But Hitler's pride in his success with the "Weser Exercise" was always accompanied by a nervous feeling that it might be reversed by a new British attack. The idea of shifting 40 percent of the Norwegian force to Dietl's command was often talked about but never carried out. Hitler took to referring to the distance between the Finnish border and Murmansk (seventy-four miles) as "laughable," as if, Mann and Jörgensen write, it would be no more than a summer promenade for Dietl's troops. The plan for a Murmansk campaign and its potential for outflanking the Russian battle line came to nothing.

Operation Barbarossa was more successful on other fronts, at least at first. The initial drive took 150,000 Soviet prisoners, 1,200 tanks, and 600 big guns. The greatest penetration was made in the south, where General Rundstedt reached Kharkhov by late September. A month later Kleist was in Rostov-on-Don and Manstein was invading the Crimea. But General Bock's armies were stopped short of Moscow by fierce Russian resistance and the onset of an early winter. As Marshal Zhukov mounted counterattacks north and south of the capital, German commanders urged a general withdrawal that would enable regrouping for the spring offensive.

This Hitler flatly refused to allow. He was shrewd enough to realize that a withdrawal would cost time and, indeed, might lead to a general disintegration of the battle line, and in view of this he had no sympathy for the ill-clad and overcommitted front-line troops. Declaring that the high command was responsible for the failure to take Moscow, he ordered that his armies stay and fight where they were. He followed this by a more ominous decision. On December 19, 1941, when his com-

mander in chief, Brauchitsch, was forced to resign for reasons of
health, he announced that he would take the command into his own
hands. In words that must have filled the hearts of his senior commanders with dread, he said that being in charge of the army was no
more than "a little matter of operational command" that "anyone can
do."[2]

III

Some idea of the results of that decision is provided by the massive
book *Hitler and His Generals*, the first complete stenographic record of
the military situation conferences from the Battle of Stalingrad to Hitler's death in Berlin. This picture of Hitler in his dealings with the military and other leaders of the German war effort shows him at his best
and worst, shrewd on technical questions (the importance, for example,
of the new Russian tank), hopelessly unreliable on non-European matters (almost everything he says about the United States sounds like a
caricature), and a total failure in his personal relations with his generals.
Hitler's basic hostility to the professional soldiers, whom he once called
"a special caste of particularly snobbish, pretentious airheads and destructive vermin . . . with no imagination, full of sterile fertility, cowardice and vanity" made genuine cooperation with the professional soldiers impossible, and conferences on the military situation were marked
by much petty criticism and sarcasm.

An exchange like the following with General von Kluge comes close
to representing the tone of the daily conferences:

General von Kluge: But I need panzer divisions, too, of course.
The Führer: Well, you don't like this garbage too much, so it's easier
 for you to give it away!
Von Kluge: What garbage?
The Führer: You said, "It's only garbage!"
Von Kluge: I didn't say that!
The Führer: Yes, it slipped from your mouth, so we're taking it away
 from you.

This sort of thing was trivial compared with the floods of rage and
contempt Hitler poured over the commanders who he believed were
disobeying his orders. In 1943 when the Sixth Army was surrounded by
the Russians at Stalingrad and its commander, Field Marshal Friedrich

Paulus, decided, after losing half of his command, to surrender, Hitler said,

> It hurts me so much because the heroism of so many soldiers is de-
> stroyed by a single spineless weakling. . . . He'll sign everything
> there. He will make confessions and appeals. You'll see: they'll walk
> down the road completely disregarding any principle—to the deep-
> est abyss.

In April 1945, when the commandant of Königsberg surrendered his position when most of his garrison was dead, Hitler sentenced him in absentia to death by hanging.

It was clear after the fall of Stalingrad that the tide of war had swung completely to the Soviet side and that Hitler's days as a strategist were over. He remained in command, however, and continued to fight all the battles from his bunker, making tactical decisions for all units on all fronts and treating his commanding officers as if they were high-salaried noncommissioned officers. His repeated exhortations to his armies to stand and fight in their places could not, however, halt the enemy's advance. By mid-1944 the British and Americans were in Italy and France and the Russians were pressing relentlessly forward along a line that ran between Smolensk and Kiev.

Hitler hoped to change the tempo of the fighting by launching a new offensive in the direction of the Ardennes in Belgium, but his plans were delayed by the attempt on his life on July 20, 1944. Among the records in *Hitler and His Generals* there is an interesting description of the aftereffects of this *Attentat* in Hitler's own words. Speaking of future travel plans, he says:

> For at least the next eight days, I won't be able to fly because of my
> ears. . . . If I get into an airplane now with the roaring and all those
> changes in pressure, it could be catastrophic. And what would hap-
> pen if I suddenly got a middle-ear infection? I would have to be
> treated. The risk of an infection is there as long as the wound is
> open. It didn't go off without affecting my head either. . . . A speech
> like the one I held at the Obersalzberg recently I wouldn't dare to
> hold today, because I might suddenly get a dizzy spell and collapse.

From these disabilities Hitler recovered, and in December he launched his long-planned counteroffensive. This was contained, not without difficulty, in what came to be known as the Battle of the Bulge.

Still undaunted, Hitler told his staff:

> Germany will either save itself or—if it loses this war—perish. I want to add right away, gentlemen, that when I say this, don't conclude that I've had even the slightest thought of losing this war. I never in my life learned the meaning of the word "capitulation," and I'm one of those who has worked himself up from nothing. . . . I only say this to make you see why I pursue my goal with such fanaticism and why nothing can weaken my resolve.

But it was too late for this kind of defiance to be effective. As the ring of Germany's enemies tightened inexorably about it, Hitler had to admit that the game was over and on April 22, 1945, he told General Jodl that he was resolved to remain and die in Berlin.

Once made, this decision was irrevocable. There were people—Hitler called them "those smart-asses that Clausewitz warned of . . . who always see the easier way as the more intelligent"—who believed he would in the end decide to continue the fight in a southern redoubt in the Obersalzberg. This he never seems to have considered seriously. "If we were to leave the world stage so disgracefully," he told his staff,

> then we would have lived in vain. It's completely unimportant if we continue to live for a while still or not. Better to end the battle honorably than to go on living in shame and dishonor for a few more months or years. . . . That's the decision: to save everything here and only here, and to put the last man into action—that's our duty.

24

The Russians Are Coming!

I

On Christmas Eve 1944, General Heinz Guderian, chief of the German army's supreme command, drove to Adolf Hitler's headquarters near Ziegenberg and informed the Führer that, according to the latest report of the military intelligence department for the eastern front, the Red Army intended to launch a major invasion of Germany from the line of the Vistula River on or about January 12. Guderian's source calculated that the enemy would possess a superiority of eleven to one in available infantry forces, seven to one in tanks, and twenty to one in both artillery and aviation. To avoid disaster he asked that as many divisions as possible be redeployed from the west, where the German Ardennes offensive had now come to a virtual halt.

It was typical of Hitler's now fixed distrust of the general staff and the officer class in general that he was unmoved by this plea. Contesting all of Guderian's estimates of Soviet strength, he shouted, "It's the greatest imposture since Genghis Khan! Who is responsible for producing all this rubbish?" To Guderian's consternation, the Führer pro-

Review of *The Fall of Berlin 1945*, by Anthony Beevor, *The New York Review of Books*, May 23, 2002, pp. 46–47. Reprinted with permission from *The New York Review of Books*. Copyright © 2002, NYREV, Inc.

ceeded to prolong the Ardennes offensive, at great cost and little result, aside from the final destruction of the Luftwaffe as an effective force, while also committing himself to a fruitless counteroffensive in Hungary. Meanwhile, the Red Army did what Guderian predicted it would do. On January 12, at 5 o'clock in the morning Moscow time, it began the concentrated drive from the Vistula that was to culminate in the last days of April with the capture of Berlin, Hitler's suicide, and the end of the war.

Antony Beevor is a British historian of great distinction and range, who has written widely on military affairs in the twentieth century. His history of the Battle of Stalingrad was awarded the Samuel Johnson Prize for Non-Fiction, the Wolfson History Prize, and the Hawthornden Prize for Literature, and has been translated into eighteen languages. To write a successor to that excellent chronicle of the savagery of modern warfare could not have been easy for its author, and it would not be fair to compare them, for *The Fall of Berlin* is a more political book than its predecessor, as it must be in view of the interest of the Western powers in the fate of Central Europe. But the drive against Berlin is its main theme, and here Beevor once more demonstrates his mastery of the sources, including newly disclosed material from Soviet archives, and his skill in describing complicated operations.

The Soviet offensive was conducted by three army groups: to the north, the 2nd Belorussian Front, commanded by Marshal Konstantin Rokossovsky, whose mission was to overrun East Prussia; in the center, on the main route to Küstrin, the Oderbruch, and the highway to Berlin, the 1st Belorussian Front, commanded by the redoubtable Marshal Georgy Zhukov, who had directed the defense of Moscow in 1941; and in the south, at the Sandomierz bridgehead on the Vistula, the 1st Ukrainian Front, commanded by Marshal Ivan Konev, probably Stalin's favorite general because of his ruthlessness, who was to advance directly westward to capture Breslau and the rich industrial areas of Silesia.

The Soviet superiority in numbers and equipment was roughly what Guderian had predicted it would be in his report to Hitler, and its initial effect was overwhelming. Marshal Konev's artillery bombardment in the first phase of his offensive used up to three hundred guns per kilometer and shattered the German defenders, leaving them, Beevor writes, "grey-faced and trembling" and ready to surrender. On the central front, the whole of Germany's Army Group Vistula, commanded inadequately by Heinrich Himmler, contained only three understrength panzer divisions. Zhukov's tank brigades swept by them to establish two bridgeheads on the Oder River in the first days of February. So rapid was the initial Soviet advance that some of Zhukov's subordinates, including his old antagonist from Stalingrad days, Vassili Ivanovitch Chuikov, criticized him for not crowning it with an immediate drive on the German capital. Zhukov, however, was concerned about a gap that had developed between his own forces and the 2nd Belorussian Front of Rokossovsky and the possibility of being outflanked. Consequently, he slowed down until this threat could be eliminated, and this enabled the Nazis to reinforce their defenses.

They did so by bringing some units from the western front and from Poland but also by calling up large numbers of the SS and creating a new Volkssturm out of elements hitherto unmobilized because of youth or age. At the same time, in order to check the onrush of Soviet tank brigades, Hitler ordered the establishment of a Panzerjagd Division, which turned out to be rather less imposing than its title, since it was composed of bicycle companies formed from the Hitler Youth. Beevor writes:

> Each bicyclist was to carry two panzerfaust anti-tank launchers clamped upright either side of the front wheel and attached to the handlebars. The bicyclist was supposed to be able to dismount in a moment and be ready for action against a T-34 or Stalin tank.

The panzerfaust did not turn out to be the wonder weapon that Heinrich Himmler claimed it was, but, detached from the bicycle, it played an important role in the German defense, and the Hitler Youth, whose members fought with patriotism and bravery, destroyed its share of enemy armor.

The movement of the defending forces was impeded by the flight of the civilian population before the invaders. Beevor describes the advancing Soviet columns as

> an extraordinary mixture of modern and medieval: tank troops in padded black helmets, their T-34s churning up the earth as they dipped and rolled with the ground, Cossack cavalrymen on shaggy mounts, . . . Lend-Lease Studebakers and Dodges towing light field

guns, open Chevrolets with tarpaulin-covered mortars in the back, and tractors hauling great howitzers, all eventually followed by a second echelon in horse-drawn carts.

The variety of conduct among the Red soldiers was almost as great as that of their equipment, but all too often it was characterized by a hatred for Germany that was expressed in widespread looting and mistreatment of civilians, especially women. Beevor writes that "altogether, at least two million German women are thought to have been raped" during the Russian invasion, and a substantial minority of these appear to have suffered multiple rape. One doctor deduced, he adds, that out of approximately 100,000 women raped in Berlin, some 10,000 died as a result, mostly from suicide. Compulsive drinking, which gravely diminished the fighting capacity of the Red Army, had a part in this primitive behavior. Soviet troops had an insatiable appetite for anything that was supposed to be alcoholic, including dangerous chemicals seized from laboratories. When they were not poisoned, Soviet soldiers often attacked women and, if they then proved to be sexually impotent because of what they had drunk, they frequently brutalized them.

This is a subject that was rarely discussed in postwar Russia and, when mentioned at all, accompanied by spurious justifications. It is hard to find an excuse, however, for the fact that neither army commanders nor the secret police (NKVD) and counterintelligence (SMERSH) that accompanied the armies and were ever vigilant for signs of lack of ideological zeal tried to monitor the private behavior of their troops toward the civilian population. After the fall of Berlin, one Soviet district commander responded to a group of German women who had come to ask for protection from repeated attacks by laughing, "That? Well, it certainly hasn't done you any harm. Our men are all healthy." Unfortunately, this was not invariably true, as many victims discovered.

II

Meanwhile, as the Red Army breached the old frontiers of the Reich, Berlin itself was in a state of disintegration. Most people did their best to maintain their old routines, going to work every day, but with two air-raid warnings a night and the public services deteriorating progressively, this became harder and harder. Many wanted to get out of the threatened capital, but Joseph Goebbels, Reich commissar for Berlin, had declared that leaving the city without official authorization was the same as desertion and would be punished accordingly. In January the SS executed members of the resistance movement who had been involved in the July plot against Hitler. Numbers of people whose only crime had been listening to foreign broadcasts were also arrested and sentenced to death. These actions demonstrated how ruthless the regime was prepared to be and how unwilling to make distinctions between kinds of opposition.

Meanwhile, contact between leaders of the Nazi movement and the public became infrequent. Goebbels, to be sure, visited troops, reviewed Volkssturm detachments, and harangued Berliners about the necessity of total war, but little was seen of Hitler. The Führer, showing the signs of the marked physical deterioration that had overtaken him since the attempt on his life, made his last speech to the German people on January 30, the twelfth anniversary of his taking over power, and then retired to the privacy of the Reich Chancellery. Here, surrounded by an intrigue-ridden camarilla, he brooded over the treason that he was sure had defeated his ambitions.

The fate that was to overcome the capital became more palpable in February and March, when Zhukov closed the dangerous gap that had separated his armies from Rokossovsky's. Their united forces now pushed into West Prussia and split Pomerania in two, and this at once opened new opportunities for a drive upon the capital city.

From the Soviet point of view, this had acquired a new urgency, for on March 7 the US Army had seized the bridge at Remagen on the Rhine, and this could be counted on, it was thought, to inspire an attempt on the part of the Western forces to get to Berlin before the Red Army. Joseph Stalin could not tolerate such an outcome. Aside from the political advantages that it would bring—Karl Marx had once said, "Who possesses Berlin possesses Germany, and whoever controls Germany, controls Europe"—he considered the seizure of Berlin an indispensable revenge for the German invasion of June 1941. It was believed by Soviet officials, moreover, that stocks of uranium, which the Soviet Union needed for its faltering nuclear program, were to be found in the Kaiser Wilhelm Institut in Dahlem in the capital. (This proved to be correct, and when the Red Army reached Dahlem on

April 24, they seized 250 kilograms of metallic uranium, three tons of uranium oxide, and twenty liters of heavy water.)

Stalin need not have been so concerned. While the British made no bones about their desire to capture Berlin, they found that the supreme commander, Dwight David Eisenhower, was not interested. This was not because he was, in the words of the British chief of staff, Sir Alan Brooke, "a most attractive personality and at the same time [had] a very very limited brain from a strategic point of view." As Beevor writes, Eisenhower wanted to win the war against Germany as quickly, and with as few casualties, as possible, so that he could turn to the war against Japan. For that enterprise he hoped to have Stalin's support and had no desire to alienate the Soviet leader by becoming involved in a competition for Berlin. Even so, Stalin was not one to take things for granted, and consequently the latter part of March was devoted to planning the assault on Berlin and bringing up the enormous amount of supplies that would be needed to support it, and on April 16 the attack began. By that time the Soviet forces amounted to 2.5 million men, backed by 41,600 guns and heavy mortars, as well as 6,250 tanks and self-propelled guns and four air armies.

It is hard to read Beevor's detailed account of the fighting that followed without feeling that the Soviet strategy was excessive and self-defeating. The Soviet plan was complicated in any case by the fact that the main concentration of Zhukov's forces lay right below the best defensive feature in the whole region, the Seelow Heights, the strength of which he had gravely underestimated. The initial Soviet artillery bombardment, which amounted to 1,236,000 rounds, did less harm to the Germans than it did to the water-logged terrain, making it almost impassable for Soviet tanks. The weather was overcast and the ground wet, and infantry units, lacking radio discipline, got lost and bumped into one another. They also suffered heavily from their own supporting artillery, and there were cases of Soviet aircraft bombing and strafing their own men because the leading rifle battalions were ignorant of the flares that should have been used to indicate their front line positions.

In addition, the medical services were overwhelmed and proved incapable of evacuating the wounded from the battlefield, which did not prevent SMERSH from pulling doctors away from their proper work to examine suspected cases of self-inflicted wounds. SMERSH seemed to operate on the principle that anything but death was suspicious, as in the samizdat song:

> The first piece of metal made a hole in the fuel tank.
> I jumped out of the T-34, I don't know how,
> And then they called me to [SMERSH].
> "Why aren't you burnt, along with the tank, you bastard?"
> "I'll definitely burn in the next attack," I answered.

This basic distrust was equaled by the callousness of the high command, which kept committing troops without any regard for losses. On the first day of fighting, the 1st Belorussian Front lost nearly three times as many men as the German defenders.

Beevor writes that the Battle of Seelow Heights was "certainly not Marshal Zhukov's finest hour." Having failed to secure the heights on the first day of fighting, he could not now hope to be in Berlin in six days as planned. When he telephoned this news to Moscow, Stalin was clearly angered and immediately ordered Marshal Konev to detach two tank armies from his siege of Breslau and to attack Berlin from the south, while Rokossovsky speeded up his crossing of the lower Oder and attacked from the north. When he learned of this, Zhukov realized that his reputation was at stake and almost desperately committed all his forces to an attack by day and night. The break came in the morning of April 18 when the German line fell apart and the road to Berlin was open. Zhukov had lost just over 30,000 men, compared with German losses of 12,000.

After the German retreat from the Seelow Heights there was no recognizable front line, and the exhausted defenders fell back in small groups that fought fiercely when attacked but with decreasing effect. The last organized German units, the panzer and mountain corps of General Theodor Busse's Ninth Army, abandoned what was left of the Oder line and, disregarding Hitler's orders to counterattack, fell back into the Spree forest. The German forces that were expected to "hurl back" Konev's two tank armies consisted of a division made up of boys in Reich service labor detachments and a small detachment of tanks from a training school. It was not surprising therefore that by April 25 the Red Army had reached Berlin and was advancing into Zehlendorf and Neukölln and Spandau.

Conditions in the city now rapidly became chaotic, with front line units racing to capture strongpoints like the zoo flak tower, which was Goebbels's headquarters, and the Reichstag, a special target for Zhukov because it was an obsession of Josef Stalin, who wanted to celebrate its capture on May Day. Rearguard troops, for their part, robbed German citizens of wrist-watches and bicycles and gave themselves over to orgies of rape. In addition, the Volkssturm and SS units that still existed demonstrated their continued loyalty to Hitler by destroying houses that showed the white flag and executing their inhabitants.

Hitler had by then lost all control over this situation. He now admitted that the war was lost and was resolved not to wait for the end. His circle of close associates was now smaller than it had been, for Hermann Goering was at Luftwaffe headquarters at Berchtesgaden, where he ruined what was left of his reputation by seeking assurances from Hitler that he would be the Führer's successor and was expelled from the party, and Heinrich Himmler, *der treue Heinrich*, was known to be trying to negotiate a settlement with Count Folke Bernadotte of Sweden that would exculpate him. But Martin Bormann was still at his post, and so was Joachim von Ribbentrop, and Magda and Joseph Goebbels had refused to leave the Reich Chancellery. With them, Hitler made his final arrangements. The well-known story of Hitler's marrying Eva Braun, of their suicide, and of their incineration in the Chancellery garden, Beevor tells with panache and piquant detail; as the dead Führer was set afire, he writes, one of the SS guards who had been drinking in the canteen saw what was going on and called to a friend, "The chief's on fire. Do you want to come and have a look?"

After the capture of the Reich Chancellery at the beginning of May, an extensive search by a SMERSH team discovered the charred bodies of Hitler and Eva Braun. Stalin immediately ordered that this news be kept strictly secret, and this *Verbot* was applied even to Marshal Zhukov. Such behavior toward his leading commander was probably due to the Soviet dictator's resentment at the popularity that Zhukov had won in the Berlin campaign, for Stalin was a malicious man who could not tolerate the victories of others even when he benefited from them. But, leaving that aside, Stalin was as usual thinking of the future, and Beevor writes that his "strategy, quite evidently, was to associate the west with Nazism by pretending that the British or Americans must be hiding [Hitler]." The European war ended as a result of German surrender on

May 7 and a formal capitulation signed in Berlin on the 8th. But the cold war was not far away, and it is clear that Stalin was already thinking of it.

25

Mission Possible

In small towns across America, in the months following the end of the
Second World War, you were apt to discover, if you went into a saloon
on a Saturday morning, a row of neatly dressed young men sitting at the
bar, each with a shot of whiskey and a glass of beer in front of him, as
well as a freshly opened pack of cigarettes and the change from a five-
dollar bill. If you seated yourself beside one of them, there would be a
decent pause until you had ordered your drink, and then he might ask,
"Were you ever in Majuro (or, as the case might be, Simpson Harbor or
Okinawa)?" Whatever you answered, he would then tell you the story
of his war.

To an entire generation of young Americans, the war was the greatest experience in their lives. It had interrupted their former existences,
taken them off to far places, shown them things they had never seen
before, and taught them things, not least about themselves. It did not
leave them easily, complicating the process of readjustment to civilian
life, and in some cases it never left them at all, so that their existences

Review of *A Quiet American: The Secret War of Varian Fry* by Andy Ma-
rino; and *Surrender on Demand*, by Varian Fry: *The New York Review of
Books*, December 2, 1999, pp. 41–43. Reprinted with permission from
The New York Review of Books. Copyright © 1999, NYREV, Inc.

were permanently burdened with a mixed sense of accomplishment and incompleteness and regret. This was the case with Varian Fry.

After the fall of France in 1940, which posed an imminent threat to thousands of German, Italian, and Polish opponents of National Socialism who had found refuge in that country, an Emergency Rescue Committee was formed and financed by a group of well-to-do private citizens in New York. The committee asked Varian Fry, at that time a thirty-two-year-old political journalist who was editor of Headline Books for the Foreign Policy Association, to go to France and make a general assessment of the refugee situation, help well-known anti-Nazi intellectuals to get to Lisbon or Casablanca, whence they could make their way to England or the United States, and identify persons who might serve as future agents for the committee.

Fry had no previous experience in this kind of activity, but he was told the assignment should not present great difficulties and was not expected to take more than two or three weeks. Instead, he remained thirteen months in France, during which time he improvised one of the most remarkable relief efforts of the war, which brought vital assistance to more than four thousand refugees and helped between 1,200 and 1,800 of them, by legal or clandestine means, to escape to freedom. This for one man was an unparalleled achievement, the more so because it was doggedly opposed by Fry's own government, which in the end forced his recall from France, and was never fully appreciated by his own committee, which compelled him to resign from its membership after his return home.

In 1945, Fry published a book about his mission in France under the title *Surrender on Demand*, a reference to the nineteenth article of the Franco-German Armistice of June 23, 1940, which stipulated that the French government was "obliged to surrender on demand all Germans named by the German Government in France, as well as in French possessions, Colonies, Protectorate Territories and Mandates." His account of how he had worked to prevent the implementation of that article was widely reviewed in the press, but, given the distractions caused by the war's end, less widely read. A new edition, sponsored by the US Holocaust Memorial Museum, was published two years ago.

Now, on the basis of new research and many interviews with Fry's collaborators in France, Andy Marino has written a book which, if far inferior to Fry's in style—Marino never misses an opportunity to use "like" in place of "as" or "as if," and formulations like "animosity between he and Breton" are not uncommon—and clumsy in organization, provides interesting new information about Fry's clients and his relations with official authority, as well as a balanced analysis of his failures of sympathy and tact in his relations with his colleagues in New York.

Fry arrived in Marseille on August 15, 1940, with a list of two hundred names of persons who were at high risk of being handed over to the Nazis by the Vichy government and whose escape he was supposed to facilitate. They included Konrad Heiden, the author of the first serious study of Hitler; the novelists Heinrich Mann and Lion Feuchtwanger, whose novel *Success*, about Munich in the turbulent days of 1923, deeply offended the Nazis; the poet and novelist Franz Werfel and his wife, Alma Mahler; the cabaret poet Walter Mehring; the political scientist Hannah Arendt; the biochemist and Nobel Prize winner Otto Meyerhof; the painters Chagall and Matisse; and others who the New York committee thought might be in particular danger. Fry was not sure that all of the persons on the list deserved to be there or, indeed, wanted to escape, and within days of his arrival, he became aware of others who had an equal claim on his assistance. But how to go about arranging for their escape was a mystery to him.

Nor was he reassured by an early meeting with Frank Bohn, a bluff, self-confident trade unionist who had been sent to Marseille by the American Federation of Labor with a handful of visitor's visas in his pocket and instructions to effect the escape of European labor leaders and socialists like Rudolf Breitscheid, leader of the German SPD, Rudolf Hilferding, former German Finance Minister, and the Italian Socialist leader Giuseppe Modigliani. Bohn was already deeply involved in illicit transit of refugees through Spain to Lisbon and inclined to the belief that refugees could count on the sympathy of the police and the full support of the American consular service, a conviction that Fry soon had good reason to distrust. Bohn was also making arrangements for a boat to carry his more important clients to safety and offered Fry space on it for his. Meanwhile, he suggested a division of labor, with Fry being responsible for the writers and artists and the younger members of left-wing groups and Bohn taking care of the older socialists and trade union leaders.

Fry agreed to all of this with no real confidence, suspecting that Bohn was what he called a *mythomane*, or fantasist. He was right. The much-vaunted boat never materialized, and in the end all of the responsibility for getting the anti-Nazi notables out of Vichy France became Fry's. Moreover he discovered that the news of his arrival in Marseille had aroused all sorts of exaggerated expectations among the refugee population of the city, so that dozens of people not on his original list were soon besieging him in his hotel, pleading for help. Among the first of these were young Austrian and German socialists who already had American visas and were willing to take their chances with the Gestapo and the French and Spanish police, provided they had enough money to get them from Spain to Lisbon. This Fry provided, and they all succeeded in getting there—twenty-eight of them in Fry's first two weeks. But many of the refugees had neither visas nor passports, and some, the *apatrides* who had been declared stateless by the Nazis, could not expect to get them by legal means. Fry, rapidly redefining and expanding his mission, soon discovered that he could not fulfill it without going beyond the law.

He had, very quickly after his arrival, begun to recruit a small staff to help him with the refugee flow. The first member of this was a young German economist named Hirschman, who had fought in both the Spanish civil war and the French army. Just before the surrender, his captain had called all the non-French members of his company together and told them he was going to make them all French citizens so that they would not be killed by the Nazis. Hirschman started his new life as Albert Hermant, born in Philadelphia of French parents, but Fry always called him Beamish, because of his smile, and wrote later:

> Beamish soon became my specialist on illegal questions. It was he who found new sources of false passports when the Czech passports [which Fry had been able to procure through an arrangement with the Czech Consul, Vladimir Vochoč, an ardent anti-Nazi, and which had been used in the escapes of Konrad Heiden and Otto Meyerhof] were exposed and couldn't be used any more. It was he who arranged to change and transfer money on the black bourse when my original stock of dollars gave out. And it was he who organized the guide service over the frontier when it was no longer

possible for people to go down to Cerbère on the train and cross over on foot.

Other collaborators were Franzi von Hildebrand, an Austrian aristocrat with a Swiss passport and experience in working for a refugee committee in Paris; Lena Fishman, who before the occupation had worked in the Paris office of the Jewish Joint Distribution Committee, and who wrote and took shorthand in six languages; Miriam Davenport, a Smith graduate who had been studying art in Paris and who, in addition to her other talents, was helpful in determining which of the many refugees who claimed to be artists deserved the aid they were demanding; Heinz Ernst Oppenheimer, a German-Jewish production engineer who had run a relief committee in Holland after Hitler came to power, and who volunteered to keep the books in order (he was an artist, Fry later wrote, in disguising illegal expenditures "in various ingenious ways"); and, finally, Charles Fawcett, a Georgian who had been in the American Volunteer Ambulance Corps before the armistice, and who served as doorman and reception clerk.

This was the original staff of what was set up legally in Marseille as the Centre Américain de Secours, a name that was neutral enough to disguise the organization's real purpose. It did indeed provide relief to hundreds of people for whom it could do nothing else, handing out meal tickets that Fry got from the Quakers. But its raison d'être was different. As Fry wrote, "We were . . . the only organization in France which was helping refugees escape."

This was an exacting, grueling, and dangerous job. Fry and his colleagues had to look after a refugee population that was in constant danger of being arrested by Vichy police and placed in detention camps or jail. When this happened—as it did frequently in the case of the mercurial cabarettist Walter Mehring—they had, by ingratiating themselves with authority or by bribery or by effecting jail breaks, to secure their release. They had to keep abreast of the current state of all possible routes to freedom, to adjust to sudden changes and frontier closures, and to maintain contact with agents who could help the refugees through the more difficult routes. They had to improvise constantly, so that if the Spanish frontier closed suddenly they could quickly find a way of sending their clients by boat to whatever neutral port was available.

Mission Possible

They also had to seize on the unexpected opportunity, as Fry did when he made an agreement with the British Ambassador in Spain, Sir Samuel Hoare, to lead remnants of the British Expeditionary Force in France to points on the Spanish coast where they could be picked up by ships sent by the British from Barcelona and transported to Gibraltar, on condition that ships be available also for certain Italian and Spanish refugees in his charge. And they had to guard their backs, watching lest a sudden police raid on headquarters turn up incriminating materials or that, like Frank Bohn, they commit themselves to escape plans whose promoters were motivated by greed rather than any real concern for the refugees. It was, in every sense, a high-risk enterprise, but Fry found himself relishing every aspect of it. Marino quotes him as saying: "I like the human relations of it, the hurly-burly, the sense of urgency, the innumerable complications and problems, perhaps even the danger, which has come to be like a needed drug to me."

He soon discovered that the refugees themselves were less than fully reliable. Some of them developed qualms even after they had the necessary visas, afraid of what might happen to them once they left France, and these had to be cajoled or bullied into leaving. Others set off but then disobeyed the instructions that they had been given, neglecting to secure an entry visa and to declare their assets immediately after they had crossed the Spanish frontier and therefore ending up in camps from which Fry could extract them only with difficulty and much expenditure of time. The Italian socialist Giuseppe Modigliani was willing to leave France but flatly refused to do anything illegal to accomplish that purpose lest it reflect upon the Italian socialist movement. The Germans Breitscheid and Hilferding stubbornly opposed the very idea of flight and sat about openly in a café next to their hotel, holding court and daring the police to apprehend them. When Fry attempted to reason with them, he was amazed, Marino writes, by

> the condescension and imperious naïveté of the pair. Breitscheid was still confidently waiting for the return of the Weimar Republic, when he would be welcomed back in Berlin, carried through the streets shoulder high and hailed the returning hero.

This feckless view proved tragically mistaken when Vichy policy hardened and the two were arrested and handed over to the Gestapo.

(Hilferding committed suicide in his cell; Breitscheid died in a concentration camp.)

The Werfels provided another example of this resolute refusal to admit the realities of the situation. When Fry planned a joint escape for them and the Heinrich Manns, by train to Cerbère and then over the mountains into Spain, he warned them to bring only essential belongings. When he joined them in the Gare St. Charles in Marseille, he found that the Werfels had brought seventeen pieces of luggage. He remonstrated, but Alma Werfel declared that it was all essential, for the suitcases included holograph music scores by her dead husband, Gustav Mahler, the original manuscript of Bruckner's Third Symphony, and the manuscript of Werfel's latest work in progress.

This was irritating but less so than the apparently irresistible desire of some refugees to boast publicly of their escape when they reached freedom or to spell out in detail how it had been effected. When the novelist Lion Feuchtwanger reached New York, he gave an interview that spared no detail about how he got over the Pyrenees and inspired press reports about the "vast rescue machine that has worked quietly and efficiently for Mr. Feuchtwanger and many others in similar circumstances." Fry was aghast, for the interview had ruined the camouflage that he had been seeking to preserve. Further stories in the press, encouraged by Feuchtwanger's revelations, spoke of a "secret organization which has been smuggling politicians, Jews and men of military age from France to England via Spain, Portugal, and Gibraltar." Almost immediately the Spanish border was closed, with a consequent, but fortunately only temporary, disruption of Fry's escape system.

Such incidents did not help Fry's relations with the Vichy government or, for that matter, with his own. With respect to the first of these, this was probably unavoidable. In the first months after Fry's arrival in Marseille, the policies of Vichy were still slack and undefined, and he was able to exploit this to his own advantage and, on occasion, even win the sympathy of some of its agents. But as time passed the Vichy leadership found it expedient to base their policy upon that of the Nazis, and to copy their anti-Semitic measures. The first *statut des juifs* was passed in October, calling for a census of all non-French Jews. Only days later prefects throughout the unoccupied zone were authorized to intern foreign Jews in camps or put them under house arrest, even when their papers were in order. Meanwhile, there were anti-Jewish riots in Marseille and the local bishop publicly condemned the Jews in a sermon in which he said, "Already we see the face of a more beautiful France, healed of her sores which were often the work of foreigners."

The refugee population was terrified by these developments, and with good cause. In April 1941 the police were authorized to arrest all Jews living in Marseille's hotels, who were then taken to headquarters and interrogated, in the interests of what was called "control of situation." Among those arrested was Marc Chagall, which prompted a furious intervention on the part of Fry, who called the commissioner and threatened to release the news to *The New York Times*, with consequent embarrassment for the Vichy government, unless the artist was released immediately. Chagall was free within half an hour, but others were not so lucky and were either expelled from Marseille or sent to concentration camps. Vichy now had 120 of these, and many of Fry's clients were sent to them, in miserable conditions, which he was unable to alleviate, despite a special visit to Vichy in which he put their case to highly placed ministers. He was by this time the subject of increasing harassment and pressure to return home or be arrested; and when he remonstrated with Rodellec du Porzic, the chief of police, and asked him why he was the object of this treatment, du Porzic answered, "Because you have protected Jews and anti-Nazis."

This would have been less disturbing if he had been able to count on the support of his own government, but this was not the case. He was in the business, after all, of helping refugees come to the United States, and this was not a popular idea with many Americans, including powerful officials in the State Department. To them the word "refugee" carried the connotation of troublemaker, and they were unconvinced that entry visas should be given to people who were antigovernment agitators, even if the government they opposed was evil. Moreover, some of them were probably Communists, and many of them were Jews. Assistant Secretary of State Breckinridge Long was known to be opposed to giving visas to Jews on the same grounds that would have led him to oppose their membership in his country club, and the head of the visa division at the State Department, Avra Warren, was reported to have told the consul in Lisbon, during a 1940 visit, to make sure that not a "single goddam Jew" got to America.

Fry did not share these prejudices (he was genuinely puzzled when a member of the consulate staff in Marseille asked him why he had so many Jews on his staff) and was intent only on getting entry visas for artists and writers in danger. When visas did not come he complained loudly and soon had the reputation of being a nuisance. This did not deter him, but things became more difficult when Vichy officials complained that he was using illegal means to help the refugees. The US government was intent on preventing Vichy from handing the French fleet over to the Nazis and did not want this objective to be compromised by the actions of US citizens. Soon a directive had gone out from the State Department to all consulates in France, reminding them that "this government does not repeat not countenance any activities by American citizens desiring to evade the laws of the governments with which this country maintains friendly relations." This ended any hope that Fry might count on the support of his government when he needed it, and served as the basis for constant pressure upon him, and the Emergency Rescue Committee in New York, to stop his activities. This Fry resisted stoutly. He once said, "This job is like death—irreversible. We have started something here we can't stop. We have allowed hundreds of people to become dependent on us. We can't now say we are bored and are going home." But the pressure of two governments was eventually too much even for Fry.

He was arrested on August 29, 1941, by two of du Porzic's police agents. His own government did not protest, and he went home. Not, however, without staying in Lisbon for six weeks, attempting to save yet more refugees.

Varian Fry was only thirty-seven years old when the war ended. His magnificent achievement in Marseille had already been costly: his marriage dissolved shortly after his return to America, and his connection with the Emergency Rescue Committee had ended in acrimony and mutual misunderstanding; he felt he should have had stronger support. Although he pieced together a new career and continued to work and write (including a superb and prophetic article, "The Massacre of the Jews," published in *The New Republic* of December 1942), it is hard not to conclude that the sense of mission and excitement had gone out of his life. He died in September 1967 at the age of sixty. Earlier that year, in April, in a ceremony at the French consulate in New York, he had been presented with the Croix du Chevalier of the Légion d'Honneur for services to the French resistance. He had indeed worked with the French resistance; but this citation rather missed the real point of his achievement. If he had lived to experience it, he would probably have been prouder of the fact that in 1996 he was pronounced by Israel "Righteous Among the Nations" and had a tree planted in his memory on the road leading to the Yad Vashem Museum in Jerusalem— especially since Secretary of State Warren Christopher attended the ceremony and apologized for the way in which the State Department had treated him during the Vichy days.

Coda

26

History as a Humanistic Discipline

To my considerable wonder, I find that I have been a professional historian for fifty years, if one counts from the time when I received my first advanced degree. Surprise is not an unusual sensation on such anniversary occasions. Where has all that time gone? one asks fretfully. But in this case it is compounded by the recollection that, a scant six years before taking that degree, when I matriculated at Princeton University, I had decided that, if there was one subject in the college curriculum that I would avoid like the plague, it was history. My early experience with instruction in that subject had convinced me that it was not only unrewarding but, even when comprehensible, which was not often, maddeningly dull.

I don't think this was a willful conclusion on my part. I was a reasonably diligent pupil and generally attentive to what my teachers had to tell me. But whenever they started to talk about history, I never seemed to be able to discover what they were driving at or fit what they said into any meaningful pattern or discern in it any relevance to my own world. During my six years in grade school in Toronto, Ontario, I

This essay appeared originally in *Historical Literacy: The Case for History in American Education*, edited by Paul Gagnon and the Bradley Commission for History in Schools (New York: Macmillan, 1989), pp. 122–37.

must have been subjected to a good many sessions on Canadian history. If so, I took away from them only the impression (which even in my state of innocence, I suspect, must be sadly muddled) that a Frenchman named Carshay collaborated with a general called Montcalm-and-Wolf to defeat the Americans at Queenston at a time and for reasons that were obscure. Later, when I finished my grade school education in Jersey City, New Jersey, a city founded by the Dutch and having, by my time, a large Italian population, Peter Stuyvesant and Christopher Columbus took the places of the mysterious Frenchman and the soldier with the oddly cumbersome name, although it was never clear to me why I should be interested in either of them.

The passing of the years brought confusion of a higher order. In high school I was forced to sit through a survey of American history that turned out to be an exasperatingly arid chronicle of names and dates, which disappeared from the mind as soon as they had been memorized and regurgitated in daily quizzes, an endless stream of unaccented events in which continuity and causality were ignored and the differences between the world in which we lived and the world of those other Americas, through which we raced like a scalded cat, went unremarked. The mind was left numb and unreceptive to invitations to build upon this unpromising foundation.

Strangely enough, however, while such experiences warned me to avoid anything that was formally labeled history they in no way diminished my already healthy interest in the past. Thanks to my passion for reading and my possession of a library card, I had discovered a series of storytellers whose powers were sufficient to shore my curiosity up against the depredations of the schoolteachers and those who prescribed the nature and content of the courses they taught. At an early age, and quite by accident, I had discovered that remarkable man G. A. Henty, who had, with inexhaustible energy and verve, written scores of historical romances for young readers, books whose very titles were invitations to go time-traveling: *Beric the Briton*; *The Boy Knight: A Tale of the Crusades*; *Under Drake's Flag*; *By Pike and Dyke: A Tale of the Rise of the Dutch Republic*; *Bonnie Prince Charlie*; *A Cornet of Horse: A Tale of Marlborough's Wars*; *With Clive in India*; and many more. Henty was a former soldier, which was apparent not only in his preferred themes but in his old-fashioned patriotism and emphasis upon the martial virtues, but his books always had a strong and exciting narrative line and, because he was a conscientious researcher, gave accurate descriptions of the age in which his stories were set and the historical situations in which his characters were involved. You couldn't get a very systematic knowledge of history from reading his books (you didn't, after all, go to them for that), but you did pick up a lot of fascinating miscellaneous information and, now and then, a desire to know more about something that he had described, and this sometimes led to experiments in reading that had surprising results.

This was true also of the stories of Rudyard Kipling, particularly those in the volumes entitled *Puck of Pook's Hill* and *Rewards and Fairies.* When I first picked these up, I was just old enough to suspect them of being "kids' stuff" and to expect to be repelled by whimsy, but, after Henty, Kipling's style was beguiling, and I was soon caught up in the charm and verisimilitude of his tales of two English children who were enabled by magic to travel back to pre-Roman Britain and later to meet and talk with a young centurion of a legion stationed on the Wall, a knight of the Norman Conquest, a Jewish physician and money-lender in the time of King John, a builder and decorator of the age of Henry VII, and other figures from England's past. I was later to realize that these reconstructions were all highly romanticized, but at the time I accepted them uncritically and thankfully, because they filled the past with real people rather than with the mythological figures of my Canadian days and told me in terms that I could understand about societies that were remote from my own but nevertheless connected with it.

And finally there was Sir Walter Scott, first discovered in high school, where *Ivanhoe* was a prescribed text, but then pursued on my own with mounting pleasure and excitement by means of tattered library copies of *Quentin Durward* and *Waverley* and *Rob Roy* and *Redgauntlet.*

I had, of course, no inkling in those days that my love of Scott was a pale shadow of that enthusiasm that had swept over a whole generation of readers in the early nineteenth century, had awakened a new interest in historical study, and had served as an inspiration to some who, like Leopold von Ranke, became its most distinguished practitioners. Nor would I have found it easy to explain what I found so compelling in Scott or why I came to sense that his stories were closer to the realities of the historical process than Kipling's impressionistic genre sketches or Henty's often one-dimensional adventures. Many years later, in Georg Lukács's book *The Historical Novel,* I discovered what may have been the key to my instinctive admiration. The central figures in Scott's novels, Lukács pointed out, were not heroes but average persons with whom the reader could identify, persons with "a certain, though never outstanding, degree of practical intelligence, a certain moral fortitude and decency which even rises to a capacity for self-sacrifice, but which never grows into a sweeping human passion, is never the enraptured devotion to a great cause." In the typical Scott novel, this kind of average personality is caught up in the turmoil and confusion of a time of change and transition and finds himself involved in the fortunes of opposed characters and groups whose destinies are at stake. Through his puzzled, uncommitted, but sympathetic eyes, Scott shows us the struggles and antagonisms of history, which are in turn represented by characters who in their psychology and destiny represent social trends and historical forces. "Scott's greatness," Lukács wrote, "lies in his capacity to give living embodiment to historical social types. The typically human terms in which great historical trends become tangible had never before been so superbly, straightforwardly and pregnantly portrayed." Something of this I must have sensed and found attractive.

Since all of this, however, seemed completely alien to history as it was taught in the classroom, I decided when I went to college to continue to feed my interest in the past by private reading. And in this resolve I remained firm until my sophomore year, when my closest friends informed me that if my stubbornness in this regard prevented me from hearing Walter Phelps Hall's lectures on "The Course of Europe since Waterloo," I would be depriving myself of one of the greatest intellectual experiences that Princeton had to offer. Peer pressure was no less powerful in the 1930s than it is today. I told myself that I would be disappointed again and that it would be foolish to yield, but, fortunately for me, I yielded.

"Buzzer" Hall (so-called because he was deaf and used a battery-charged hearing aid that made odd sounds when the batteries were running down) was a graduate of Yale and Columbia who came to Princeton in 1913 at the age of twenty-nine and immediately became a campus legend. He was an inspired teacher and at the lecture podium an electric presence, charging about the platform as if pursued by demons, covering the blackboard with mystifying slogans and drawings meant to represent the course of the White Nile or the insides of the British '79, pouring floods of words over the heads of his audience in a high insistent tone that was sometimes modulated into a keening lament for the inadequacies of humankind or howls of rage at the crimes and follies of their leaders. Always passionate and opinionated and challenging, Buzzer was sometimes wonderfully comic, as in those moments of exasperation or enthusiasm when he rained blows upon the blackboard with an iron-ferruled stick, the thunder of which he could not hear but which often drowned out much of what he was saying. Yet he was also admirably persuasive in his insistence that history was so important and exciting that it required a total commitment from his auditors.

It was this rather than the theatrical aspect of his lectures that impressed me, and also the fact that I found in them, for the first time in an instructional setting, what I had found so attractive in my own reading: an approach to the past in which the emphasis was not upon lifeless figures, such as Carshay and Stuyvesant, or symbolic names and dates (1066 and all that), but upon real human beings dealing with their own problems in their own time and in their own way. Walter Hall had read Scott, too (although I suspect that it was the romantic aspect of the novels that attracted him rather than the qualities that Lukács admired), and he had gone to college at a time when apprentice historians still read Hippolyte Taine, and a lot of it had stuck. He did not, perhaps, believe, as Taine did, that history was a science like physiology and zoology, a kind of applied psychology, for he was too idealistic to share Taine's materialism. But he was inclined to agree that the study of history should begin with individuals and that its goal should be to inquire into the transformations they underwent under the influence of heredity, context, and time, and he would certainly have subscribed to that passage which Stuart Hughes has cited from Taine's *History of English Literature,* where Taine wrote:

> When we read a Greek tragedy, our first care should be to picture to ourselves the Greeks, that is, the men who lived half naked, in the gymnasia, or in the public squares, under a glowing sky, face to face with the most noble landscapes, bent on making their bodies

nimble and strong, on conversing, discussing, voting, carrying on patriotic piracies, but for the rest lazy and temperate, with three urns for their furniture, two anchovies in a jar of oil for their food, waited on by slaves, so as to give them leisure to cultivate their understanding and exercise their limbs, with no desire beyond having the most beautiful town, the most beautiful possessions, the most beautiful ideas, the most beautiful men. . . . A language, a legislation, a catechism, is never more than an abstract thing: the complete thing is the man who acts, the man corporeal and visible, who eats, walks, fights, labours.

In his lectures on European history in the nineteenth and twentieth centuries, Walter Hall began with the assumption that the laws and doctrines and reforms and revolutions of those centuries were made by, and in turn affected, human beings. He taught history, in short, as a humanistic discipline, and so compellingly that in the end I decided to follow his example.

The humanistic studies take their name from the term "humanism," which originally referred to a tendency among thinkers during the Renaissance, like Petrarch, Boccaccio, and Lorenzo Valla, to emphasize classical studies and to seek to return to classical ideals and forms, but has been defined in a more general sense as any system of thought or action that assigns a predominant interest to the affairs of men as compared with the supernatural or the abstract. From this latter definition, it is clear that, among the academic disciplines, history has no exclusive right to be called a humanistic study, for university schools of humanities include others that are concerned with human beings and their activities, philosophy and the literature and arts departments, for example, and, among the so-called behavioral sciences, political science, economics, sociology, psychology, anthropology, and others. These other disciplines, however, are concerned with human beings in a selective and partial way—the political scientists study *zoon politikon* and the economists Economic Man, with scant attention to his other interests and capacities—and some of them are inclined to view men and women collectively rather than in their individuality, divesting them, as the sociologists often do, of personality in order to see them as typical members of groups or classes. Even the philosophers and the students of literature are apt to become so fascinated by the derivations and connections of ideas and the language, conventions and forms of poetry and the novel, that they tend to forget at times that the works they study were the products of real people in specific ages. And sometimes, as in the case of the deconstructionists of our time, this forgetfulness is deliberate. It is the historian alone who is interested in human beings in all of their activities, capacities, and quiddities and is best qualified to declare, with the Roman dramatist Terence, that nothing human is alien to him.

This claim will perhaps seem excessive to anyone who remembers the comparatively narrow scope of historical instruction, even at major universities, fifty years ago, and the predominance of the kind of political history that concentrated on the fortunes of the Great Powers—what the irreverent called "drum and trumpet history"—and the statesmen who charted their courses in world politics that had prevailed for much longer than that. Part of the blame for this must be attributed to the nature of the times, for the whole period from 1860 to 1945 was, in the Western world at least, a period of domestic and international violence and change, and historiography tended to reflect this in its choice of themes. The narrowness of range was to be explained in part also by the fact that, before the invention of mechanical means for the easy duplication of documents, few researchers had the energy to go beyond the political files in archival collections, so that whole areas of human experience went uninvestigated. Finally, lack of imagination, reinforced by the prejudices of the time, had a lot to do with it, making certain lines of inquiry—notably the role of women in history and the role of minorities in national cultures—seem to be unpromising and without significance. It is true that smallness of view was not characteristic of the most eminent of historians. One thinks of the astonishing range of J. G. Droysen's *Alexander the Great* and Jacob Burckhardt's *The Age of Constantine* and Theodor Mommsen's *Roman History,* works that not only presented persuasive assessments of the characters and careers of the main figures in their stories, but gave remarkably detailed portraits of the age in which they lived, which included descriptions of social stratification, trades and industry, agriculture, religion, money, the institutions and economy of war, architecture, art and literature, public morality, crime, cuisine, the overlapping of civilizations, the Jews and other minorities, and other aspects of life in the Mediterranean and

Middle Eastern areas. This sort of thing represented historical humanism in the grand manner, but it was not within the competence of the
average practitioner of the discipline, whose range, like that of the of-
ferings in the departments in which they taught, remained modest.

In our own time, the scope of historical investigation has been so
greatly expanded that the conscience of historians need not suffer when
they describe their calling as truly humanistic. Since the end of World
War II, their profession has benefited from a democratization of attitude, caused not least of all by the transformation of sexual attitudes,
and a massive increase of research capacity that is largely due to the
computer revolution. It should now be recognized more generally than
it is that, if it is to make good its claim to be the queen of the humanities, history must focus its attention, both in research and classroom
instruction, upon the role, not only of the movers and shakers in history, but upon that of men and women of every class and condition, including racial and ethnic minorities in society, and that, since computer-
ized research techniques now make it possible to digest and analyze
statistical and social data that were unmanageable and hence inaccessi-
ble to earlier generations of scholars, there are no insuperable obstacles
to assigning to these formerly forgotten groups their proper place in the
historical record.

One should perhaps linger for a moment over the new vistas
opened up for historians by the computer. Bernard Bailyn has written
in the introduction to what will be a large-scale work entitled *The Peo-
pling of British North America,* that the movement of thousands of people
from the area that stretches from Prussia to the Danube and from the
Hebrides to Africa across the Atlantic to the seaboard communities and
the forests and valleys of North America was "the greatest population
movement in early modern history and yet . . . our understanding of
this great westward transfer of people is a blur, lacking in structure,
scale, and detail. We know only in the vaguest way who the hundreds of
thousands of individuals who settled in British North America were,
where precisely they came from, why they came, and how they lived out
their lives." How rapidly this situation is now changing as a result of
computer analysis of data gathered from emigration records, genealogical sources, local histories, town records, personal diaries, and newspapers can be seen in Bailyn's first volume, *Voyagers to the West,* which not

only gives a quantitative and structural analysis of what is now seen clearly as a more complicated population movement than had been formerly imagined but also provides micronarratives in which the fortunes of selected individuals and families are traced from their origins to their final destinations in ways that illustrate the whole range of experiences and frustrations and successes of the emigrants.

New possibilities breed new attitudes. In the recent interest in what the Germans call *Alltagsgeschichte,* or everyday history, one can detect the belief that historians should not believe that the world of great political and economic decisions and of ideological conflict is essentially any worthier of their attention than the way in which ordinary people lead their lives and, indeed, that a knowledge of the songs that are sung in the back streets may throw new light on the structure and cohesiveness of society. This is not to recommend that history teachers, in particular, turn their attention away from the "big questions" of state and class formation, of religion and churches, of industrialism and its human effects, and of the basic causes and results of such movements as national socialism, for the thoughts and behavior of people in even the smallest spaces in society are to a large extent determined by these things. But there is no doubt that everyday history brings a concreteness and specificity to the past that is not always found in the description of longtime trends. As Hans-Ulrich Wehler has written, "a colorful, plastic history of individual and collective experiences, happenings, modes of perception, behavioral dispositions and actions (such as is made possible by the study of workers in specific trades, utopian societies, outsiders in society like beggars and vagrants, and other special groups that have attracted the attention of enthusiasts for *Alltagsgeschichte)* broadens the understanding of the past and stimulates the fantasy as well as the intellect."

The new democratization of attitude has affected even the most traditional forms of historical writing for the better. Military history, for example, until very recently concentrated largely upon the so-called decisive battles, which were always seen from the standpoint of the generals conducting them, and the strategies they had devised, or from that of the posterity that benefited or suffered from their results. How the common soldier felt about all this was left to the novelists and the poets, some of whom proved more successful than the historians in conveying a sense of the realities of modern war, as Stendhal's account of the battle of Waterloo in *The Charterhouse of Parma* and Stephen Crane's masterful story *The Red Badge of Courage* make clear enough. Recently, however, the British historian John Keegan has shown, in his brilliant and exciting *The Face of Battle,* that historical imagination and skill in using sources are perfectly capable of revealing the experiences and feelings of the ordinary man-at-arms at Agincourt or the Somme and his *Mask of Command* is a fascinating and original study of the complex relationship between the commander and his troops, illustrated by the cases of Alexander, Wellington, Grant, and Hitler.

Admittedly, many schoolteachers and course planners will doubt the advisability of including much military history in their curricula, but its total exclusion is hardly advisable in view of the importance of war as an agency for historical change and the undeniable interest that many students have in it. Recently, a German newspaper, the *Frankfurter Allgemeine Zeitung,* has been distributing to writers, artists, and other prominent public figures an elaborate questionnaire that was popular in the nineteenth century and was filled out by such people as Karl Marx, John Stuart Mill, and Marcel Proust. One of the questions was "What military achievements do you most admire?," and many of the recent respondents to the questionnaire either left this blank or used the occasion to say how much they hated war. One respondent, however, wrote, "Building the Roman roads." He was perhaps a historian who remembered the Via Aurelia ran all the way from Rome to distant Gaul—"It's twenty-five marches to Narbo," Kipling wrote in "Rimini," one of his poems about the Roman army, "It's forty-five more up the Rhone"—and that it and the many other roads built by the legions long outlasted the Empire and served as a network of communication between localities that would otherwise have languished in total isolation during the medieval period. Historian or not, his answer reminds us that there is more to war than killing, and that imaginative approaches can make the historical role of military establishments a rewarding aspect of historical study.

Concerning historical instruction, whether written or oral, three special problems are worth at least cursory consideration: the effective mode or style of communication; the question of bridging the gap that lies between the time of the historian or the teacher and that of the events that are his subject; and, related to this, the role of moral judgments in historical instruction.

With respect to the first of these, it goes almost without saying that the story or narrative form has the most attractive appeal to readers and students and is the most effective method of covering large stretches of time, of demonstrating connections, of delineating lines of continuity, and of presenting dramatic illustrations of the disruption caused by change. But this linear form of historical discourse is generally better at explaining how events took place in time than why they did so, and even the most effective practitioners of the narrative form, or perhaps *especially* the most effective, are prone to omitting or minimizing the importance of facts and circumstances that interfere with its dramatic sweep. To guard against this propensity of the storyteller and its own inherent weaknesses, the narrative form must be reinforced by other techniques that facilitate the explanation of the origins of events, the operation of cause and effect, and the similarities and dissimilarities between analogous developments, and which monitor the generalizations that the narrator makes and keeps them within the range of plausibility. Such techniques include the rigorous analysis of contingent and apparently irrelevant factors (useful in any case to correct the persistent human assumption that events have single causes) and the employment of comparative techniques that test the plausibility of notions of singularity and reveal patterns of behavior and development. (Thus, one is apt to be more cautious in making generalizations about nineteenth-century British liberalism if one has also studied liberalism in France, Switzerland, and Italy, and one is likely also to discover things not revealed by absorption in the single case.)

It is here that the historian can often find assistance in the methods of other disciplines, particularly the social sciences. If he is dealing with the inflationary period in the Weimar Republic, for example, he would be well advised to consult what economists have written about the general causes and characteristics of inflationary spirals; if he intends to describe a particularly complicated diplomatic crisis, it may be helpful for him to read what Alexander L. George has written about the anatomy of crises as revealed by comparative case studies of such political phenomena; and in general, he should remember that sociologists can tell him a great deal about bureaucracies and social stratification and psychologists about the behavior of crowds. He has no good reason, therefore, to be parochial or scornful of what others have to teach him. On the other hand, he must guard against becoming so entranced with what the social sciences are doing that he begins to base his approach upon theirs or even adopt their literary style, with its use of nouns as adjectives and verbs and its barbaric inventions, which often defeat the precision they are meant to enhance. The business of the social sciences is different from his own, which, as Siegfried Kracauer once wrote, is "to elude not only the Scylla of philosophical speculations with their wholesale meanings but also the Charybdis of the sciences with their natural laws and regulations" and to seek to deal with "the particular events, developments, and situations of the human past," a formulation in which the emphasis should be placed upon the words "particular" and "human."

In general, the nature of the period being studied, the materials available, and the skill and imagination of the historian will determine the most effective mode of presenting the story to his readers and students. Whatever his ultimate choice, however, he must of course be guided by their knowledge and interests and be prepared to build on the former and motivate and heighten the latter. He must never forget that it is the approval of his audience and not that of his colleagues that should be in the front of his mind. Jacob Burckhardt was surely making a wise decision when he wrote, as an apprentice historian, "At the risk of being considered unscientific by the population of pedants, I am firmly determined from now on to write in a *readable* fashion. . . . Against the sneers of the contemporary scholarly generation, one must armor oneself with a certain indifference, so that one will perhaps be bought and read, and not merely be the subject of bored note-taking in libraries." A humanistic discipline deserves to be presented in a humane way, as a story about human beings in circumstances, told with grace and energy, its analytic rigor heightened by clarity and logic, its argument persuasive rather than strident or bullying.

Special problems are posed by the distance that exists between the historian and the events that he describes. The Hungarian historian Michael de Ferdinandy once wrote that the humanistic nature of historical scholarship was nowhere more strikingly demonstrated than in its subjective character, in the fact that what we call history exists only because human beings think about it. "Without the historian—whether chronicler or reader," Ferdinandy wrote, "without the intelligent (understanding) eye which observes and assesses the past, there is no history, only a *caput mortuum,* the inert mass of data and past conditions of something that has been. Only through this eye does the dead material take on life again and order and articulate itself and emerge again within us as a living picture of the once existent." But it does so, he continued, in a way that is determined by the qualities of the observing eye, by the intellectual and historical situation of its time, and by its view of the future.

It is clear that this relationship can be productive of much confusion and erroneous generalization about the past that really existed long before our generation came along to observe it, and the facile analogies that our politicians are fond of making between present and past situations are not the only form that such error assumes. It is all too easy and too tempting to make the real past a mere backward extension of our own times, peopled by individuals who might wear clothing different from our own but who are essentially like us in their fundamental attitudes and motivations, in the passions that move them and in the ordering of their priorities. It does not, of course, take much reflection to convince us that this could not possibly be true, and that there are vast differences between the thought processes of inhabitants of twentieth-century New Hampshire and those of their forebears at the end of the seventeenth century, who witnessed and accepted without surprise a degree of savagery in their quotidian existence that is scarcely comprehensible to us. But we often forget this, in small and sometimes important ways, when we are talking or writing about the past. To prevent this requires a high degree of caution and self-criticism as we approach the past, the utmost fidelity to existing sources, a determined and imaginative search for new ones, and a plenitude of the quality that we call empathy, which permits us to feel our way, if we are lucky and work hard enough at it, into the culture of the age that we set out to study and describe.

One of the greatest mistakes to which we are prone as we think about the past is the assumption of inevitability of result. In his inaugural lecture as professor of history at the University of Jena on May 27, 1787, on the theme "What is and to what end do we study universal history?" Friedrich Schiller began by saying, "The very fact that we find ourselves here at this moment, that, characterized as we are by this level of national culture, this language, these moral attitudes, these *bürgerliche* advantages, and this measure of intellectual freedom, we have gathered here, is perhaps the result of all previous world events: the whole of world history would at least be necessary to explain this single moment." In a limited sense—namely, the sense that we are the result of the past—the great poet was doubtless correct. But if he was intimating that history necessarily tended to this end, he was of course doing grave injustice to the richness and variety of the past (for surely the evolution of Chinese and Indian culture was not driven by the determination to produce a Friedrich Schiller), to say nothing of denying freedom of will to generations of individuals who made the history of his own country. To forget that the present is the result of many developments that might have taken a different course and of decisions that might not have been made, or not at the same time or in the same way, is seriously to foreshorten our historical perspective and to indulge in linear thinking of the most restricted kind. The duty of the historian, the contemporary German scholar Thomas Nipperdey once said, is to restore to the past the options it once had. To do so, moreover, is a marvelously effective way of teaching history, for few things engage students more than opportunities to argue about the reasons why such and such things occurred in history rather than quite different ones.

More difficult than any of the problems discussed so far is the question of whether the historian is called upon, in his writing or teaching, to pass moral judgments upon past actions or individual actors. This is a question of the utmost delicacy and one capable of arousing the most violent controversy among professional historians. In the nineteenth century, Lord Acton insisted that it was the historian's duty to "suffer no man and no cause to escape the undying penalty which history has the power to inflict on wrong," and said of scholars who passed over crime and injustice without comment that "the strong man with the dagger is followed by the weak man with the sponge." In our own century the general tendency among historians has been either to ignore the moral obligation that Acton called for or to insist that, since moral values change from age to age, the historian is best advised to practice a "value-free" kind of history, being rigorous and objective in his presentation of the facts and letting his readers or students make their own judgments.

Yet, as Gordon Wright said in his presidential address to the American Historical Association in 1978, this kind of argument will probably give teachers of history who live in the age of Watergate (we may strengthen his argument by adding in the age of Irangate and Pentagon defense contract scandals) some twinges of self-doubt about their classroom obligations. Most of the people involved in these escapades were holders of university degrees and must have had some exposure to the humanistic disciplines. If so, they seem not to have derived from them any sense of moral values or civic responsibility, and this raises serious questions about the nature of the instruction they received. Were their delinquencies perhaps in part due to too much "value-free" instruction? With apparent approval, Wright quoted the British historian C. V. Wedgwood's words: "History dispassionately recorded nearly always sounds harsh and cynical. History is not a moral tale, and the effect of telling it without comment is, inevitably, to underline its worst features: the defeat of the weak by the strong, the degeneration of ideals, the corruption of institutions, the triumph of intelligent self-interest." A surfeit of this sort of thing is bound to make it easier for people to rationalize crime and immorality by arguing that that is the way of the world.

If history is a humanistic discipline, is not one of its principal functions to promote humane values? And can it do that effectively without reprobating the crimes against humanity with which history is filled? When the "greatness" of Julius Caesar is discussed, does not the historian have an obligation to point to the needless barbarity of the Gallic Wars—the lopping off of the hands of tens of thousands of enemy warriors; the extirpation of whole tribes of innocent men, women, and children for no other purpose than to enhance the political fortunes of the Roman commander? Granted that the chief end of historical instruction is to make students understand the past, surely it is unreasonable to suppose that to understand is to forgive? After he has explained the circumstances that led so many Germans to give their support to Adolf Hitler in the early 1930s, is not the practitioner of a humanistic discipline justified in finding those representatives of the world of culture and learning who, like the philosopher Martin Heidegger, called upon their colleagues to rally to the Nazi cause and those German scientists who collaborated in Hitler's atrocities especially culpable and worthy of condemnation?

Obviously not everyone will think so, but the question should at least be pondered by anyone who considers himself a humanist. It is clear enough that history teachers should not become preachers of morality. But they must, it seems to me, have a moral instinct that is strong enough to recognize that there are limits to objectivity. Aside from that, the search for historical truth should be suffused with a commitment to deeply held humane values and a warm and instinctive sympathy for such qualities as fortitude, steadfastness, endurance, civic virtue, dedication to the greater good, and service to humanity when they are embodied in historical movements and personalities. The recognition of such qualities in historical instruction can be an effective way of reprobating their opposites.

People of a practical turn of mind—politicians, for example—often ask what are the lessons that history has to offer them. In response to a publisher who wanted him to write a short book on the subject, Charles A. Beard, the Columbia University historian, answered that he could summarize such lessons in four sentences:

1. Whom the gods would destroy, they first make mad with power.
2. The mills of God grind slowly, yet they grind exceedingly small.
3. The bee fertilizes the flower it robs.
4. When it is dark enough, you can see the stars.

This answer does not satisfy the politicians, who are apt to make up historical lessons of their own to fit their private agenda; and it may not satisfy many beginning students of history, who will ask insistently why, if there are no specific and tangible benefits in sight, they should study it at all. For anyone who regards history, not as a practical science, but as a humanistic discipline, the answer is clear enough. You should study history because it is good for you. By telling you about how other individuals and societies lived in history, it gives you a vicarious experience and thus makes you a more complete human being. It is a source of reassurance in time of discouragement, for it tells you that other people before you had problems and perplexities and yet managed, because the human spirit is indomitable, to survive them. It is, as the Roman historian Livy once said,

[T]he best medicine for a sick mind, for in history you have a record of the infinite variety of human experience plainly set out for all to see, and in that record you can find for yourself and your country both examples and warnings: fine things to take as models, base things, rotten through and through, to avoid.

Finally, it provides you with an extension of your own life and a connectedness that gives it a greater significance in the stream of history, making you a vital link in the great process that connects the remotest past with the most distant future. In this concept there is a grandeur that transfigures the brevity of individual existence. This is what Schiller meant in his inaugural lecture when, answering the question "What is and to what end do we study universal history," he said:

History, insofar as it accustoms human beings to comprehend the whole of the past and to hasten forward with its conclusions into the far future, conceals the boundaries of birth and death, which enclose the life of the human being so narrowly and oppressively, and, with a kind of optical illusion, expands his short existence into endless space, leading the individual imperceptibly over into humanity.

Reference Matter

Notes

Editors' Introduction

1 Gordon A. Craig, *The Germans* (New York: Meridian Books, 1982), p. 7.
2 For Craig's account of the genesis of his career, see "History as a Humanistic Discipline," the final essay in this volume.
3 Gordon A. Craig, "Sir Llewellyn Woodward (1890–1971)," *Yearbook of the American Philosophical Society* (1971), pp. 200–201. Woodward was one of the four teachers to whom Craig intended to dedicate a collection of his essays written during the 1980s. The others were Walter Phelps Hall, the Princeton professor whose influence he recalls in "History as a Humanistic Discipline"; B. Humphrey Sumner, the British diplomatic historian, his tutor at Oxford; and Raymond James Sontag, who taught both George Kennan and Gordon Craig at Princeton, and whose classic *Germany and England: Background of Conflict, 1848–1894* was one of the models for Craig's own work in diplomatic history.
4 For an example of how careful Craig was in his moral judgments, see the delicately balanced assessment of the Swiss role in the Second World War, included in this volume.
5 See James J. Sheehan, "Gordon Alexander Craig (1913–2005)," in *Tact and Intelligence: Essays on Diplomatic History and International Relations* (Palo Alto: SPOSS, 2008), pp. vii–xii.
6 For Taylor on Craig, see "The German Army in Politics," in *Europe: Grandeur and Decline* (Harmondsworth: Penguin, 1967). For Craig on Taylor, see "Europe's Perpetual Quadrille," *Saturday Review*, July 15, 1955, p. 28; "Provocative, Perverse View of Pre-1939, " in *Origins of the*

Second World War: A. J. P. Taylor and His Critics, ed. William Rogers Lewis (New York: John Wiley & Sons, 1972); and *The Germans*, p. 71.

7 Taylor's description of Macaulay's style is cited by David Cannadine, "Troubled Troublemaker: The Vanity, Resentment, and Brilliance of A. J. P. Taylor," *Times Literary Supplement*, February 4, 1994, p. 3.

8 For the great historians' literary styles and strategies, see John Clive, *Not by Fact Alone: Essays on the Writing and Reading of History* (New York: Alfred A. Knopf, 1989); Felix Gilbert, *History: Politics or Culture? Reflections on Ranke and Burckhardt* (Princeton: Princeton University Press, 1990); and Peter Gay, *Style in History: Gibbon, Ranke, Macaulay, Burckhardt* (New York: W. W. Norton, 1991).

9 Cannadine, "Troubled Troublemaker," p. 4.

10 Ibid., p. 3.

11 Fritz Stern, "Can One Explain the 'Demonic'?" *Encounter*, June 1979, p. 58.

12 "The Political Leader as Strategist," perhaps the masterpiece among the essays in this volume, applies Clausewitzian criteria to the assessment of the principal leaders of both the First and the Second World Wars. For incisive comments on this essay, see Scott D. Sagan's review of *Makers of Modern Strategy: From Machiavelli to the Nuclear Age*, ed. Peter Paret, "Arms and Ideas," *The New Republic*, September 8, 1986, p. 37.

13 Gordon A. Craig, "Political and Diplomatic History," in *Historical Studies Today*, ed. Felix Gilbert and Stephen R. Graubard (New York: W. W. Norton, 1972), p. 360.

14 Ibid.

15 One of the shrewdest comments on the centrality of intellectual history in Craig's work comes from the pen of the great historian of France, Richard Cobb, reviewing *Germany 1866–1945*: "His book is not so much about the German people . . . as about the intellectuals, the educated men, the terrible university professors who betrayed their trust, who rejected doubt, and who turned their backs on truth, a *trahison des clercs* on a national scale with, unfortunately for others, international repercussions. Any history of the German Reich *has* to be intellectual, for its central theme *has* to be the development of ideas and ambitions divorced from everyday realities and of abstractions that deny the evidence of common sense and of historical experience." See Richard Cobb, "A Culture That Went Wrong," *The Spectator*, November 4, 1978, p. 18.

16 As Charles Maier suggested in his review of Craig's *Germany 1866–1945*, in *The New Republic*, October 7, 1978, Craig combined "a Rankean concern with international rivalry and a Tacitus-like moral preoccupation with the corruptions of power."

[17] See his classic essay "Engagement and Neutrality in Weimar Germany," *Journal of Contemporary History*, 2: 2 (April 1967), pp. 49–63.

[18] See Barry M. Katz, *Foreign Intelligence: Research and Analysis in the Office of Strategic Services 1942–1945* (Cambridge: Harvard University Press, 1989), p. 166.

[19] See, for example, the first two essays in this volume, and his splendid book on liberalism in nineteenth-century Switzerland, *The Triumph of Liberalism: Zurich in the Golden Age, 1830–1869* (New York: Scribner, 1988).

[20] For Craig's refusal to accept a "demonic" interpretation of the role of power in German history, see *The Politics of the Unpolitical: German Writers and the Problem of Power 1770–1871* (New York: Oxford University Press, 1995), p. xii.

[21] Gordon A. Craig, *Theodor Fontane: Literature and History in the Bismarck Reich* (New York: Oxford University Press, 1999), p. xii.

[22] Craig delivered this lecture for the Library of Congress Symposium on Knowledge and Power, on 15 June 1988. There is a typescript of the lecture in the Gordon Alexander Craig Papers (SC 467) in the Department of Special Collections, Stanford University Libraries. This important passage, which summarizes much of Craig's thinking on the relationship between intellectuals and power in Germany, continues as follows: "Nietzsche's warning, after the victory over France, that to confuse power and culture would encourage the eventual victory of barbarism and his reminder that the obsession with power merely propagated stupidity and deprived the nation of material and intellectual resources that should be put to better use, had no power to deter generations of scholars from Dahlmann and Treitschke to Max Weber and Dietrich Schäfer from idealizing the *Machtstaat* and giving it undeviating support even in its most bellicose moods. During the Wilhelmine period, the professoriate more than justified its description as the loyal bodyguard of the Hohenzollerns: during the Weimar Republic it engaged in a *trahison des clercs* that was as stupid as it was shameful. Unable to reconcile itself to a regime of democratic freedom, it did what it could to weaken the republic's foundations and then delivered itself, with relief and enthusiasm, into the hands of the Nazis and lent its talents to their purposes."

[23] Jacob Burckhardt, *Force and Freedom: Reflections on History* (New York: Pantheon Books, 1943), p. 96.

[24] For examples of civic virtue and fortitude in this volume, see *inter alia* the essays on Moses Mendelssohn, Max Weber, and America's Scarlet Pimpernel, Varian Fry.

[25] See, for example, Gordon A. Craig, "German Unification in Historical Perspective," *Proceedings of the American Philosophical Society*, 135: 1 (March 1991), pp. 369–84.

Chapter 2

[1] *Plagues and Peoples* (Garden City, NY: Anchor/Doubleday, 1976), p. 231.

Chapter 3

[1] Marianne Weber, *Max Weber, Ein Lebensbild* (Tübingen: Verlag J .C. B. Mohr/Paul Siebeck, 1926), p. 212.

[2] See my article "The Kaiser and the Kritik" in *The New York Review*, February 18, 1988, pp. 17–20. [Reprinted in *Politics and Culture in Modern Germany: Essays from the New York Review of Books* (Palo Alto: SPOSS, 2000), pp. 66–78.]

[3] Richard Baxter, 1615–1691, the English nonconformist clergyman whom Weber regarded as the outstanding writer on Puritan ethics.

[4] Max Weber, *The Protestant Ethic and the Spirit of Capitalism*, translated from the German by Talcott Parsons, with an introduction by Anthony Giddens (London: Unwin-Hyman, 21st impression, 1990), p. 155.

[5] "Zwischenbetrachtung: Theorie der Stufen und Richtungen Religiöser Weltablehnung," in Max Weber, *Die Wirtschaftsethik der Weltreligionen Konfuzianismus und Taoismus: Schriften, 1915–1920 (Max Weber Gesamtausgabe*, Abeilung I, vol. 19, edited by Hedwig Schmidt-Glintzer in collaboration with Petra Kolonko (Tübingen: Verlag J. C. B. Mohr/Paul Siebeck, 1989).

[6] Ibid., p. 488.

[7] Ibid., p. 512.

[8] Marianne Weber, *Max Weber, Ein Lebensbild*, p. 466.

[9] Ibid., p. 494.

[10] The translation is by Mr. Scaff in *"Zwischenbetrachtung," Max Weber Gesamtausgabe*, Abteilung I, vol. 19, p. 517ff.

[11] See Friedrich Nietzsche, *The Birth of Tragedy and the Genealogy of Morals*, translated by Francis Golffing (Garden City, NY: Doubleday, 1956), p. 284ff.

[12] See Wolfgang J. Mommsen, *Max Weber and German Politics, 1890–1920*, translated from the German by Michael S. Steinberg (University of Chicago Press, 1984); and my article "The Kaiser and the Kritik," *The New York Review*, February 18, 1988, p. 20.

[13] Johann Wolfgang Goethe, *Werke, Hamburger Ausgabe in 14 Bände*, edited by Erich Trunz (Munich: C. H. Beck Verlag, 1981), vol. IV, p. 400; vol. X, p. 177ff.

Chapter 4

1 Conrad Alberti, *Die Alten und die Jungen: Sozialer Roman* (Leipzig: W. Friedrich, 1889), chapter 1.

2 Quoted in Victor Lange, "Ausdruck und Erkenntnis: Zur politischen Problematik der deutschen Literatur seit dem Expressionismus," *Die Neue Rundschau*, (1963), p. 96ff.

3 See the entry dated October 26, 1930: Harry Graf Kessler, *Das Tagebuch 1880–1937*, vol. 9, 1926–1937, ed. Roland S. Kamzelak and Ulrich Ott (Stuttgart: J.G. Cotta, 2004), p. 389.

4 Susanne Miller and Heinrich Potthoff, eds., *Die Regierung der Volksbeauftragten, 1918–19* (Düsseldorf: Droste, 1966), Document No. 105, p. 249. See also Gordon A. Craig, "Prussianism and Democracy: Otto Braun and Konrad Adenauer," chapter 4 of *The End of Prussia* (Madison: University of Wisconsin Press, 1984).

5 The last few words of this sentence were illegible in the only extant copy of the text of Gordon Craig's lecture. The phrase that concludes the sentence, "lost by default," is an interpolation by the volume editors.

6 Klaus Bergmann, *Agrarromantik und Grossstadtfeindschaft* (Meisenheim a. Glan: Hain, 1970).

7 Wilhelm Schäfer, *Die dreizehn Bücher der deutschen Seele* (Munich: G. Müller, 1923).

Chapter 5

1 See my article "Becoming Hitler" in *The New York Review*, May 19, 1997. [Reprinted in *Politics and Culture in Modern Germany: Essays from the New York Review of Books* (Palo Alto: SPOSS, 2000), pp. 134–40.]

Chapter 6

1 Hans-Peter Schwarz, *Adenauer: Der Staatsmann, 1952–1967* (Stuttgart: Deutsche Verlags-Anstalt, 1991), p. 987

2 Lorenz Stucki, "Adenauer in Nöten," *Die Weltwoche* (Zürich), November 5, 1954.

Chapter 7

1 These aspects of Scottish history are recounted in rich detail and lively prose in Magnus Magnusson, *Scotland: The Story of a Nation* (New York: Atlantic Monthly Press, 2000). More comprehensive and scholarly but also more uneven, because it is a work by several hands, is *The New Penguin History of Scotland from Earliest Times to the Present Day*, ed. R. A. Houston and W. W .J. Knox (London: Allen Lane, Penguin, 2001).

2 Michael Fry, *The Scottish Empire* (East Lothian: Tuckwell, 2001; Edinburgh: Birlinn, 2001).

3 Cited by John Mackenzie, "Hearts in the Highlands," *Times Literary Supplement*, January 25, 2002, p. 11.

4 Mackenzie, "Hearts in the Highlands," p. 11.

5 *A Drunk Man Looks at the Thistle*, ll. 736–38.

6 Allan Massie in *The Times Literary Supplement*, May 20, 1994, p. 24.

Chapter 8

1 Arthur Moeller van den Bruck (1876–1925) was a German cultural historian and right-wing nationalist, best known for his book *Das Dritte Reich* (1923), the title of which the Nazis appropriated. *Der Preußische Stil* (1916) became one of the chief inspirations of the Juni-Club of the Jungkonservativen ("young conservative movement") in Germany. The classic study of Moeller's thought and influence is Fritz Stern, *The Politics of Cultural Despair: A Study in the Rise of Germanic Ideology* (Berkeley: University of California Press, 1961).

2 The *Neue Wache* (New Guard House) is a building in central Berlin, located on the north side of the *Unter den Linden*.

3 Arthur Moeller van den Bruck, *Der Preußische Stil* (Munich: Bergstadtverlag Wilhelm Gottlieb Korn, 1953), pp. 11–12.

4 Ibid., pp. 114–15.

5 See *Treitschke's History of Germany in the Nineteenth Century* (London: Jarrold & Sons, 1915).

6 See Friedrich Nietzsche, *Beyond Good and Evil: Prelude to a Philosophy of the Future*, chapter 6, section 209.

7 Moeller van den Bruck, *Der Preußische Stil*, pp. 197–98.

8 Ibid., p. 211.

9 Oswald Spengler, *Preussentum und Sozialismus* (Munich: C. H. Beck, 1919), p. 5. Spengler (1880–1936) is best known, of course, as the author of *Der Untergang des Abendlandes* [*The Decline of the West*], a jeremiad that achieved worldwide success in the aftermath of the First World War. See the classic study by H. Stuart Hughes, *Oswald Spengler: A Critical Estimate* (New York: Scribner, 1952).

10 Ibid., p. 103.

11 Johann Gottfried Schadow (1764–1850) was a German sculptor whose teacher Jean-Pierre-Antoine Taessart (1727–1788) was the court sculptor for Frederick the Great.

12 For Marwitz, see Gordon A. Craig, "The Failure of Reform: Stein and Marwitz," *The End of Prussia* (Madison: University of Wisconsin Press, 1984), pp. 8–26.

[13] In *The End of Prussia*, on p. 49, Gordon Craig quotes a definition of this term by the Catholic bishop of Mainz, Wilhelm Emanuel Freiherr von Ketteler, an opponent of Bismarck: "By *Borussianismus*, we understand an *idée fixe* about Prussia's calling, a vague conception of a world mission imposed on Prussia, tied up with the conviction that this calling and task are absolutely necessary ones . . . and that it is impermissible to oppose [them] in the name of law or history."

Chapter 9

[1] On this, see Theodor Fontane, *Wanderungen durch die Mark Brandenburg*, vol. II (Munich: Carl Hanser Verlag, 1960), p. 284ff.

[2] Christopher Duffy, *The Military Life of Frederick the Great* (New York: Atheneum, 1986), p. 132.

[3] Ibid., p. 181.

[4] Wilhelm Dilthey, *Gesammelte Schriften*, vol. III, ed. by Paul Ritter (Leipzig: Teubner, 1927), p. 100ff.

[5] Hans I. Bach, *The German Jew: A Synthesis of Judaism and Western Civilization, 1730–1930* (New York: Oxford University Press, 1984), p. 44.

[6] Alexander Altmann, *Moses Mendelssohn: A Biographical Study* (Tuscaloosa: University of Alabama Press, 1973), pp. 15–25.

[7] Peter Gay, *The Enlightenment: An Interpretation*, vol. II, *The Science of Freedom* (New York: Knopf, 1969), p. 458.

[8] Ibid., vol. I, *The Rise of Modern Paganism* (New York: Knopf, 1966), p. 11.

[9] Theodor Schieder, *Friedrich der Grosse. Ein Königtum der Widersprüche* (Frankfurt a. Main: Propyläen Verlag, 1983), p. 105; *Die werke Friedrichs des Grossen*, ed. Gustav Berthold Volz, vol. VII (Berlin: Hobbing, 1913), especially pp. 106–107.

[10] Richard Dietrich, ed., *Politische Testamente der Hohenzollern* (Munich: Deutscher Taschenbuch Verlag, 1981), p. 174.

[11] Schieder, *Friedrich der Grosse*, p. 307.

[12] Ibid.

[13] See Theodore Bestermann, *Voltaire* (New York: Harcourt, Brace & World, 1969), pp. 92, 572.

[14] Richard Dietrich, ed., *Politische Testamente*, p. 167. This passage has been omitted from the *Testamente* as printed in Volz, ed., *Die Werke Friedrichs des Grossen*, vol. VII, p. 148.

[15] Richard Dietrich, ed., *Politische Testamente*, p. 281.

[16] Schieder, *Friedrich der Grosse*, pp. 465–72.

[17] *Moses Mendelssohn zur 200jährigen Wiederkehr seines Geburtstages*, herausgegeben von der Encyclopaedia Judaica (Berlin: L. Schneider, 1929), p. 19.

[18] Altmann, *Moses Mendelssohn*, pp. 264–65.

[19] Ibid., p. 275ff.

[20] *Mendelssohn zur 200jährigen Wiederkehr*, p. 81.

[21] Altmann, *Moses Mendelssohn*, pp. 30, 67–68, 71–72.

[22] For Lessing's appreciation of this point, see his play *Die Juden*.

[23] George L. Mosse, *German Jews Beyond Judaism* (Bloomington: Indiana University Press, 1985), chapter 1.

[24] Bach, *The German Jew*, p. 44.

Chapter 10

[1] See my article "Becoming Hitler," *The New York Review*, May 29, 1997. [Reprinted in *Politics and Culture in Modern Germany: Essays from The New York Review of Books* (Palo Alto: SPOSS, 2000), pp. 134–40.]

[2] *Founder: A Portrait of the First Rothschild and His Time* (New York: Viking, 1996); see my review, "Prophets," in *The New York Review*, January 9, 1997. [Reprinted in *Politics and Culture in Modern Germany: Essays from The New York Review of Books* (Palo Alto: SPOSS, 2000), pp. 229–38.]

[3] Cited in Gordon A. Craig, *The Politics of the Unpolitical* (New York: Oxford University Press, 1995), p. 132ff.

Chapter 11

[1] Thomas Babington Macaulay, *History of England from the Accession of James the Second* (5 vols., 1849–61), vol. III, Introduction.

[2] Dean Acheson, *Sketches from Life* (New York: Harper, 1961), pp. 16–17. Lord Bullock, *Ernest Bevin, Foreign Secretary, 1945–1951* (London: Heinemann, 1983), p. 88.

[3] Stanley Hoffmann, *Decline or Renewal? France Since the 1930s* (New York: Viking Press, 1974), pp. 231, 236, 427, 433.

[4] Johann Peter Eckermann, *Gespräche mit Goethe in den letzten Jahren seines Lebens* (Munich: W. Goldmann, 1984), pp. 152, 408f.

[5] Cited in Rudolf von Thadden, "Das schwierige Vaterland," in *Die Identität der Deutschen*, ed. Werner Weidenfeld (Munich: C. Hanser, 1983), p. 52.

[6] Heinrich Heine, *Werke*, ed. Martin Greiner (2nd edition, 2 vols., Köln: Kiepenheuer & Witsch, 1962), vol. II, p. 583.

[7] Gordon A. Craig, *Über die Deutschen* (Munich: C. H. Beck, 1982), p. 19.

[8] Richard Wagner, "Was ist deutsch?" in *Ausgewählte Schriften und Briefe*, ed. Alfred Lorenz (2 vols., Berlin, 1938), vol. II, p. 332.

[9] W. M. Simon, *Germany in the Age of Bismarck* (London: George Allen & Unwin, 1968), p. 154; K. Frantz, *Der Föderalismus* (Mainz: F. Kircheim, 1879), esp. pp. 220ff, 299f.

[10] Theodor Schieder, *Das deutsche Kaiserreich von 1871 als Nationalstaat* (Köln: Westdeutscher Verlag, 1961).

[11] Walther Bußmann, *Treitschke, Sein Welt- und Geschischtsbild* (Göttingen: Musterschmidt, 1952), p. 334; Heinrich von Treitschke, *Zehn Jahre Deutsche Kämpfe* (Leipzig, 1874), p. 280.

[12] Helmuth Plessner, *Die verspätete Nation* (Stuttgart: W. Kohlhammer, 1959), pp. 85–88.

[13] Thomas Nipperdey, "Nationalidee und Nationaldenkmal in Deutschland im 19. Jahhundert," in *Gesellschaft, Kultur, Theorie* (Göttingen: Vandenhoeck und Ruprecht, 1976), pp. 171, 172f.

[14] Bernd Faulenbach, *Ideologie des deutschen Weges: Die deutsche Geschichte in der Historiographie zwischen Kaiserreich und Nationalsozialismus* (Munich, C.H. Beck, 1980), p. 172.

[15] Ibid., p. 173.

[16] Ibid., p. 255.

[17] Erich Marcks, *Männer und Zeiten*, vol. II (Leipzig: Quelle & Meyer, 1922), p. 393.

[18] Plessner, *Verspätete Nation*, p. 87; Gordon A. Craig, *Deutsche Geschichte, 1865–1945* (Munich: C. H. Beck, 1980), p. 425ff.

[19] Thadden, "Das schwierige Vaterland," p. 55.

[20] Botho Strauß, *Der junge Mann* (Munich: Deutscher Taschenbuch Verlag, 1984), pp. 180–81.

[21] [A television miniseries broadcast by NBC in the United States in 1978. Although some critics charged that it trivialized the subject, it won several awards in the United States and made a considerable impact when it appeared on German television in 1979.]

[22] Saul Friedländer, *Reflections of Nazism: An Essay on Kitsch and Death*, translated from the French by Thomas Weyr (Bloomington and Indianapolis: Indiana University Press, 1993), p. 19. See also Botho Strauß, *Paare Passanten* (Munich: C. Hanser Verlag, 1984), p. 180.

[23] Hans Mommsen, "Die Last der Vangenheit," in *Stichworte zur "Geistigen Situation der Zeit,"* ed. Jürgen Habermas (2 vols., Frankfurt am Main: Suhrkamp, 1979), vol. I, p. 183f.

[24] Karl Dietrich Bracher, *Theodor Heuß und die Wiederbegründung der Demokratie in Deutschland* (Tübingen: Wunderlich, 1965).

[25] Heine, *Werke*, vol. II, p. 500.

[26] Friedrich Nietzsche, *Unzeitgemäße Betrachtungen* (Stuttgart: A. Kröner, 1964), p. 105.

Chapter 12

[1] See Goethe's comments on this in Johann Goethe, *Goethes Sämtliche Werke: Jubiläumsausgabe in 40 Bänden*, ed. Eduard von der Hellen, 40th ed.

(Stuttgart and Berlin: J.G. Cotta, 1902), p. 139, which are balanced by his insistence that, by promoting cultural rivalry among German rulers, disunity had its positive side (*Conversations with Eckermann*, October 23, 1828).

[2] See Richard Hamann and Jost Hermand, *Naturalismus: mit 59 Abbildungen und 10 farbigen Tafeln*, 2nd ed. (Berlin: Akademie-Verlag, 1968), p. 284.

[3] Ibid., pp. 278–82.

[4] On this, see especially Robert Minder, "Deutsche und französische Literatur—inneres Reich und Einbrüderung des Dichters," in *Kultur und Literatur in Deutschland und Frankreich: Fünf Essays* (Frankfurt am Main: Insel-Verlag, 1962), pp. 5–43.

[5] Erich Auerbach, *Mimesis: The Representation of Reality in Western Literature* (Princeton: Princeton University Press, 1953), p. 452ff.

[6] Nigel Hamilton, *The Brothers Mann: The Lives of Heinrich and Thomas Mann, 1871–1950 and 1875–1955* (New Haven: Yale University Press, 1979), p. 213.

[7] Klaus Vondung, *Das Wilhelminische Bildungsbürgertum: Zur Sozialgeschichte seiner Ideen* (Göttingen: Vandenhoeck & Ruprecht, 1976), pp. 30–33.

[8] Heinrich Mann, *Essays* (Hamburg: Claassen, 1960), pp. 15ff, 39ff, 82ff.

[9] Theodor Fontane, *Sämtliche Werke*, ed. Edgar Gross, 24 vols. (Munich: C. Hanser, 1959), vol. 8, p. 283 (*Der Stechlin*).

[10] Cited in Walter Müller-Seidel, *Theodor Fontane: Soziale Romankunst in Deutschland* (Stuttgart: J. B. Metzler, 1975), p. 100.

[11] Hans-Heinrich Reuter, *Fontane*, 2 vols. (Munich: Nymphenburger Verlagshandlung, 1968), vol. 1, p. 192.

[12] Ibid., pp. 190, 215ff, 221, 229.

[13] Theodor Fontane, *Sämtliche Werke*, ed. Edgar Gross, vol. 16, p. 496 (*Aus den Tagen der Okkupation*).

[14] Ibid., p. 485ff.

[15] Reuter, *Fontane*, vol. 1, p. 483.

[16] Fontane, *Sämtliche Werke*, vol. 8, p. 251 (*Der Stechlin*).

[17] Ibid., vol. 3, pp. 170, 205 (*Irrungen, Wirrungen*).

[18] Reuter, *Fontane*, vol. 2, p. 669.

[19] Ibid., p. 595.

[20] Kenneth Attwood, *Fontane und das Preußentum*, (Berlin: Baltica Verlag, 1970), p. 276.

[21] Theodor Fontane, *Sämtliche Werke*, vol. 7, p. 25ff. (*Frau Jenny Treibel*).

[22] Ibid., vol. 4, p. 41 (*L'Adultera*).

[23] Ibid., vol. 2, pp. 383–84 (*Schach von Wuthenow*).

[24] Konrad Wandrey, *Theodor Fontane* (Munich: Beck, 1914), p. 285.

[25] Fontane, *Sämtliche Werke*, vol. 7, pp. 373–75. (*Effi Briest*).

[26] Reuter, *Fontane*, vol. 1, pp. 92, 416ff.

27 Fontane, *Sämtliche Werke*, vol. 7, p. 28 (*Frau Jenny Treibel*).

28 Ibid., p. 71.

29 Ibid., vol. 8, p. 62 (*Der Stechlin*).

30 *Fontanes Briefe*, ed. Gotthard Erler, 2 vols. (Berlin: Aufbau-Verlag, 1968), vol. 1, p. 445.

31 Reuter, *Fontane*, vol. 2, p. 643.

32 *Fontanes Briefe*, vol. 2, p. 172.

33 Reuter, *Fontane*, vol. 2, p. 700.

34 Robert Minder, *Dichter in der Gesellschaft: Erfahrungen mit deutscher und französischer Literatur* (Frankfurt am Main: Insel, 1966), p. 151.

35 Georg Lukács, *Deutsche Realisten des 19. Jahrhunderts* (Berlin: A. Francke Ag. Verlag, 1959), p. 306.

36 Reuter, *Fontane*, vol. 2, p. 628.

37 *Fontanes Briefe*, vol. 2, p. 395ff.

38 Fontane, *Sämtliche Werke*, vol. 8, pp. 154, 168 (*Der Stechlin*).

39 *Fontanes Briefe*, vol. 2, pp. 417–20.

40 Minder, *Dichter in der Gesellschaft*, p. 152.

41 See Joachim Remak, *The Gentle Critic: Theodor Fontane and German Politics, 1848–1898* (Syracuse: Syracuse University Press, 1964).

42 Mann, *Essays*, p. 158.

43 Hamilton, *The Brothers Mann*, p. 32.

44 Ibid., p. 212.

45 Müller-Seidel, *Theodor Fontane*, p. 316; Ulrich Weisstein, *Heinrich Mann*. (Tübingen: M. Niemeyer, 1962), p. 22ff.

46 Carl E. Schorske, *Fin-de-Siècle Vienna: Politics and Culture* (New York: Vintage Books, 1980).

47 Heinrich Mann, *Zwei Romane* (Berlin: Aufbau, 1966), p. 183 (*Im Schlaraffenland*).

48 Ibid., p. 368ff.

49 Siegfried Kracauer, *From Caligari to Hitler: A Psychological History of German Film* (Princeton: Princeton University Press, 1947), pp. 215–18.

50 Friedrich Nietzsche, *Götzendämmerung* (Stuttgart: Kröner, 1964), p. 125.

51 Mann, *Zwei Romane*, p. 403ff. (*Professor Unrat*).

52 Ibid., p. 513.

53 Ibid., p. 546ff.

54 Ibid., p. 518.

55 See the interesting analyses of the trilogy in Weisstein, *Heinrich Mann*, pp. 111–41; and R. Travis Hardaway, "Heinrich Mann's *Kaiserreich* Trilogy and the Democratic Spirit," *Journal of English and German Philology*, 53 (1954): 319–33.

56 Heinrich Mann, *Der Untertan: Roman* (Munich, 1969), p. 47.

57 Klaus Schroeter, *Heinrich Mann in Selbstzeugnissen und Bilddokumenten* (Hamburg: Reinbek, 1967), p. 90.

58 Heinrich Mann, *Briefe an Karl Lemke und Klaus Pinkus,* (Hamburg: Claassen, 1964) (to Lemke, December 10, 1948).

59 Gottfried Benn, *Essays, Reden, Vorträge,* 2nd ed. (Wiesbaden: Limes, 1962), p. 583ff.

60 See Hildegard Brenner, *Ende einer bürgerlichen Kunst-Institution: Die politische Formierung der Preussischen Akademie der Künste ab 1933* (Stuttgart: Deutsche Verlags-Anstalt, 1972).

61 Mann, *Essays,* p. 13. ("Geist und Tat," 1910).

Chapter 13

1 Peter Gay, *The Naked Heart: The Bourgeois Experience from Victoria to Freud* (New York: W. W. Norton, 1995), p. 216.

2 Wolf Lepenies, *Die drei Kulturen: Soziologie zwischen Literatur und Wissenschaft* (Munich: Carl Hanser Verlag, 1985), p. 308.

3 Carl E. Schorske, *Fin-de-Siècle Vienna: Politics and Culture* (New York: Vintage Books, 1980).

4 Matthew Arnold, *Selected Prose,* ed. P. J. Keating (Harmondsworth: Penguin, 1970), p. 161.

5 Matthew Arnold, *Culture and Anarchy,* ed. J. Dover Wilson (Cambridge: Cambridge University Press, 1971), pp. 39, 43.

6 Matthew Arnold, *Schools and Universities on the Continent* (London: Mac-Millan, 1868).

7 See Baudelaire, *Oeuvres Complètes* (Paris: Gallimard, 1976), vol. II, pp. 351ff, 415ff. It has been suggested that Baudelaire was being ironical, and that his dedication of the *Salon de 1846* in particular is a "comic dedication." (See Charles Rosen and Henri Zerner, "The Unhappy Medium," *The New York Review,* May 27, 1982, p. 51.) The editors of the *Oeuvres Complètes* take the line that Baudelaire was serious and was in essence arguing that the artist and the bourgeois needed each other; see vol. II, p. 129ff.

8 Letters, *The New York Review,* April 1, 1982, p. 47.

Chapter 14

1 See Lawrence A. Scaff, *Fleeing the Iron Cage: Culture, Politics and Modernity in the Thought of Max Weber* (Berkeley: University of California Press, 1989), pp. 228–29.

2 Friedrich Nietzsche, *Unzeitgemässe Betrachtungen* (Stuttgart: Kröner Verlag, 1964), pp. 50–51.

3 *Gold and Iron: Bismarck, Bleichröder, and the Building of the German Empire*

(Knopf, 1977); *The Politics of Cultural Despair: A Study in the Rise of Germanic Ideology* (Berkeley: University of California Press, 1961).

Chapter 15

1 This essay makes use of the following sources: Günter Grass, *Die Blechtrommel* (Darmstadt and Neuwied: Hermann Luchterhand Verlag, 1959); idem, *The Tin Drum,* trans. Ralph Manheim (New York: Random House, 1961); John Reddick, *The "Danzig Trilogy" of Gunter Grass* (New York: Harcourt Brace Jovanovich, 1974); Hans Magnus Enzensberger, "Wilhelm Meister, auf Blech getrommelt," in *Von Buch zu Buch: Günter Grass in der Kritik,* ed. Gert Loschütz (Neuwied and Berlin: Luchterhand, 1965), 8–12; Michael Minden, "A Post-Realist Aesthetic: Günter Grass, 'Die Blechtrommel,'" in *The German Novel in the Twentieth Century: Beyond Realism,* ed. David Midgley (Edinburgh: Edinburgh University Press, 1993), pp. 149–63; Patrick O'Neill, ed., *Critical Essays on Günter Grass* (Boston: G. K. Hall, 1987); and Hans Dieter Zimmermann, "Günter Grass: Die Blechtrommel (1959)," in *Deutsche Romane des zwanzigsten Jahrhunderts,* ed. Paul Michael Lützeler (Königstein/Ts.: Athenäum, 1983), pp. 324–39.

Chapter 17

1 Heinrich von Kleist, *Sämtliche Werke und Briefe,* ed. Helmut Sembder (2 vols., Munich: C. Hanser, 1961), vol. II, p. 479.

2 *Berliner Abendblätter,* ed. Heinrich von Kleist (facsimile edition with an epilogue by Helmut Sembdner) (Stuttgart: Cotta, 1965), numbers for 1 and 22 October 1810.

3 On Unruh, see Albert Soergel and Curt Hohoff, *Dichtung und Dichter der Zeit. Von Naturalismus bis zur Gegenwart* (new ed., 2 vols., Düsseldorf, 1963), vol. II, pp. 245–54; and Georg Gustav Wieszner, "Der Dichter und Redner in der Zeit," in Fritz von Unruh, *Mächtig seid Ihr nicht in Waffen: Reden.* Mit einem Begleitwort von Albert Einstein (Nürnberg: H. Carl, 1957).

4 Unruh, *Reden,* p. 147.

5 Otto von Corvin, *Ein Leben voller Abenteuer,* ed. Hermann Wendel (Frankfurt am Main: Frankfurter Societäts-Druckerei, 1924), p. 77. In contrast, Unruh described the cadet corps as an "early model of the concentration camps," in *Reden,* p. 147.

6 Corvin, *Leben,* p. 264.

7 Ibid., p. 136.

8 Ibid., p. 267.

9 Ibid., p. 369.

[10] Ibid., p. 370.

[11] Ibid., p. 434.

[12] Ibid., p. 435.

[13] Ibid., p. 423ff.

[14] Corvin admired Emma Herwegh's courage and common sense. See ibid., p. 435; on her missions in search of Hecker, see ibid., p. 439ff. and *1848: Briefe von und an Georg Herwegh*, ed. Marcel Herwegh (Münich: A. Langen, 1898), pp. 155–77.

[15] See Corvin, *Leben*, pp. 458–78, where the legends of Herwegh's cowardice, to which Heinrich Heine contributed, are strongly denied.

[16] Ibid., pp. 506–35.

[17] For the Badanese campaign of 1849, see *inter alia* Willy Real, *Die Revolution in Baden 1848/49* (Stuttgart: W. Kohlhammer, 1983), especially pp. 106–75; Josef Becker, Lothar Gall et al., *Badische Geschichte* (Stuttgart: Theiss, 1979), p. 58ff.; Veit Valentin, *Geschichte der deutschen Revolution* (2 vols., Berlin: Ullstein, 1930), vol. II, p. 526ff.; *Denkwürdigkeiten des Generals Franz Sigel aus den Jahren 1848 und 1849*, ed. Wilhelm Blos (Mannheim: J. Bernsheimer, 1902); Karl Schurz, *Lebenserinnerungen*, vol. I, (Berlin: G. Reimer, 1911), p. 134ff.

[18] On Rastatt during the siege, see Corvin, *Leben*, pp. 556–610; Schurz, *Lebenserinnerungen*, vol. I, p. 136ff.

[19] Sigel, *Denkwürdigkeiten*, p. 20ff; Valentin, *Deutsche Revolution*, vol. I, p. 491.

[20] *1848: Briefe*, p. 250.

[21] Valentin, *Deutsche Revolution*, vol. II, p. 171.

[22] Real, *Revolution*, pp. 160–62.

[23] *Meyers Neues Lexikon* (1947).

[24] Valentin, *Deutsche Revolution*, vol. II, pp. 537–39; Schurz, *Lebenserinnerungen*, vol. I, last chapter; Werner Kaegi, *Jakob Burckhardt, eine Biographie*, vol. III (Basel: B. Schwabe [1947–82], p. 212f.; Karl Dändliker, *Geschichte der Stadt und des Kantons Zürich*: Schulthess 1912), p. 486; Otto Henne, *Gottfried Kinkel, ein Lebensbild* (Zuruck: Schmidt, 1883).

[25] See W. H. Chaloner and W. O. Henderson, *Engels as Military Critic* (Manchester: Manchester University Press, 1959), p. x, n. 3.

[26] Gustav Mayer, *Friedrich Engels aus seiner Frühzeit, 1820–1851* (Berlin: J. Springer, 1920), p. 70, and *Friedrich Engels, eine Biographie* (2nd rev. ed., The Hague, 1934), vol. I, p. 68ff.

[27] Friedrich Engels, *Die deutsche Reichsverfassungskampagne*, ed. Rolf Dlubek (Berlin, 1969), p. 105.

[28] *Briefwechsel zwischen Friedrich Engels und Karl Marx, 1844 bis 1883*, ed. August Bebel and Eduard Bernstein (4 vols., Stuttgart: J. H. W. Dietz, 1921), vol. I, p. 106. For brief summaries of Engels's role in the

campaign, see August Happich, *Friedrich Engels als Soldat der Revolution* (Leipzig: R. Noske, 1931), p. 29ff., and Mayer, *Engels*, vol. I, pp. 342–50.

29 *Engels-Marx Breifwechsel*, vol. I, 188.

30 Wilhelm Rüstow, *Der deutsche Militärstaat vor und während der Revolution* (facsimile of 1850 ed., Osnabrück: Biblio Verlag, 1971), p. 170f.

31 On all this, see Peter Wiede, *Wilhelm Rüstow, 1821 bis 1878. Ein Militärschriftsteller der deutschen Linken* (Inaug. Diss., Philosophische Fakultät, Universität München, 1957), chapter 1; and Marcel Herwegh, *Guillaume Rüstow, un grand soldat, un grand caractère* (Paris: Editions Victor Attinger, 1935), pp. 24–34.

32 Ferdinand Lassalle, *Nachgelassene Briefe und Papiere*, ed. Gustav Mayer (6 vols., Osnabrück: Biblio Verlag, 1967), vol. V, p. 15.

33 Herwegh, *Rüstow*, pp. 45–48; Wiede, *Rüstow*, pp. 45–53.

34 For details, see Wiede, *Rüstow*, p. 55ff.

35 An amusing description of the occasion on which Rüstow first met Lassalle is to be found in Jakob Baechtold, *Gottfried Kellers Leben. Seine Briefe und Tagebücher*, vol. II (Berlin: Hertz, 1894), p. 320f. On the Italian plan, see Wiede, *Rüstow*, pp. 414–19; Lassalle, *Nachgelassene Briefe*, vol. V, pp. 7, 15, 27f, 44 ff.

36 Engels, *Reichsverfassungskampagne*, p. 116.

37 In the desperate campaigns of 1862 and 1863, heroes of the Baden revolution repeatedly distinguished themselves. In December 1862, Karl Schurz commanded the 3. Division of Franz Sigel's reserve corps in the failed attack across the Rappahannock, and in the following May Alexander Schimmelpfennig led a brigade in Schurz's division at Chancellorsville, a bloody fight in which Colonel Friedrich Hecker seized his regiment's flag and led a bayonet charge to relieve Stonewall Jackson's pressure on the Union line.

38 Wiede, *Rüstow*, p. 78.

39 Georges Rapp, Viktor Hofer and Rudolf Jaun, *Der schweizerische Generalstab* (3 vols., Basel: Helbing & Lichtenhahn, 1983), vol. I, p. 7; vol. II, pp. 23, 39, 50; vol. III, no. 499.

40 Ibid., vol. II, pp. 64, 83 (on staff rides), 141, 142, 143, 147, and, on selection process, pp. 162–164.

41 See Gordon A. Craig, "Delbrück, the Military Historian," in *Makers of Modern Strategy from Machiavelli to the Nuclear Age*, ed. by Peter Paret (Princeton: Princeton University Press, 1986), p. 328f.

42 *Engels-Marx Briefwechsel*, vol. II, p. 228.

43 Sigmund Neumann and Mark von Hagen, "Engels and Marx on Revolution, War and the Army in Society," in *Makers of Modern Strategy*, p. 267.

44 Ibid., p. 279.

[45] That Engels had a low regard for militia is shown in his comments on the American Civil War in a letter to Marx in January 1868: *Engels-Marx Briefwechsel*, vol. IV, pp. 12–13.

[46] Friedrich Engels, *Herrn Eugen Dührings Umwälzung der Wissenschaft* (9. ed., Stuttgart: J. H. W. Dietz, 1919), pp. 176–77.

Chapter 18

[1] Carl von Clausewitz, *On War*, ed. and trans. Michael Howard and Peter Paret, rev. ed. (Princeton: Princeton University Press, 1984), p. 607.

[2] David Fraser, *Alanbrooke* (London: Atheneum, 1982), p. 215.

[3] Edward Spears, *Prelude to Victory* (London: Jonathan Cape, 1939), p. 377f.

[4] Gerhard Ritter, *Staatskunst und Kriegshandwerk* (Munich: R. Oldenbourg, 1964), vol. 3, p. 586.

[5] Ibid., p. 241.

[6] Ibid., p. 383ff.

[7] A. J. P. Taylor, *Politics in Wartime* (New York: Atheneum, 1965), p. 21.

[8] Roy Jenkins, *Asquith: Portrait of a Man and an Era* (New York: Chilmark Press, 1964), p. 387.

[9] Ibid., p. 328.

[10] E. L. Woodward, *Great Britain and the War of 1914–1918* (London: Methuen, 1967), pp. 148–49.

[11] Quoted by Robert Graves in *The Observer,* March 1, 1959.

[12] Leon Wolff, *In Flanders Fields* (New York: Viking Press, 1958), p. 184.

[13] Lord Newton, *Lord Landsdowne: A Biography* (London: Macmillan, 1929), p. 468.

[14] Jere King, *Generals and Politicians* (Berkeley: University of California Press, 1951), p. 242.

[15] Spears, *Prelude to Victory*, p. 377.

[16] C. Bugnet, *Rue St Dominique et GHQ* (Paris: Plon, 1937), p. 273.

[17] On all of this, see Harvey A. DeWeerd, "Churchill, Lloyd George, Clemenceau," in *Makers of Modern Strategy*, ed. Edward Mead Earle (Princeton: Princeton University Press, 1943), p. 303.

[18] General Jean Jules Mordacq, *Le Ministère Clémenceau* (Paris: Plon, 1930), vol, 2, pp. 363–67.

[19] Ibid., especially p. 308ff.

[20] David Lloyd George, *War Memoirs* (London: Nicholson and Watson, 1933–37), vol. 6, p. 3421.

[21] Generaloberst Franz Halder, *Kriegstagebuch,* ed. Hans-Adolf Jacobsen (Stuttgart: W. Kohlhammer, 1962), vol. 3, pp. 354, 356-59; *Hitler als Feldherr* (Munich: Münchener Dom-Verlag, 1949), pp. 15, 45.

[22] Percy Ernst Schramm, *Hitler: The Man and the Military Leader,* trans. and ed. Donald S. Detweiler (Chicago: Quadrangle Books, 1971), p. 198.

[23] Ibid.

[24] Andreas Hillgruber, *Hitlers Strategie: Politik und Kriegfuhrung 1940–1941* (Frankfurt am Main: Bernard & Graefe Verlag, 1965) and "Der Faktor Amerika in Hitlers Strategie 1938–1941," in Hillgruber, *Deutsche Grossmacht-und Weltpolitik im 19, und 20. Jahrhundert* (Düsseldorf: Droste, 1977).

[25] Erich von Manstein, *Verlorene Siege* (Bonn: Athenäum Verlag, 1955), p. 305ff.

[26] These sentences repeat what I have said in *Germany, 1866–1945* (Oxford and New York: Oxford University Press, 1978), p. 721.

[27] Barry A. Leach, *German Strategy against Russia, 1939–1941* (Oxford: Clarendon Press, 1973), p. 78f.

[28] Halder, *Kriegstagebuch*, vol. 2, pp. 261, 320, 336. That a large proportion of the army leadership did not worry about such distinctions is shown by Jürgen Förster in his essay in *Das Deutsche Reich und der Zweite Weltkrieg,* ed. Milit Forschungsamt, vol. 4; *Angriff auf die Sowjetunion* (Stuttgart: Deutsche Verlags-Anstalt, 1983).

[29] Trumbull Higgins, *Hitler and Russia* (New York: Macmillan, 1966), p. 156.

[30] Ibid., pp. 209–10.

[31] Halder, *Kriegstagebuch*, vol. 3, p. 489.

[32] Schramm, *Hitler*, p. 203f.

[33] Basil Liddell Hart, "The Military Strategist," in A. J. P. Taylor, Robert Rhodes James, J. H. Plumb, Basil Liddell Hart, and Anthony Storr, *Churchill Revised* (New York: Dial Press, 1969), p. 197. See also Ronald Lewin, *Churchill as Warlord* (New York: Stein and Day, 1973), p. 13.

[34] Gordon Wright, *The Ordeal of Total War* (New York: Harper & Row, 1968), p. 238f.; Lewin, *Churchill*, p. 32 .

[35] John Connell, *Wavell: Soldier and Statesman* (London: Harcourt, Brace & World, 1964), p. 256.

[36] R. W. Thompson, *Generalissimo Churchill* (New York: Scribner, 1973), p. 100.

[37] Connell, *Wavell*, p. 421.

[38] Thompson, *Churchill*, p. 120f.

[39] Major General Sir John Kennedy, *The Business of War* (London: Hutchinson, 1957), p. 108. It should be noted that Churchill continued to be excessively critical of his commanders in the field and that Brooke, after listening to his abuse of Montgomery and Alexander in July 1944, "flared up and asked him if he could not trust his generals for five

minutes instead of continuously abusing and belittling them." Fraser, *Alanbrooke,* p. 442.

[40] For the full development of this relationship, see *Roosevelt and Churchill: Their Secret Wartime Correspondence,* ed. Francis L. Loewenheim, Harold D. Langley, and Manfred Jonas (New York: Saturday Review Press, 1975). See also *Churchill and Roosevelt, The Complete Correspondence,* ed. Warren F. Kimball, 3 vols. (Princeton: Princeton University Press, 1984).

[41] See above all Mark S. Watson, *Chief of Staff: Pre-War Plans and Preparations* (Washington, D.C.: Center of Military History, 1950).

[42] Winston S. Churchill, *The Grand Alliance* (Boston: Houghton Mifflin, 1950), pp. 625, 643.

[43] Lord Ismay, *Memoirs* (New York: Viking Press, 1960), p. 116.

[44] Fraser, *Alanbrooke,* pp. 231–32; Lewin, *Churchill,* p. 127ff.

[45] Liddell Hart, "The Military Strategist," p. 215; Fraser, *Alanbrooke,* p. 311ff.

[46] Fraser, *Alanbrooke,* pp. 384–92.

[47] Maurice Matloff and Edwin S. Snell, *Strategic Planning for Coalition Warfare, 1941–1942* (Washington, D.C.: Center of Military History, 1953), 272–73.

[48] See *On War,* book 1, chapter 1, and, especially, book 8, chapter 6.

[49] *The Papers of Dwight David Eisenhower: The War Years,* ed. Alfred Chandler, 5 vols. (Baltimore: Johns Hopkins University Press, 1970), vol. 4, pp. 2592–95.

[50] *Roosevelt and Churchill,* p. 548. On the growth of Churchill's fears in this regard, see Herbert Feis, *Churchill, Roosevelt, Stalin: The War They Waged and the Peace They Sought* (Princeton: Princeton University Press, 1957), p. 338ff.

[51] See Gordon A. Craig, "Roosevelt and Hitler: The Problem of Perception," in *Deutsche Frage und europäisches Gleichgewicht: Festschrift für Andreas Hillgruber zum 60. Geburtstag,* ed. Klaus Hildebrand and Reiner Pommerin (Cologne and Vienna: Böhlau, 1985).

[52] Robert Dallek, *Franklin D. Roosevelt and American Foreign Policy, 1932–1945* (New York: Oxford University Press, 1979), p. 321.

[53] Fraser, *Alanbrooke,* p. 230.

[54] Kent Roberts Greenfield, *American Strategy in World War II: A Reconsideration* (Baltimore: Johns Hopkins University Press, 1963), p. 52f.

[55] Ibid., p. 53.

[56] Feis, *Churchill, Roosevelt, Stalin,* pp. 54-55.

[57] On all this, see Forrest G. Pogue, *George C. Marshall: Organizer of Victory, 1943–1945* (New York: Viking Press, 1973).

[58] Gordon A. Craig and Alexander L. George, *Force and Statecraft: Diplomatic Problems of Our Time* (New York: Oxford University Press, 1983), p. 101ff.

Chapter 20

[1] See my article, "'A Talented Amateur,'" in *The New York Review*, February 28, 2002, p. 26.

Chapter 21

[1] Max Frisch, *Stiller: Roman* (Frankfurt am Main: Suhrkamp Verlag, 1963), p. 292.
[2] Gottfried Keller, *Züricher Novellen: Aufsätze* (Basel: Diogenes, 1978), p. 278ff.
[3] Adolf Muschg, *Die Schweiz am Ende, Am Ende die Schweiz: Erinnerungen an mein Land vor 1991* (Frankfurt am Main: Suhrkamp Verlag, 1990), p. 173.

Chapter 22

[1] *Hitler, 1889–1936: Hubris* (New York: Norton, 1998).
[2] *I Will Bear Witness: A Diary of the Nazi Years, 1933–1941* and *I Will Bear Witness: A Diary of the Nazi Years, 1942–1945*, translated by Martin Chalmers (New York: Random House, 1998 and 1999). These appeared earlier in German, as *Ich will Zeugnis ablegen bis zum letzten: Tagebücher 1933–1945* (Berlin: Aufbau Verlag, 1995).

Chapter 23

[1] Hans-Adolf Jacobsen, *Dokumente zur Vorgeschichte des Westfeldzuges 1939–1940* (Göttingen: Musterschmidt, 1956), p. 6.
[2] Ian Kershaw, *Hitler, 1936–1945: Nemesis* (New York: Norton, 2000), p. 412.

Index